I0473070

Drawn & Courted

Four pamphlets of drawing suggestions created for the Oakville OASIS Drawing Bee, in the Oakville OASIS Drawing Bee,
by R. David Foster.

TEXTBOOK --A--

Warm Ups
Split the Area :
  Simple
  & Complex
Split the Angle :
  Simple
  & Complex
Land the Circle :
  Simple
  & Complex
2D vs. 3D - Isometric Cube
Doodling - Faces, Plants, Animals

from
Drawing on the Right Side of the Brain
Vases and Faces
Meeting Edges
Blind Contour
  & Contour Drawing
Negative Space
Upside Down Drawing
Sighting Proportions

Portraits
Eye Line ½ of Face /
  Ears - Eye Line to Base of Nose
Eyes
Ears
Noses
Mouths
Hair
Full Face VS. Profile

Head Rotation
Centre Line, Ear Line,
  Eye Line, Nose Line, & Mouth Line
21 Spheres
21 Heads

Still Life
Sphere, Cylinder, Cone, Box
Textures
Highlights, Full Light, Back Lights & Shadows
Plants
Crotch Angle

TEXTBOOK --B--
Visual Vocabulary

People -
Eyes,
Ears,
Noses,
Mouths,
Hair
Head Shapes
Hands
Feet
Body Types
Clothing & Drapery

Animals -
Breeds, Species *1*
Breeds, Species 2

Plants -
Trees,
Shrubs,
Grasses,
Flowers
Vegetables

Mechanical -
Vehicles *1*
Vehicles 2
Machines,
Tools,
Toys,
Appliances,
Furniture,
Architecture,
Roads & Pavings,
Bridges and Structures

Geological -
Mountains,
Soils,
Rocks,
Gravels

Topographic and Landscapes
Topographic and Landscapes 1
Topographic and Landscapes 2

Textures -
Leaves, Needles & Barks
Scales
Grasses, Hair & Fur
Feathers

Drapery -
Gravity & Rigidity,
Folds,
Flow

TEXTBOOK --C--
Simple Perspective

Illustration of Visualizing in Three Dimensions
Isometric Cube - 2D vs. 3D
Orthographic Projection,
Isometric Projection,
Oblique Projection &
Perspective Projection

Theory
Horizon is at viewers eye level
Picture Plane perpendicular to the Line of Sight
Limits of the chosen Picture Plane
Panning : curved picture plane
Parallel Planes with Parallel Lines

Architectural
1, 2 & 3 Vanishing Point(s) Perspective
Additional Vanishing Points for parallel planes with
  parallel lines *1*
Additional Vanishing Points for parallel planes with
  parallel lines 2
Additional Vanishing Points for parallel planes with
  parallel lines *3*
Receding Lengths -
  telephone poles
  "boxes"

Light Source and Shadows
Circles, Ellipses & Arcs

Creative Perspective
Escher
Salvador Dali

Figure Drawing in Perspective
Boxing in for Arcs, Cylinders and Spheres 1
Boxing in for Arcs, Cylinders and Spheres 2
Portrait,
Head,
Shoulders,
Hips
Foreshortening

TEXTBOOK --D--
Landscapes

Topographic
Hills,
Plains and
Mountains -
  Ranges in Perspective
  Shadows
Lakes,
Rivers, and
Waves -
  Lake
  Shore
  River
Snow
Architecture in the Landscape -
  Variety of Vanishing Points
  Shadows

Atmospheric
Contrast & Detail
Clouds and Skies
Precipitation -
  Rain
  Snow

Day and Night
Overcast,
Sunlit,
Artificial Light - Streetlights
Dawn and Dusk
Contrast and Detail -
  Day
  Night

EPILOGUE -
Placing a Perfect Sphere in Perspective, in a Graphically Calculated Perfect Cube.

DEDICATED
with sincere appreciation and love
to
Gwen . .
. . and presented for
all secular faithfull.

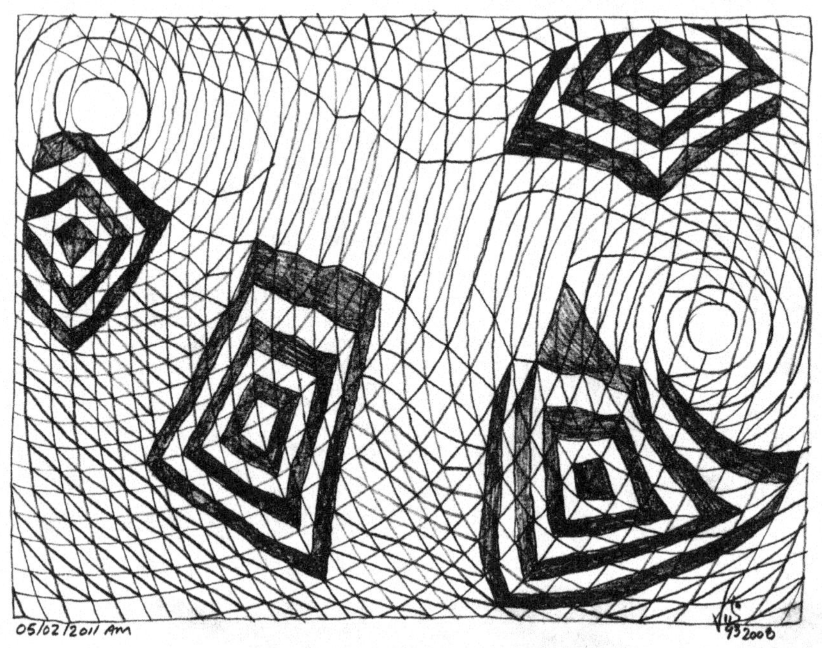

All the drawings in this book were created by R. David Foster. Almost all the drawings were completed entirely in the Oakville OASIS Drawing Bee, from the author's imagination, in an effort to stimulate hesitant Oakville OASIS Drawing Bee participants to get going on drawing at the weekly meetings with coffee on Monday mornings beginning in March 2010, and funded by the Canadian Mental Health Association - Halton Region Branch, in Oakville, Ontario, Canada. The only drawings **NOT** completed in the Drawing Bee are the ones under the heading "Other Drawings", the drawings in the Epilogue, and the images taken from the 35mm animated film **HYPOTHERMIA** / My Kayak Prayer, which were still all created by R. David Foster.

This Oakville OASIS Drawing Bee drawing group continues to meet in Oakville, now led by Paul Tomas.

A light website is at ***https://sites.google.com/site/oasisdrawingbee/*** .

To date about almost three comic books have almost been completed by Drawing Bee participants. One comic book was completed by Jomo Powell a few years ago.

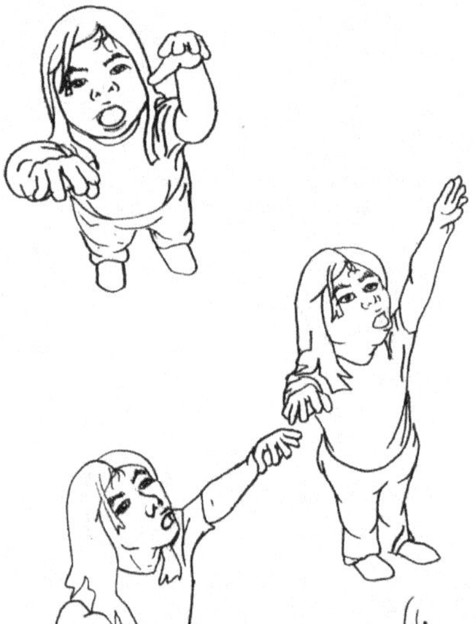

04/18/2011 AM

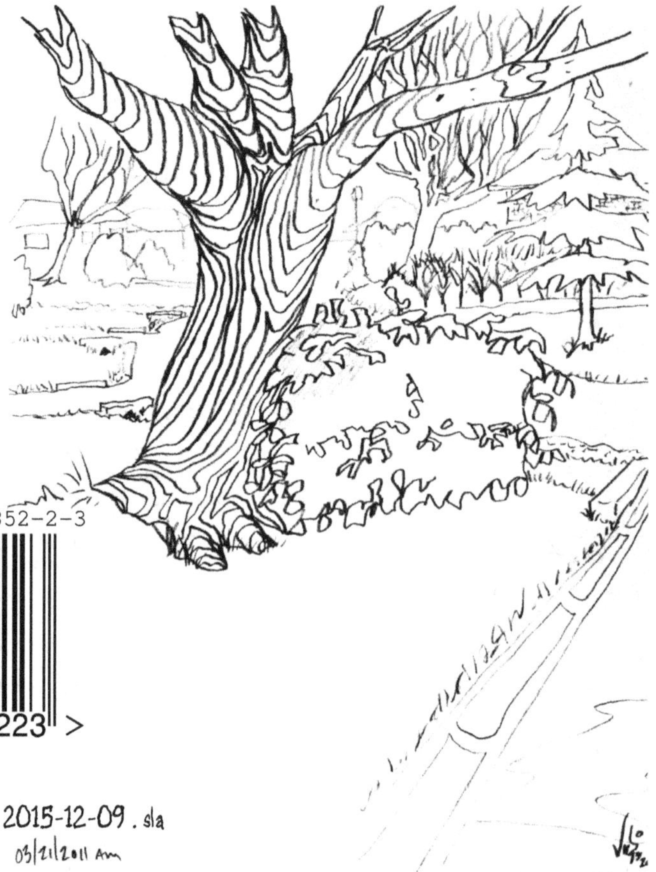

ISBN 978-0-9917852-2-3

9 780991 785223 >

Drawn & Courted
ISBN 978-0-9917852-2-3
Self-published by R David Foster, Oakville, Ontario, Canada; through Lulu.com.
 First Edition --A, B, C, D-Ep-- 021 2015-12-09 .sla

03/21/2011 AM

Discounts on bulk orders of this book may be substantial for providing this book as a textbook for instruction, and may be ordered by emailing vid932008@gmail.com. Again, in the case of hardship, email the author, David Foster, at vid932008@gmail.com for special arrangements.

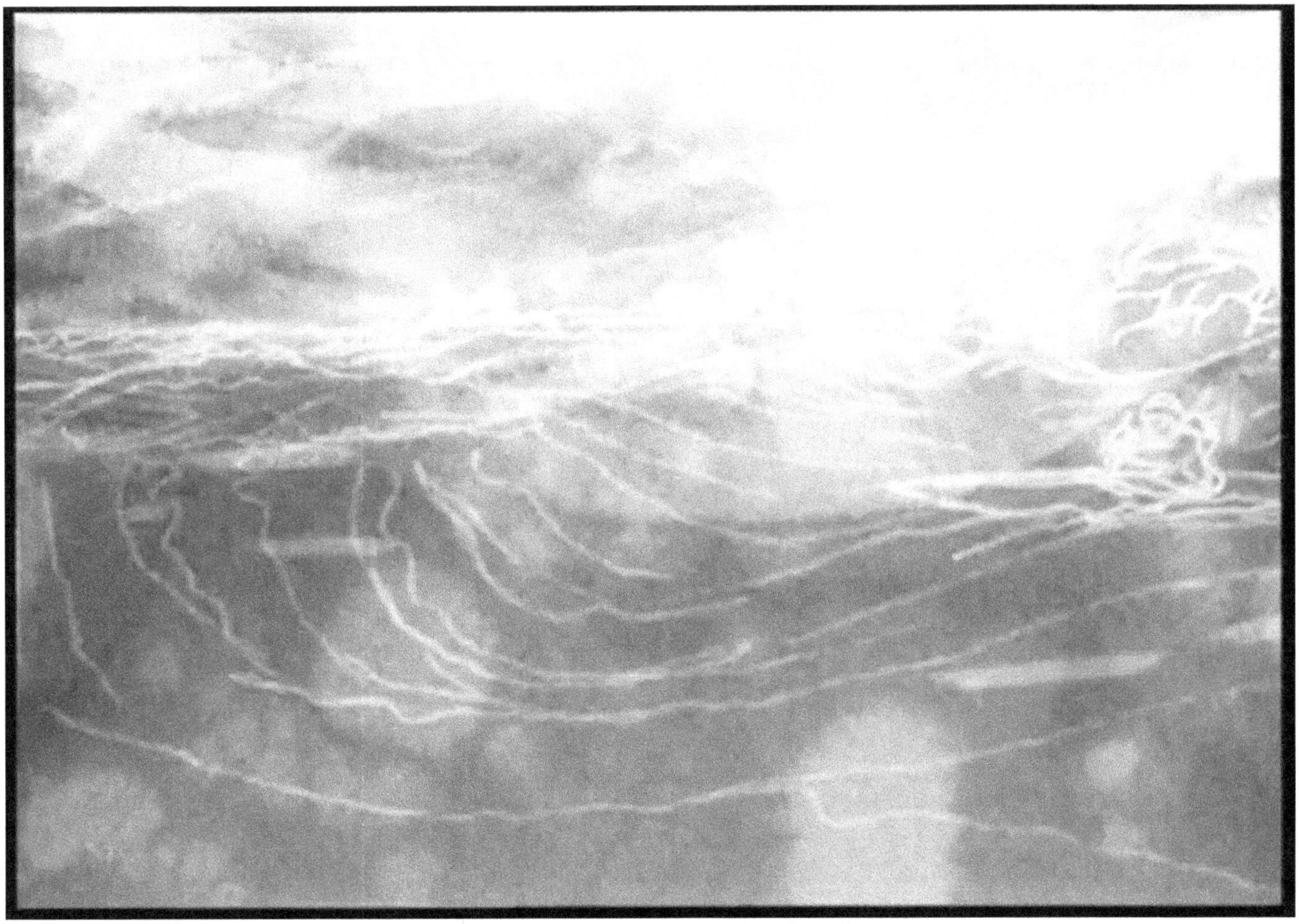

Warm Ups / Drawing on the Right Side of the Brain / Portraits / Still Life

Textbook --A--

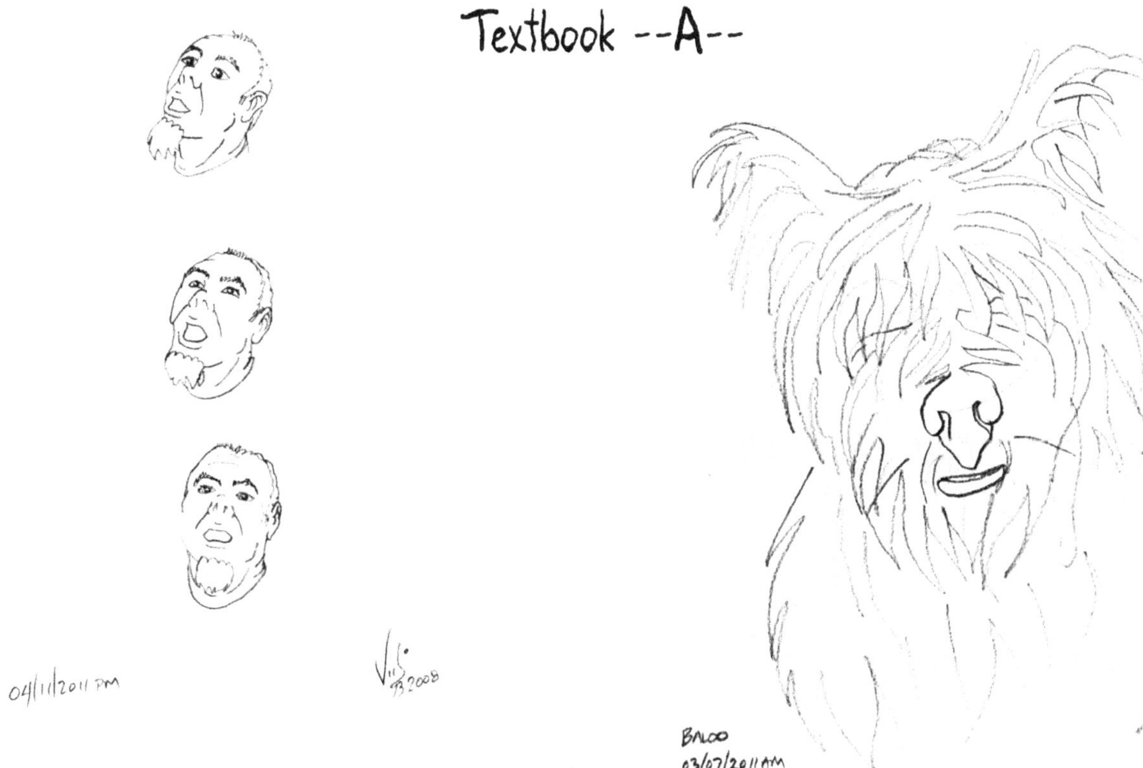

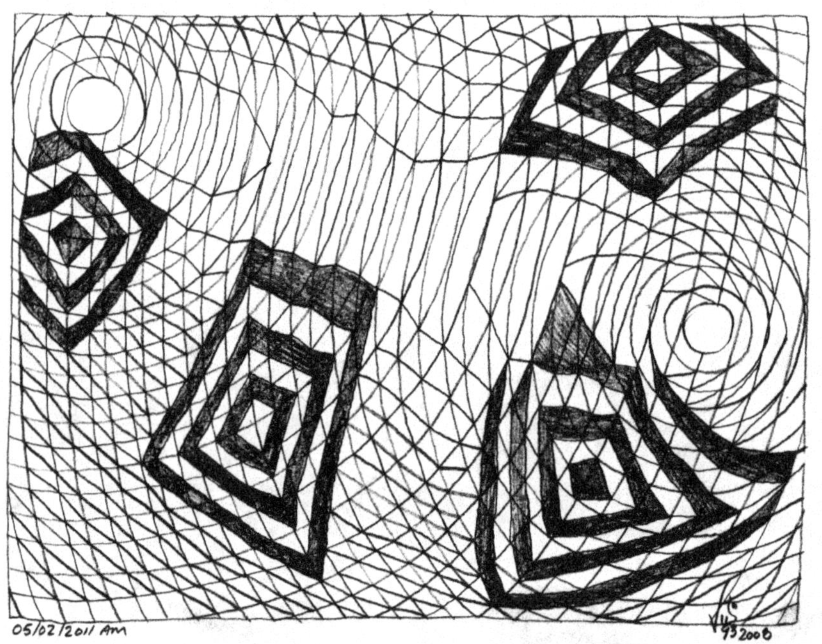

IMAGE CREDITS:

Front cover and Textbook Cover pages:
top: A still image from the animated film HYPOTHERMIA / My Kayak Prayer, © R David Foster 2008 .
lower right: R . David Foster in the OASIS Drawing Bee on date as noted .
lower left: R . David Foster in the OASIS Drawing Bee on date as noted, Character Development drawing for the animated film HESUS JOY CHRIST / Matthew's Five's Nine .

Previous Page (Textbook Cover page):
same as front cover .

This Page, copyright page, and pages after Textbook Cover pages:
Top left: R . David Foster in the OASIS Drawing Bee on date as noted . .
Lower left: R . David Fsoter in the OASIS Drawing Bee on date as noted, Character Development drawing for the animated film HESUS JOY CHRIST / Matthew's Five's Nine .
Lower right: R . David Foster in the OASIS Drawing Bee on date as noted .

Outside back Cover:
Top: R . David Foster on site sketch on the Cross of Victory Pilgrimage on date as noted .
Lower Right Side: R . David Foster in the OASIS Drawing Bee on date as noted .

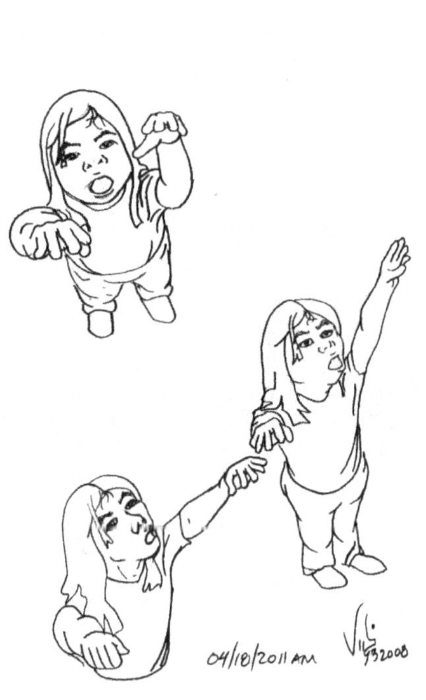

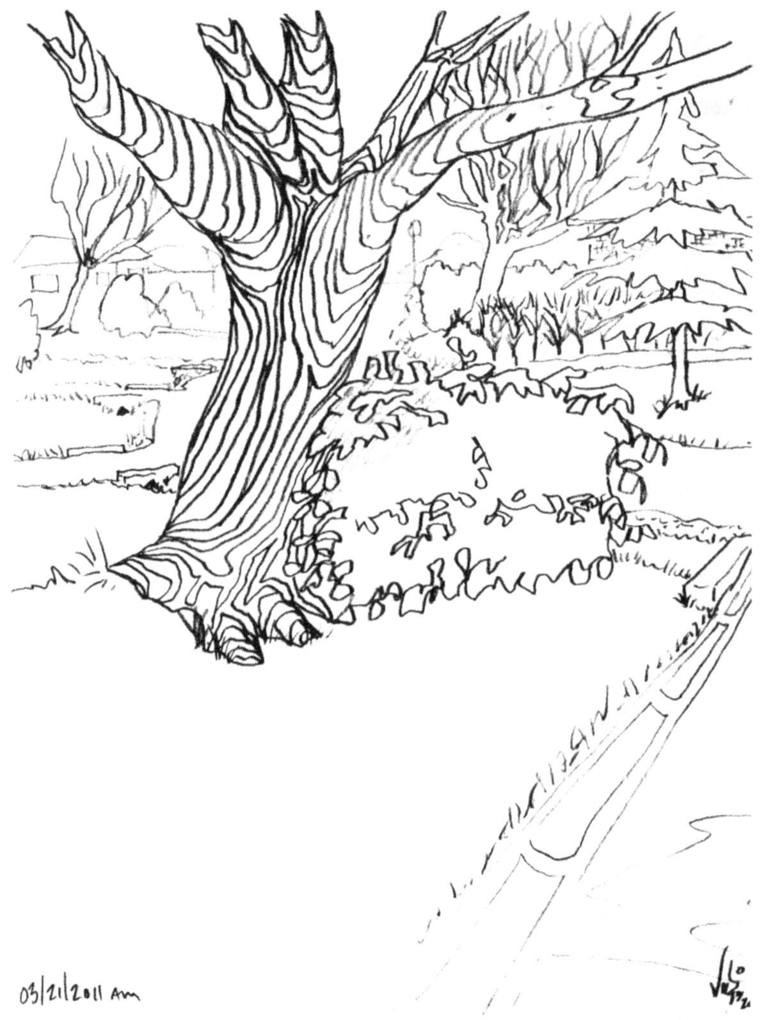

03/21/2011 Am

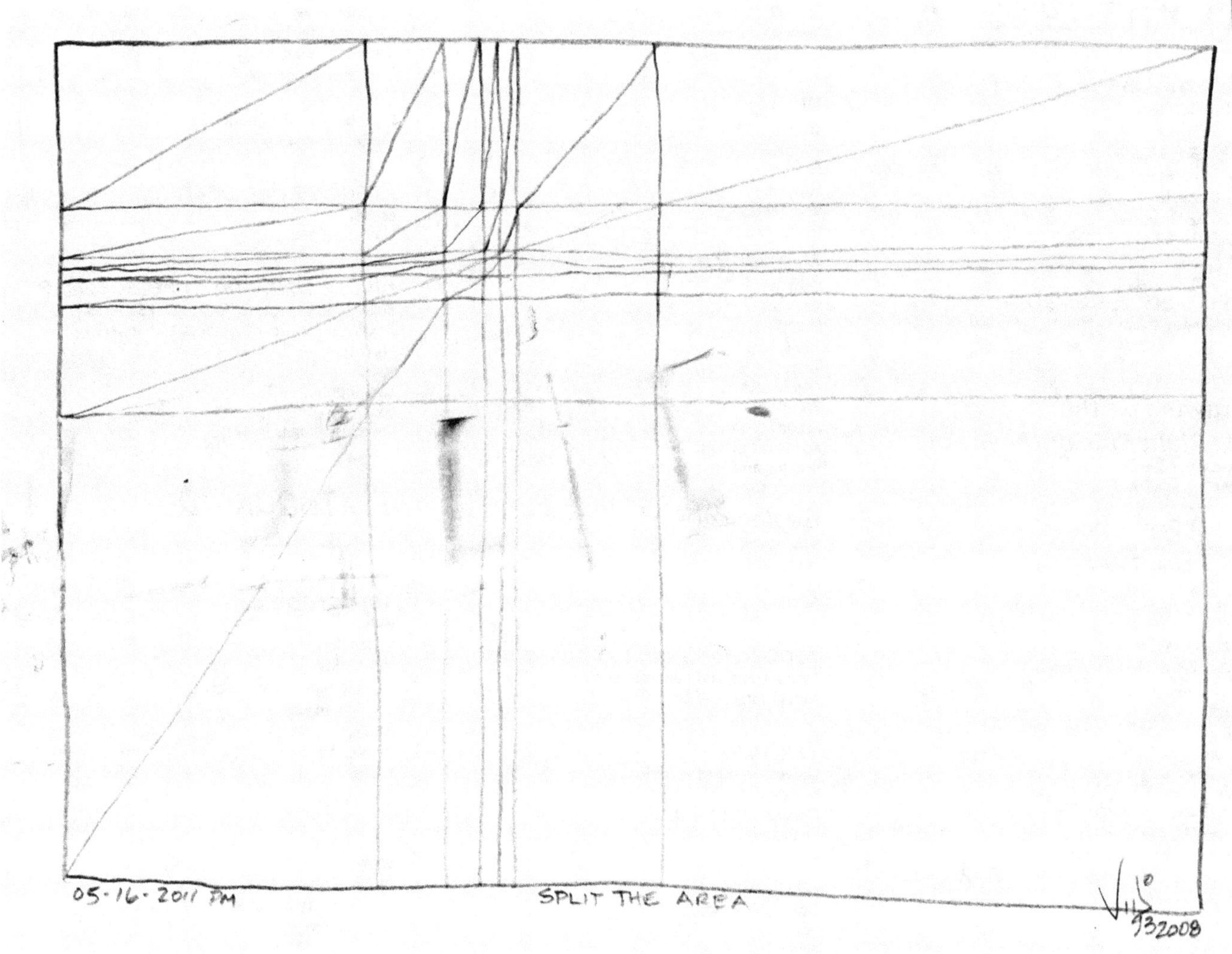

Warm Ups :--

Split the Area - Simple

The idea of this exercise is to develop one's draftsmanship to cultivate an ability to judge spacing, draw straight lines, and test these skills by drawing the diagonal lines between the intersections.

First draw a line halfway across the page, then split the two halves you just created, and continue to split the halves as you create them. Then begin again by drawing perpendicular to what you have just completed. Finally, test your drawing by drawing the diagonals between the intersections of the perpendicular lines. If your drawing is solid the diagonals should be fairly straight lines.

TO FULLY APPRECIATE THE IMPORTANCE OF THIS EXERCISE, SKIP AHEAD TO THE EPILOGUE, PAGES 147 TO 153. AS A SPORT, THE SKILLS DEVELOPED BY PRACTICING THIS EXERCISE ARE ESSENTIAL TO THE GOOD DRAFTSMANSHIP ABSOLULTELY NECESSARY TO ACHIEVE AN ARBITRARY GOAL SUCH AS PLACING A SPHERE IN PERSPECTIVE.

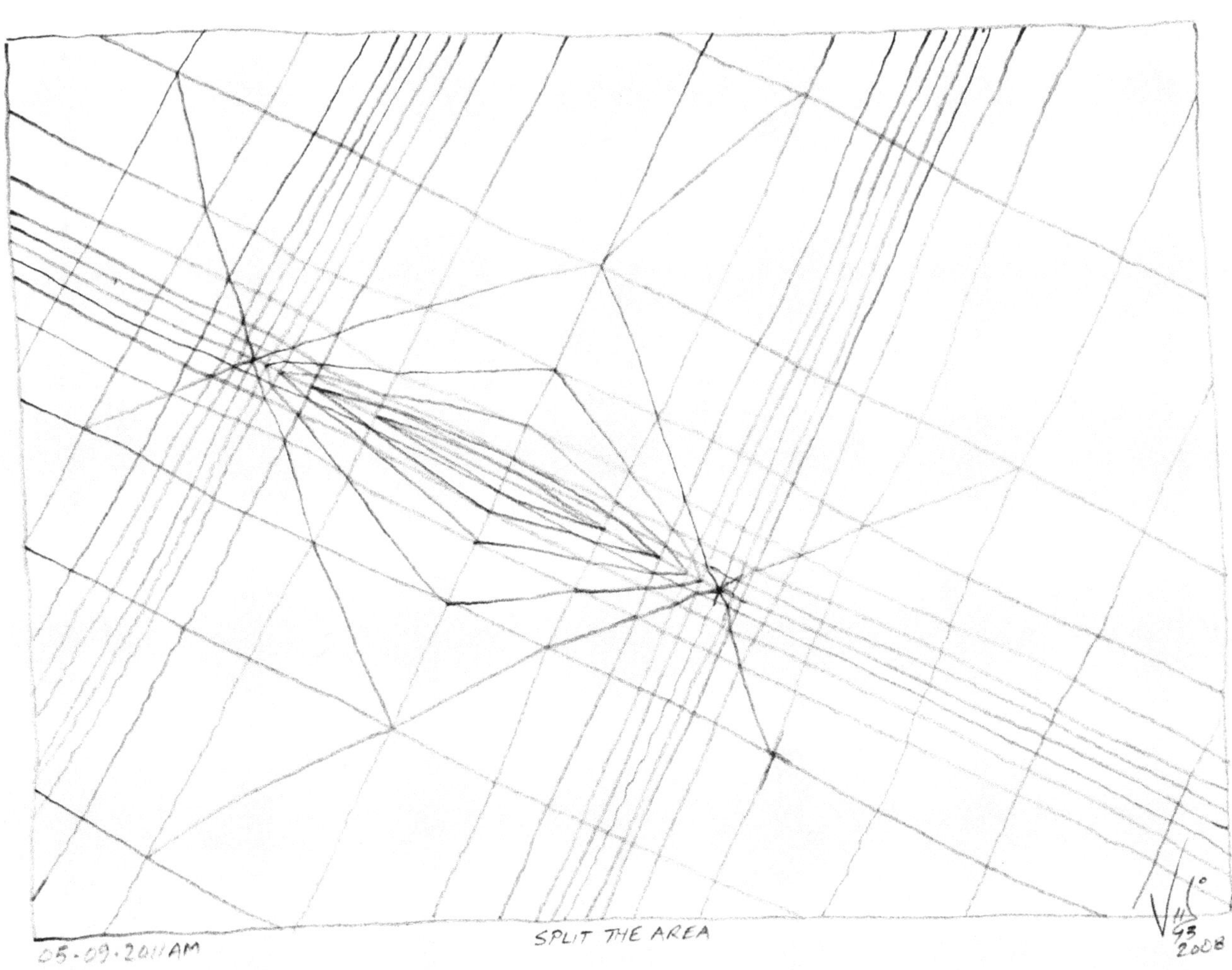

Warm Ups :--

Split the Area - Complex

The idea of this exercise is still to develop one's draftsmanship to cultivate an ability to judge spacing, draw straight lines, and test these skills by drawing the diagonal lines between the intersections.

First draw a line diagonally halfway across the page, then split the two halves you just created, diagonally, and continue to split the halves as you create them. Then begin again by drawing perpendicular to what you have just completed. Finally, test your drawing by drawing the diagonals between the intersections of the perpendicular lines. If your drawing is solid the diagonals should be fairly straight lines.

TO FULLY APPRECIATE THE IMPORTANCE OF THIS EXERCISE, SKIP AHEAD TO THE EPILOGUE, PAGES 147 TO 153. AS A SPORT, THE SKILLS DEVELOPED BY PRACTICING THIS EXERCISE ARE ESSENTIAL TO THE GOOD DRAFTSMANSHIP ABSOLULTELY NECESSARY TO ACHIEVE AN ARBITRARY GOAL SUCH AS PLACING A SPHERE IN PERSPECTIVE.

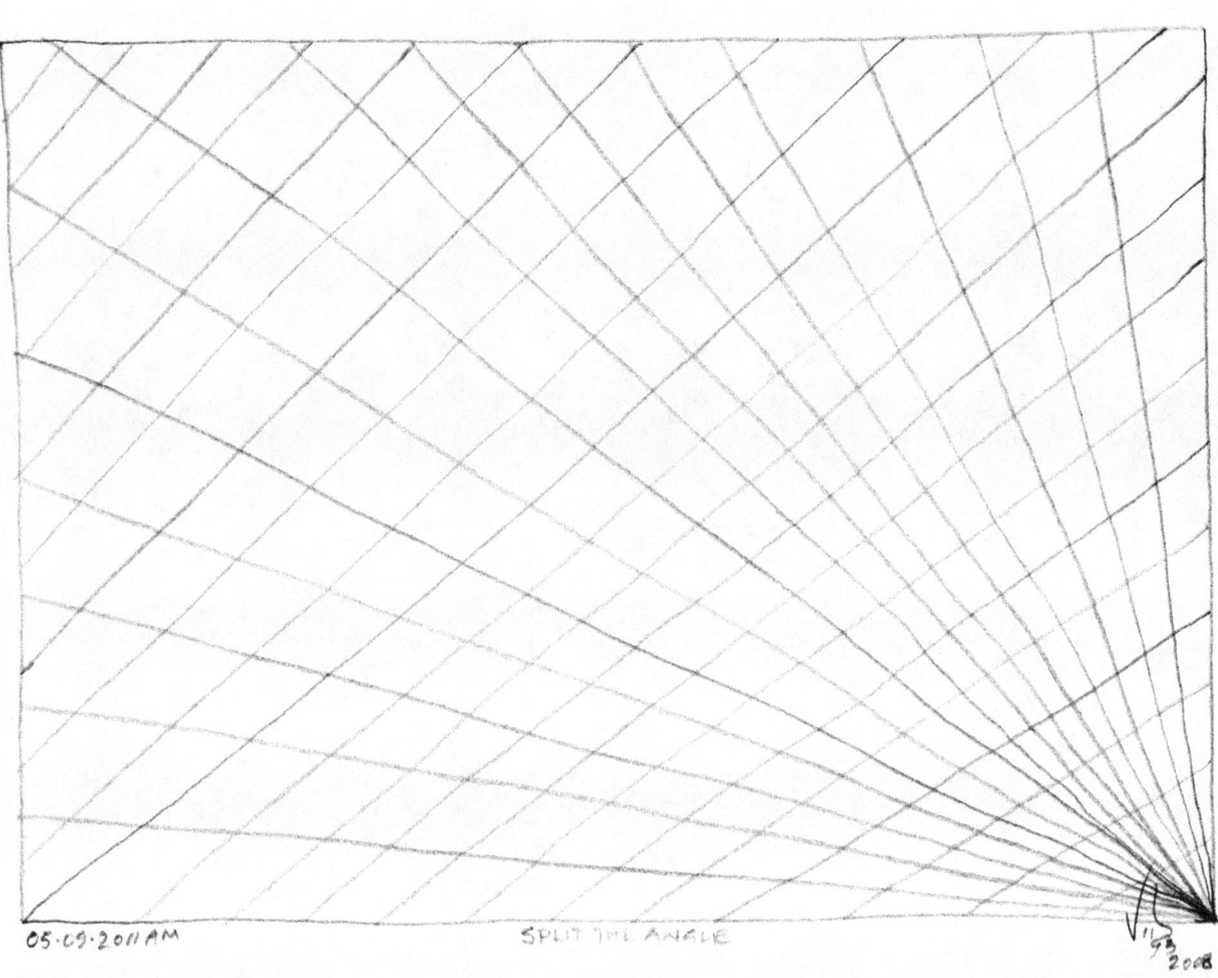

Warm Ups :--

Split the Angle - Simple

The idea of this exercise is to develop one's draftsmanship to cultivate an ability to judge spacing, draw straight lines, and test these skills by drawing the connecting lines between the intersections. As well, this exercise improves one's ability to place lines that are not parallel, and is excellent practice for freehand perspective drawing.

First draw a line splitting the 90 degree angle at a corner of the page into two 45 degree angles, and continue splitting the angles as you create them. Then do the same for another corner. Finally, test your drawing by drawing more lines connecting the intersections of the lines from the two corners.

If your drawing is solid the lines connecting the intersections should flair consistently with few jogs to break up a consistent flair.

This is also good practice keeping track of your lines to help with freehand perspective drawing.

TO FULLY APPRECIATE THE IMPORTANCE OF THIS EXERCISE, SKIP AHEAD TO THE EPILOGUE, PAGES 147 TO 153. AS A SPORT, THE SKILLS DEVELOPED BY PRACTICING THIS EXERCISE ARE ESSENTIAL TO THE GOOD DRAFTSMANSHIP ABSOLULTELY NECESSARY TO ACHIEVE AN ARBITRARY GOAL SUCH AS PLACING A SPHERE IN PERSPECTIVE. AS WELL, PAGES 101 TO 103 PRESENT THE NECESSITY OF THE SKILLS DEVELOPED IN THIS EXERCISE !

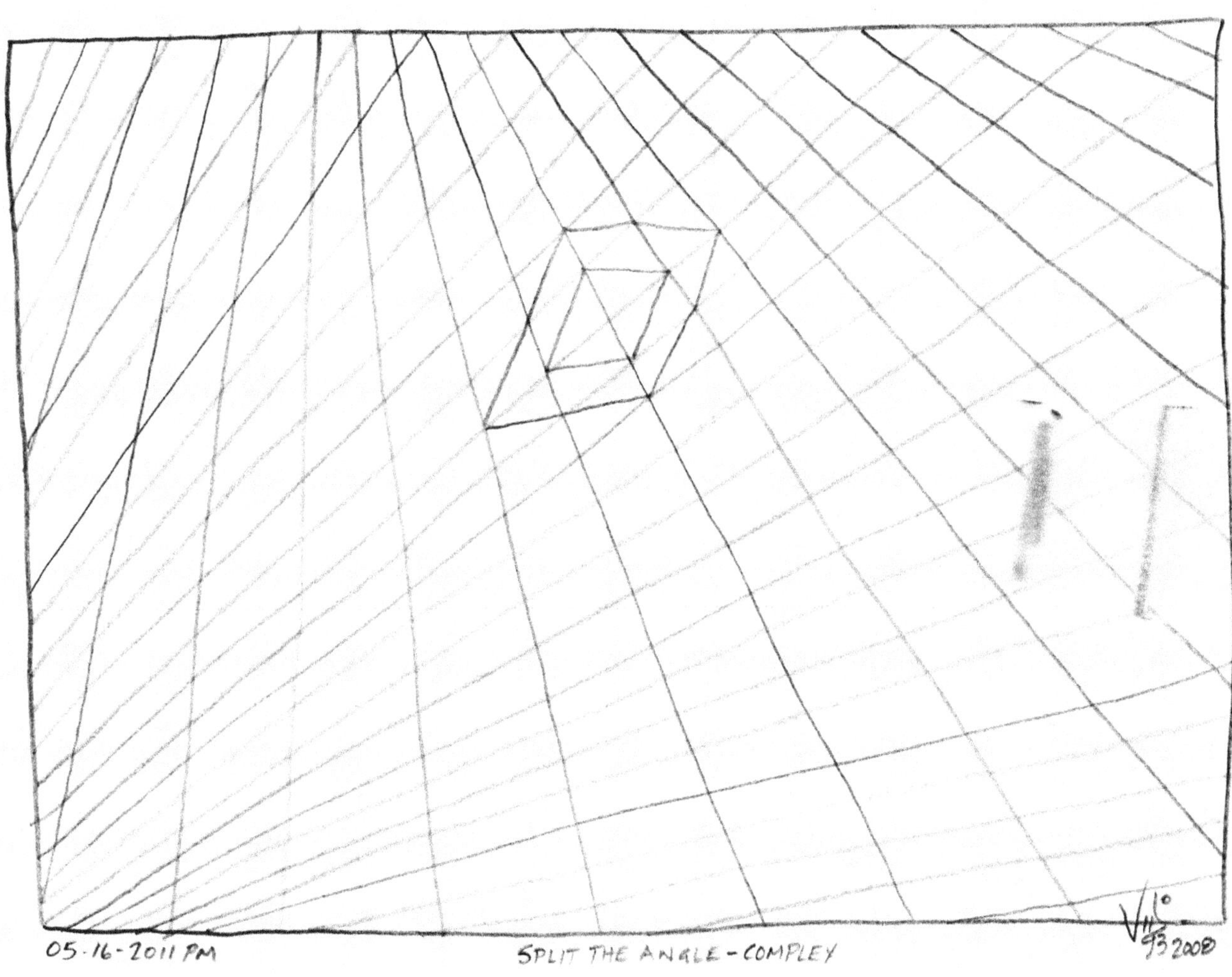

05-16-2011 PM SPLIT THE ANGLE - COMPLEX

Warm Ups :--

Split the Angle - Complex

Once one is comfortable with the previous Split the Angle exercise, and is able to place a line consistently between two lines that are not parallel, this exercise will challenge that ability .

First draw a line across the page at any angle, then draw another line at an angle to the first line . The lines should not cross . Continue by drawing a line midway between the first two lines, splitting the angle created by the first two lines . Continue splitting the angle created by the lines drawn, leaving the area outside of the first two lines until you have established the lines between the first two, and can project a single point of convergence of all the lines that is off the page .

Finally, connect the intersections with lines . If the drawing is consistent these lines should not have any jogs and will be consistent in one way or another .

TO FULLY APPRECIATE THE IMPORTANCE OF THIS EXERCISE, SKIP AHEAD TO THE EPILOGUE, PAGES 147 TO 153. AS A SPORT, THE SKILLS DEVELOPED BY PRACTICING THIS EXERCISE ARE ESSENTIAL TO THE GOOD DRAFTSMANSHIP ABSOLULTELY NECESSARY TO ACHIEVE AN ARBITRARY GOAL SUCH AS PLACING A SPHERE IN PERSPECTIVE. AS WELL, PAGES 101 TO 103 PRESENT THE NECESSITY OF THE SKILLS DEVELOPED IN THIS EXERCISE !

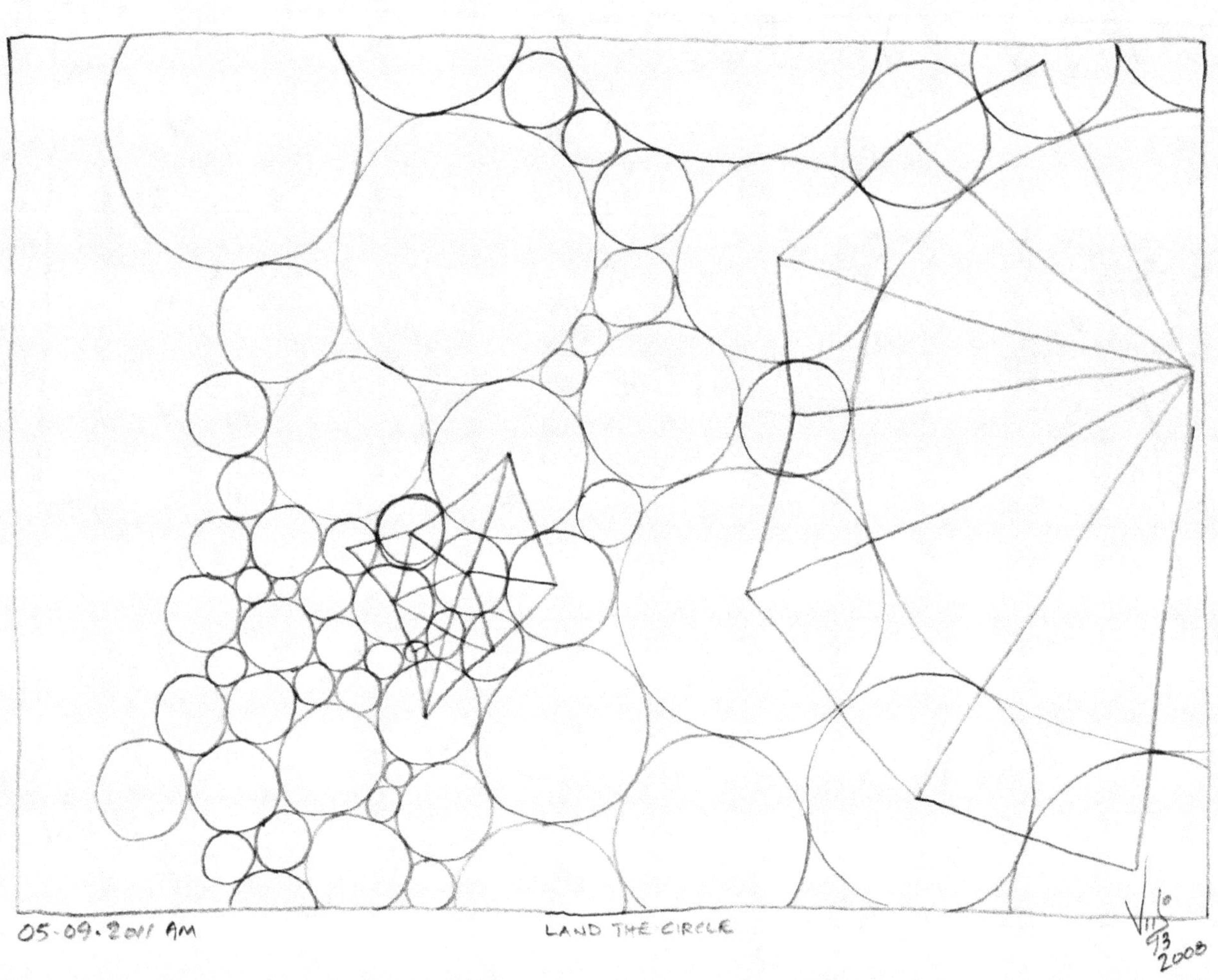

Warm Ups :--

Land the Circle - Simple

This is an exercise in drawing clean, consistently round circles . Instead of willy nilly circle drawing, this exercise forces one to place clean circles of a certain size exactly in a certain place .

Begin by drawing a clean circle anywhere in the page . Then draw a second circle tangent (touching) the first circle . Continue by drawing a third circle tangent to both other circles . Continue drawing tangent circles to more or less fill the page . A clean circle ic one that doec not have any "hookc" where it ic closed .

Drawing clean accurate circles is essential to drawing people as a circle is the base of drawing a portrait . As well, once one is proficient at drawing circles they may continue on to drawing clean ellipses as they are able to judge and place a smooth curve .

Finally, test your drawing by drawing lines between the centres of the circles . These lines should pass precisely through the point where the two adjacent circles touch .

TO FULLY APPRECIATE THE IMPORTANCE OF THIS EXERCISE, SKIP AHEAD TO THE EPILOGUE, PAGES 147 TO 153. AS A SPORT, THE SKILLS DEVELOPED BY PRACTICING THIS EXERCISE ARE ESSENTIAL TO THE GOOD DRAFTSMANSHIP ABSOLULTELY NECESSARY TO ACHIEVE AN ARBITRARY GOAL SUCH AS PLACING A SPHERE IN PERSPECTIVE.

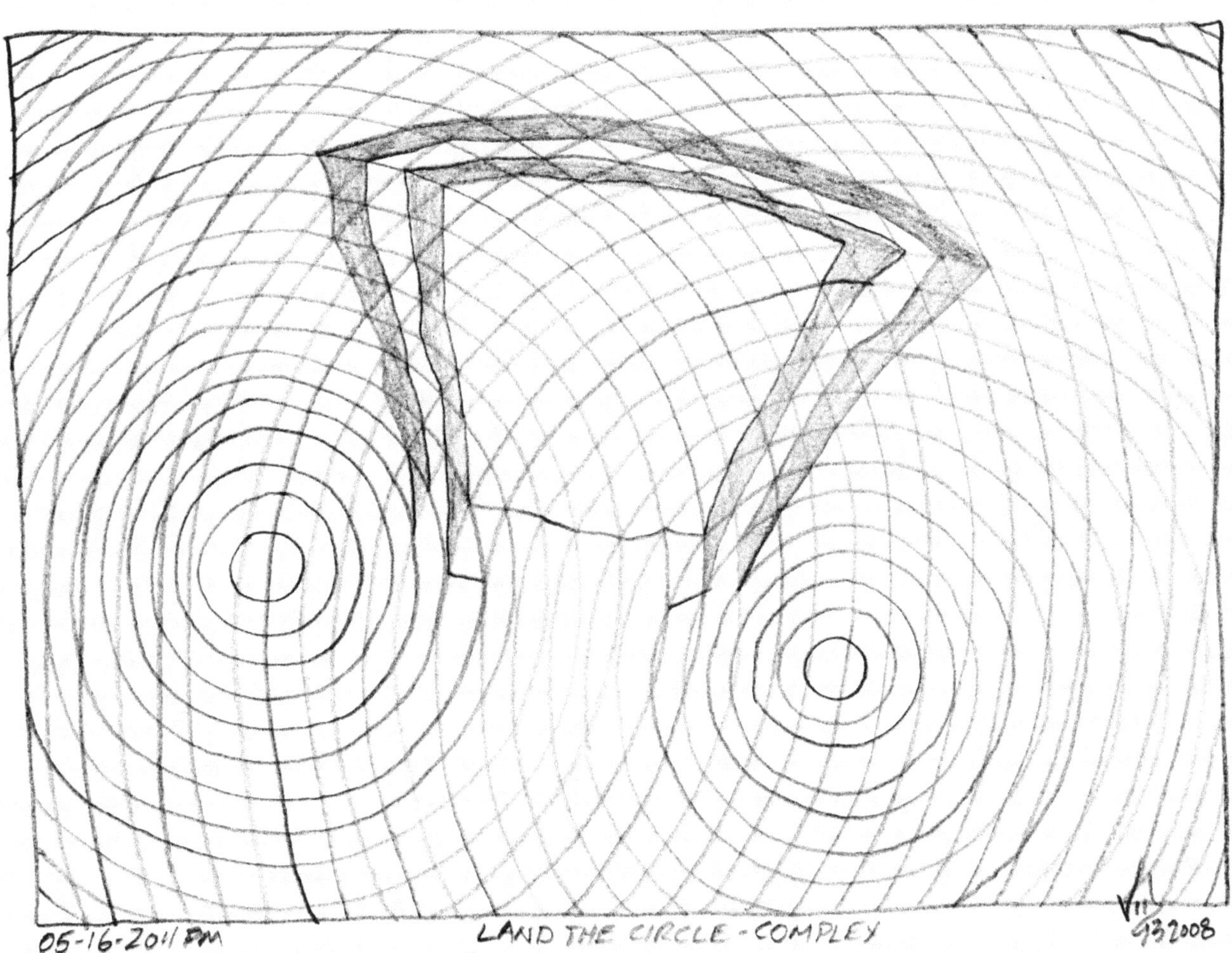

Warm Ups :--

Land the Circle - Complex

This is an exercise in drawing clean, consistently round circles. Instead of willy nilly circle drawing, this exercise again forces one to place clean circles of a certain size exactly in a certain place.

Begin by drawing a clean small circle anywhere in the page. Then draw a second circle around the first circle. Continue by drawing more and more circles outside of the first circles. Leave a bit of space between the circles, and then once the page is filled, go back and draw more circles in between the circles. This is called "inbetweening" and helps to maintain consistency. Then draw another small circle with a different centre location, and fill the page again with circles concentric with the second small circle you just drew.

Drawing clean accurate circles is essential to drawing people as a circle is the base of drawing a portrait. As well, once one is proficient at drawing circles they may continue on to drawing clean ellipses as they are able to judge and place a smooth curve.

Finally, test your drawing by drawing lines between the intersections of the circles. These lines should flair consistently, with very few jogs, if the circles are even and consistent.

TO FULLY APPRECIATE THE IMPORTANCE OF THIS EXERCISE, SKIP AHEAD TO THE EPILOGUE, PAGES 147 TO 153. AS A SPORT, THE SKILLS DEVELOPED BY PRACTICING THIS EXERCISE ARE ESSENTIAL TO THE GOOD DRAFTSMANSHIP ABSOLULTELY NECESSARY TO ACHIEVE AN ARBITRARY GOAL SUCH AS PLACING A SPHERE IN PERSPECTIVE.

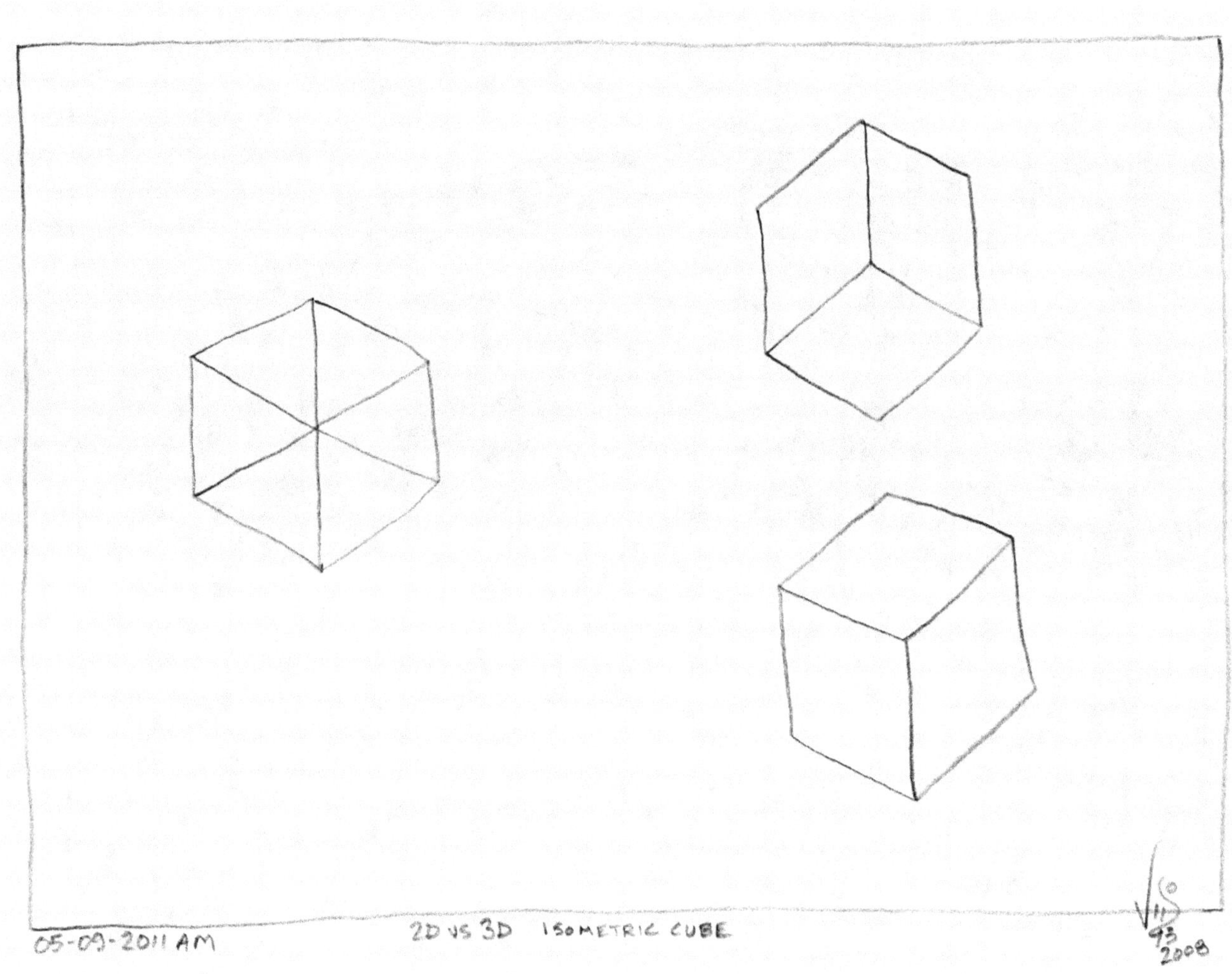

Warm Ups :--

Isometric Cube :
- 2D vs . 3D

This exercise illustrates two different ways of looking at the drawing piece of paper . One way is to see pencil lines on paper, and the other way is to see the paper as a window into a three dimensional space, and drawing becomes just tracing the image of the three dimensional world that exists beyond the window of the paper, onto that window, or paper .

Begin by drawing a clean equilateral (three sides the same length) triangle with one side absolutely vertical . Continue by drawing adjacent equilateral triangles until the entire shape forms a hexagon of six equilateral triangles . At this point it looks like a flat hexagon or perhaps looking down on a flat pie .

But if one erases three alternating (do not erase adjacent lines) interior lines, of which one is vertical, the image takes on the look of a box in three dimensions . This shift in one's perception must be noted and cultivated so that it can be made to happen at will .

This is a very simple exercise but it is essential as a means to keep track of the image that otherwise easily becomes a jumble of lines if one cannot perceive such a drawing as a three dimensional image .

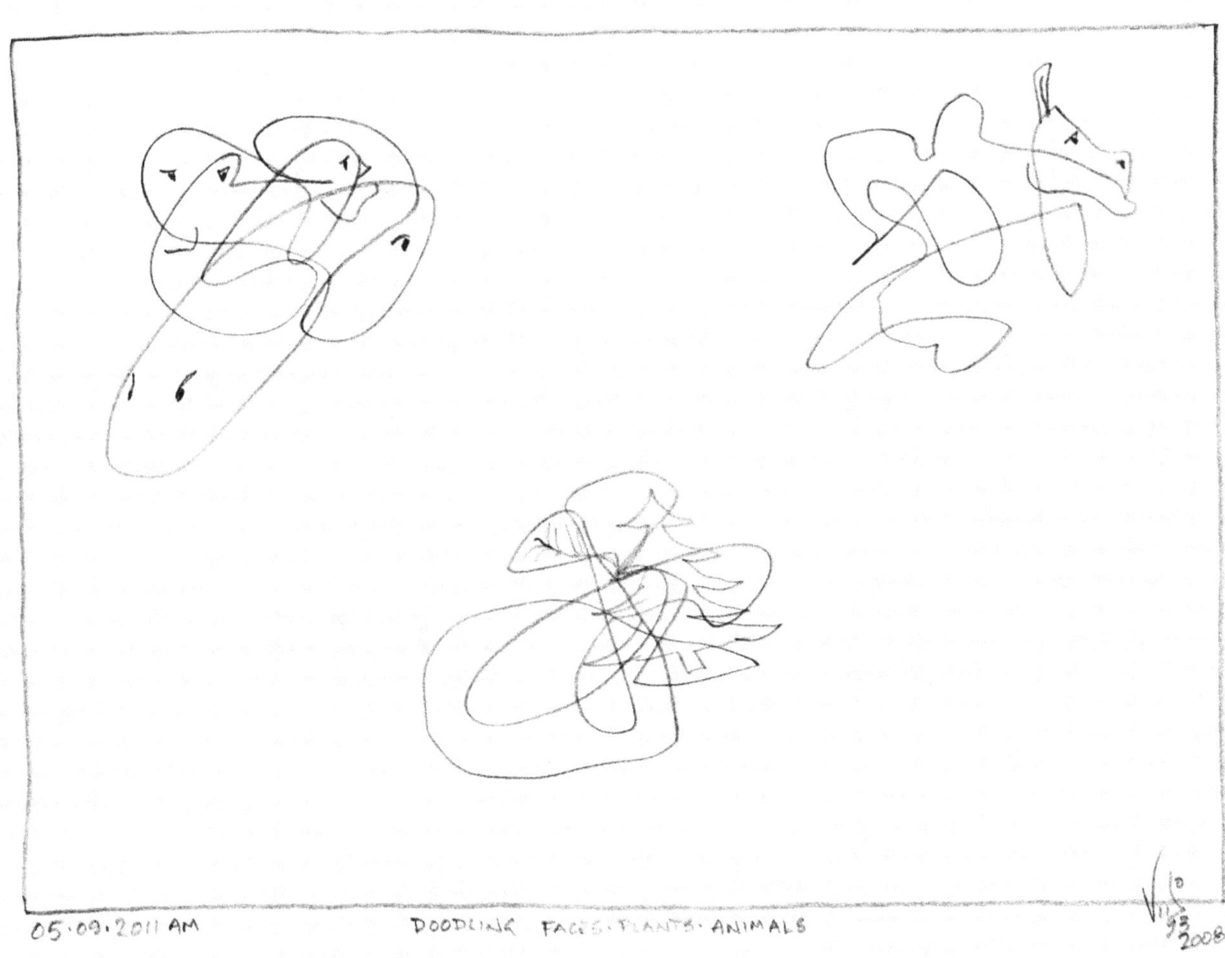

Warm Ups :--

Doodling :,
- Faces, Plants, Animals

This is an exercise in seeing an image in the page. This is important because if you cannot see the image through the page it is very difficult to construct a solid three dimensional image.

Begin by scribbling randomly in a fair size portion of the page. Then try to see a face in the scribble you just drew. There has to be at least one in any scribbled line. Continue by drawing features such as eyes, nose and mouth, to confirm the image of a face that you found in the scribble. Then see if you can make more images of faces in the same scribble.

Do the same again and try to find images of plants and then again to find images of animals.

This forces one again, to see three dimensions through the window of a two dimensional piece of paper. It also challenges one to expand their visual vocabulary.

This is the end of the Warm Up section. Any of these exercises are something one can do when they are feeling uninspired and don't know what to draw. They are mostly technical and do not present much of a creative challenge, which may be what one needs when they first sit down to draw on a Monday morning. : >

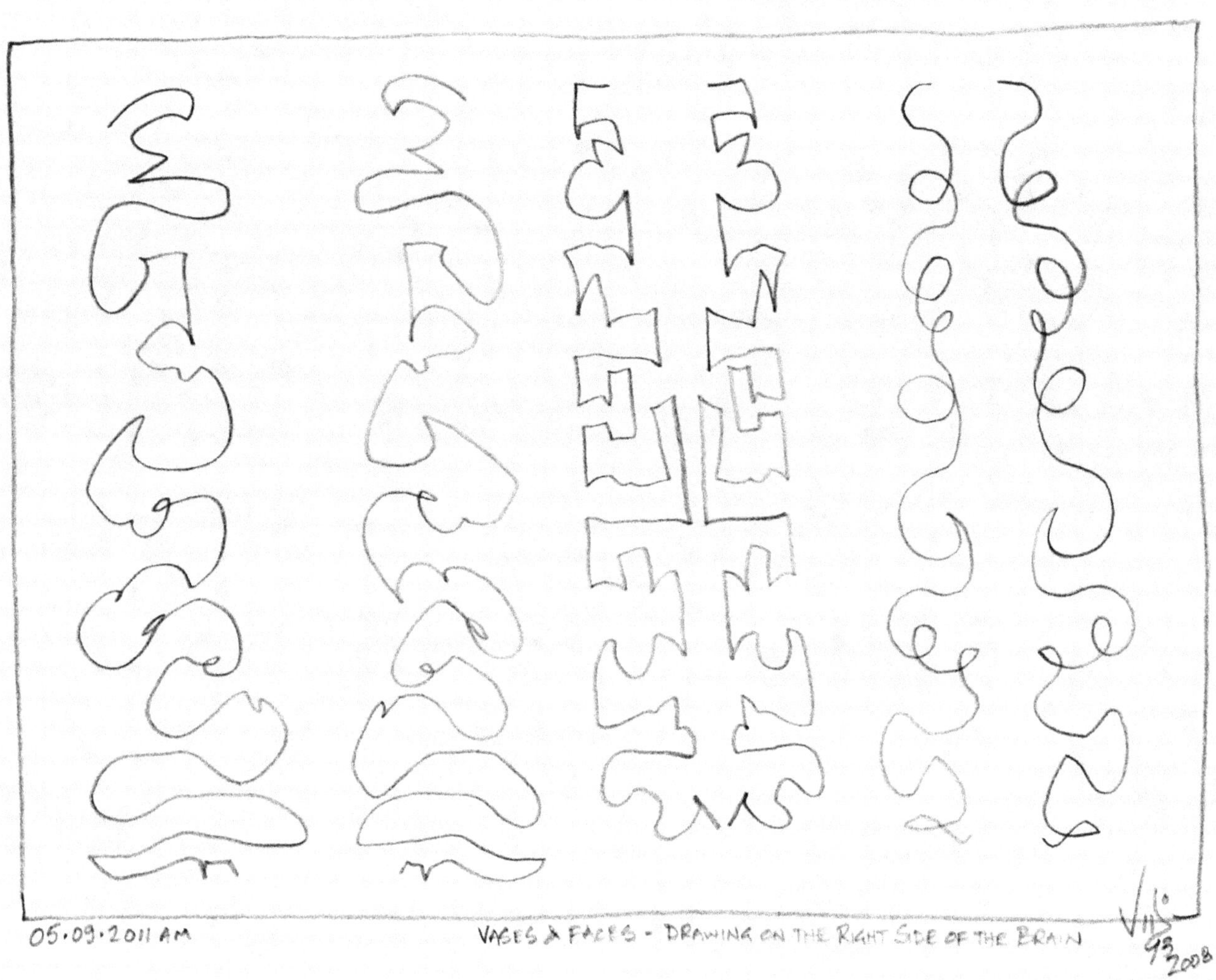

05.09.2011 AM
VASES & FACES - DRAWING ON THE RIGHT SIDE OF THE BRAIN
93
2008

Vases & Faces:

from ***Drawing on the Right Side of the Brain***
which is a book written by Betty Edwards and is readily available at book stores. I have taken seven exercises from this book, which I feel incorporate essential skills in which any person trying to draw needs to be proficient. These skills are the hardest to learn, and the most effective at improving one's ability and enjoyment of drawing. Practice these exercises earnestly and frequently.

This is an exercise forcing one to think visually. Most people have a strong tendency to rush through this incorrectly or get stumped and very frustrated with this exercise.

Begin by scribbling randomly down one side of the page.

Then, down the right side of the page, draw the mirror image of the scribble you just drew.

Use the example of the image above to get the idea. There are three pairs of lines, in the image, and each pair is two lines that are the mirror, or opposite, image of the other.

Drawing on the Right Side of the Brain Author: ***Betty Edwards***
ISBN-13: **9780874775136** ISBN-10: **0874775132** Edition: **Revised** Binding: **Paperback**
Publisher: **Tarcher** Published: **May 1989** List Price: **$15.95**

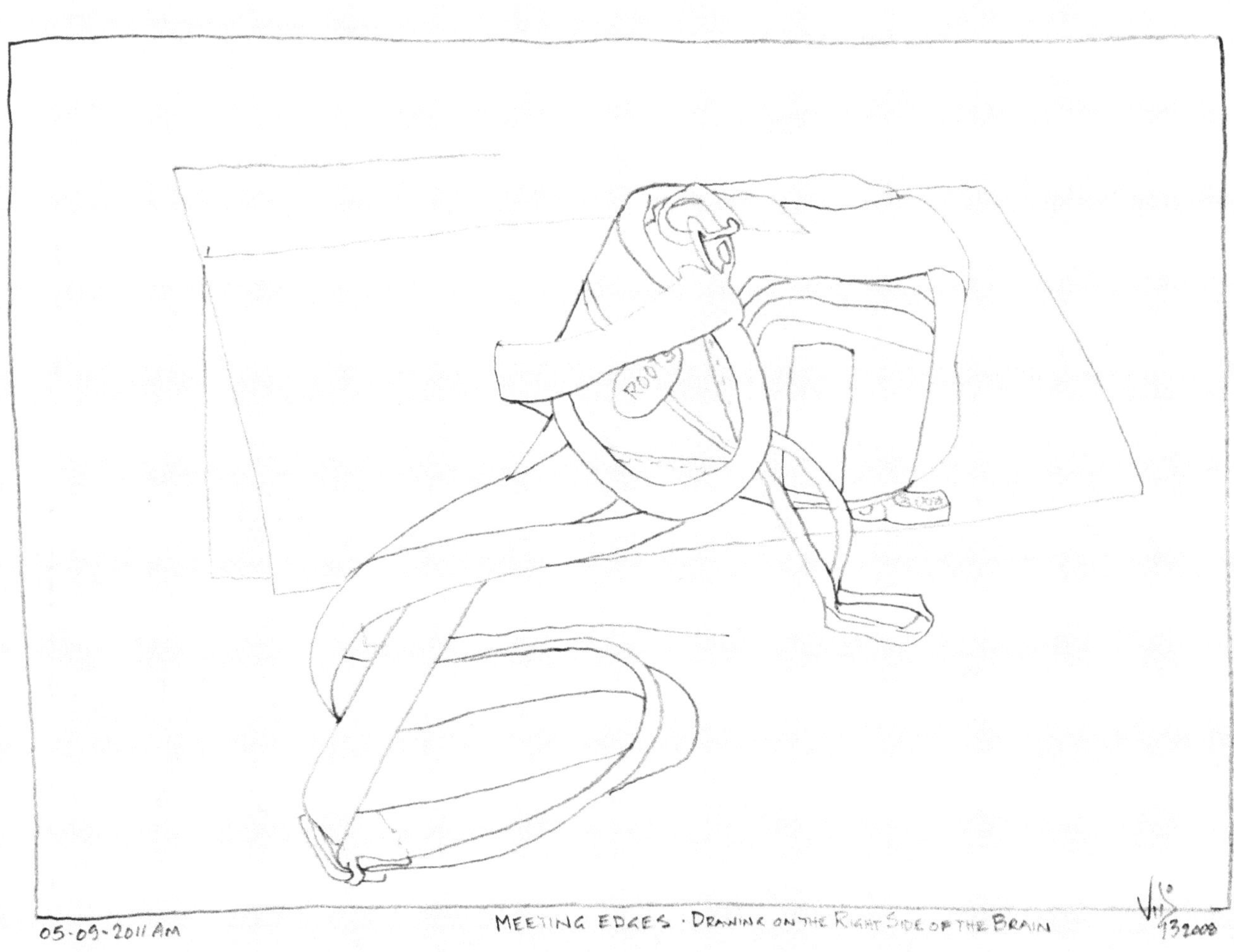

ROOTS
05-09-2011 AM
MEETING EDGES · DRAWING ON THE RIGHT SIDE OF THE BRAIN

Meeting Edges:

from ***Drawing on the Right Side of the Brain***

Paying attention to the larger image and how parts relate to other parts, in a drawing, is what this exercise is about .

Any area of an image that can be defined by an outer edge, meets other areas that can be defined by an outer edge, at some edge that can be drawn as a line . These areas can be viewed as pieces of a puzzle so that drawing the image becomes tracing the outlines of the puzzle pieces . This tracing of the margin defining, simultaneously, two separate puzzle pieces, forces one to think visually and use the skills practiced in the previous exercise " Vases & Faces" .

As this is the first real observation and production of a finished drawing, choose a subject that is more or less arbitrary and generally some sort of jumble . This will force one to observe rather than implement a symbol for the subject . Good subjects are a pile of pencils or a crumpled piece of paper . Bubble wrap has been used effectively for this exercise, and if you can get some, try it if you dare . :P

Drawing on the Right Side of the Brain Author: ***Betty Edwards***
ISBN-13: **9780874775136** ISBN-10: **0874775132** Edition: **Revised** Binding: **Paperback**
Publisher: **Tarcher** Published: **May 1989** List Price: **$15.95**

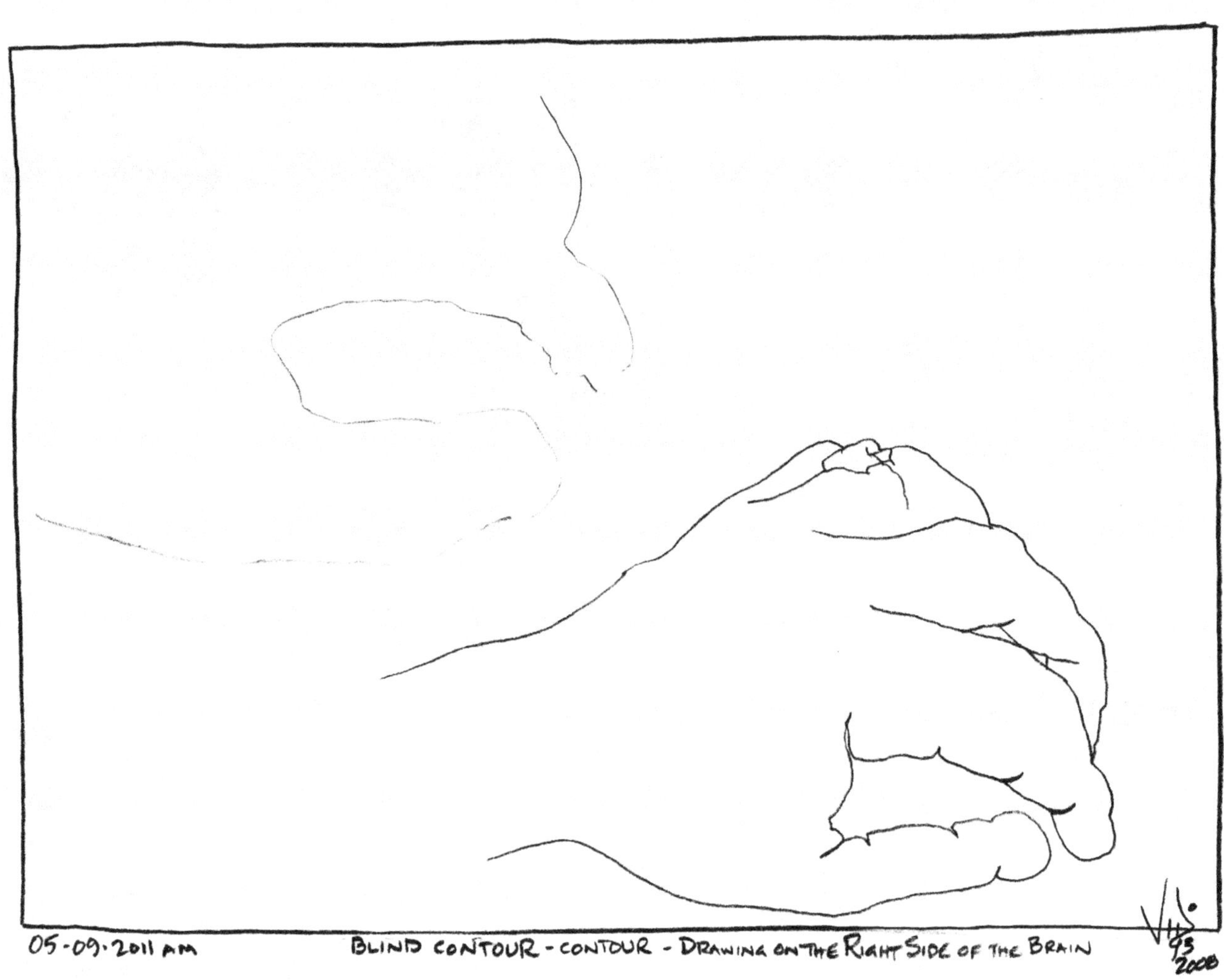

Blind Contour & Contour Drawing:

from ***Drawing on the Right Side of the Brain***

This is an exercise forcing one to observe. The whole point of this exercise is to observe, with any drawing produced being incidental.

Begin by tracing the contours that traverse something organic, usually your off hand, while only looking at your hand and not looking at your drawing ever. This is why it is called "Blind Contour", as you are blind to your drawing. You may need to tape your paper down to keep it from moving as you draw.

Just have your pencil move on the paper in the same way that your eye follows along any contour it can find that traverses the subject, your off hand. You may also draw the outline of your hand by again, having your pencil move simultaneously and in the same way that your eye moves along the contour. If this exercise is done correctly, without peeking, one will end up with a jumble of very interesting lines.

Contour drawing is the same except you may look at your drawing to line up lines and adjust proportions. Nevertheless, the point of this exercise is to observe, observe, observe!

Drawing on the Right Side of the Brain Author: ***Betty Edwards***
ISBN-13: **9780874775136** ISBN-10: **0874775132** Edition: **Revised** Binding: **Paperback**
Publisher: **Tarcher** Published: **May 1989** List Price: **$15.95**

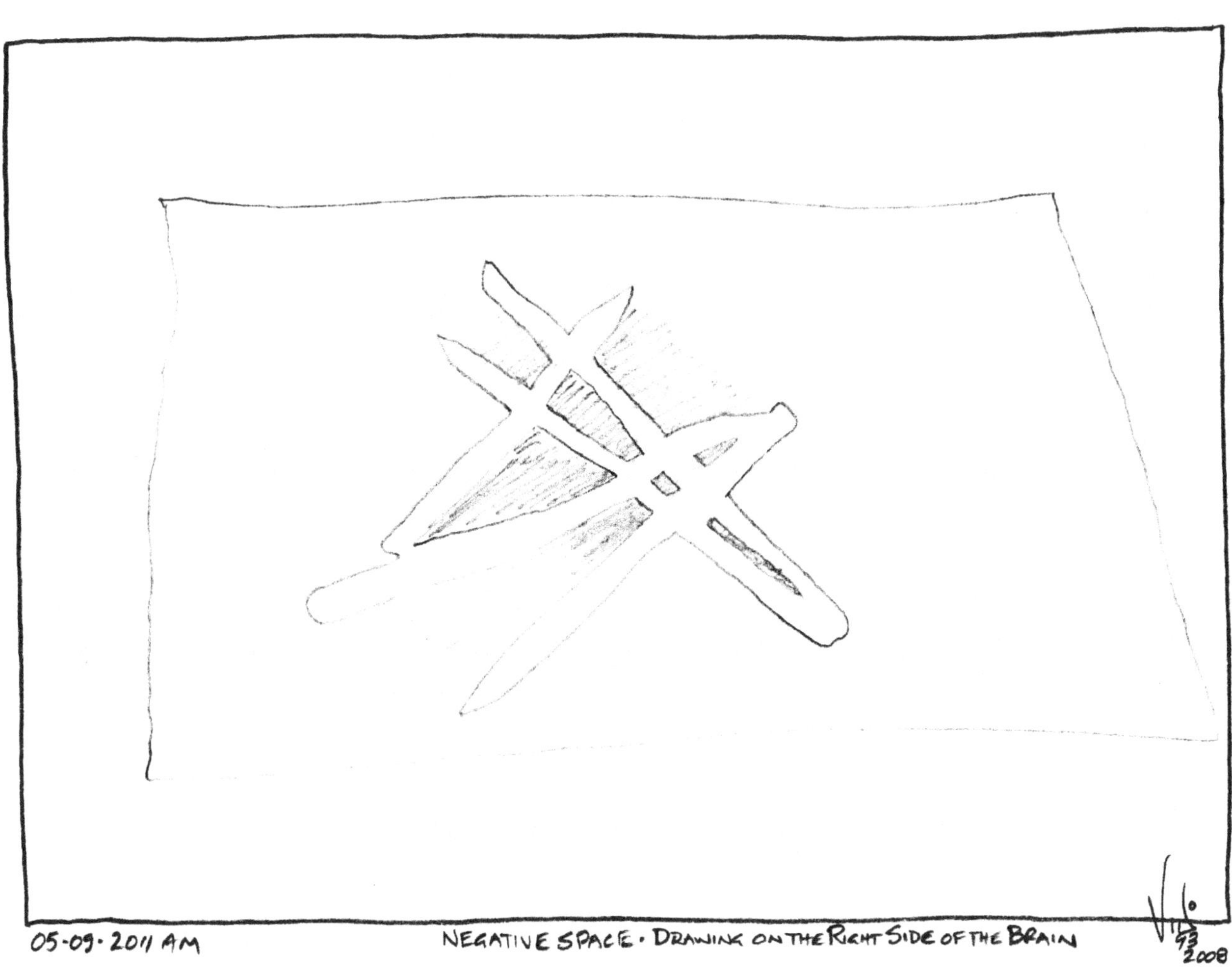

05-09-2011 AM
NEGATIVE SPACE • DRAWING ON THE RIGHT SIDE OF THE BRAIN
2008

Negative Space:
from ***Drawing on the Right Side of the Brain***

This is another exercise forcing one to observe. The point of this exercise is to look at the spaces between the objects you are drawing, and draw the blank (negative) spaces rather than the objects (positive spaces).

A pile of pencils, scraps of torn papers in a pile, or a chair are all good subjects to draw with this exercise. Remember to draw the empty spaces rather than the objects. Get the shape and size of the space, rather than the objects that form the "negative" space.

If you are drawing a chair, draw all the spaces between the legs and within the back of the chair, and then once that is done complete the drawing by drawing the outer edge of the chair image to hold all the negative spaces together.

This exercise forces one to see the real shapes rather than reiterate a symbol of a chair. The angle and the orientation of the chair will come through in the drawing if one is faithful to observing and drawing the negative spaces formed by the chair.

Drawing a pile of papers or a pile of pencils will confound the urge to reiterate a symbol, and although not as recognizable as a chair, will still facilitate an interesting drawing. Remember - observe, observe, observe!

Drawing on the Right Side of the Brain Author: ***Betty Edwards***
ISBN-13: **9780874775136** ISBN-10: **0874775132** Edition: **Revised** Binding: **Paperback**
Publisher: **Tarcher** Published: **May 1989** List Price: **$15.95**

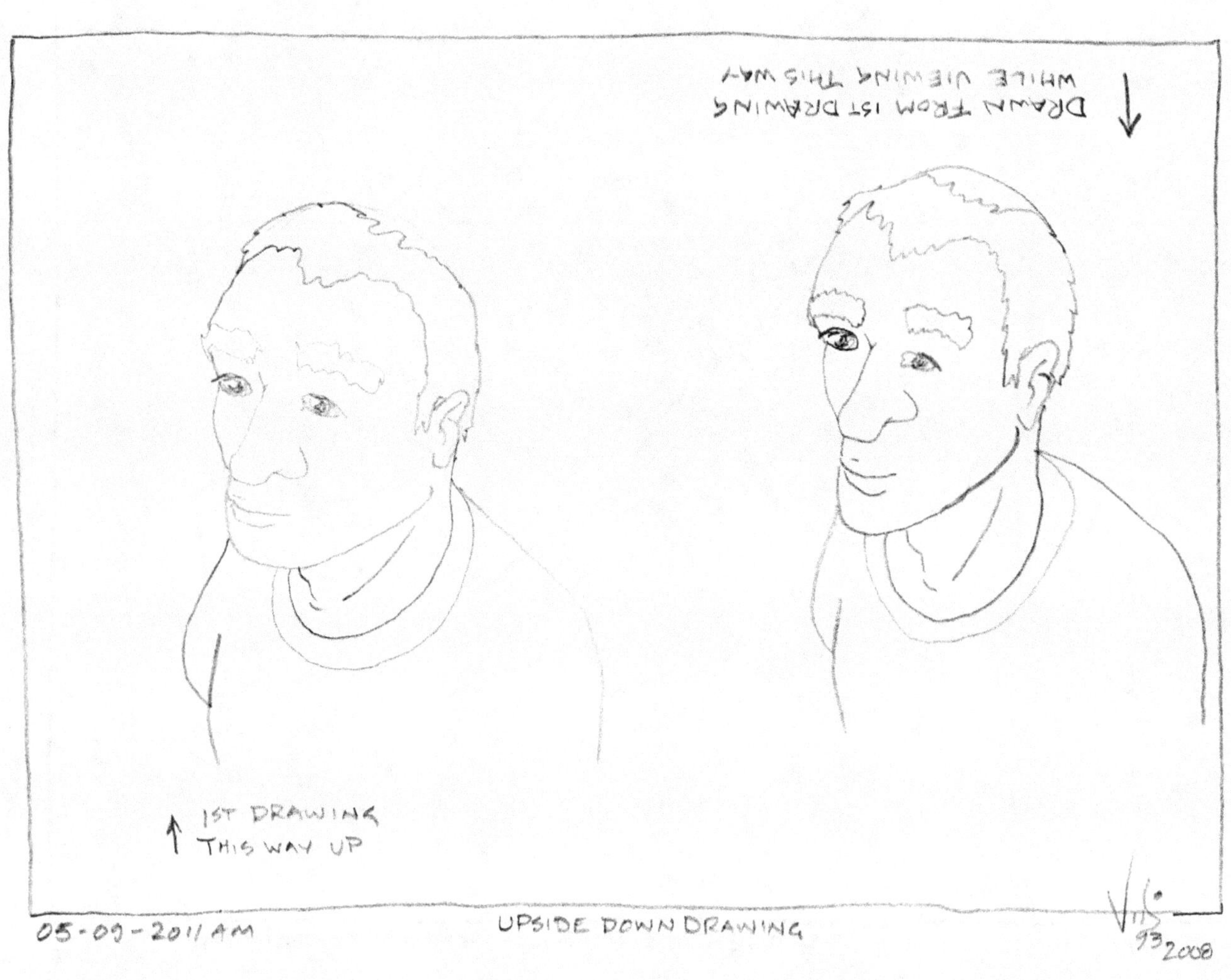

Upside Down Drawing :

from ***Drawing on the Right Side of the Brain***

Instead of seeing the image for what it is - an identifiable object, turning the drawing upside down to copy it changes the image into a jumble of lines and shapes, and this allows the mind to duplicate the actual shapes and lines rather than substitute a known symbol for the identified object . The greater the complexity of the original drawing being copied, the more astounding the result of copying it when it is viewed upside down .

Drawing on the Right Side of the Brain Author: ***Betty Edwards***
ISBN-13: **9780874775136** ISBN-10: **0874775132** Edition: **Revised** Binding: **Paperback**
Publisher: **Tarcher** Published: **May 1989** List Price: **$15.95**

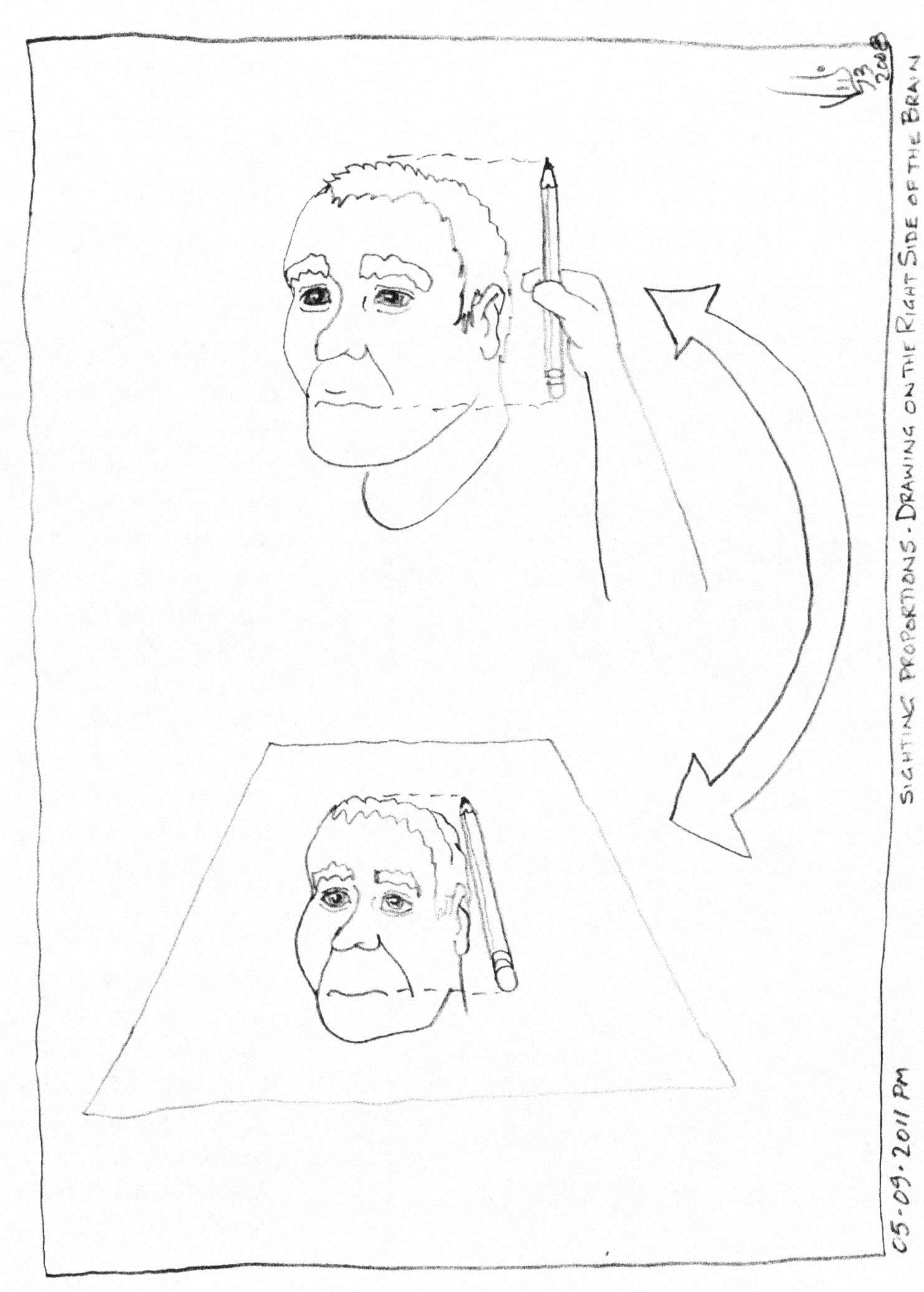

Sighting Proportions:

from ***Drawing on the Right Side of the Brain***

This is an often misunderstood process and is difficult to describe in a single drawing. In this case I have illustrated how one may transfer a distance from sighting to the drawing.

What the process of sighting is really about, is comparing measurements as they are sighted and then maintaining the same proportions in the drawing. An example of this would be if the distance between the eyes is half a pencil and the height of the head is a full pencil, then on the drawing the distance between the eyes should be half of the height of the head.

This is the end of the section referring to the book ***Drawing on the Right Side of the Brain***

Drawing on the Right Side of the Brain Author: ***Betty Edwards***
ISBN-13: **9780874775136** ISBN-10: **0874775132** Edition: **Revised** Binding: **Paperback**
Publisher: **Tarcher** Published: **May 1989** List Price: **$15.95**

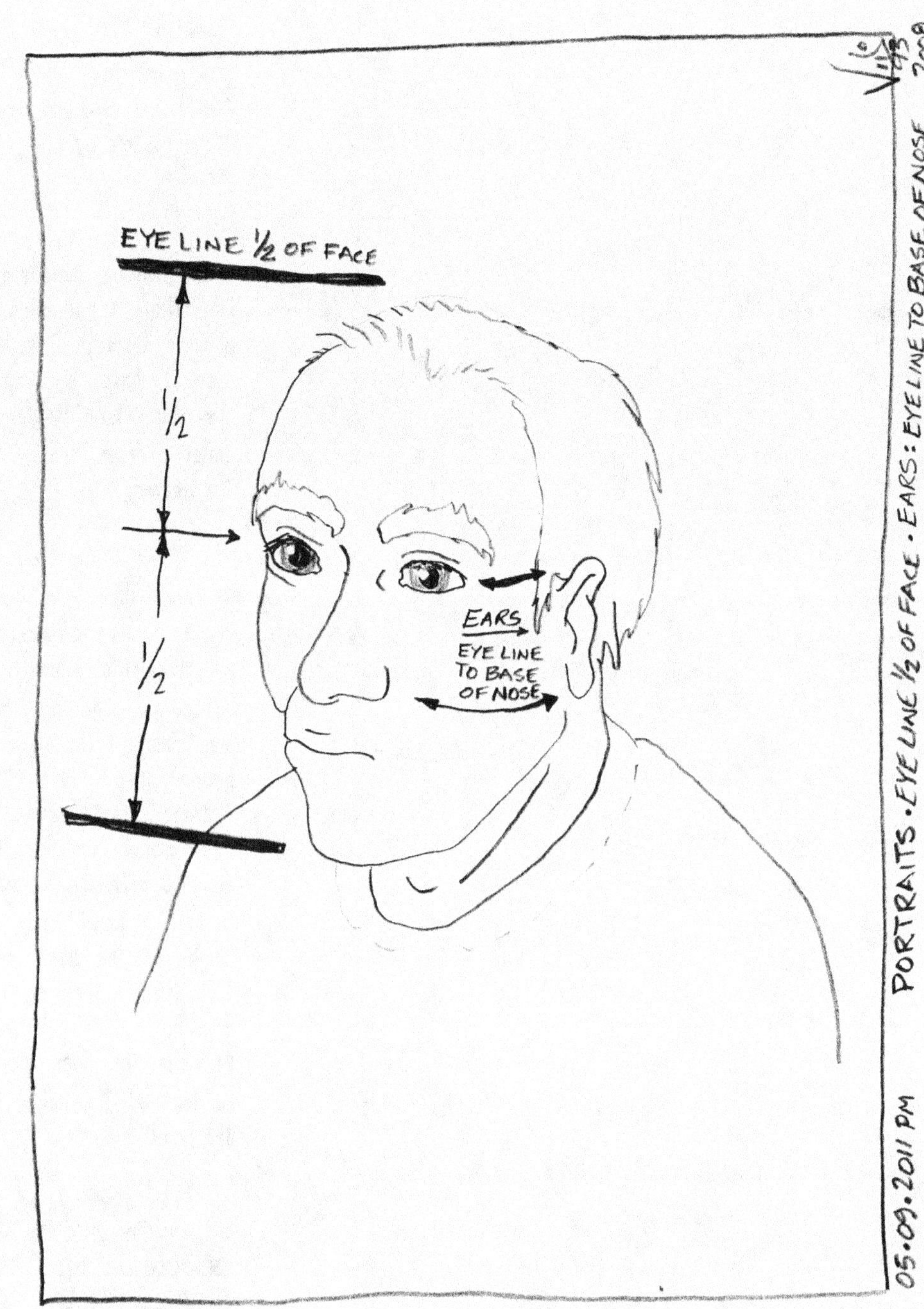

Portraits

Eye Line
Half of Head Height

Ears :
Eye Line to
Base of Nose

An example of proportions in an image is the relatively constant relationship between the position of the eyes in the whole of the head. Keep in mind that the eyes are halfway up the head, and the hair may be much higher than the top of the head. One has to judge the actual top of the skull when placing the eyes.

There are always variations which can be identified when one is actually observing the subject.

The ears are another relatively constant proportion that extends from the eye line to the base of the nose. This proportion, again will vary with actual drawing subjects, and checking these proportions will disclose whether this rule is true with a specific drawing subject.

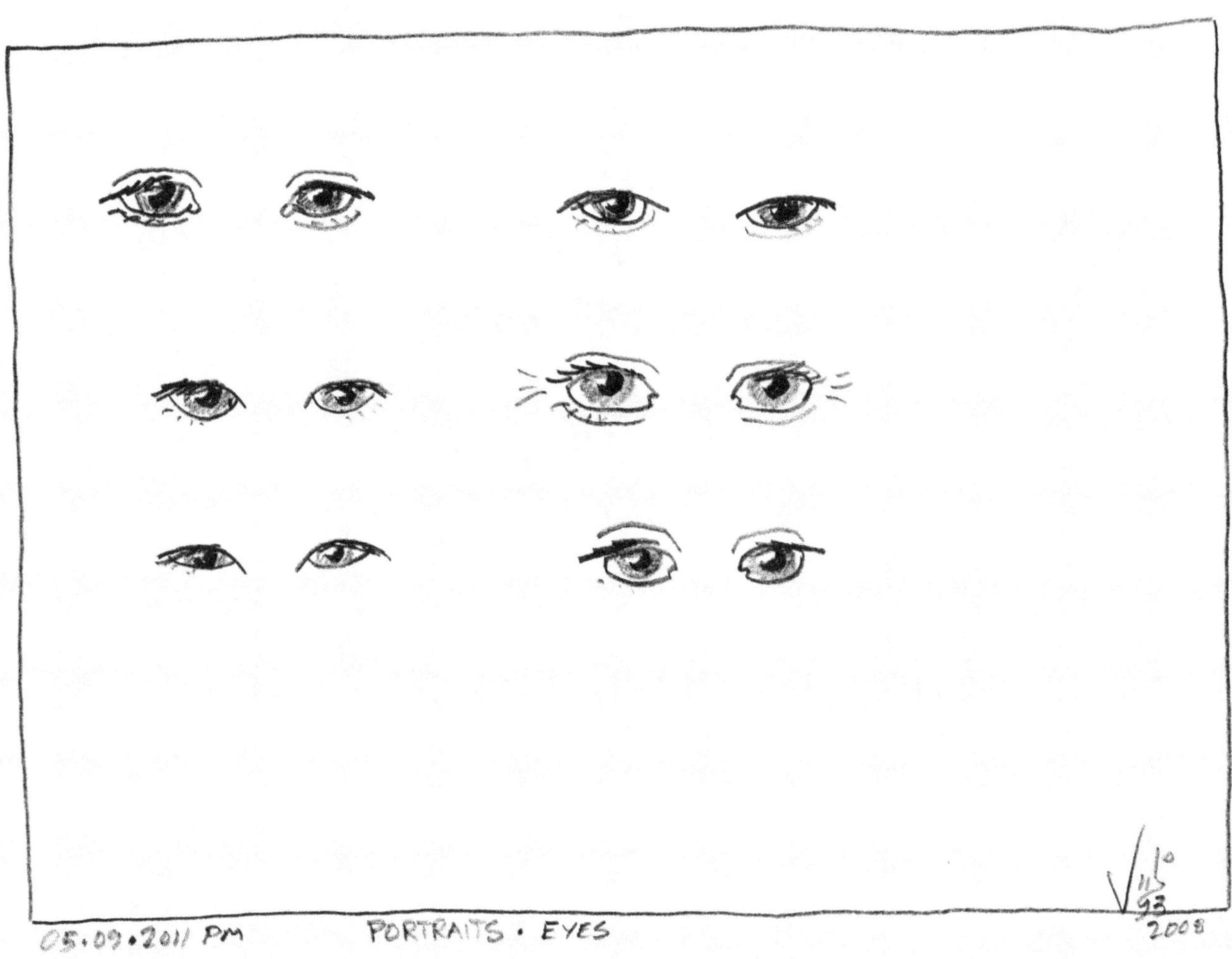

Portraits

Eyes

Eyes are the first of many items in a portrait that must be observed carefully to create a likeness. When drawing from life use the Drawing on the Right Side of the Brain exercises of negative space and vases and faces. One can draw the shape above the eye and the shape between the eye and the nose. Often one eye will be open more than another, and this can establish a mood. Also check for the presence of creases or folds above and below the eye, in the eyelids.

Regular deliberate observation of people one meets from day to day will help to increase one's Visual Vocabulary so that one may recall many types of eyes when drawing from the imagination.

One can copy these eyes to start, but take the opportunity as it comes to carefully observe the eyes of people you meet.

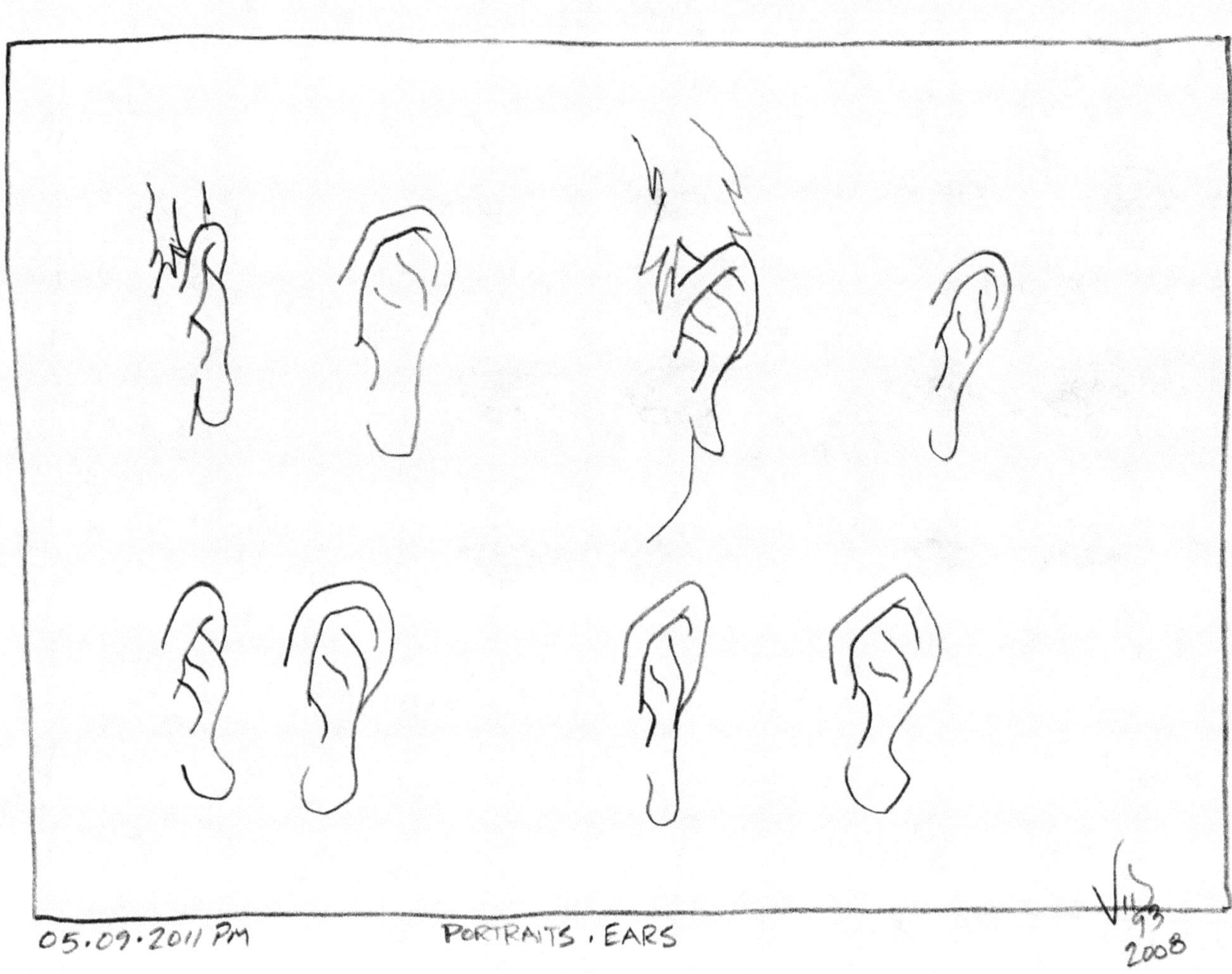

Portraits

Ears

Ears are a second of many items in a portrait that must be observed carefully to create a likeness. When drawing from life use the Drawing on the Right Side of the Brain exercises of negative space and vases and faces. One can draw the shape around the ear and the shape between the ear and the hair line. Often one ear will be different from the other, and this can establish a mood.

Regular deliberate observation of people one meets from day to day will help to increase one's Visual Vocabulary so that one may recall many types of ears when drawing from the imagination.

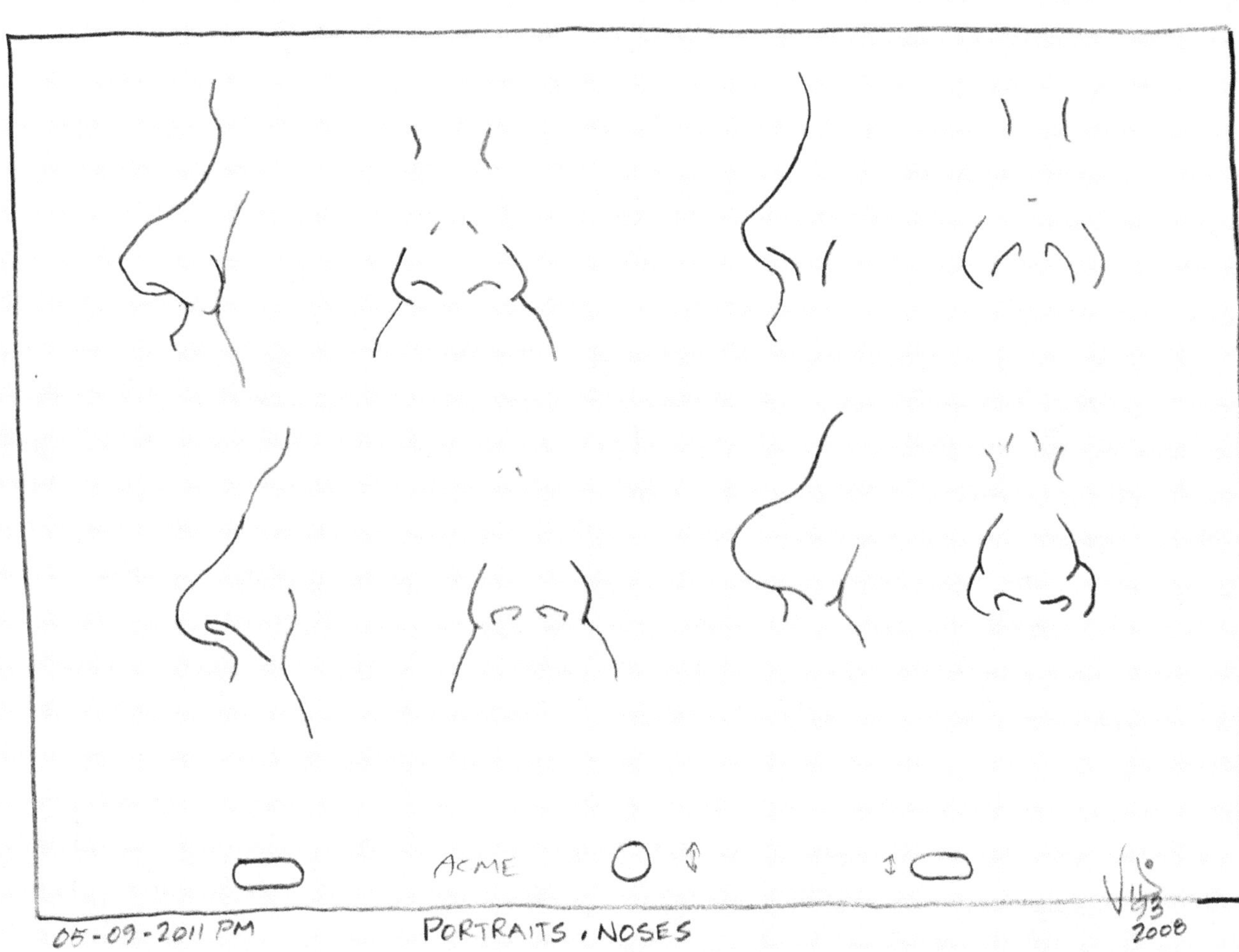

Portraits

Noses

Noses are a third of many items in a portrait that must be observed carefully to create a likeness. When drawing from life use the Drawing on the Right Side of the Brain exercises of negative space and vases and faces. One can draw the shape around the nose and the shape between the ear and the mouth. Often one side of the nose will be different from the other, and this can establish a mood.

Regular deliberate observation of people one meets from day to day will help to increase one's Visual Vocabulary so that one may recall many types of noses when drawing from the imagination.

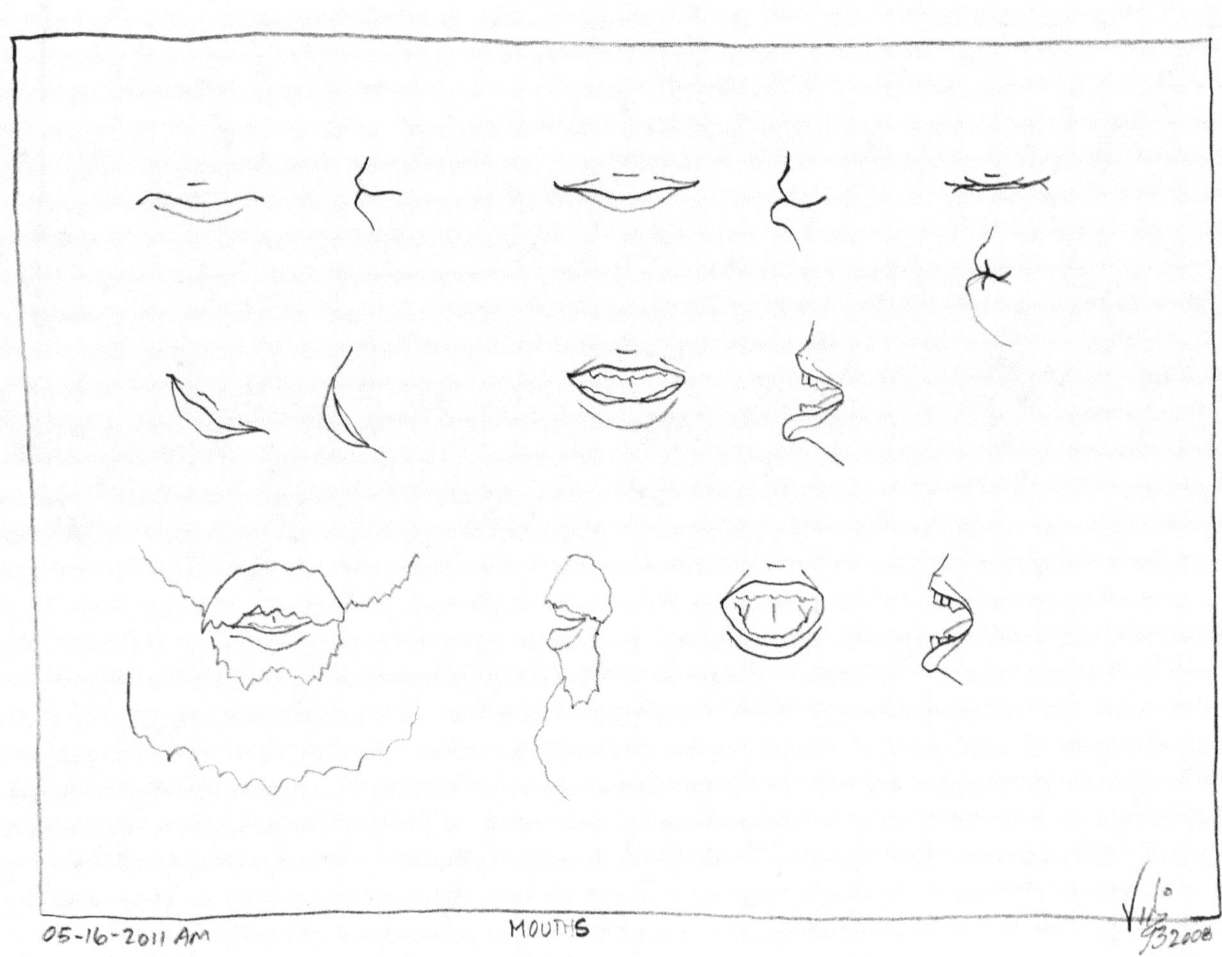

Portraits

Mouths

Mouths are a fourth of many items in a portrait that must be observed carefully to create a likeness. When drawing from life use the Drawing on the Right Side of the Brain exercises of negative space and vases and faces. One can draw the shape around the mouth and the shape between the nose and the chin, and the mouth. Often one side of the mouth will be different from the other, and this can establish a mood.

Regular deliberate observation of people one meets from day to day will help to increase one's Visual Vocabulary so that one may recall many types of mouths when drawing from the imagination.

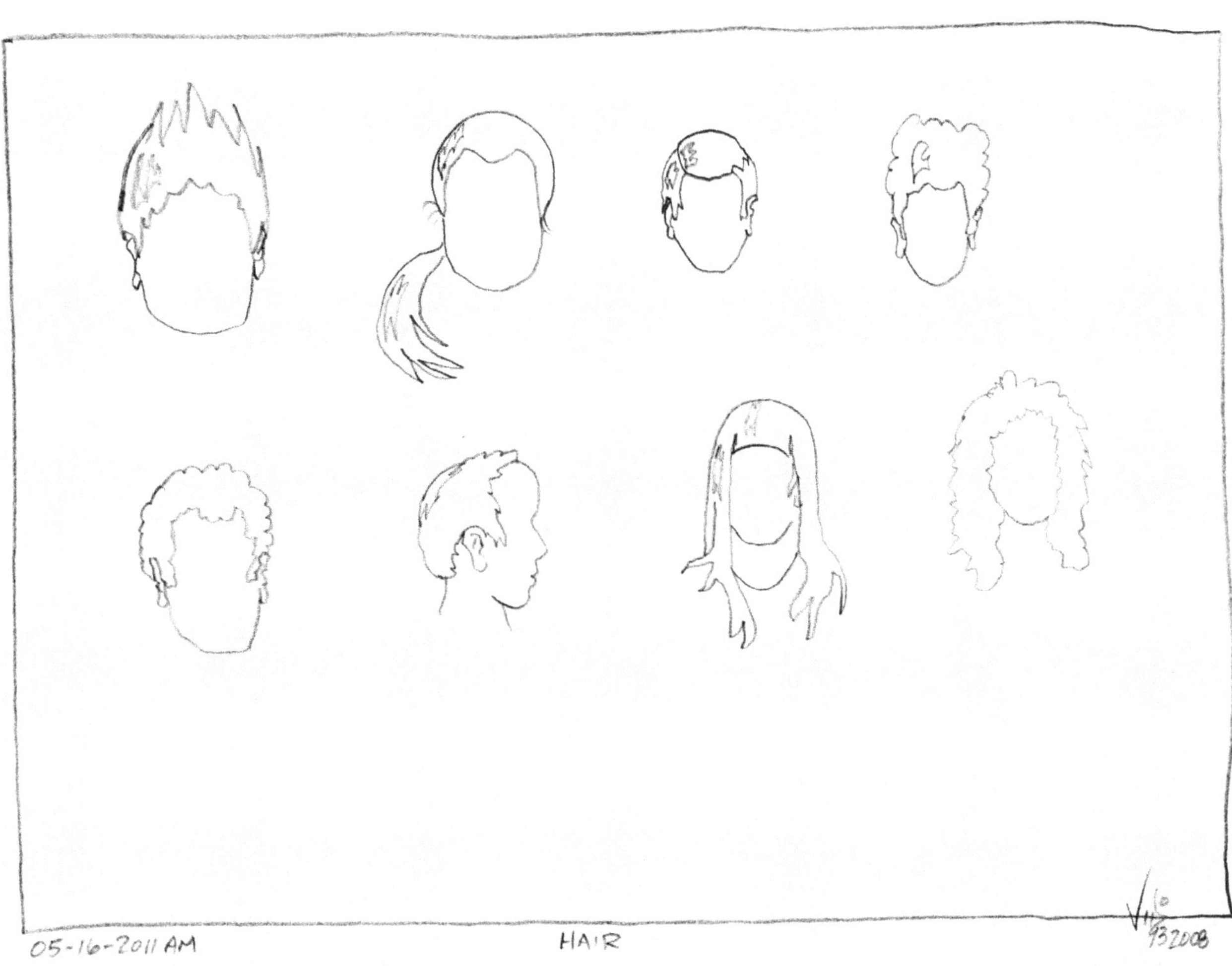

Portraits

Hair

Hair styles are a fifth and the final item addressed in this book, of many and far more portrait items that must be considered in any portrait, and all items must be observed carefully to create a likeness. When drawing from life use the Drawing on the Right Side of the Brain exercises of negative space and vases and faces. One can draw the shape of the forehead and cheeks to achieve a likeness of how the hair is positioned around the face. Very often one side of the hair will be different from the other, such as when the hair is parted on one side and this can establish a mood.

Regular deliberate observation of people one meets from day to day will help to increase one's Visual Vocabulary so that one may recall many types of hair styles when drawing from the imagination.

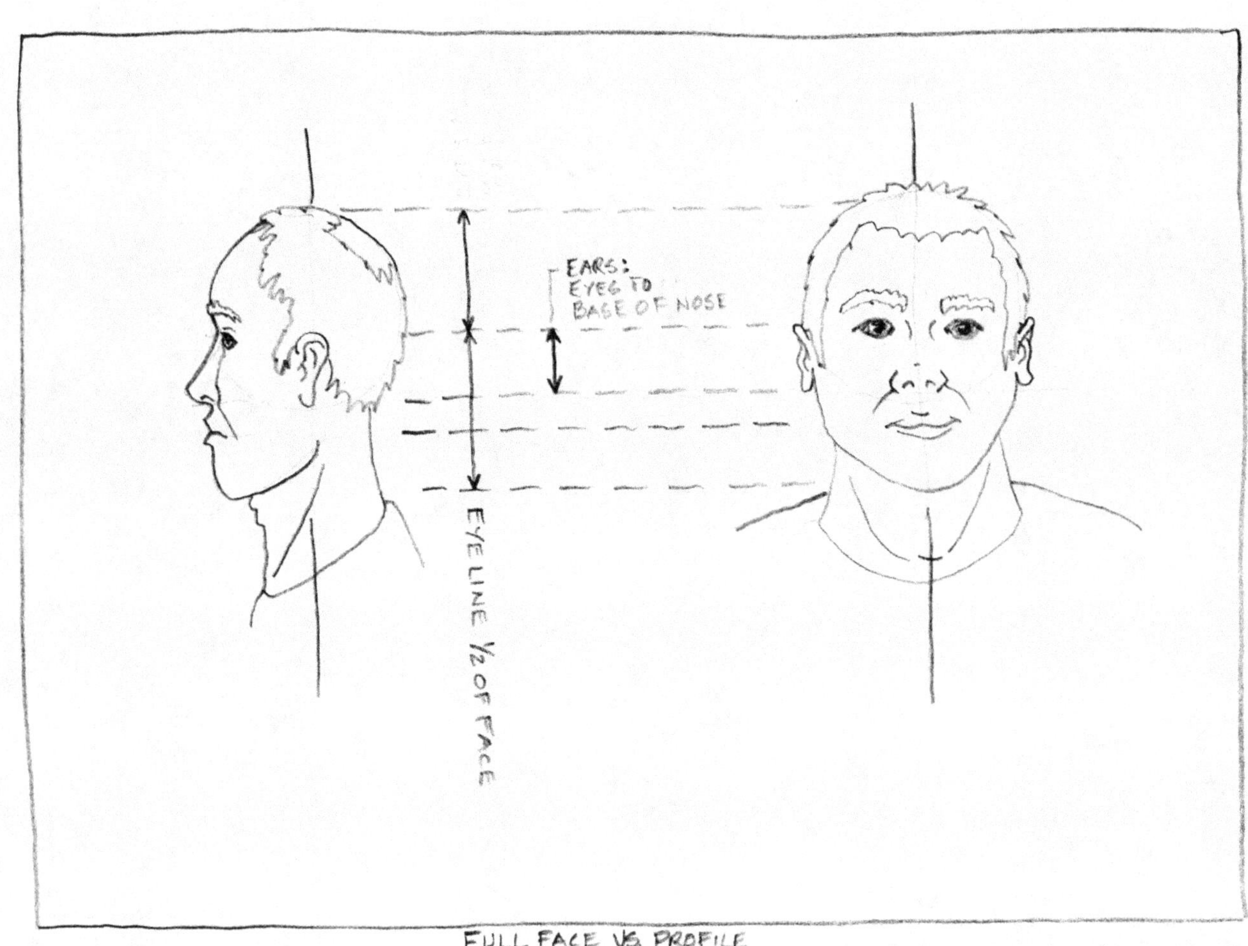

FULL FACE VS. PROFILE

Portraits

Full Face versus Profile

The proportions that exist in one view must be maintained in all views in which they appear .

Use the vases and faces exercise to capture the line of the profile, with all it's ins and outs .

One may have a weasel face and another a square face . The bridge and tip of the nose are another area to pay attention to .

Regular deliberate observation of people one meets from day to day will help to increase one's Visual Vocabulary so that one may recall many types of profiles when drawing from the imagination .

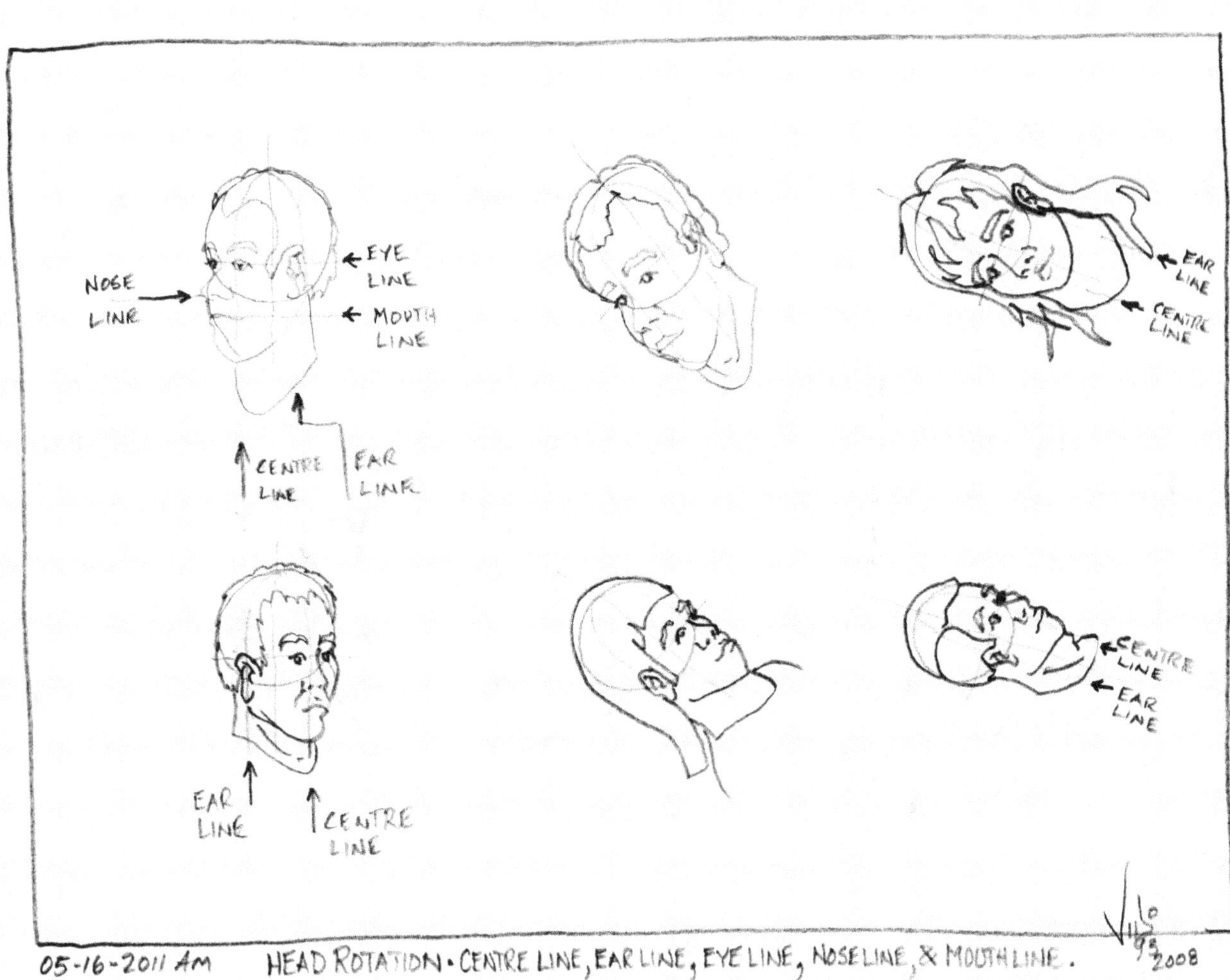

05-16-2011 AM HEAD ROTATION • CENTRE LINE, EAR LINE, EYE LINE, NOSE LINE, & MOUTH LINE. 2008

Portraits

Head Rotation
Centre Line, Ear Line, Eye Line, Nose Line and Mouth Line

Once one has established a full face view and a profile view, rotating the head into different views will be more achievable .

When placing the vertical lines of the centre of the face and the centre of the ears, keep in mind that one will be closer to the edge and the other will be closer to the centre .

Regular deliberate observation of people one meets from day to day will help to increase one's Visual Vocabulary so that one may recall many types of heads when drawing from the imagination .

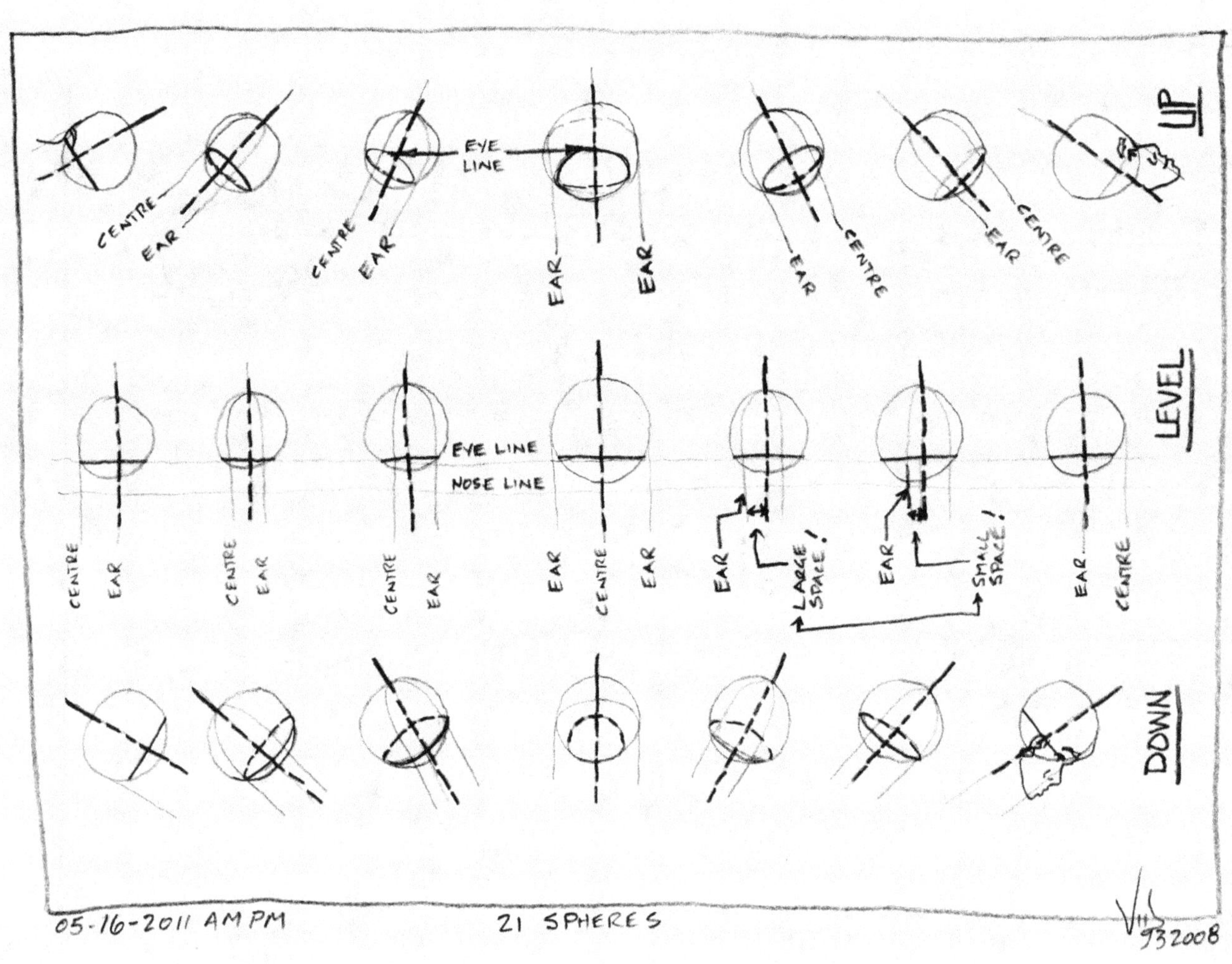

Portraits

Head Rotation : 21 Spheres

Once one has established a full face view and a profile view, rotating the head into different views will be more achievable .

When placing the vertical lines of the centre of the face and the centre of the ears, keep in mind that one will be closer to the edge and the other will be closer to the centre .

If one has problems when placing the lines to rotate a sphere, practice is necessary before one will be able to rotate a head .

Regular deliberate observation of people one meets from day to day will help to increase one's Visual Vocabulary so that one may recall many types of heads when drawing from the imagination .

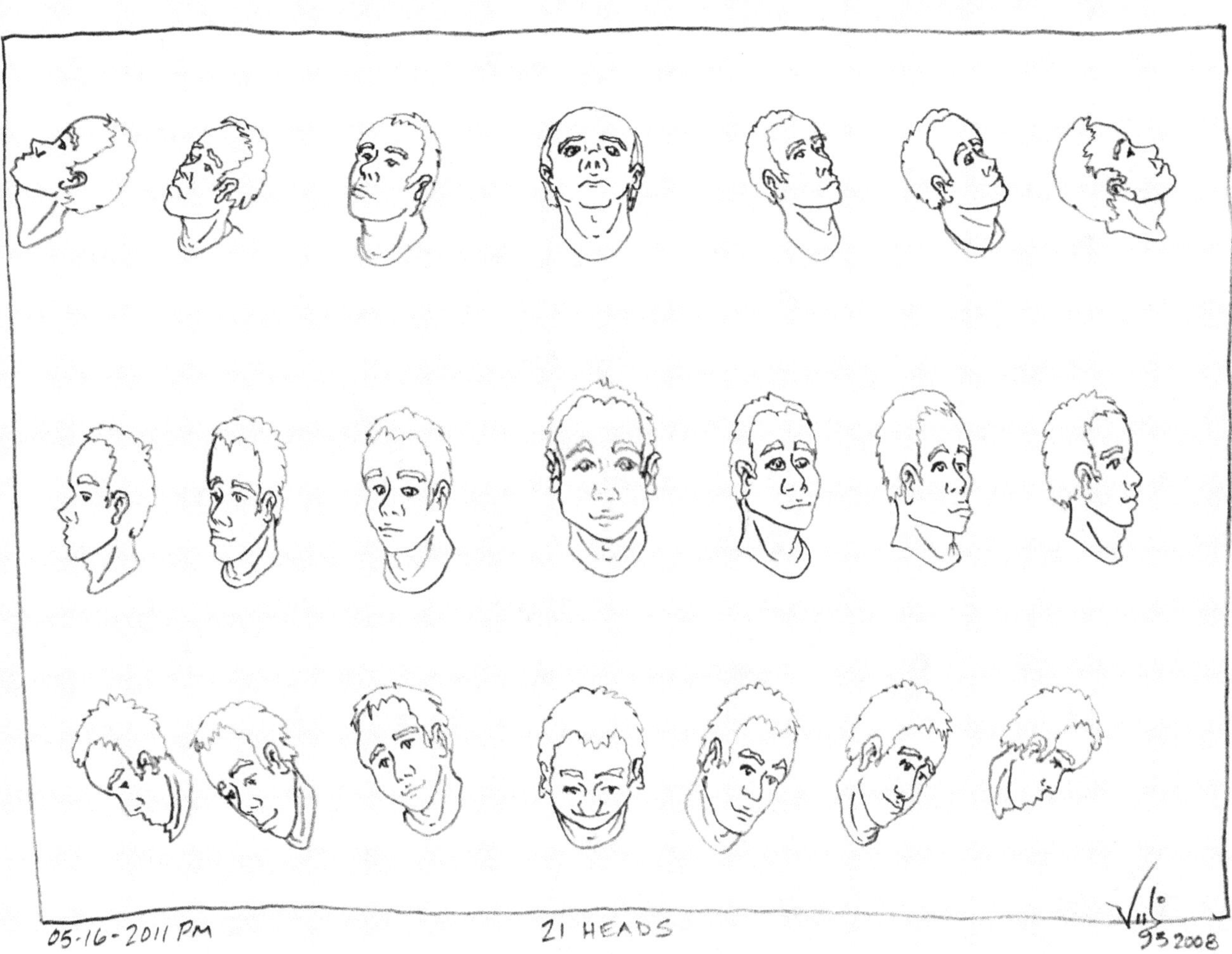

Portraits

Head Rotation : 21 Heads

Once one can rotate a sphere, rotating the head into different views will be more achievable .

When placing the vertical lines of the centre of the face and the centre of the ears, keep in mind that one will be closer to the edge and the other will be closer to the centre .

If one has problems when placing the lines to rotate a sphere, practice is necessary before one will be able to rotate a head .

Regular deliberate observation of people one meets from day to day will help to increase one's Visual Vocabulary so that one may recall many types of heads when drawing from the imagination .

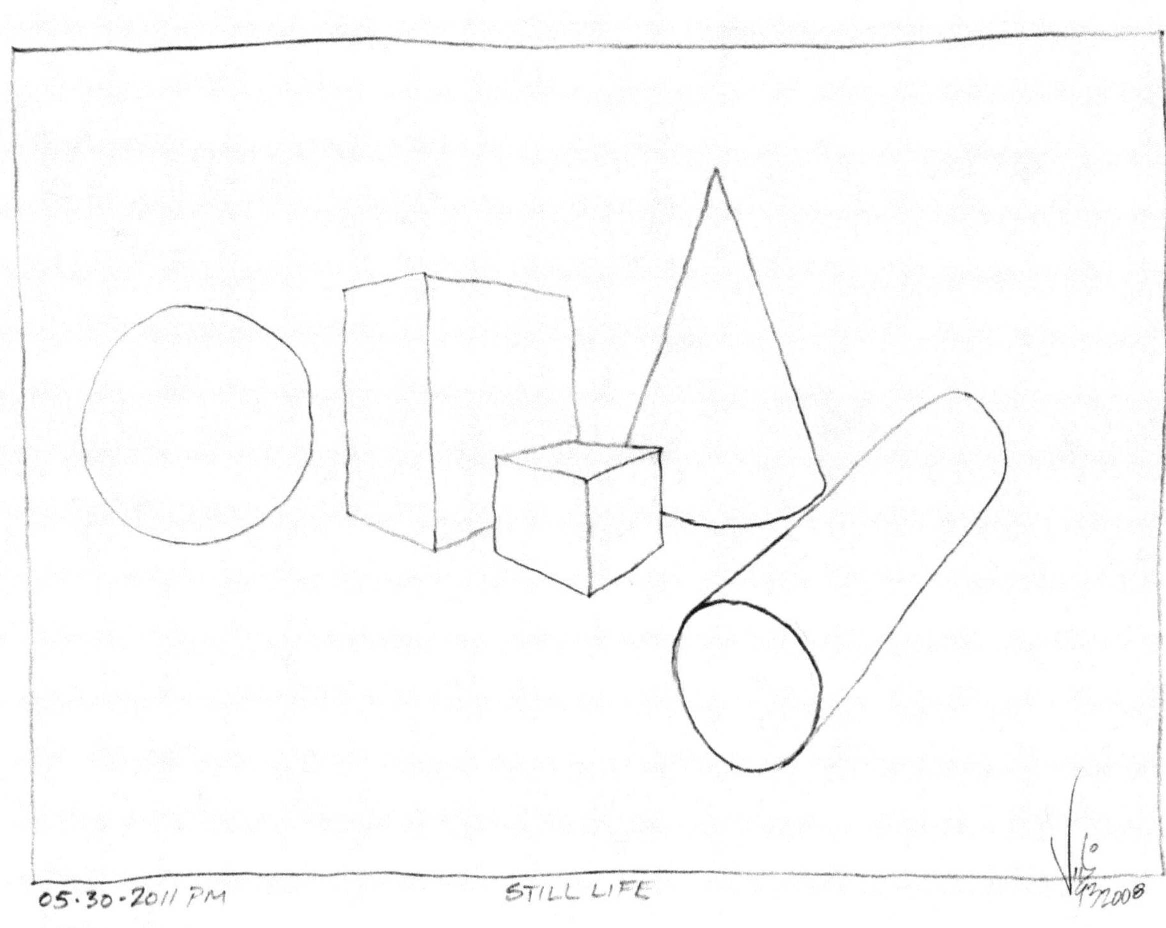

Still Life:

Sphere, Cylinder, Cone & Box

These four basic three dimensional shapes are the basis for most items that may be drawn. Variations of these basic shapes will keep one's still life drawing solid.

Perspective is very important when creating a three dimensional representation, and this will be discussed thoroughly later in this pamphlet. For now, use careful observation and practice the exercises from the book Drawing on the Right Side of the Brain when creating a three dimensional environment.

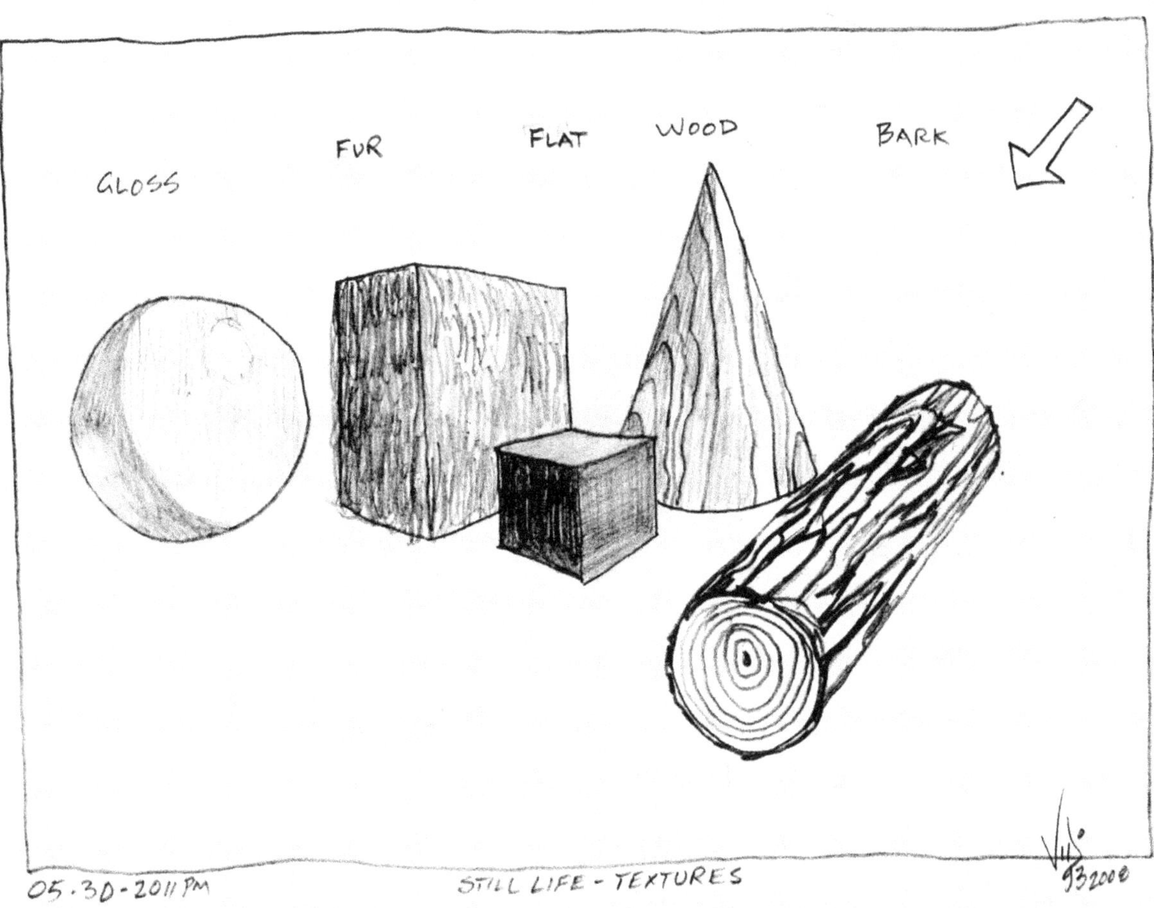

Still Life:

Textures

These four basic three dimensional shapes are the basis for most items that may be drawn but textures are what must be illustrated in drawing them . Shading is very important, but I chose textures first to emphasis that it is the textures that one must illustrate, when portraying light and shadow .

For now, use careful observation and practice the exercises from the book Drawing on the Right Side of the Brain when creating a three dimensional environment .

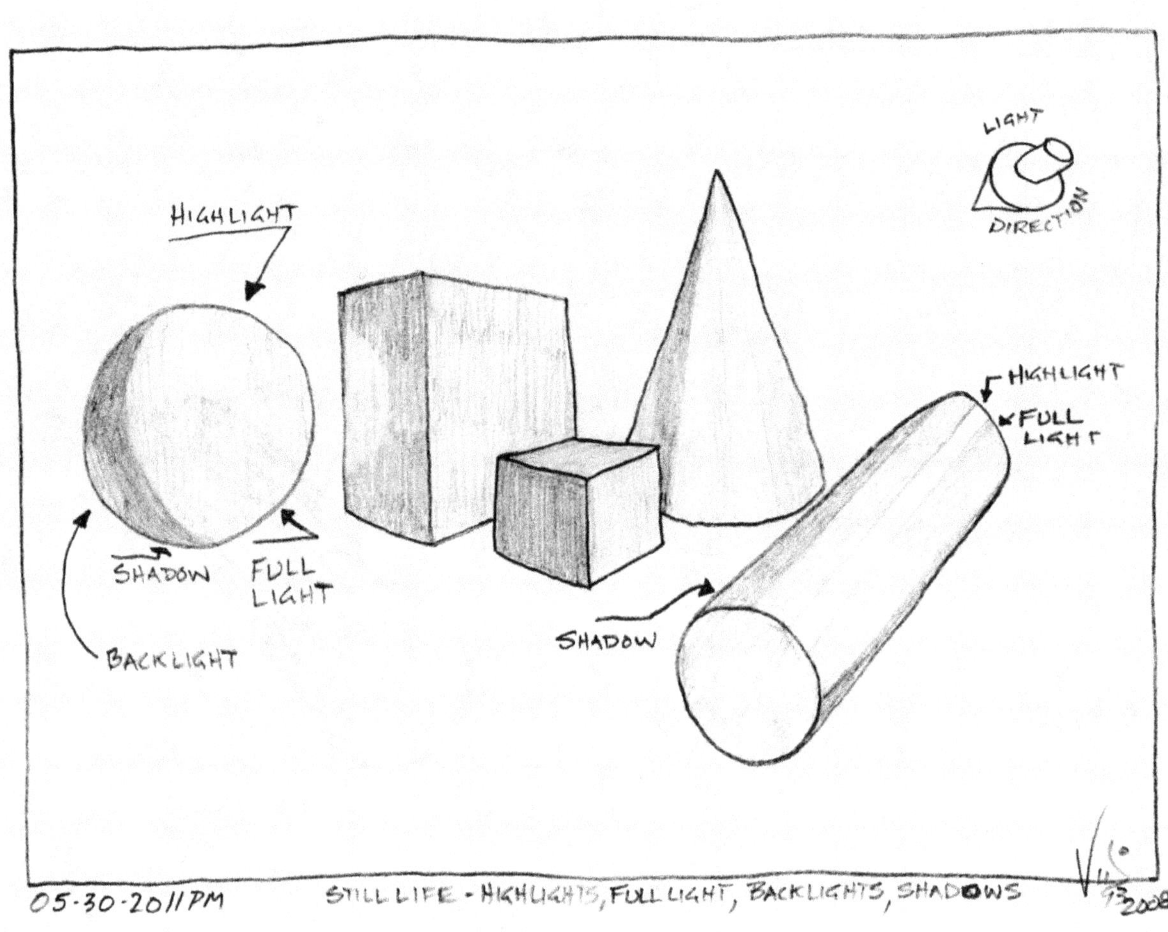

Still Life:

Highlights, Full Lights, Back Lights and Shadow

These four levels of light and shade are the basis for most items that may be drawn. Combinations of these four levels of shading will keep one's still life drawing solid.

Highlights are the brightest and lighter in value than the colour of the object. Full light is the true colour and value of the object. Back lights are lighter than shadows because light is being reflected from other objects into the shadow area. Shadows are the darkest.

Keep clear distinctions between these four levels of shading, especially in bright direct light.

Use careful observation and practice the exercises from the book **Drawing on the Right Side of the Brain** when creating a three dimensional environment.

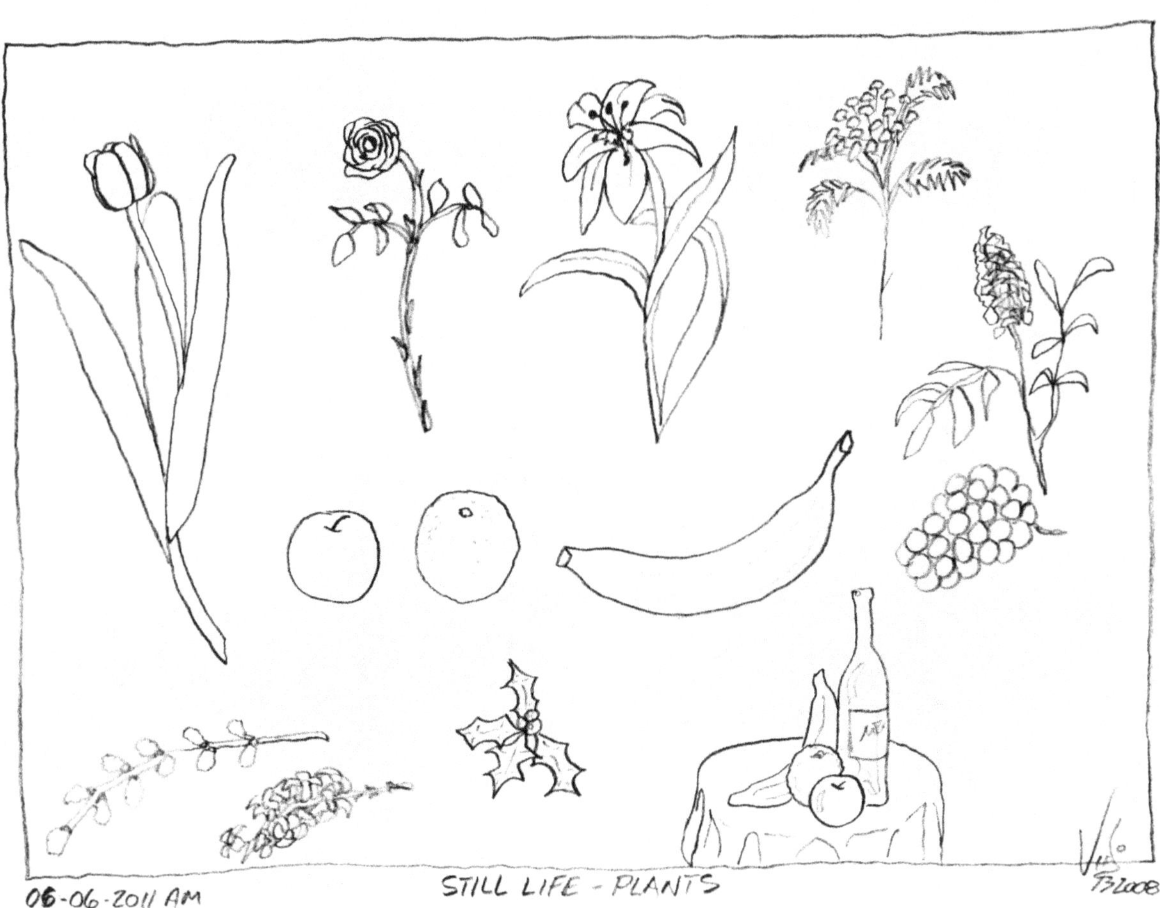

Still Life:
Plants

Copying drawings of plants is a good way to start, but never forget that careful observations are essential and can be made everywhere, even when not drawing.

For now, use careful observation and practice the exercises from the book ***Drawing on the Right Side of the Brain*** when creating a three dimensional environment.

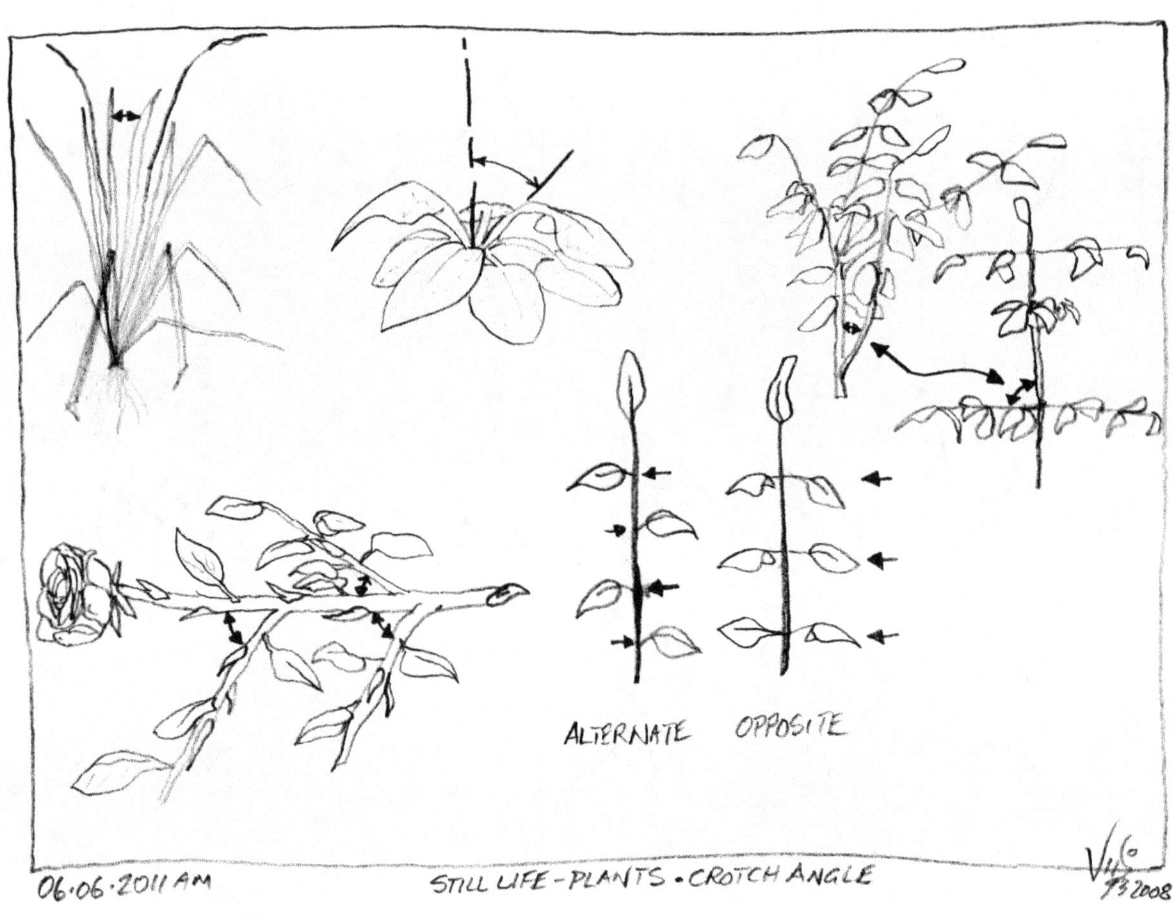

Still Life:

Plants : Crotch Angle

An important thing to observe and keep in mind when drawing plants, is the crotch angle, or the angle formed where two limbs of the plant or even grass join .

Plant identification books may have a question and answer system for identifying various plants, that narrows down the options . This process is very good for clarifying the structures of plants . An example is the identification of opposite or alternate branching structures .

For now, use careful observation and practice the exercises from the book ***Drawing on the Right Side of the Brain*** when illustrating an organic environment .

Keep on Drawing:

This is the first of a series of pamphlets created for the Oakville OASIS Drawing Bee, and this series is intended to overcome the hurdle of beginning to draw. When one is faced with what they are going to do all day, they can flip through these pamphlets and get engrossed with the ideas of what they could be drawing.

Drawing skills are very transferable to other areas of life, but the most important transferable skills are the emotional ones of accepting one's shortcomings and carrying on to overcome them with practice and an acceptance of their level of ability. No one ever got better at anything by not practicing.

As well, as the mind becomes involved in the drawing, there is a peace and almost relaxed atmosphere created, which is refreshing and beneficial to the rest of one's day.

A friend from secondary school, who went on to become an actuary, told me he thinks of me when he is bored, and wonders what I would do in such a boring situation. I was known for coming up with interesting activities, when called upon. Drawing is a great activity that anyone can do and it fills the time as well as refreshes the spirit, if one can get started and involved.

Finally, one rule I like to promote is for anyone who is critical of their drawing skill, and that is to never throw out a drawing, just hide it or put it away if one is frustrated. This is because when one completes a drawing, they are very much aware of how far the drawing came short of the image they had in their mind. But after a period of time, they forget the image they had in their head and will only see their accomplishments that they achieved in the drawing. This is encouraging and promotes further drawing.

<u>Drawing on the Right Side of the Brain</u> Author: ***Betty Edwards***
ISBN-13: **9780874775136** ISBN-10: **0874775132** Edition: **Revised** Binding: **Paperback**
Publisher: **Tarcher** Published: **May 1989** List Price: **$15.95**

The book cited above, is great at getting one better at drawing, but eventually, your visual vocabulary will need to be expanded, and as far as anatomy goes, I cannot recommend a better reference than the book cited below.

<u>Atlas of Human Anatomy for the Artist</u> Author: ***Stephen Rogers Peck***
ISBN-13: **9780195030952** ISBN-10: **0195030958** Edition: **1** Binding: **Paperback**
Publisher: **Oxford University Press** Published: **February 1982** List Price: **$19.95**

I would strongly recommend studying this book on anatomy, by memorizing the names of all the bones in the body, as well as the names of all the muscles in the body, so that you will be more fluent in the language of drawing people.

Other Drawings

Aug 8, 2011

. . my 1979 two man tent, drawn from life, on site during the Cross of Victory Pilgrimage 2011 -
- walking from Burlington to Martyrs' Shrine, Midland, Ontario .

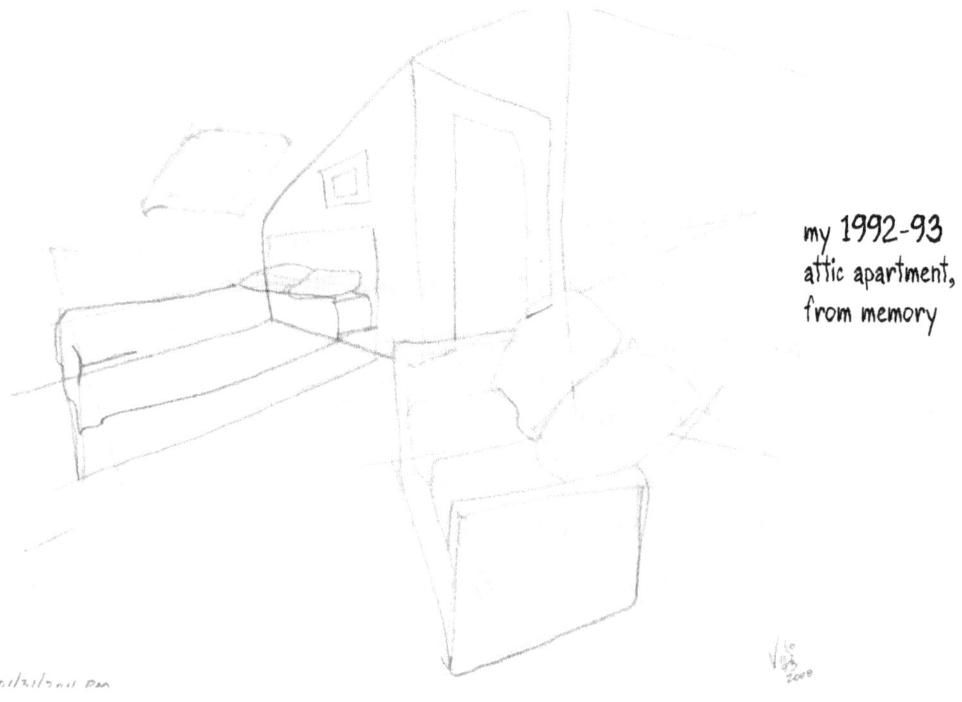

my 1992-93 attic apartment, from memory

TEXTBOOK --A--

Warm Ups

from
Drawing on the Right Side of the Brain

Portraits

Still Life

Drawing on the Right Side of the Brain Author: ***Betty Edwards***
ISBN-13: **9780874775136** ISBN-10: **0874775132** Edition: **Revised** Binding: **Paperback**
Publisher: **Tarcher** Published: **May 1989** List Price: **$15.95**

R David Foster

- began the Oakville OASIS Drawing Bee in March 2010, with funding from the Canadian Mental Health Association (CMHA), Halton Region Branch, and it continues today with Paul Tomas leading it. Before that, around 2005, David ran a workshop in drawing and watercolour painting, again under CMHA at the request of Clarisse Berardicurti. His other accomplishments are a 35mm animated film entitled **HYPOTHERMIA / *My Kayak Prayer*,** completed in 2008, that was supported by the Liaison of Independent Film of Toronto and the Ontario Arts Council. He is now devoting the largest portion of his available time to his animated series HESUS JOY CHRIST , of which there are 5 episodes completed. He regularly updates his blog entitled . . . . . .

Vid'93 Bein' To Wordie . . . . . . at ***www.vid93.blogspot.com*** .

David is currently a member of the Oakville Arts Council, and the Art Gallery of Burlington (AGB) - Burlington Fine Arts Association. He attends the Wednesday Sketch Group, at the AGB when he is available and inspired and appreciates the opportunity to practice life drawing, portrait drawing, and still life drawing, from life.

David has always drawn, with the exception being when he was in high school, when he only practiced technical drawing or drafting. So his self taught experience far exceeds his formal artistic education, giving due credit to his father's generous exposure and encouragment towards art, and the benefits of the exercises provided by the book ***Drawing on the Right Side of the Brain***, by Betty Edwards. David achieved honours in the Art Fundamentals Intensive program at Sheridan College in Oakville, Ontario, before being accepted into the Classical Animation Program in 1993, only to fail out by the end of first year. The Art Fundamentals instructors did not want him to waste his talent in Animation, but he had a love for the potential of the medium of Animation, which exceeded the discouragement of the animation instruction.

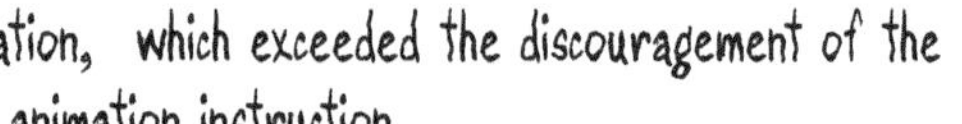

Search **"vid932008"** *on* **www.google.ca** *for a website with all of it !*

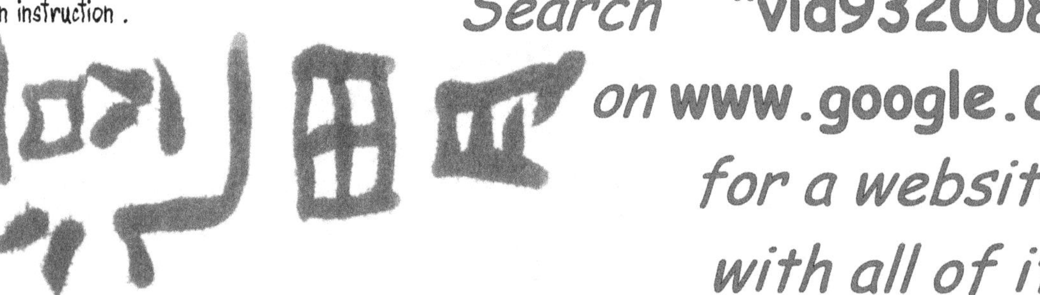

vid932008@gmail.com

www.vid93.blogspot.com

http://sites.google.com/site/vid932008/

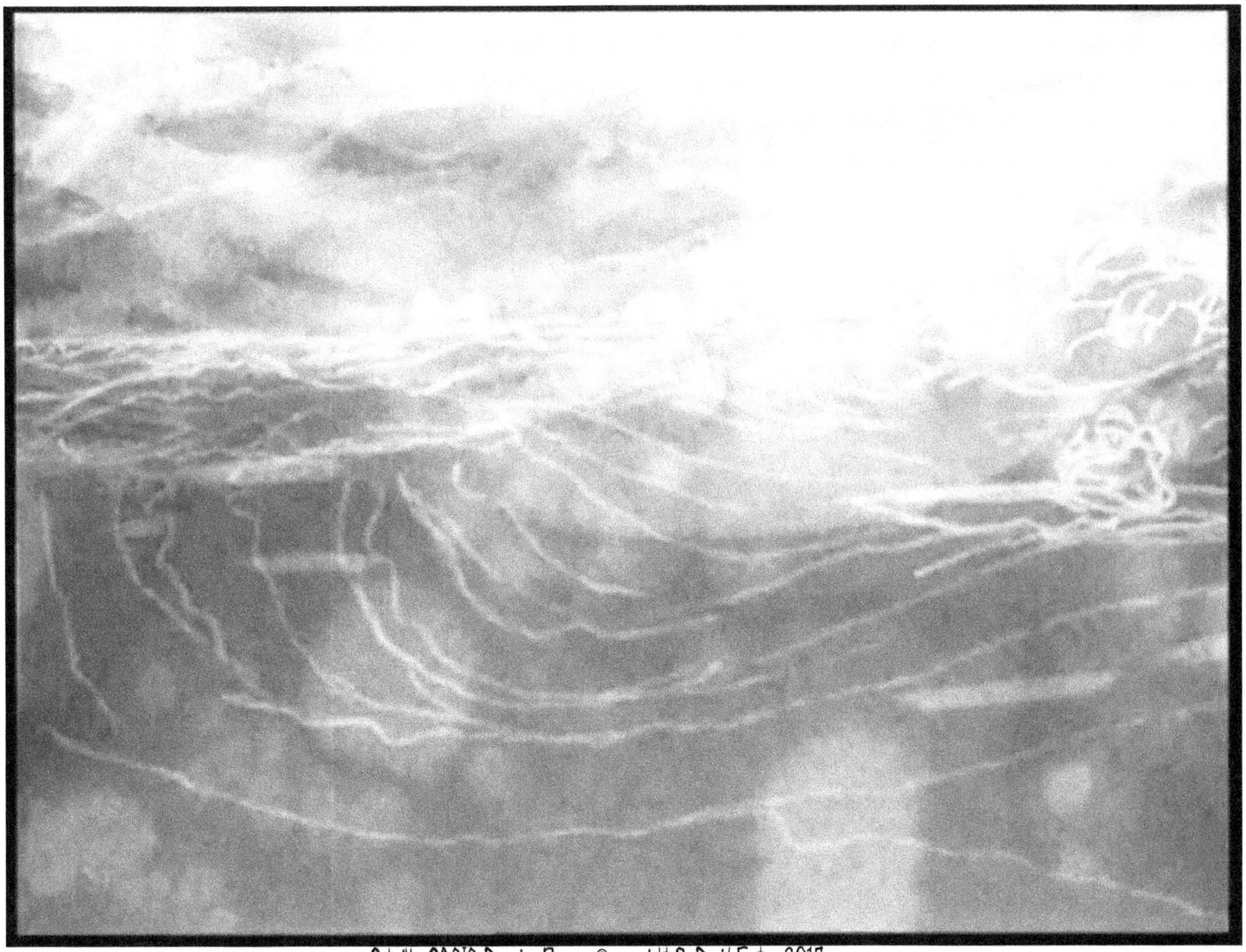

Oakville OASIS Drawing Bee © copyright R. David Foster 2015

VISUAL VOCABULARY

Textbook --B--

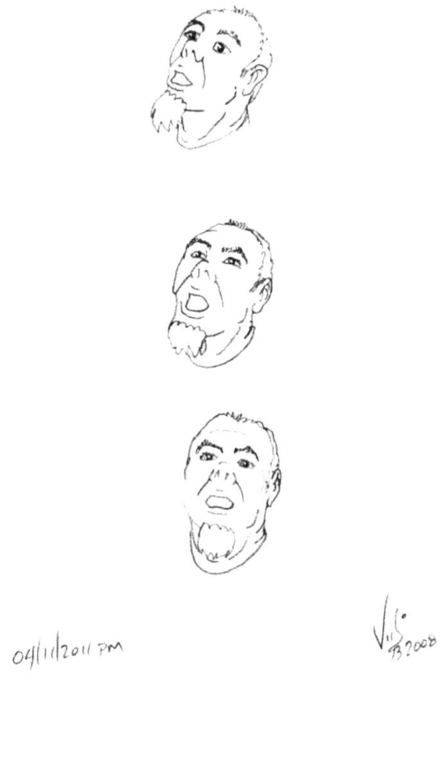

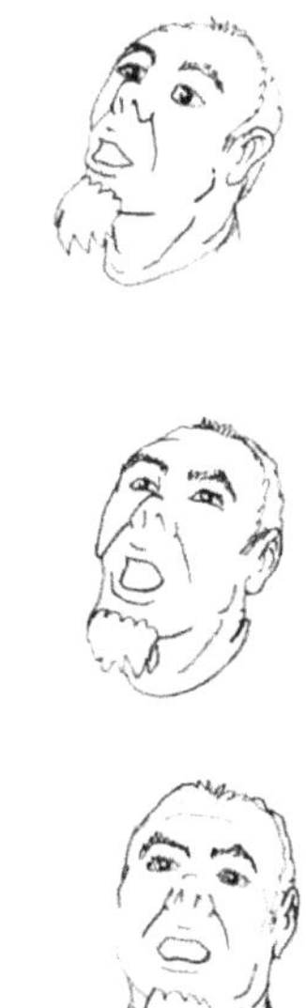

04/11/2011 PM

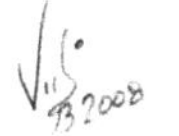

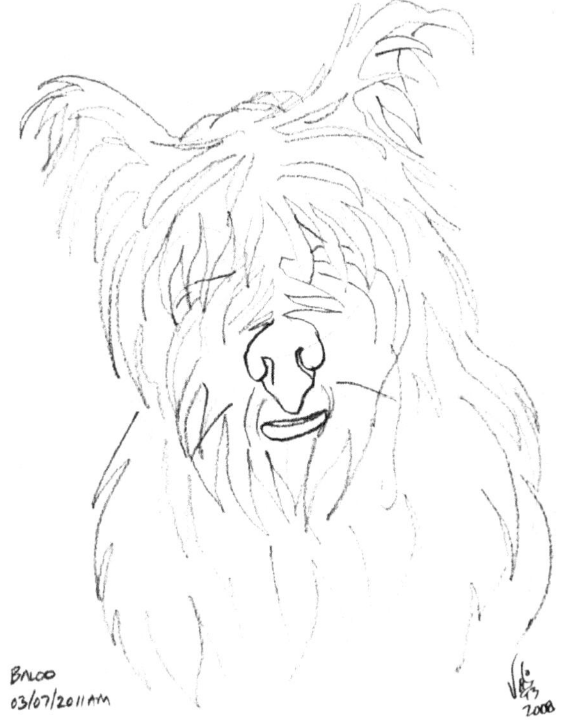

05/02/2011 AM

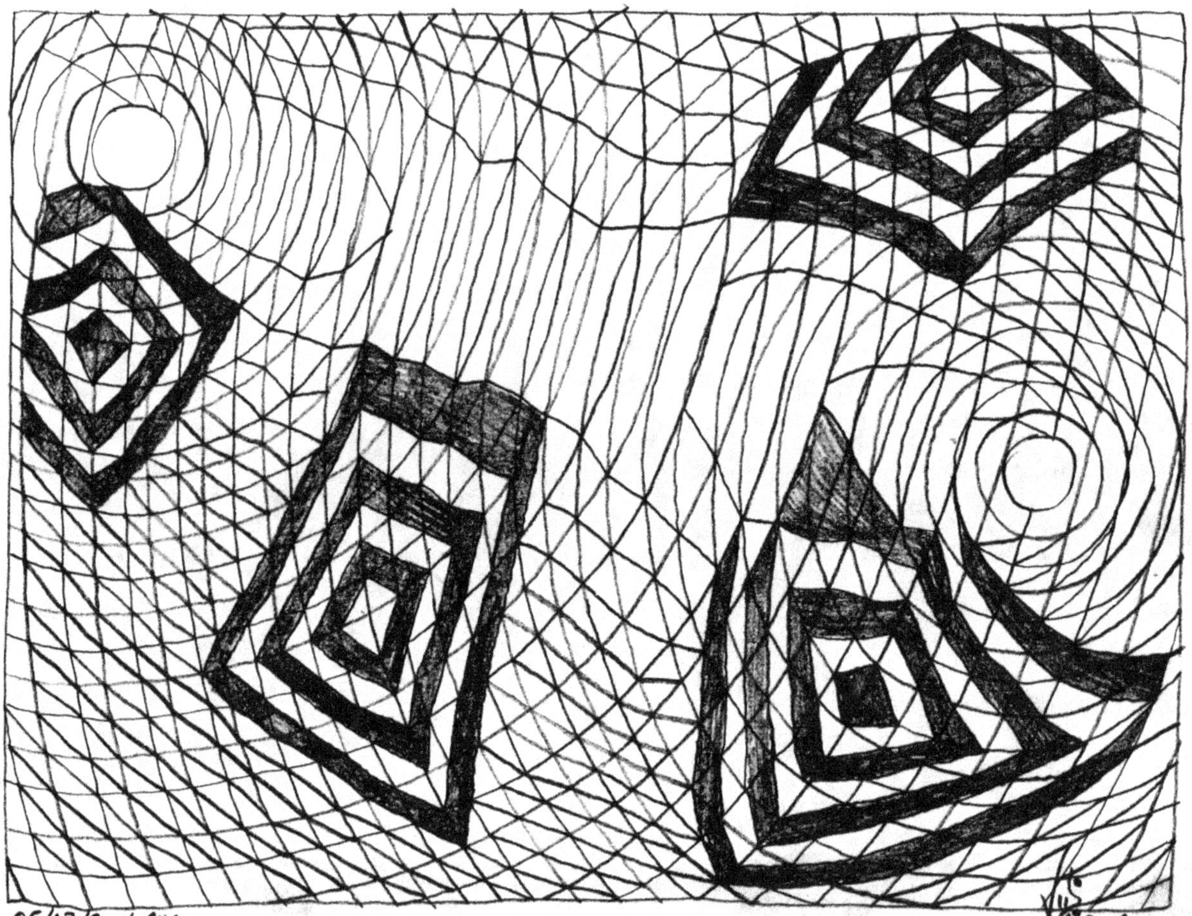

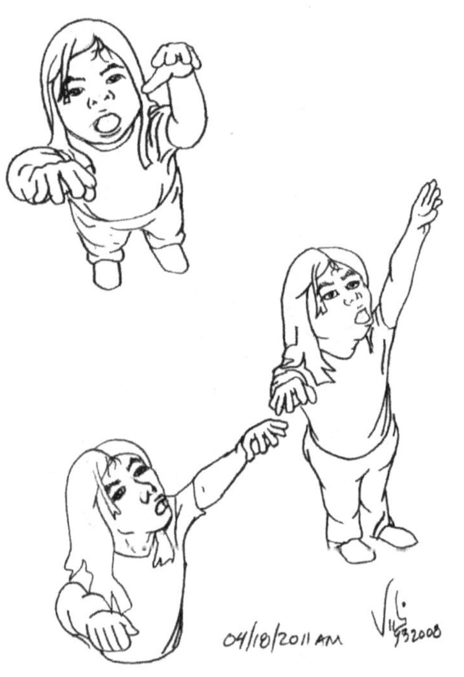
04/18/2011 AM

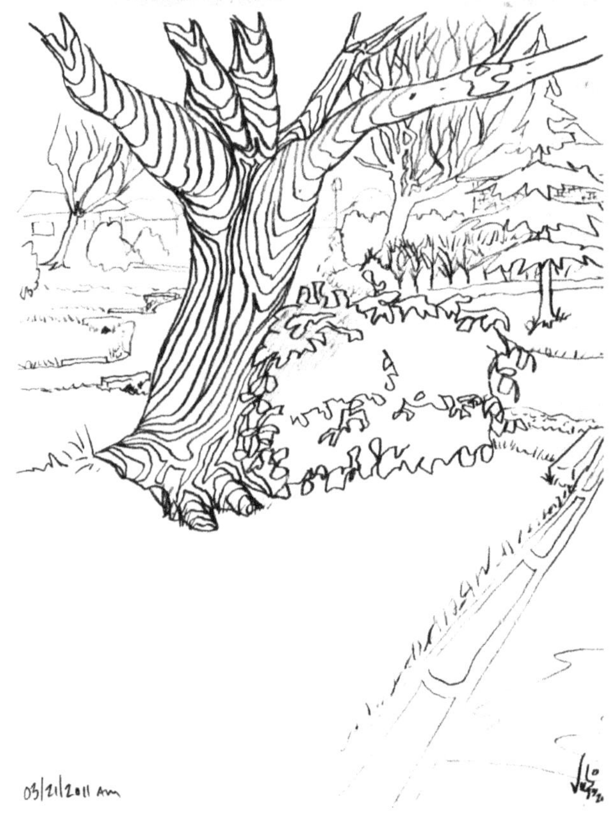
03/21/2011 Am

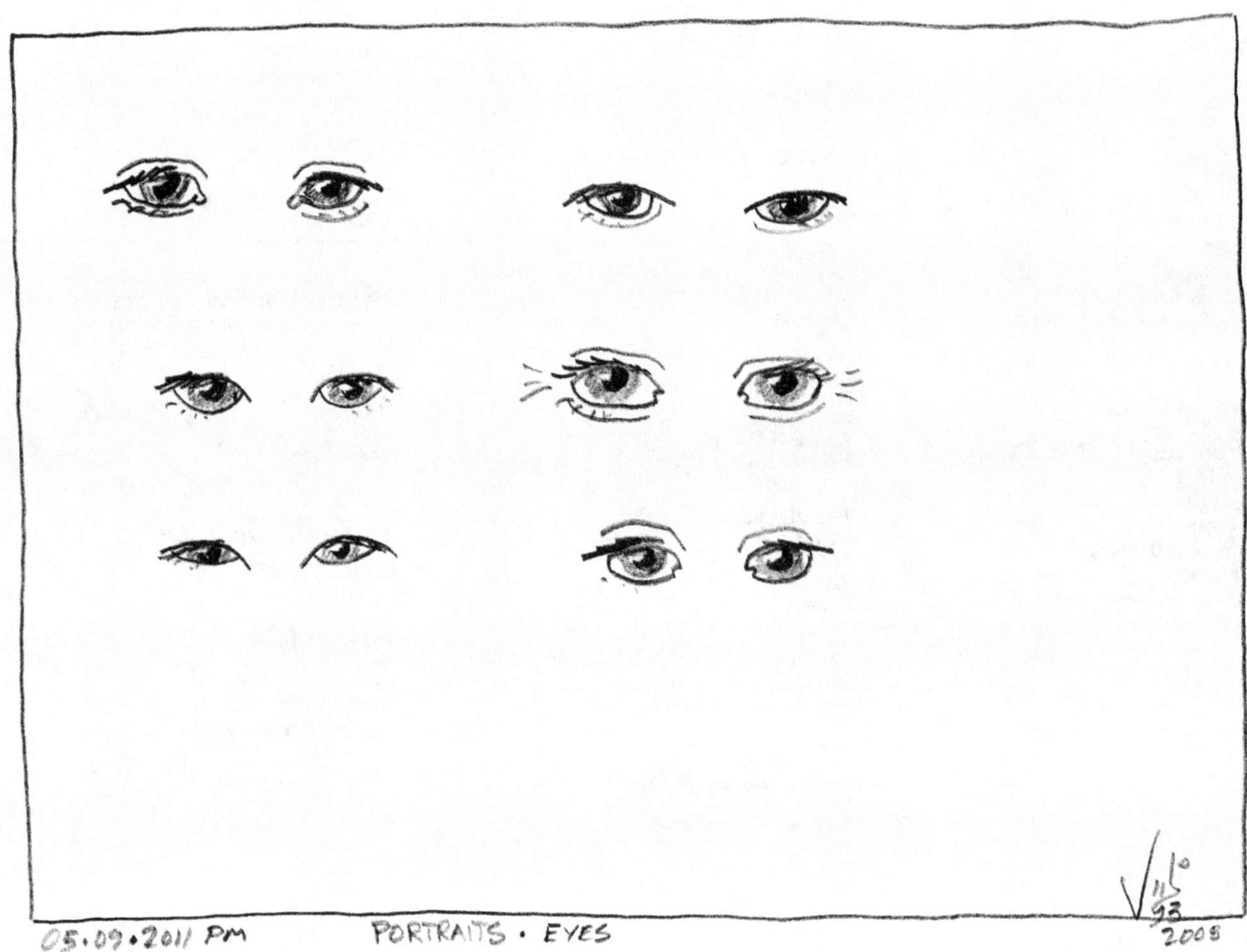

from Textbook --A-- Portraits:

Visual Vocabulary

People : Eyes

Eyes are a first of many items in a portrait that must be observed carefully to create a likeness. When drawing from life use the **_Drawing on the Right Side of the Brain_** exercises of negative space and vases and faces. One can draw the shape above the eye and the shape between the eye and the nose. Often one eye will be open more than another, and this can establish a mood. Also check for the presence of creases or folds above and below the eye, in the eyelids.

Regular deliberate observation of people one meets from day to day will help to increase one's Visual Vocabulary so that one may recall many types of eyes when drawing from the imagination.

One can copy these eyes to start, but take the opportunity as it comes to carefully observe the eyes of people you meet.

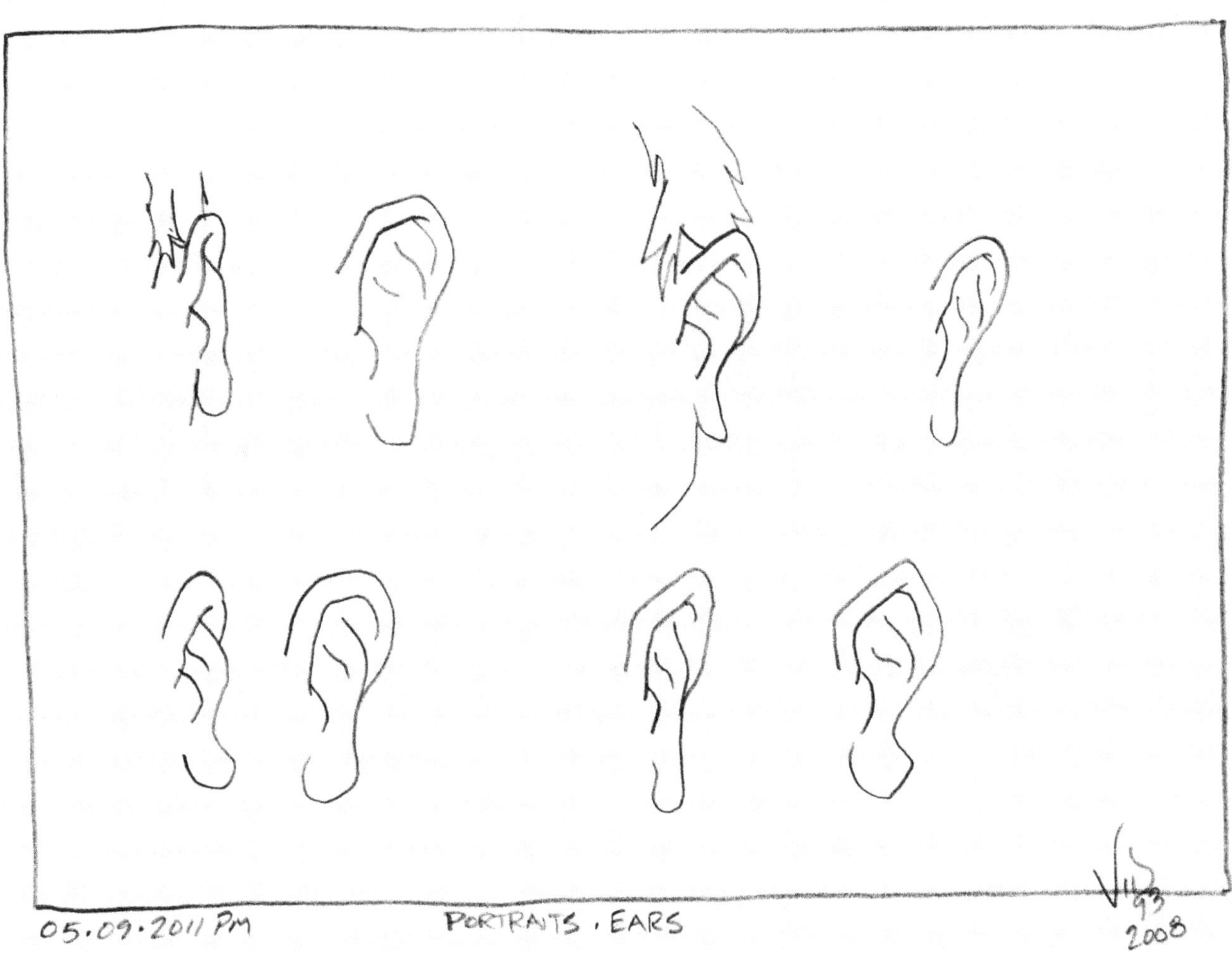

from Textbook --A-- Portraits:

Visual Vocabulary

People : Ears

Ears are a second of many items in a portrait that must be observed carefully to create a likeness. When drawing from life use the ***Drawing on the Right Side of the Brain*** exercises of negative space and vases and faces. One can draw the shape around the ear and the shape between the ear and the hair line. Often one ear will be different from the other, and this can establish a mood.

Regular deliberate observation of people one meets from day to day will help to increase one's Visual Vocabulary so that one may recall many types of ears when drawing from the imagination.

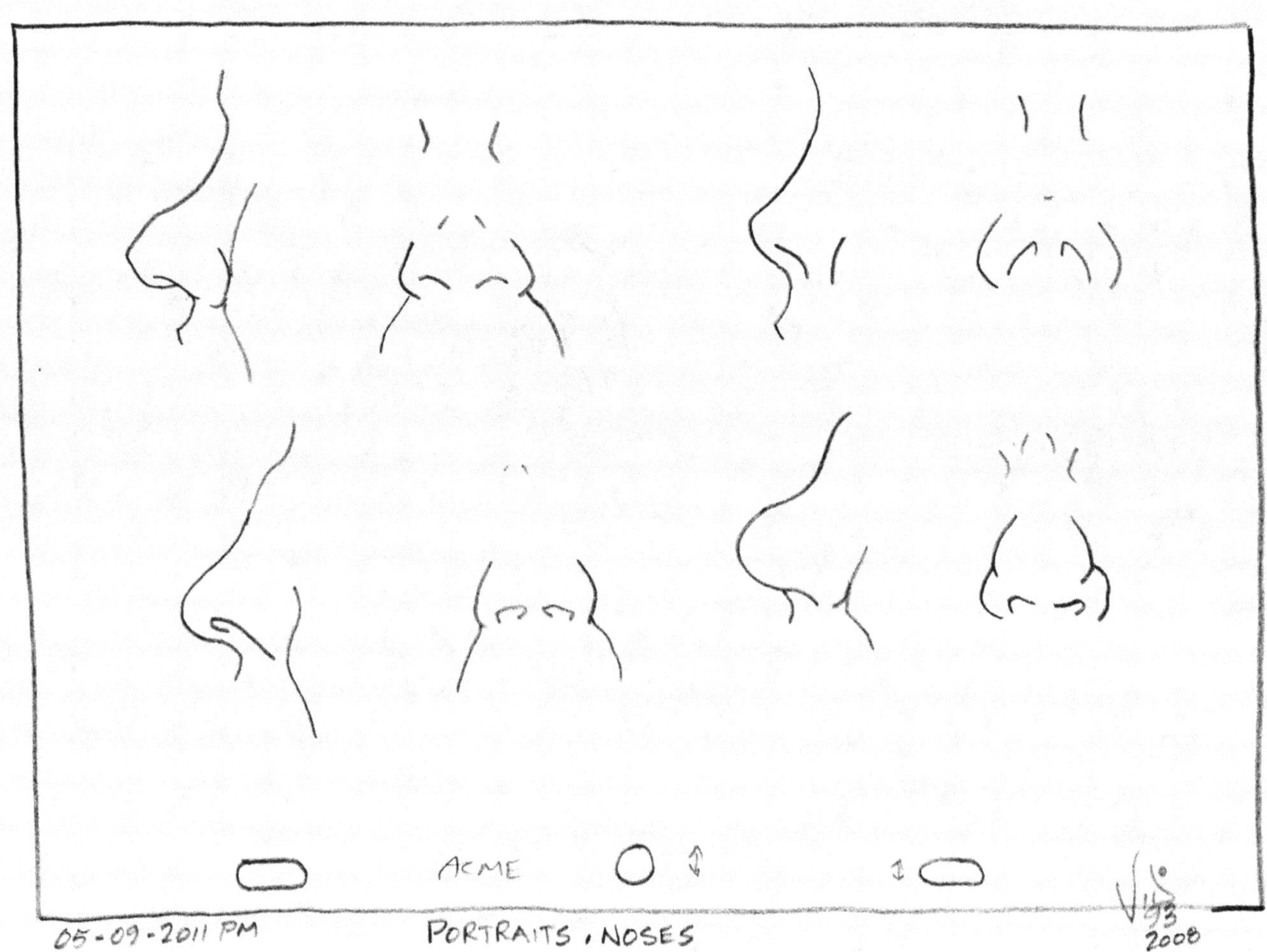

from Textbook --A-- Portraits:

Visual Vocabulary

People : Noses

Noses are a third of many items in a portrait that must be observed carefully to create a likeness. When drawing from life use the ***Drawing on the Right Side of the Brain*** exercises of negative space and vases and faces. One can draw the shapes around the nose and the shapes between the nose and the mouth. Often one side of the nose will be different from the other, and this can establish a mood.

Regular deliberate observation of people one meets from day to day will help to increase one's Visual Vocabulary so that one may recall many types of noses when drawing from the imagination.

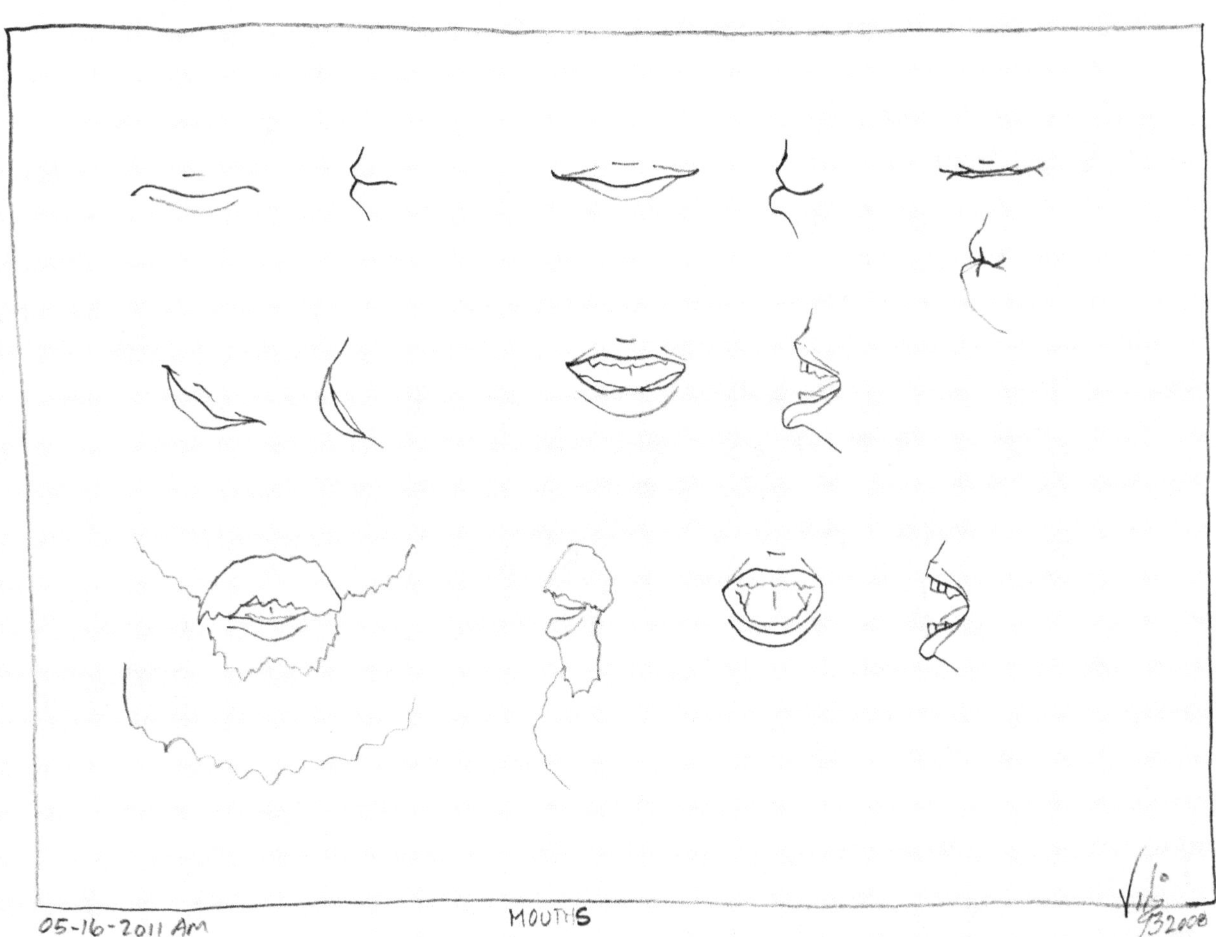

from Textbook --A-- Portraits:

Visual Vocabulary

People : Mouths

Mouths are a fourth of many items in a portrait that must be observed carefully to create a likeness. When drawing from life use the ***Drawing on the Right Side of the Brain*** exercises of negative space and vases and faces. One can draw the shapes around the mouth and the shapes between the nose and the chin, and the mouth. Often one side of the mouth will be different from the other, and this can establish a mood.

Regular deliberate observation of people one meets from day to day will help to increase one's Visual Vocabulary so that one may recall many types of mouths when drawing from the imagination.

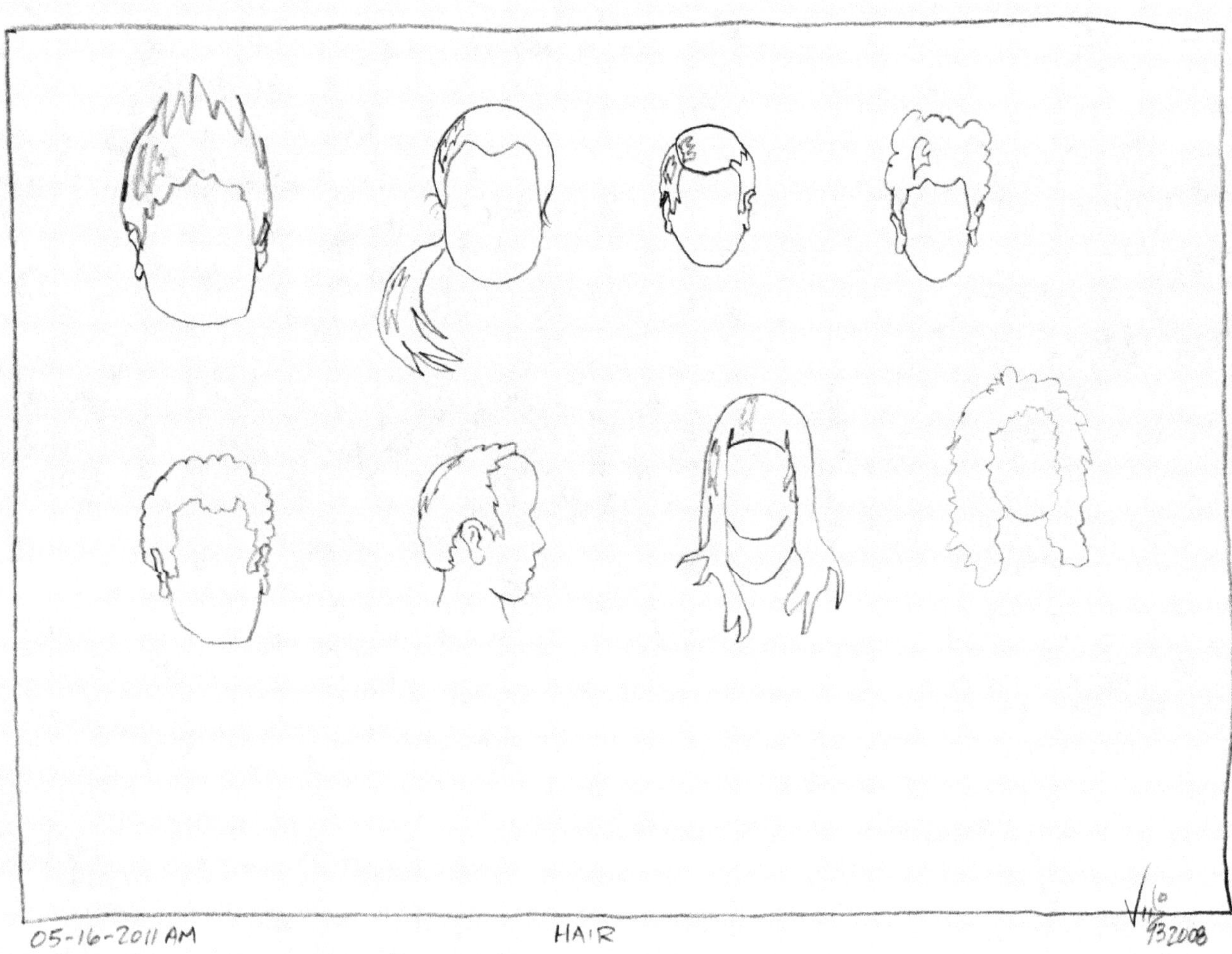

from Textbook --A-- Portraits:
Visual Vocabulary

People : Hair

Hair styles are a fifth and the final item addressed in this book, of many and far more portrait items that must be considered in any portrait, and all items must be observed carefully to create a likeness. When drawing from life use the ***Drawing on the Right Side of the Brain*** exercises of negative space and vases and faces. One can draw the shapes of the forehead and cheeks to achieve a likeness of how the hair is positioned around the face. Very often one side of the hair will be different from the other, such as when the hair is parted on one side, and this can establish a mood.

Regular deliberate observation of people one meets from day to day will help to increase one's Visual Vocabulary so that one may recall many types of hair styles when drawing from the imagination.

These two sections are dealt with more thoroughly in Textbook --A--

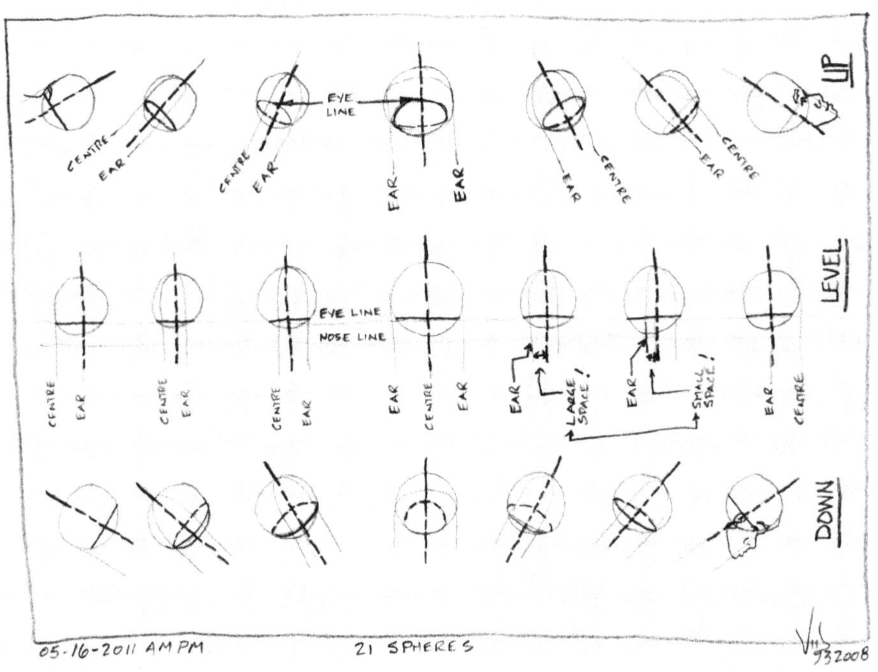

from Textbook --A -- Portraits:

People :
Head Rotation : 21 Spheres

Once one has established a full face view and a profile view, rotating the head into different views will be more achievable .

When placing the vertical lines of the centre of the face and the centre of the ears, keep in mind that one will be closer to the edge and the other will be closer to the centre .

If one has problems when placing the lines to rotate a sphere, practice is necessary before one will be able to rotate a head .

Regular deliberate observation of people one meets from day to day will help to increase one's Visual Vocabulary so that one may recall many types of heads when drawing from the imagination .

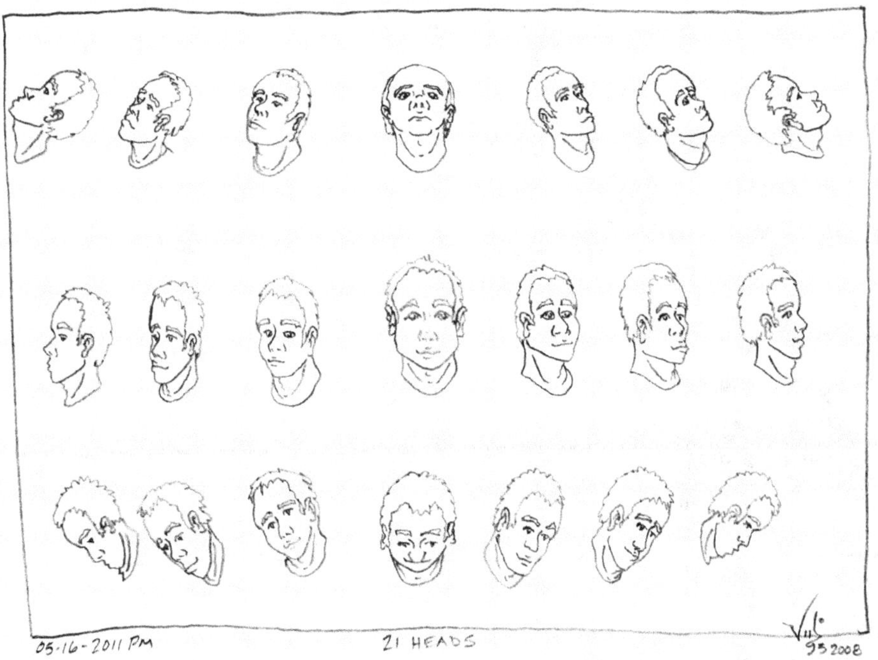

from Textbook --A -- Portraits:

People :
Head Rotation : 21 Heads

Once one can rotate a sphere, rotating the head into different views will be more achievable .

When placing the vertical lines of the centre of the face and the centre of the ears, keep in mind that one will be closer to the edge and the other will be closer to the centre .

If one has problems when placing the lines to rotate a sphere, practice is necessary before one will be able to rotate a head .

Regular deliberate observation of people one meets from day to day will help to increase one's Visual Vocabulary so that one may recall many types of heads when drawing from the imagination .

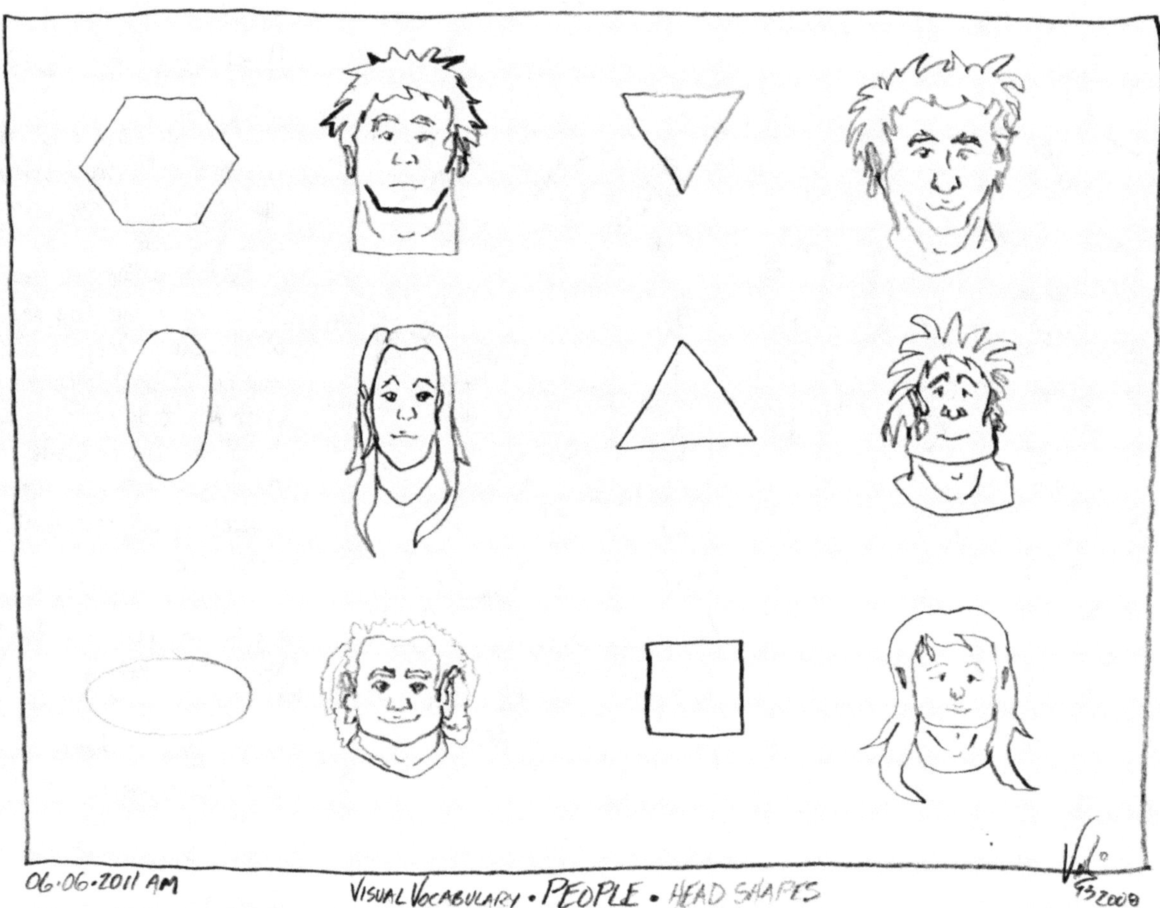

Visual Vocabulary:

People : Head Shapes

Cultivate an awareness of any head as a whole and learn to identify head shapes by the basic shapes such as square, round, triangular, horizontal oval, vertical oval or even a hexagon . This also applies to profile views, and there may be a great difference in the same head between the shape of the frontal view and the shape of the profile view .

Hair style can greatly affect the shape of the head, and one should look at the shape of the face and the parts of the face, as well as the whole head .

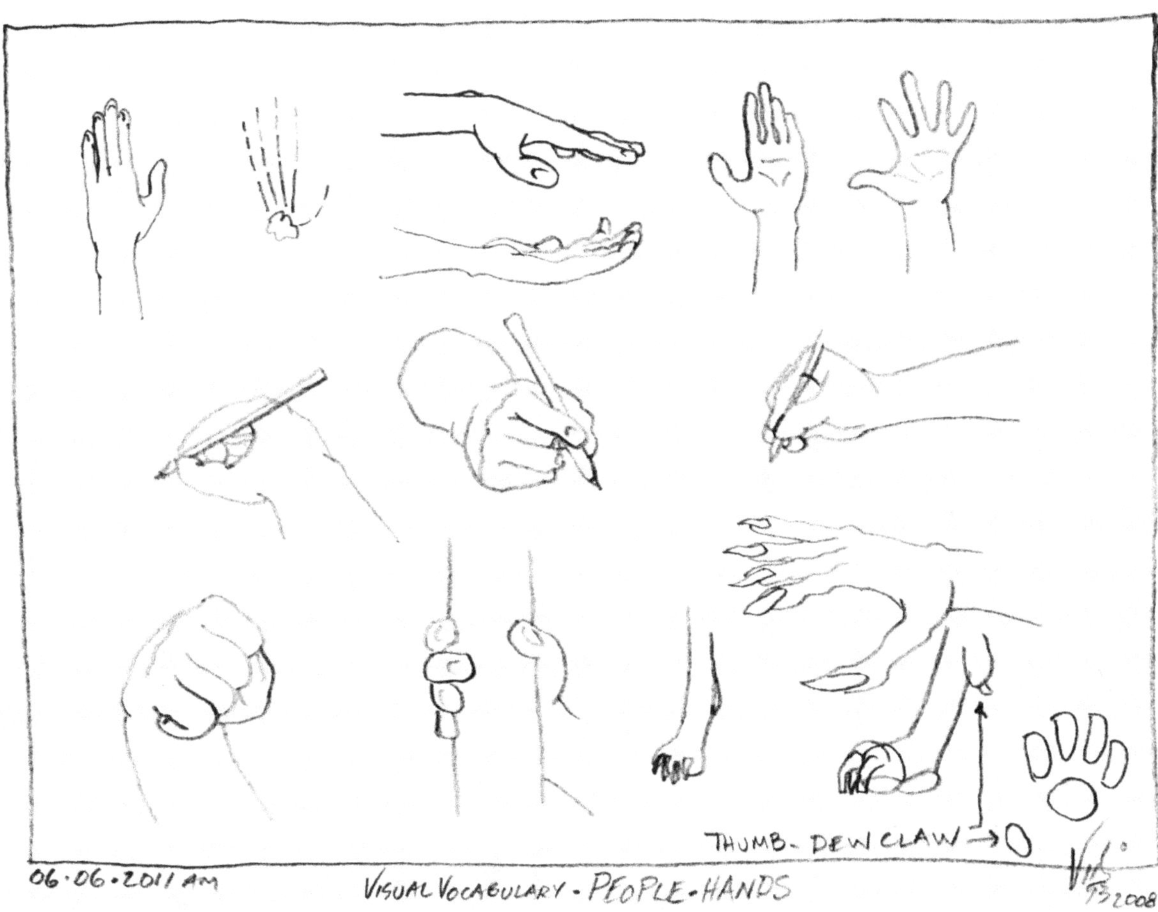

Visual Vocabulary:

People : Hands

Cultivate an awareness of hands as a whole and learn to identify hand shapes by the basic shapes such as square, round, triangular, horizontal oval, vertical oval or even a hexagon .

Observe the arcs that occur in the hand and maintain those arcs in the various different views and position of the hands you are drawing . Look for these arcs when observing and maintain them in your drawing .

Hands are a great thing to draw, as well as feet, when one is just warming up . Let your imagination flow and try to come up with as many different hand positions as you can in your drawings .

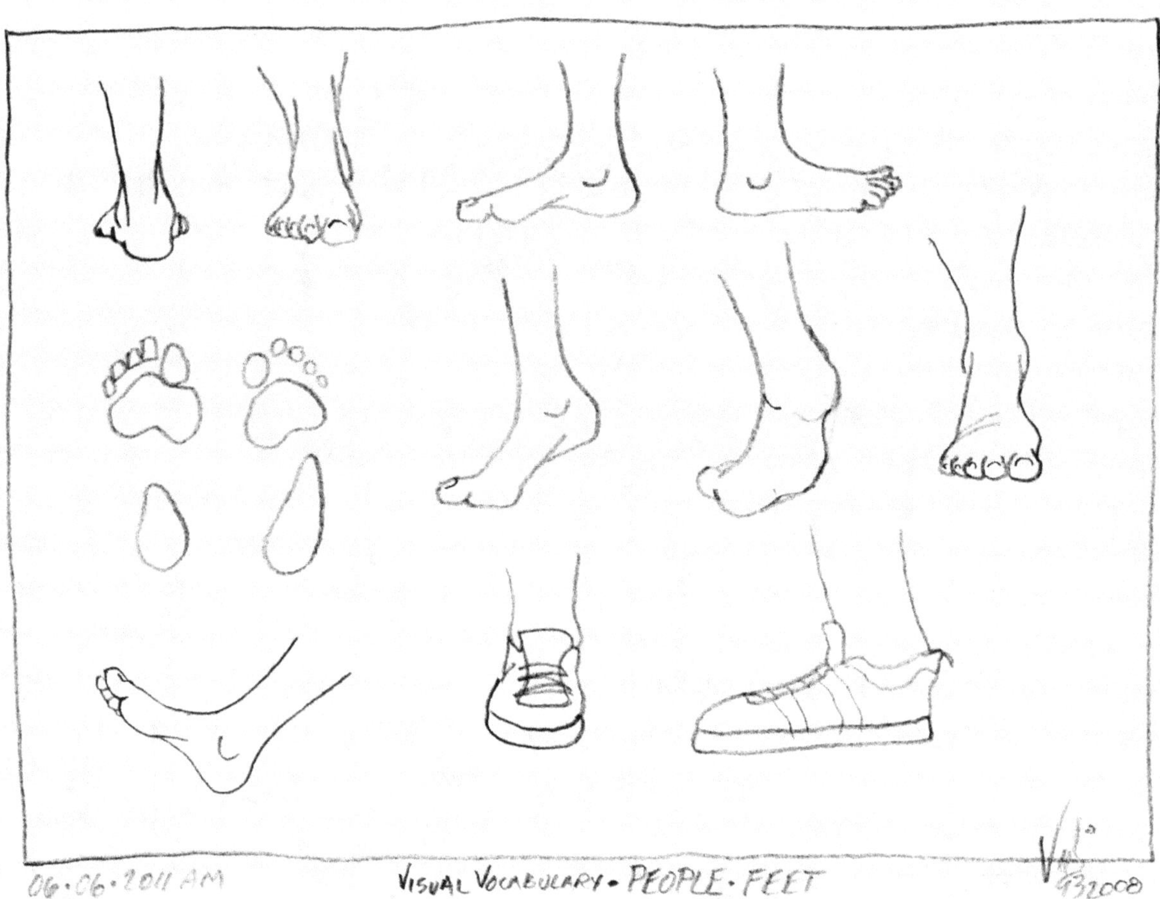

Visual Vocabulary:

People: Feet

Cultivate an awareness of feet as a whole and learn to identify foot shapes by the basic shapes such as square, round, triangular, horizontal oval, vertical oval or even a hexagon .

Observe the arcs that occur in the foot and maintain those arcs in the various different views and positions of the feet you are drawing . Look for these arcs when observing and maintain them in your drawing .

Feet are a great thing to draw, as well as hands, when one is just warming up . Let your imagination flow and try to come up with as many different foot positions and views as you can in your drawings .

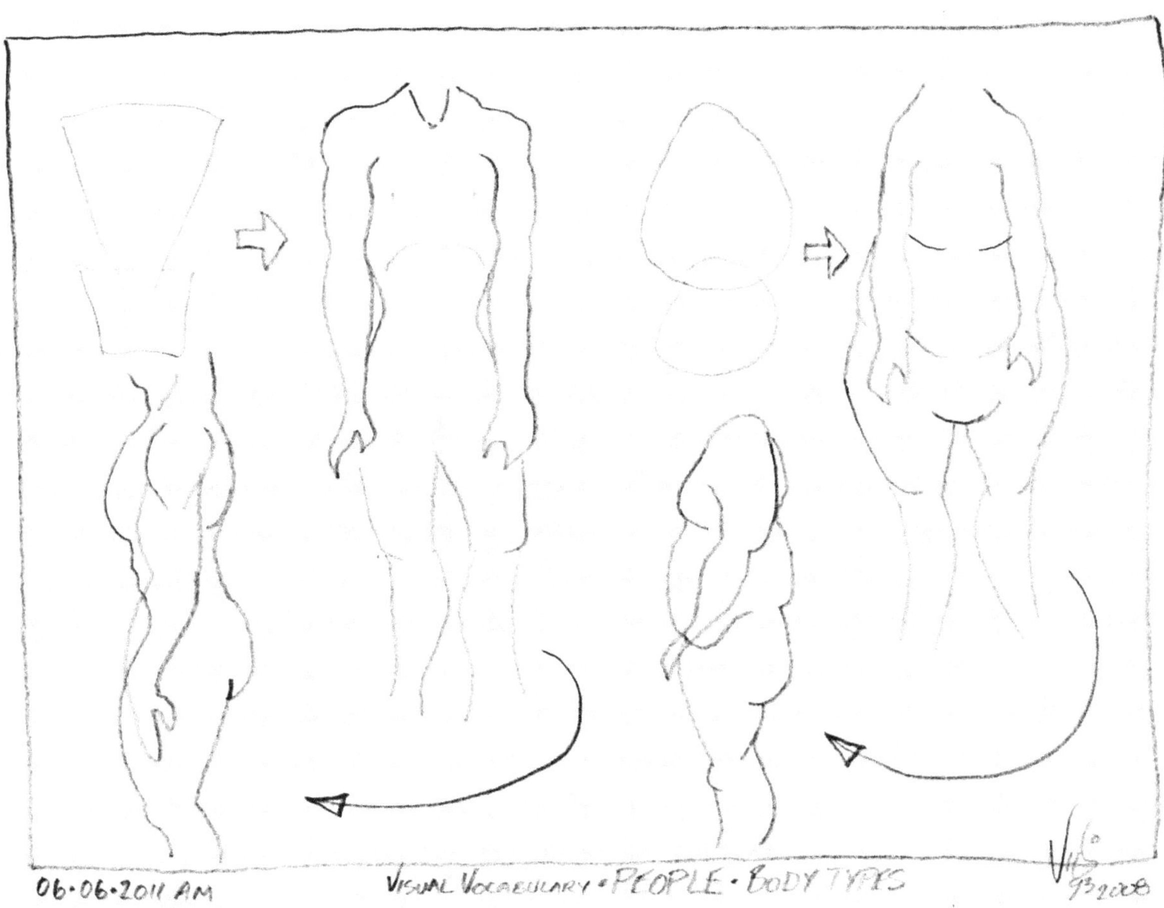

Visual Vocabulary:

People: Body Types

Cultivate an awareness of body shapes as a whole and learn to identify body shapes by the basic shapes such as square, round, triangular, horizontal oval, vertical oval or even a hexagon .

Observe the arcs that occur in the body and maintain those arcs in the various different views and positions of the body you are drawing . Look for these arcs when observing and maintain them in your drawing .

Daily identification of body shapes as you go through your day, coming across people when you walk down the street, will improve your ability to draw characters from your imagination . Let your imagination flow and try to come up with as many different body types as you can in your drawings .

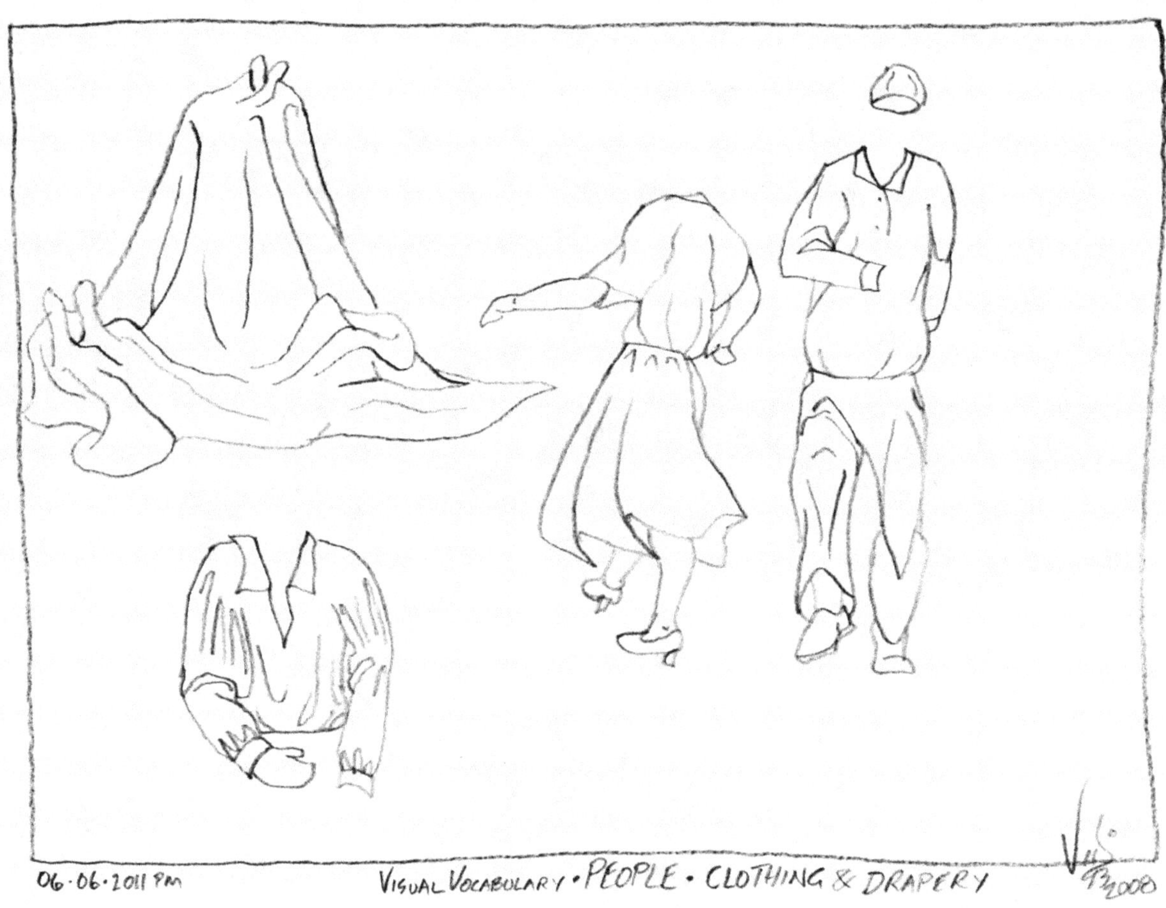

Visual Vocabulary:

People: Clothing & Drapery

Cultivate an awareness of clothing and various drapery, as most illustrations of people will require the subject to be clothed. Having said that, clothes are not as challenging as people to draw, and regular observation will quickly cultivate a repertoire of how clothes and other drapery hang, fold, and bunch. One may find it harder to learn the various types of clothing people employ than learning how to hang the clothing.

Let your imagination flow and try to come up with as many different types of clothing as you can in your drawings.

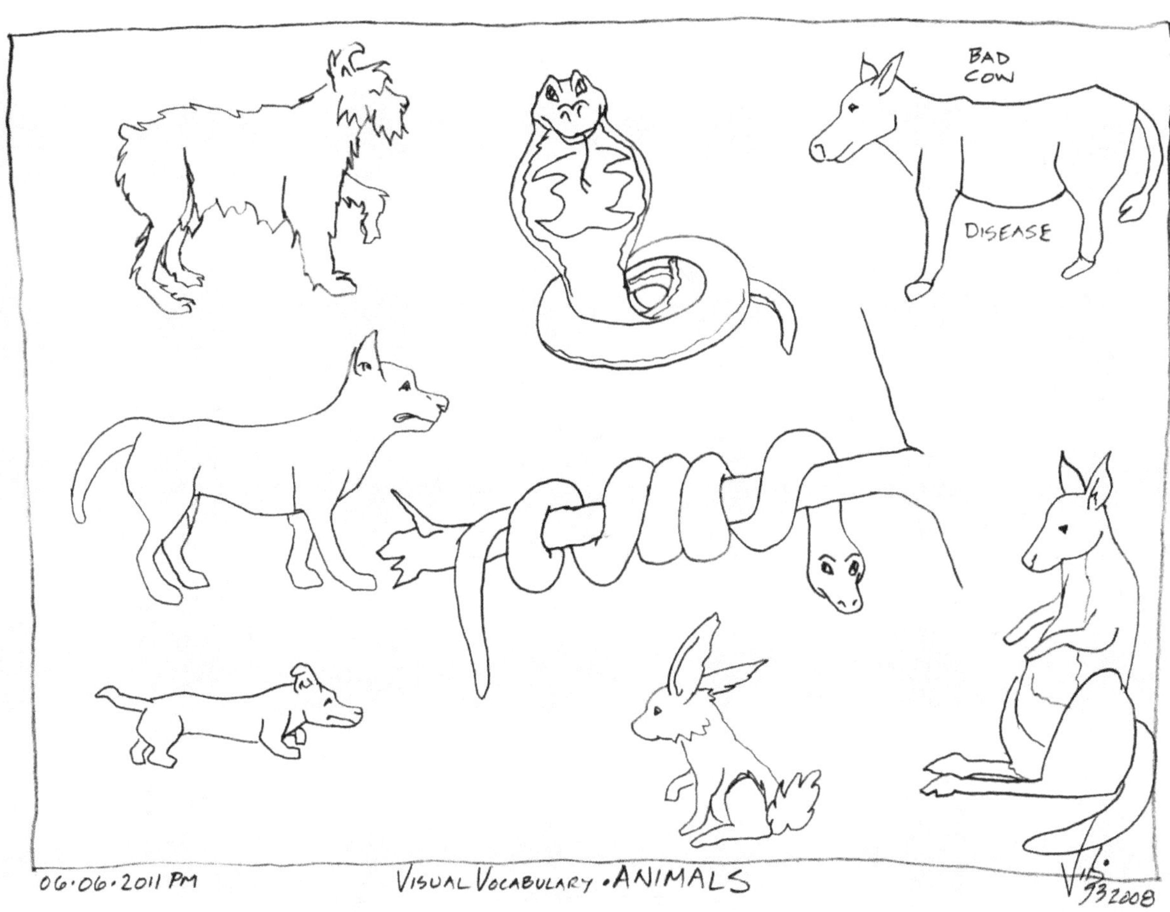

Visual Vocabulary:

Animals: Breeds, Species 1

Cultivate an awareness of different animals and notice how they compare anatomically, as this will help you distinguish a cow from a dog or a horse . Admittedly, my cow drawing above looks more like a dog . I will take the next opportunity I have to observe the differences between a cow and a dog .

Observe the arcs that occur in the body and maintain those arcs in the various different views and positions of the body you are drawing . Look for these arcs when observing and maintain them in your drawing .

Daily identification of body shapes as you come across animals, when you walk down the street, will improve your ability to draw animals from your imagination . Let your imagination flow and try to come up with as many different animals as you can in your drawings .

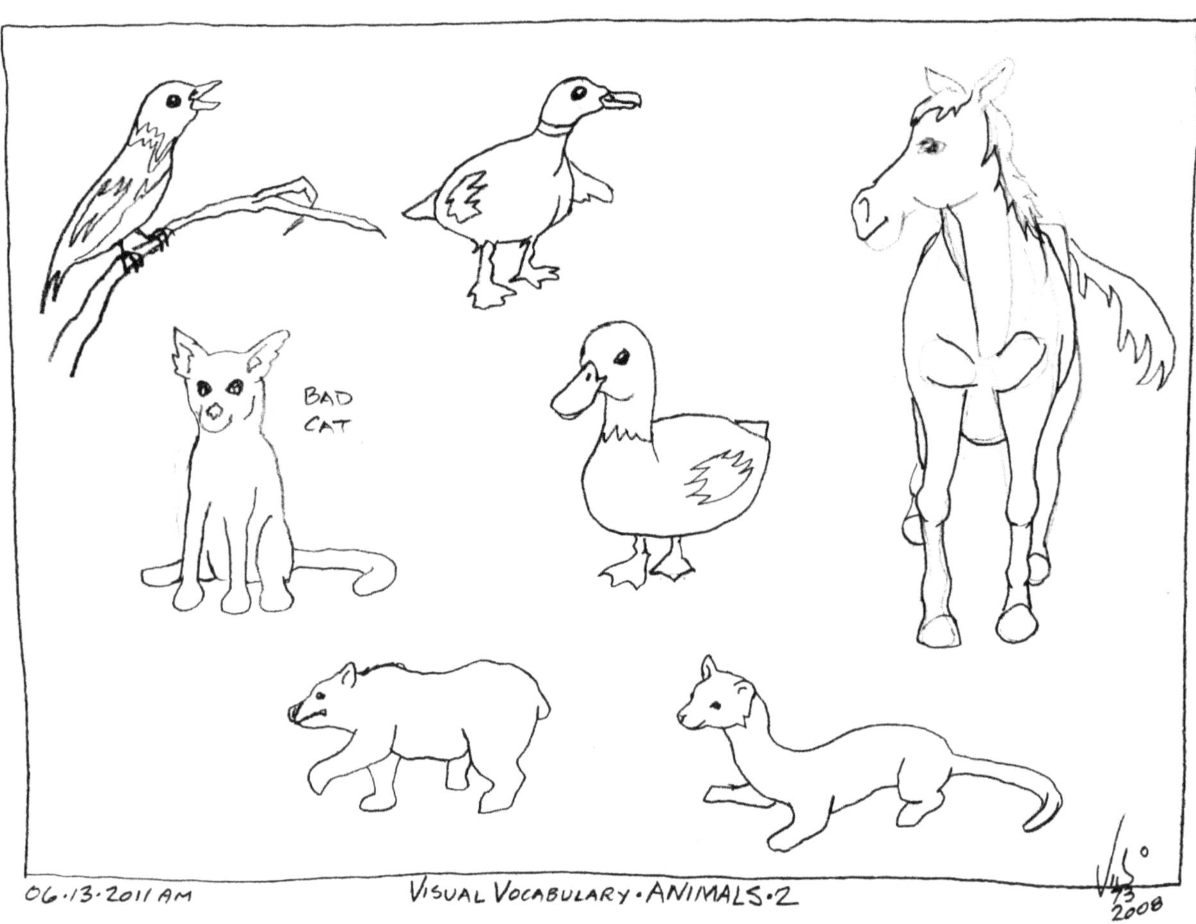

Visual Vocabulary:

Animals: Breeds, Species 2

As well as a large variety of animals, try to draw a wide variety of views of the animals you choose to draw, and then draw a wide variety of poses of those animals.

Some animals, like horses, have a lot of intricate details to illustrate, but other animals, like hamsters, are just as challenging as one doesn't want a drawing of a puff of fur, but rather an identifiable animal. The overall total shape can be very important on a simple animal.

At this point, one may become aware of how a drawing may appear wrong even when it is correct. A part of a drawing may look wrong, until one looks at the drawing as a whole. This is more common than one may expect.

Finally, one may find that there is a lot to draw when considering animals, as I have found I can fill a book with drawings of dogs and horses, but perhaps I should consider observing and drawing cats, to improve.

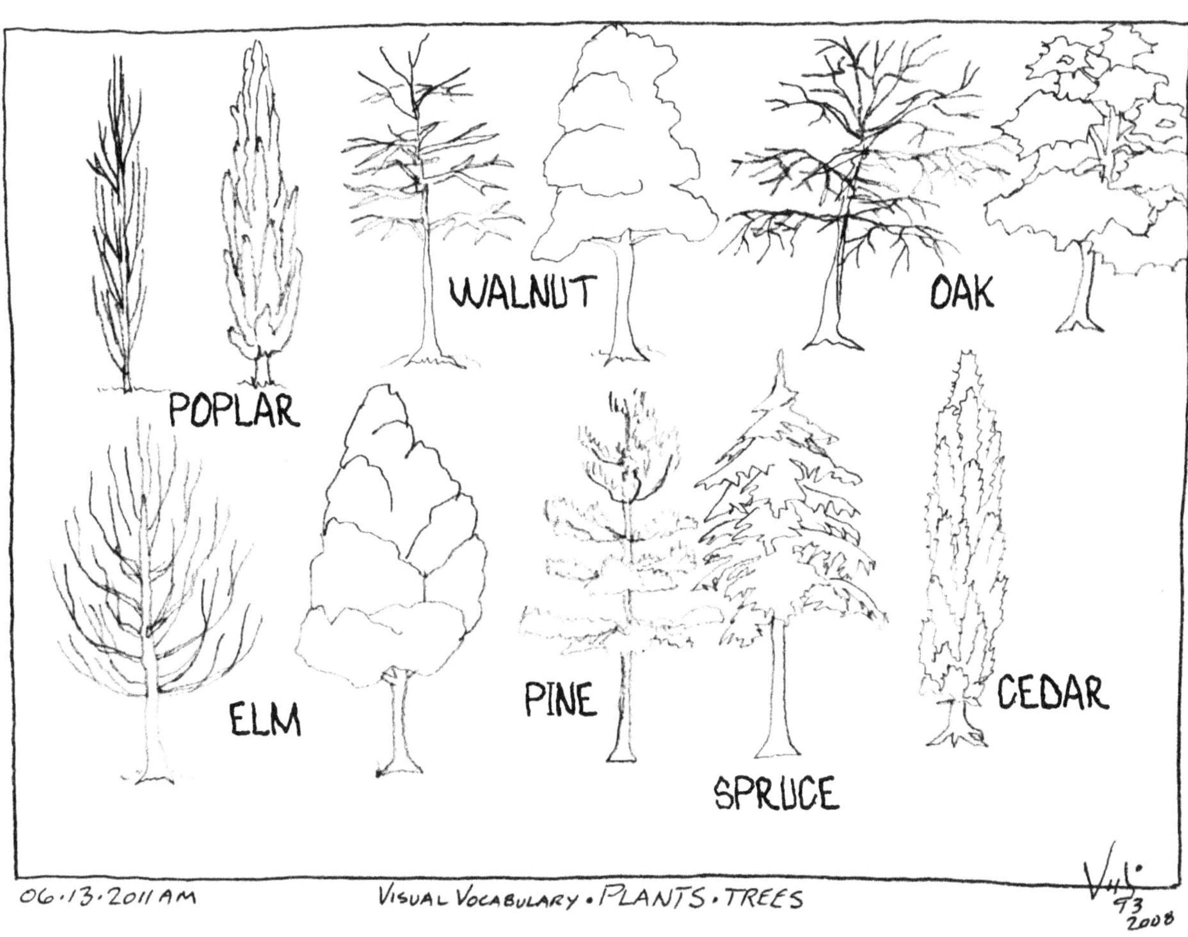

Visual Vocabulary:

Plants: Trees

A tree is not just a homogeneous mass of leaves stuck on the top of a trunk ! There are many different forms of trees and maintaining these forms can add a lot of character to one's drawing .

Once again, the crotch angle is the important thing to keep in mind, even if one is drawing a tree full of foliage, as the branches determine what the foliage will be like . The crotch angle is the angle between the branch and the trunk . A poplar, has a very small crotch angle, and this means most of its branches point straight up . On the other hand, a walnut or an oak have almost a perpendicular crotch angle, as the branches point out almost horizontally .

Even the branches of the branches maintain a similar crotch angle as the rest of the tree .

Evergreens are similar, but notice whether the branches point up as in a scotch pine, or down as in a spruce . Cedars have branches that point up .

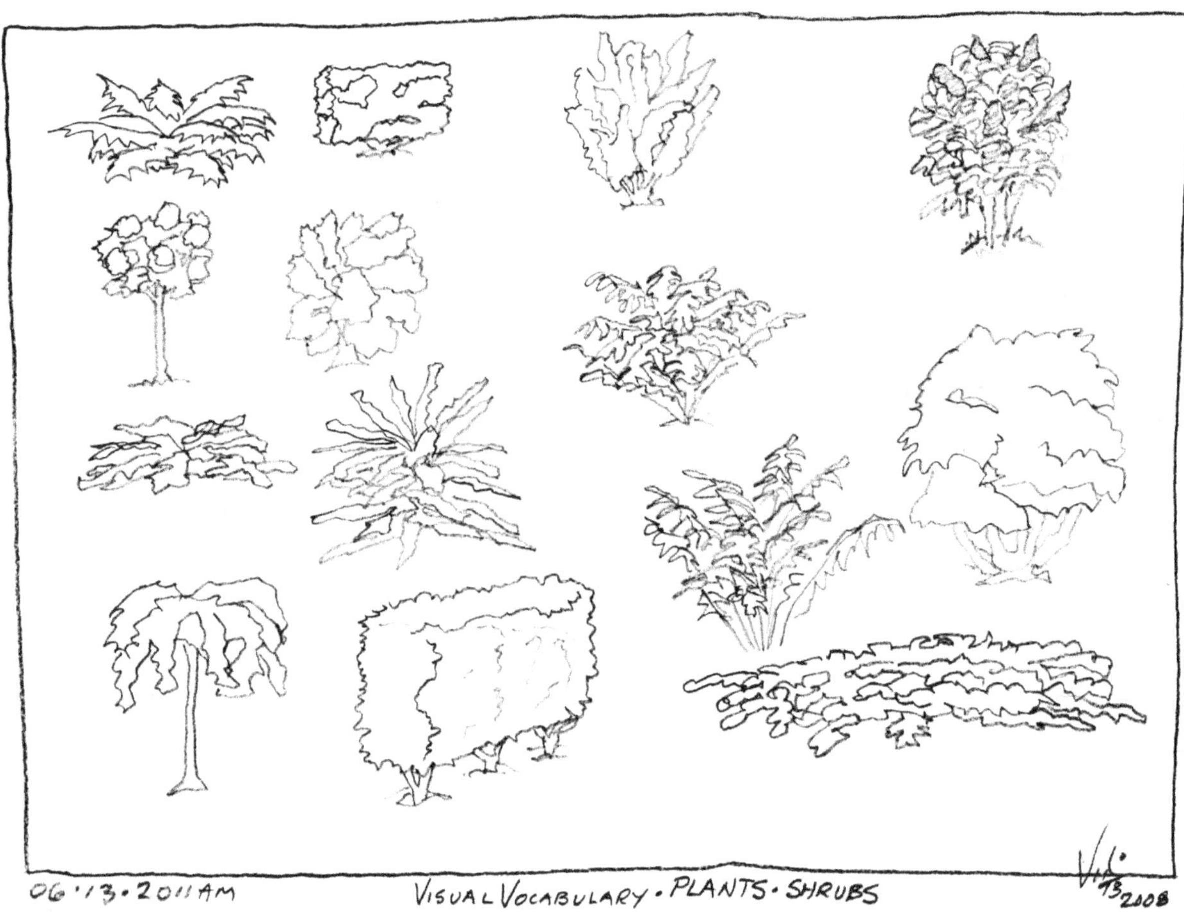

Visual Vocabulary:

Plants: Shrubs

Once again, the crotch angle of a shrub has a great deal to do with the overall shape and look of a shrub .

Some shrubs have branches that come off of a trunk, horizontally, at ninety degrees to the upright trunk, and others have branches that just point more or less up from a common stump .

Other shrubs have very horizontal branches out from a common stump, such as a juniper . And then there are the carpet type of shrubs that almost spread out over the ground .

A shrub can be cultivated to look like a ball at the top of a stick . Hedges are pruned to be box like .

In the wild, a shrub will grow toward the light, and the shaded area of a shrubs foliage will be very sparse .

Keep in mind the texture of the foliage . Round leaves create a different foliage texture than pointed leaves or evergreens . As well, a juniper has a different foliage texture than a yew .

Just start drawing whatever you can imagine, and you will notice more the next time you see actual shrubs .

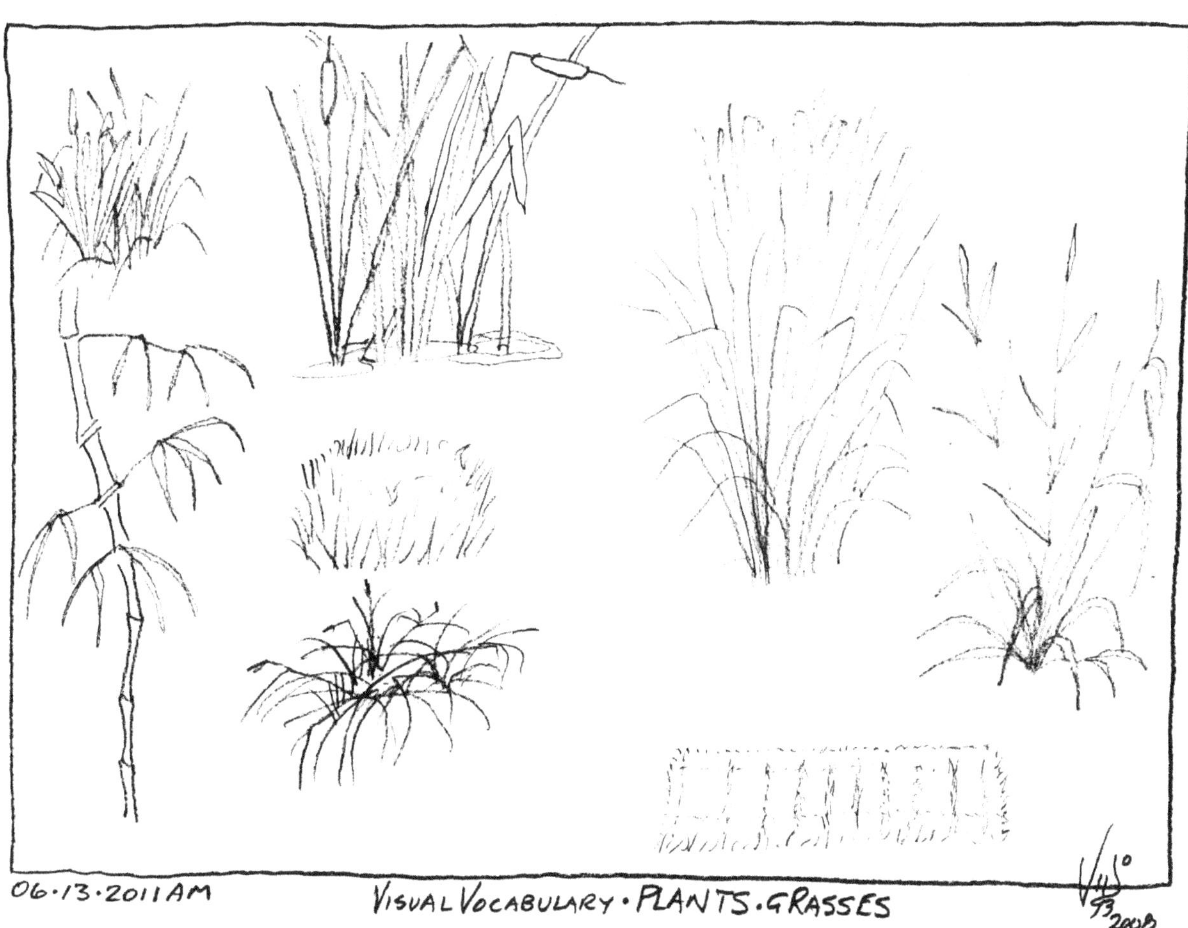

Visual Vocabulary:

Plants: Grasses

There is still an angle in the proliferation of a clump of grass that can be taken as a crotch angle .

Ornamental grasses range from short clumps to clumps that are over one's head in height .

All grasses may have grain heads if allowed to mature . Many grasses have "leaves" or stalks that branch off of the main stalk .

Many grasses have long, large blades that curve over at a certain height and in the wind, a field may look like waves on the ocean .

Even southern Ontario has many large grasses that are structured as bamboo, with nodes and leaves off of the nodes . They are tall and hollow like bamboo . I have seen this type of grass in cultivated landscapes as a large shrub .

Many grasses, both small and large, have nodes where blades of grass branch off . These grasses may be rooted in clumps, so this will determine the angle at which they jut up out of the ground .

A lawn may be illustrated by representing the mowed lines, as mowing pushes the blades one way or another, and leaves bent blades where the wheels of the mower pass .

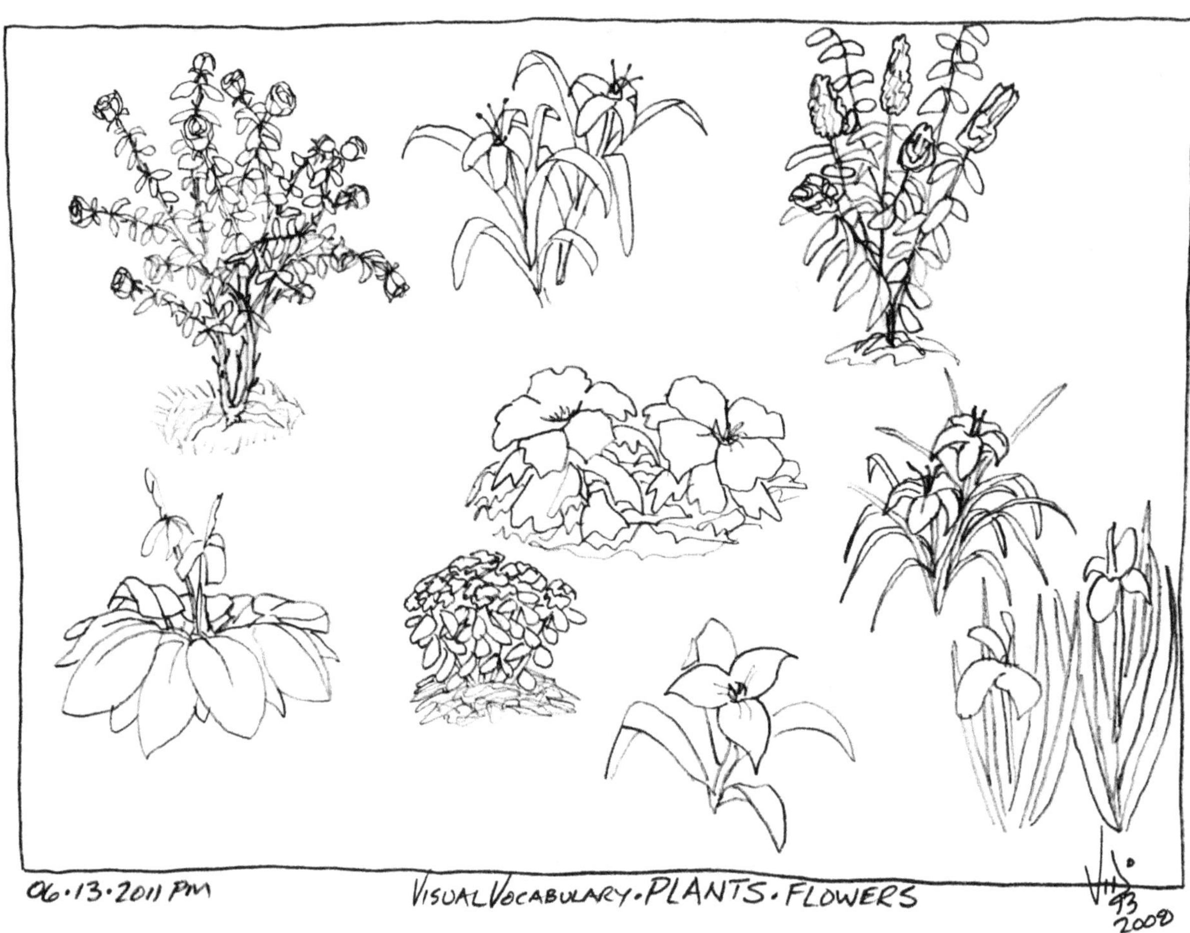

Visual Vocabulary:

Plants: Flowers

Once again, there is a crotch angle in flowers, whether a shrub or a clump of stalks.

Tulips and irises rise up out of a clump mostly vertically. Lilies have stalks that rise out of a stump or clump. Roses and lilacs are shrubs with flower heads. Trilliums are close to the ground. I will have to observe trilliums next time I see them, as I can't remember what their leaf structure is like.

The actual flowers have petals, stamens and other parts. A tulip has closed petals in a bulb shape. The petals of lilies arch back away from the centre and their stamens point straight out of the flower, with clumps of pollen. Roses are tight clumps of petals in a flattened bulb shape that curve away from the centre at their tips.

Petunias have petals with irregular edges and the plant stays close to the ground, with spreading leaves. Again, I will have to observe them next time I have the chance.

Hostas are a cultivated large plant made up of large spreading pointed leaves from a clump, and have flower stalks sticking up from the centre.

A plant nursery catalog, if it has pictures or photographs, can be a great reference had for free.

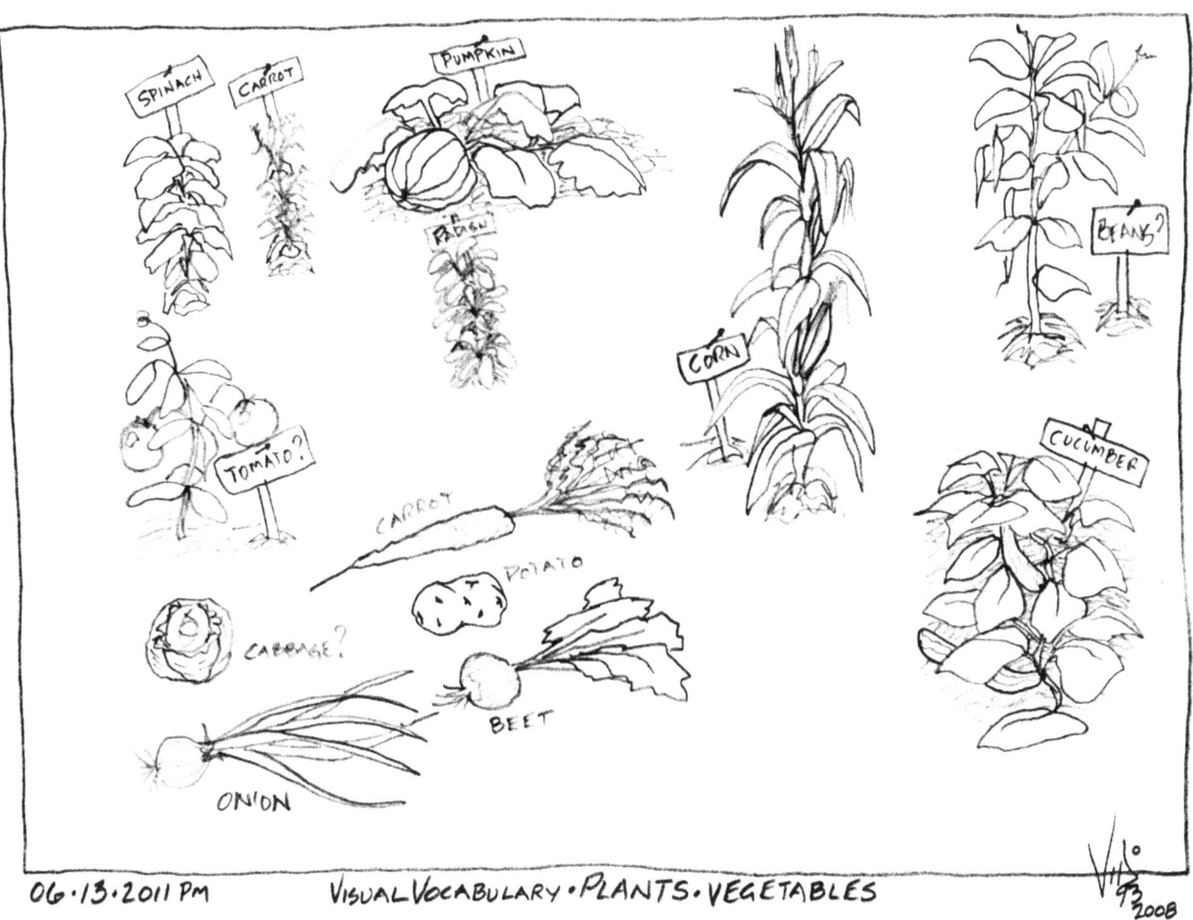

Visual Vocabulary:

Plants: Vegetables

Vegetables are a great test of how well one can draw from memory, as everyone has seen vegetables, if only in a grocery store or fridge . Try as well, to remember what they look like on the plant, when they are growing .

I will have to seek out an opportunity to observe bean plants and tomato plants, as I found I had very little idea of what they look like .

Pumpkins and cucumbers or zucchini grow on vines and have a pale side next to the ground . A cucumber has a tapered long oval shape, and pumpkins are flatter on the ground side but otherwise spherical, with longitudinal grooves .

Carrots, onions and potatoes are fairly easy, as they are commonly found in the fridge . A carrot, in the ground, has a frilly leaf structure that sticks almost straight out of the carrot . I can't remember what a potato plant looks like .

Beets and spinach, I seem to remember, have irregular leaves on stalks coming out of a clump or common root .

I have not included fruit, (yes, a tomato is a fruit), as they were in the still life drawing, but try again to draw an apple, orange, pear, banana and some grapes, as those are easy to remember . If you do, next time you see one you will notice more of the details .

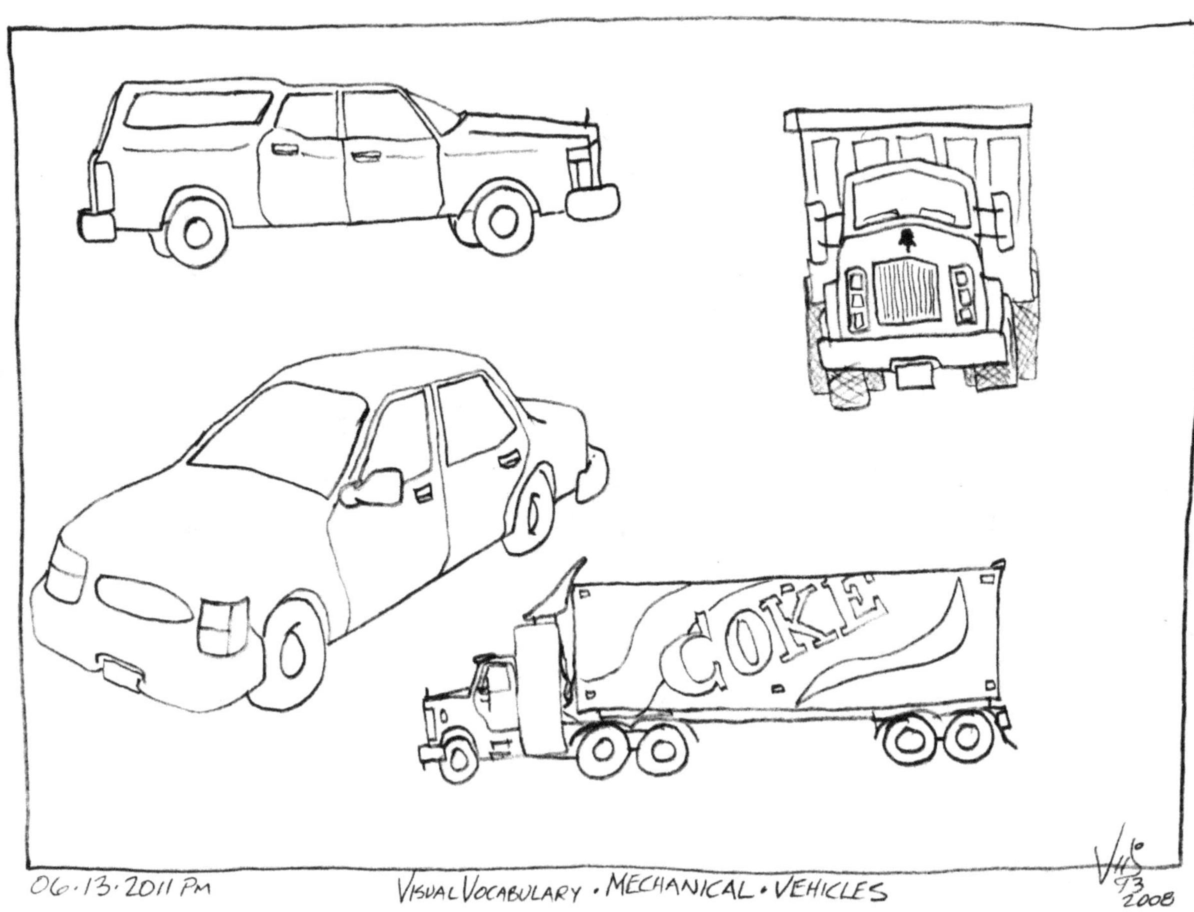

Visual Vocabulary:

Mechanical: Vehicles - 1

There are a wide variety of vehicles one can draw, from tractor trailer rigs, to buses, as well as cars .

Car styles have changed greatly over the last century, and I am familiar with cars from the late seventies until today . In the nineties cars became more streamlined without hard edges . In the forties the bubble shape was dominant before the hard straight lines of the fifties became the norm .

Try to draw what you can remember, as again, if you have made an attempt, you will notice more the next time you see in person what you were trying to draw . Try to remember what your family's car was like when you were a child, as it probably made a big impression on you .

Vans, buses and trucks, are not here as examples but are still another subject worth attempting .

If you can remember a vehicle, try drawing it from a number of different angles .

Finally, don't forget things like the front grill, headlights, brake lights, signal lights, side mirrors, rear view mirror, bumpers, windshield wipers and door handles, as well as windows . Trucks may have running boards or ladders up to the cab . Buses have their unique doors, windows and painting scheme .

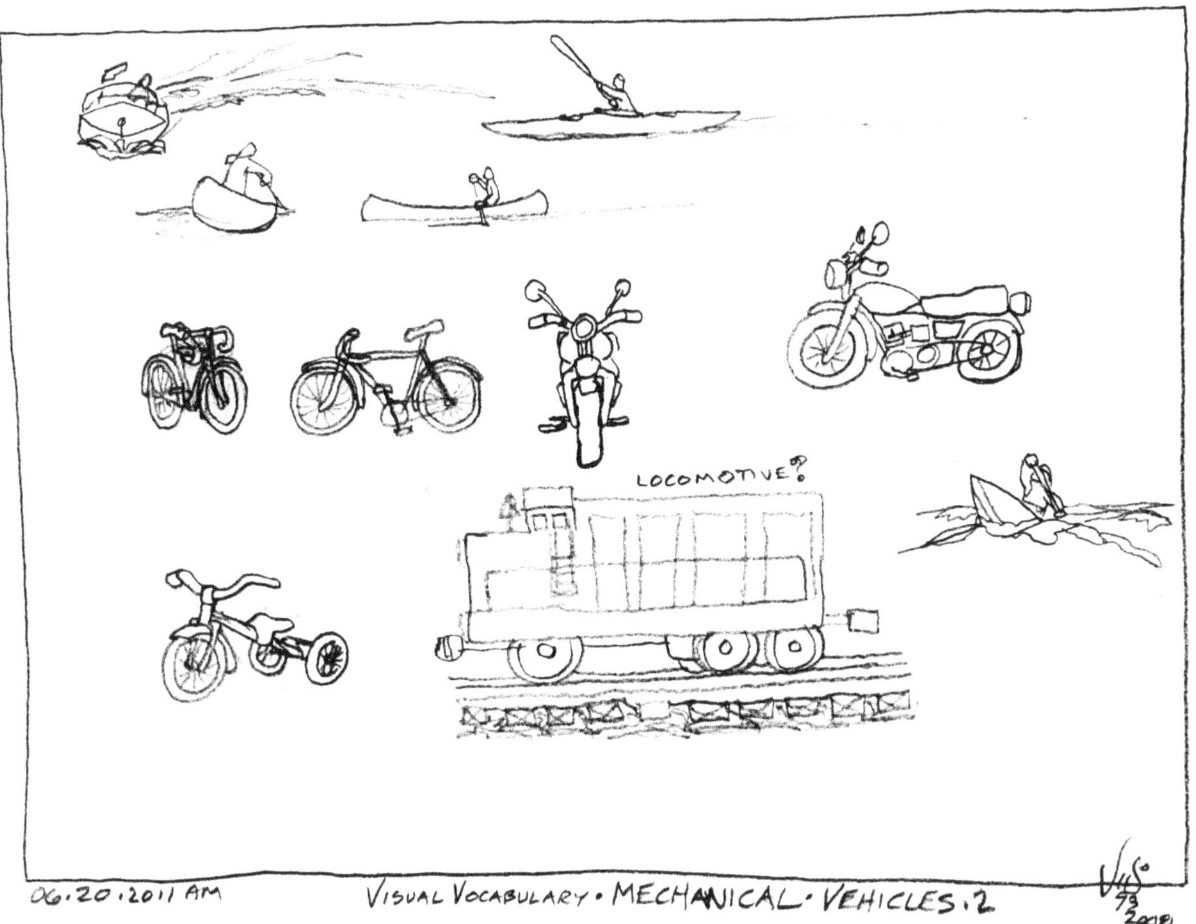

Visual Vocabulary:

Mechanical: Vehicles - 2

Not all vehicles are motorized, and don't forget watercraft.

Bicycles can be a very intricate subject to draw. Motorcycles require sufficient details to make them look correct. Nevertheless, draw what you can and be sure to observe bicycles and motorcycles next time you see them.

Watercraft can vary greatly. The smooth curves of a canoe or kayak require an accurate clean line. Drawing the paddler requires thinking to figure out where everything goes and what is happening.

Motorboats also vary greatly, so attempt to draw the easiest boat you can remember. Sailboats can be very complicated too, and ships are so large it is hard to choose what to show and fit in the details.

Locomotives, as in train engines, are something I see regularly but I just couldn't recall enough to get one looking correct.

Tricycles are a simple vehicle that is still challenging to draw, as there are a lot of intersecting straight and curved lines, as in bicycles. If you feel you are confident, draw them from a number of angles, and put riders on them.

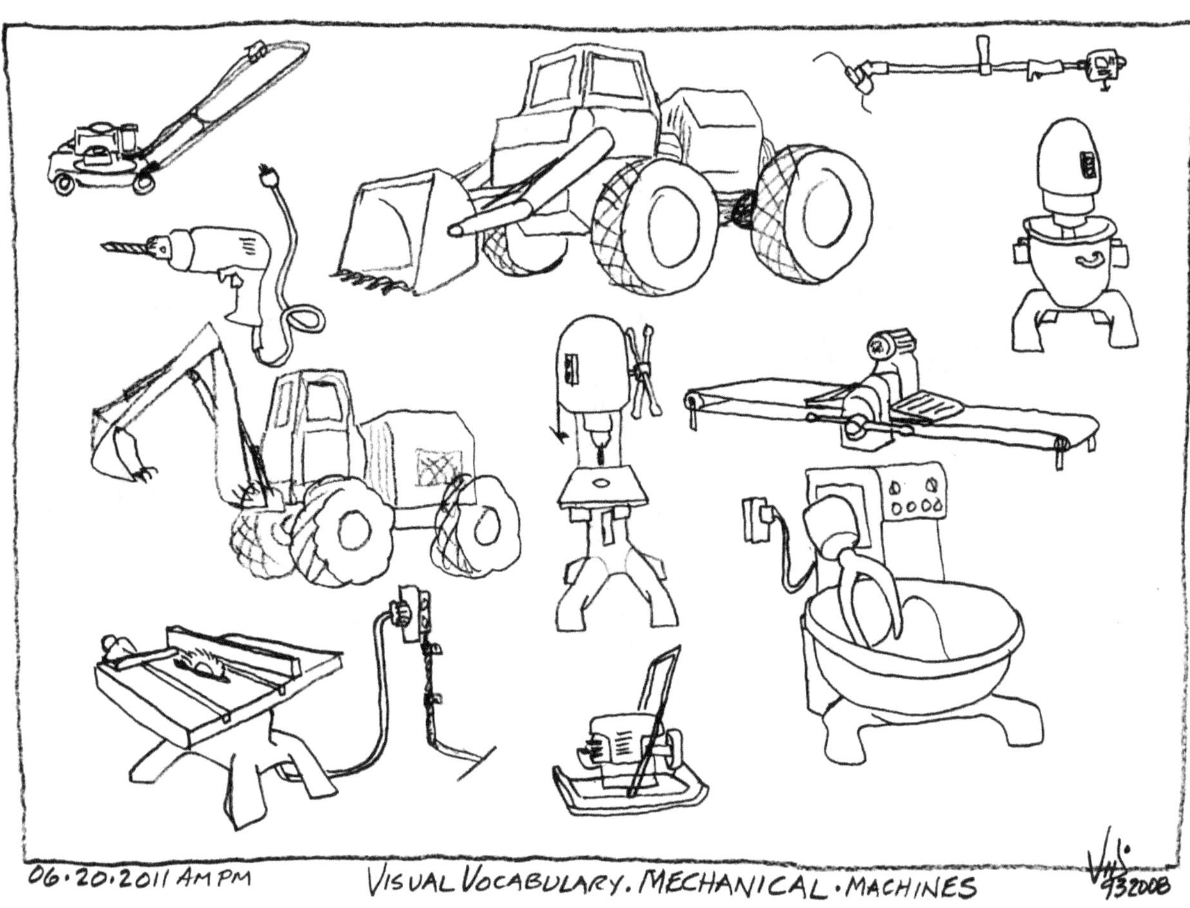
06.20.2011 AM PM   VISUAL VOCABULARY. MECHANICAL.MACHINES

Visual Vocabulary:

Mechanical: Machines

Industrial or commercial work experience can be a wealth of ideas of what kind of machines are out there. I have worked in a small bakery and kitchens and as an electricians helper. This has given me a lot of ideas of machines. Some I have left out are riding lawn mowers, including a stand up riding lawn mower, and commercial stoves and kitchen appliances.

Watch out for my front end loader and backhoe - they are not correct, as I couldn't figure out all the hydraulics on the buckets. This would be a good subject to go out and sketch, or search out on the internet.

Other subjects could be graders, and bucket trucks, and tankers and rail cars and cranes.

Locomotives, as in train engines, are something I see regularly but I just couldn't recall enough to get one looking correct.

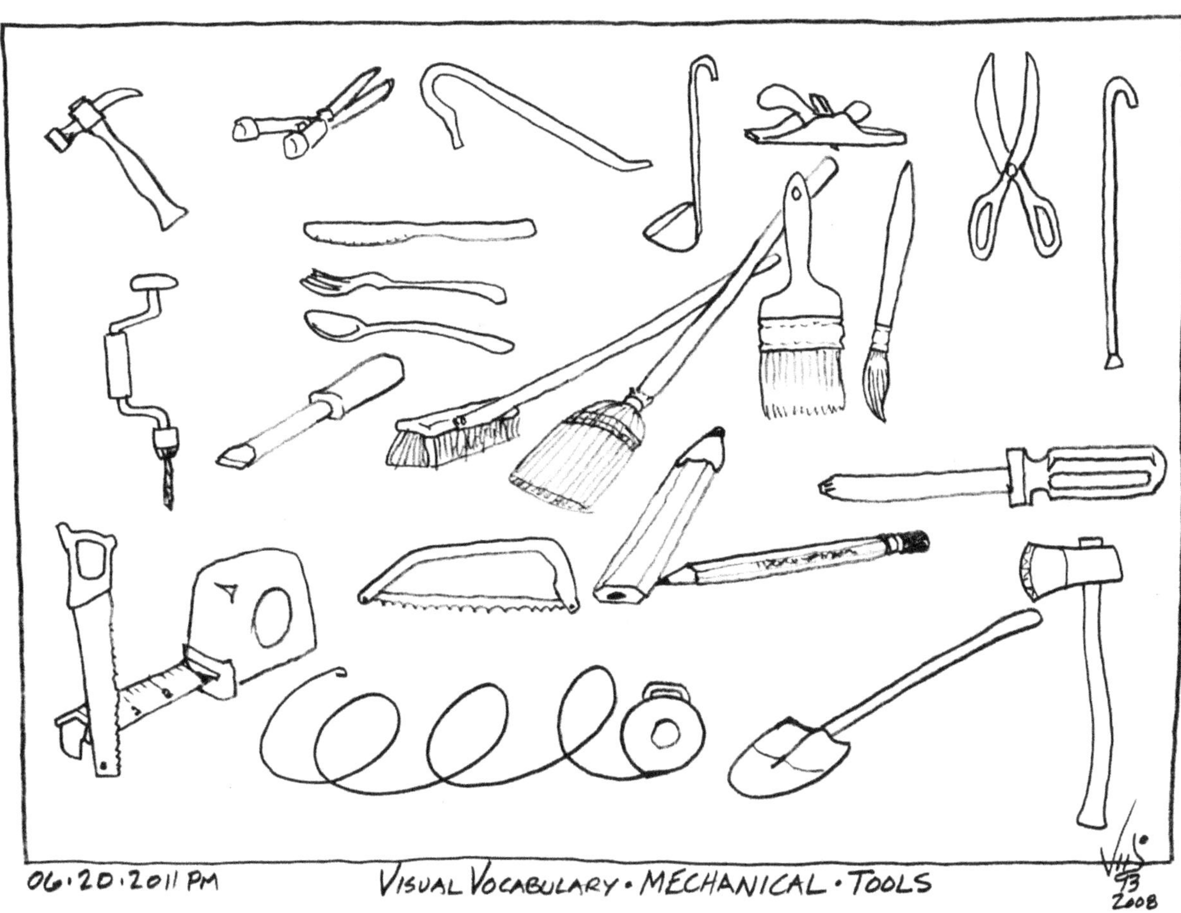

Visual Vocabulary:

Mechanical: Tools

Tools are a handy thing to draw if you have any around, in case you can't rack your brain to come up with what any of them look like. The are essentially an extension of one's hand, so try drawing them being used in the hand of the craftsman.

Utensils are a kind of tool not to be overlooked. There are a great many different designs manufactured and almost no two are alike!

Try drawing them from all different angles, to practice foreshortening. Draw the hands as they use the tools. An obvious example is to draw your hand holding the pencil you are drawing with!

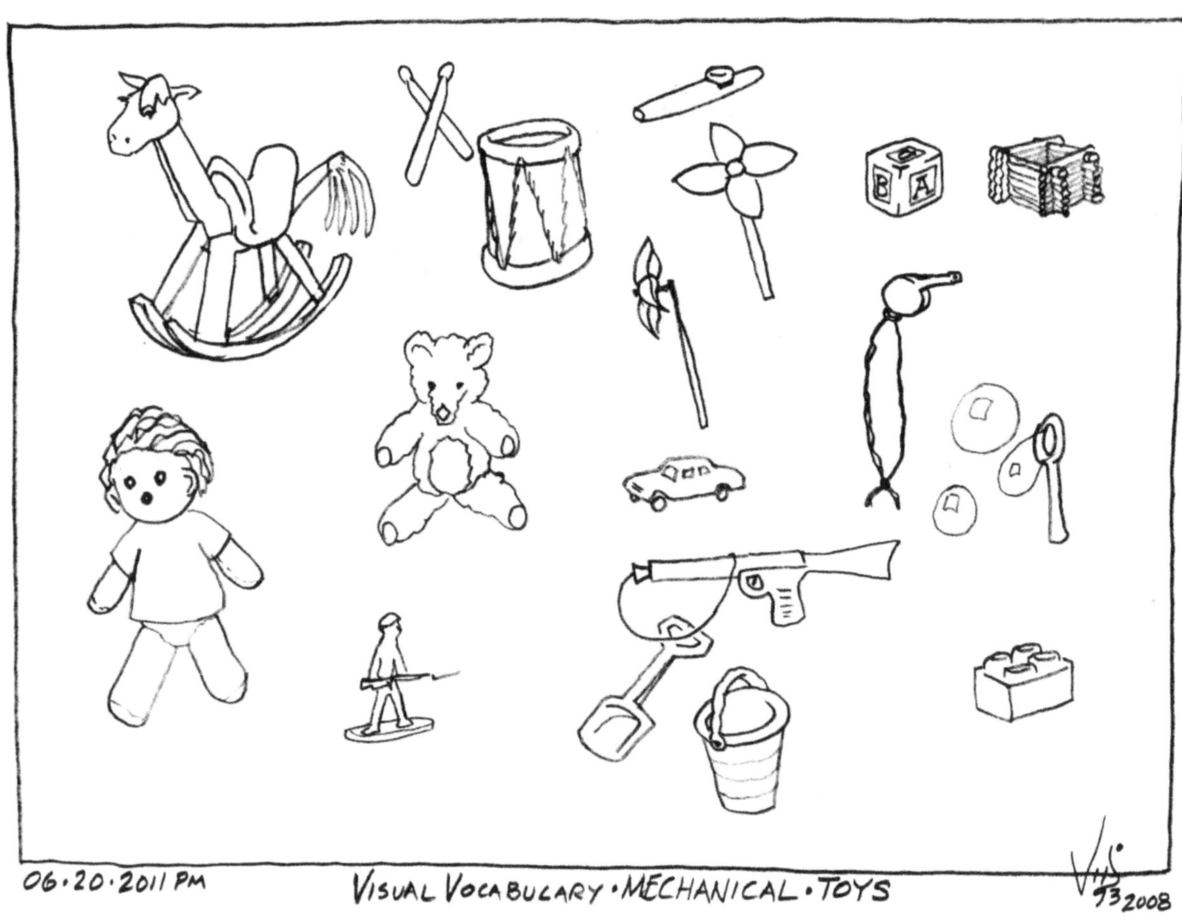

Visual Vocabulary:

Mechanical: Toys

Toys can be very difficult to remember, and they tend to look like the real thing rather than a toy. As well, modern child's toys are either complex or not much to draw.

If you are in your tv room, try drawing the game console. Then draw it from memory. Sports equipment is not heralded as a toy but if you are famillar with a sport or two, draw the equipment and field or arena. Sports are a great thing to try to illustrate, especially if you have experience playing one or two.

Try to remember the toys you grew up with, and then draw them. I had blocks, but that wouldn't be too challenging to draw. Lego was a favourite toy, but that doesn't make much of a drawing. Toy soldiers are good to draw, but they end up looking like real soldiers.

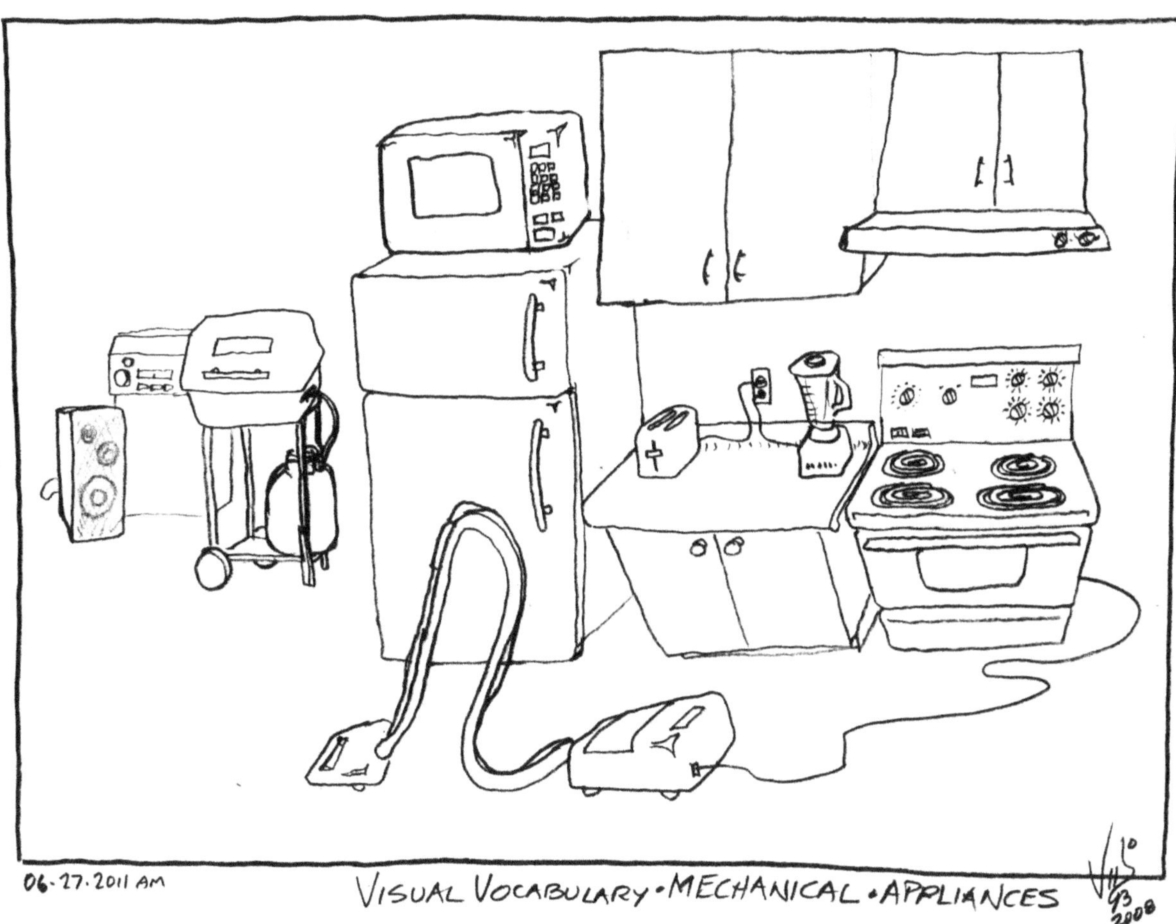

Visual Vocabulary:

Mechanical: Appliances

Appliances are another everyday item one may draw, but can you draw one from memory ? That is what Visual Vocabulary is - having a large number of items in your visual toolbox that you can draw from memory .

The perspective is slipping in this drawing, but you get the idea . Draw whatever you can see from your dining table or kitchen table . Try to get the whole shebang into one drawing, then draw it all again from memory . There is always something to draw !

Even in any room of your home there are a wealth of drawing possibilities . If it is too easy to draw something because it is so simple, try drawing it from memory in a way that it is identifiable as to what it is .

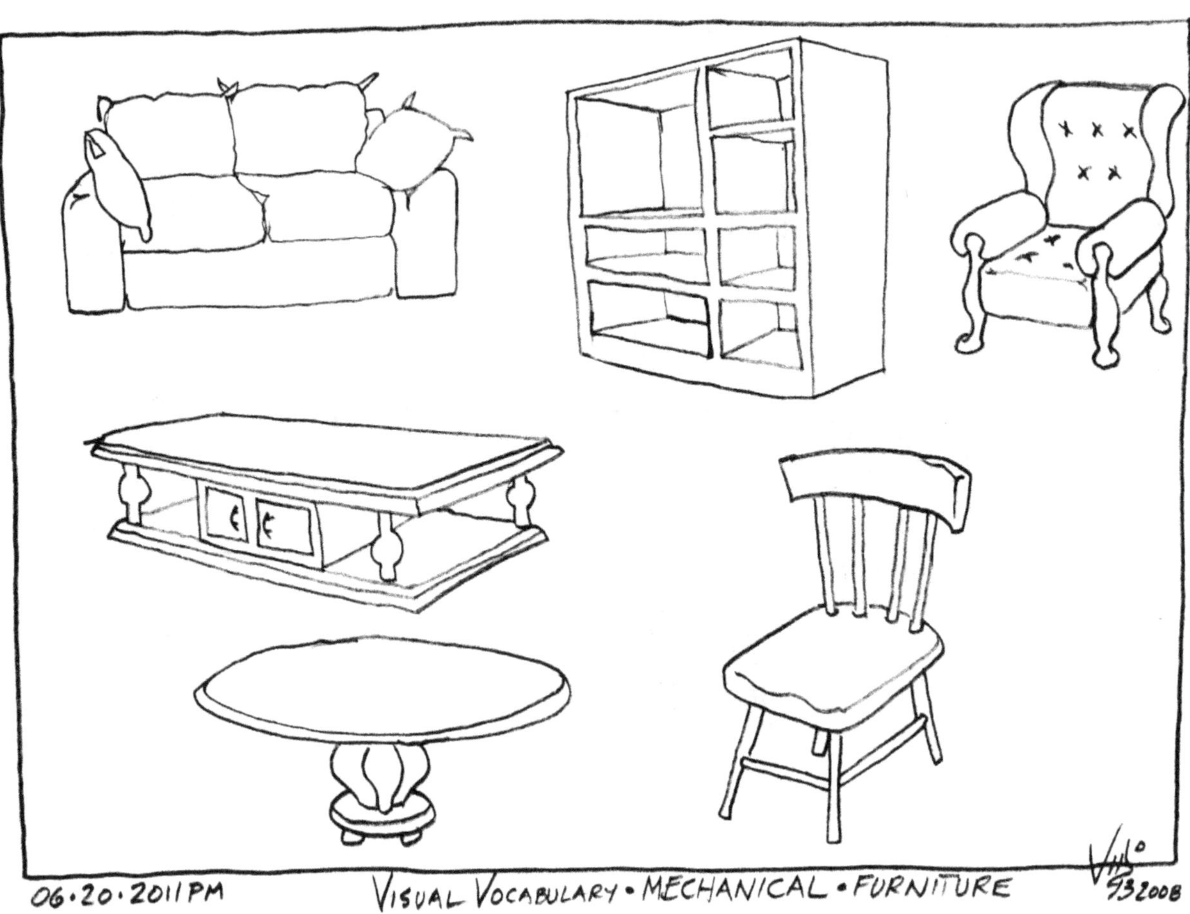

Visual Vocabulary:

Mechanical: Furniture

You see it everyday, but can you draw any of it from memory ? Can you draw it with consistent perspective ?

How do you draw a cushion or pillow so that it looks like what it really is, rather than a puff of smoke or a cloud ? Upholstery is a whole other topic to draw. Even hard furniture like chairs have a range of criss-cross angled parts. Can you draw a solid chair or a solid coffee table ?

There are many other furnishings that could be drawn if one just begins to notice them throughout the day. Your doctor's waiting room is ripe for drawing. How about a bank with the teller wickets or the train station with the ticket sales window. I suppose even the furnishings on the bus or train would count as they are something that could be drawn. Even the mall food court has a variety of furnishings.

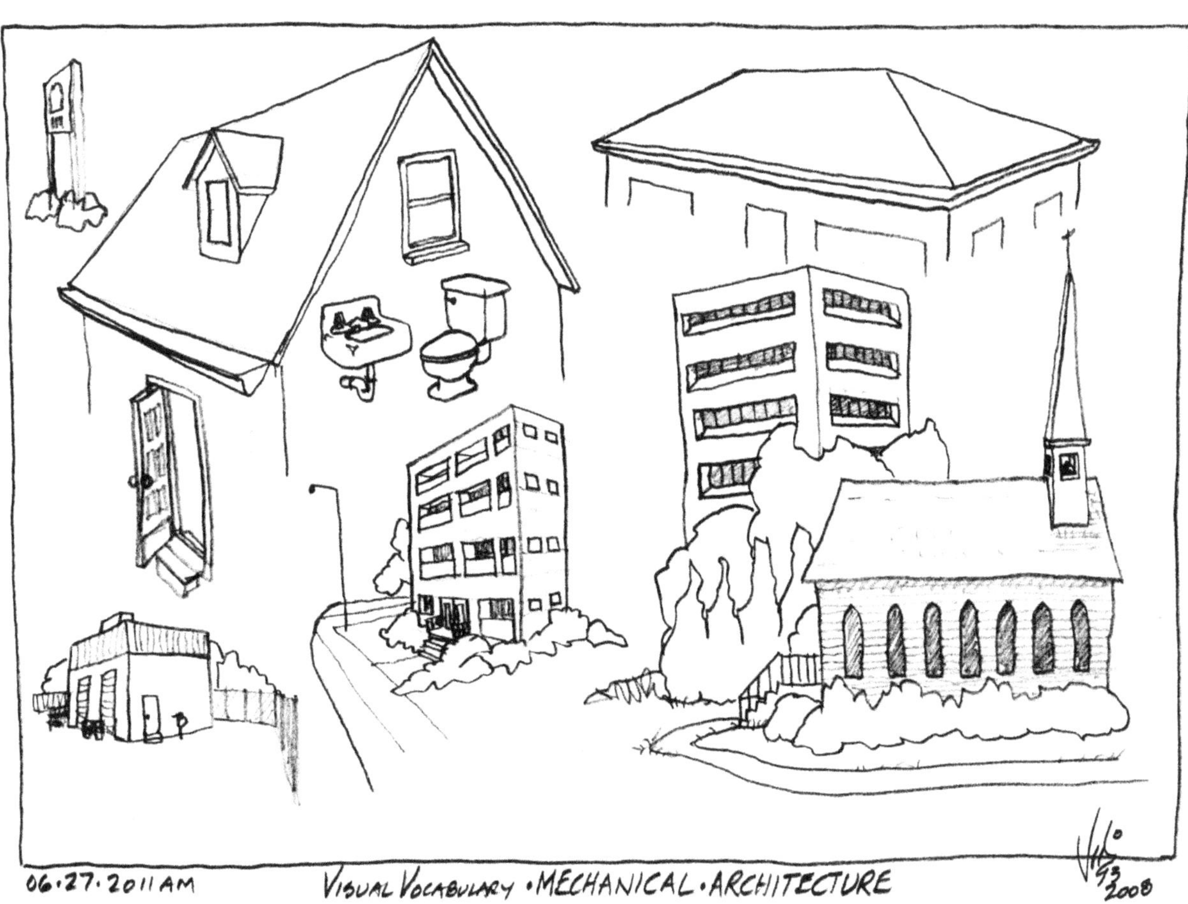

06·27·2011 AM
VISUAL VOCABULARY ·MECHANICAL·ARCHITECTURE
2008

Visual Vocabulary:

Mechanical: Architectural

This may be dubious as a mechanical category item, but nevertheless, it is another topic worthy of a draftsperson's attention. There are buildings all around us, and they are all greatly different from one another, at least in Oakville.

As well as a typical house there are many other buildings, with furnishings, that one could draw. Some examples are industrial, service, hospitals, malls, fast food restaurants, convenience stores, grocery stores, apartments, churches, schools, and street scenes, complete with signs, streetlights, trees, hydro poles and transformers, not to mention gutters, sewer grates and manholes.

And don't forget to regularly draw all these types of structures from memory, as this will improve your observation next time you see the real thing.

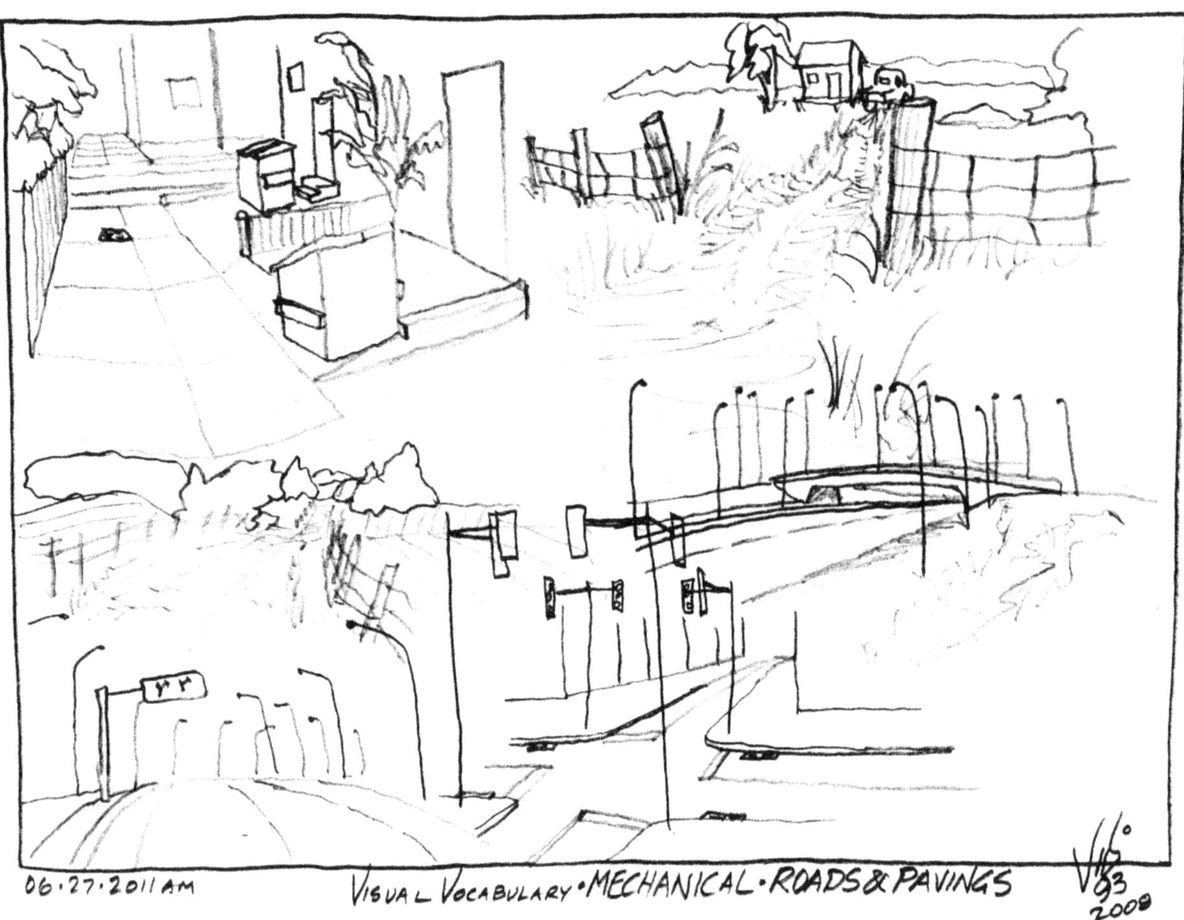

Visual Vocabulary:

Mechanical: Roads and Pavings

Roads are a very large scale drawing subject . They are just so big that laying them out on the page is the hardest part . Draw the streets you travel daily, from memory, to begin with, before moving on to topics entirely from memory, such as the last time you were out in the countryside .

Observe the different pavings in different weather and daylight conditions, when you can, and make mental notes to use the next time you are in front of a blank paper holding a pencil and trying to think of what to draw . The textures of concrete, asphalt and gravel are all different and developing a way to illustrate each type of paving is well worth the effort .

The illustration of the traffic intersection quickly becomes very complex well before all the details are added . Just the traffic control street furniture is enough to keep one busy, let alone streetlights, curbs and hydro structures ! Don't forget one could people the scene and include traffic such as cars trucks and bicycles .

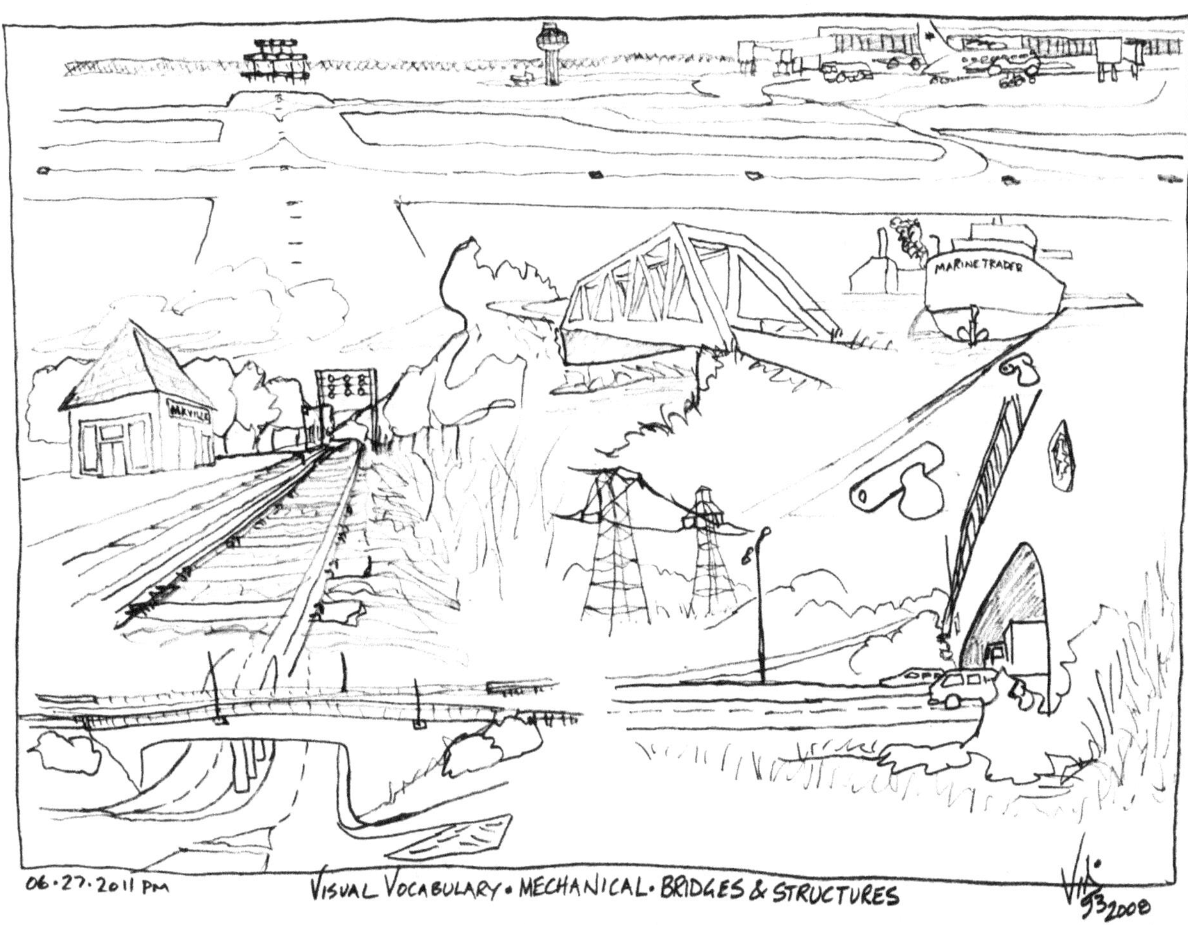

Visual Vocabulary:

Mechanical: Bridges and Structures

Here I have illusrated an airport, train station, truss bridge, wharf, underpass and an overpass. Don't stop there though - draw whatever structures you can think of !

When the subject is so large that it is lost in the drawing, the little details can make a big difference in allowing the viewer to identify the subject. Consider the airport drawing - if it didn't have airliners. The wharf without a ship would only have the moorings to suggest that the perspective line was the edge of a wharf ! Even just a bit of grass on a slope really helps to identify the truss bridge and the overpass. The perspective and curves of the underpass, as illustrated in the curb lines and the painted dotted lane separation lines, make this look like what it is.

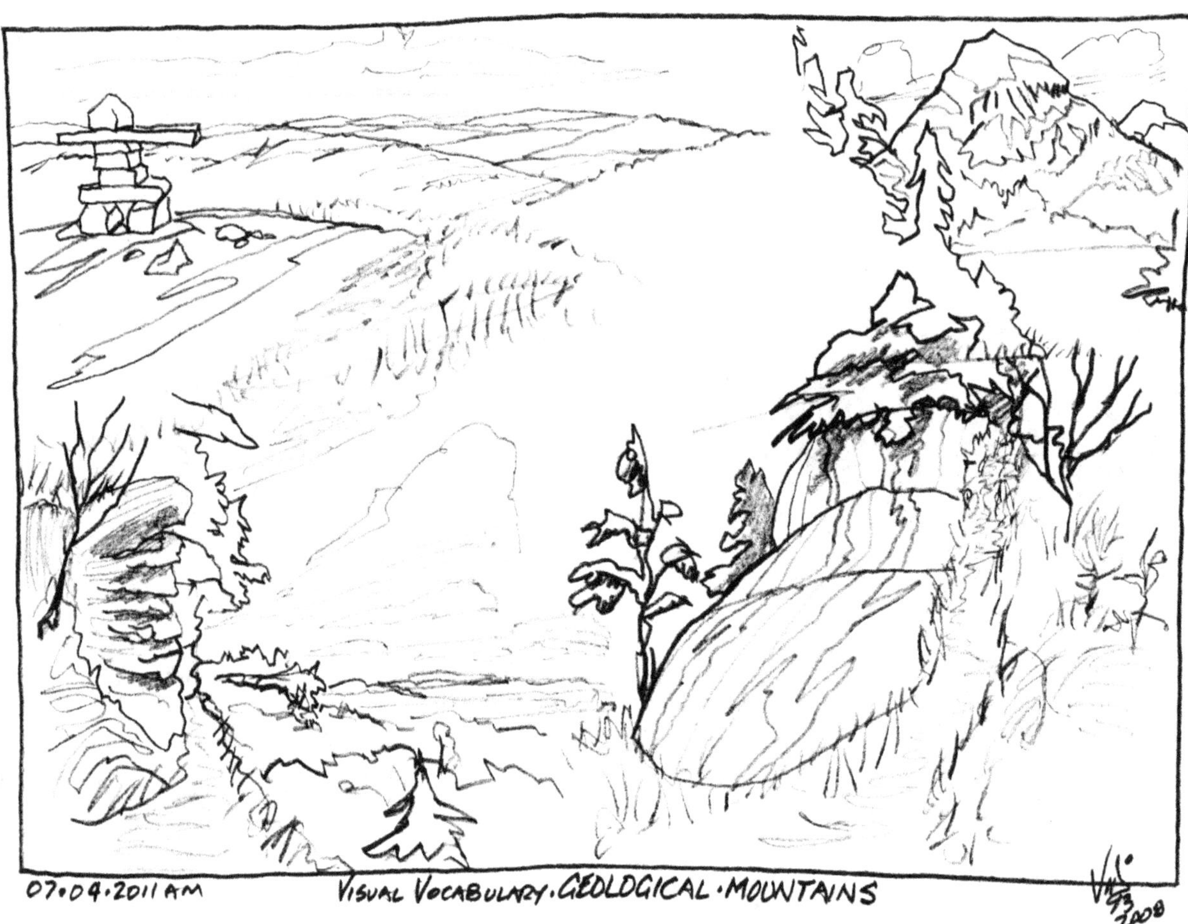

07.04.2011 AM VISUAL VOCABULARY. GEOLOGICAL. MOUNTAINS

Visual Vocabulary:

Geological: Mountains

Sure, there is the classical pointed snow-capped mountain as illustrated in the top right, but consider the other types of mountains that are older and more rounded, and don't forget the local ones - escarpments !

The inukshuk in the top left illustration gives this drawing away as being in the tundra, but there are even taller mountains, similar to what is found in between the fjiords of Scotland and Sweden, in the tundra of northern Quebec and Labrador .

The escarpment has a typical layered type of rock outcrop that make a drawing of it identifiable . And the canadian shield around Ottawa and into Algonquin Park provides bare outcrops of striated rock that are easy to identifiably illustrate .

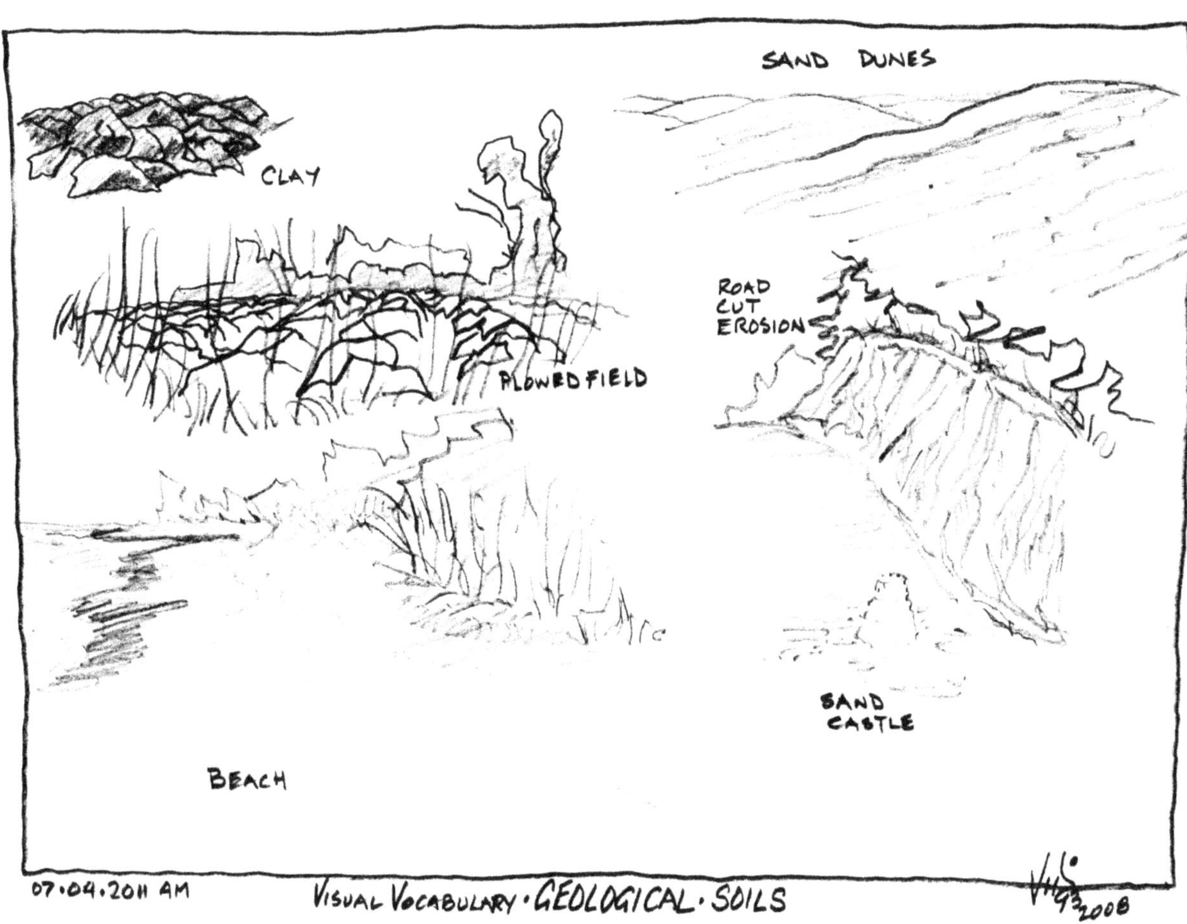

Visual Vocabulary:

Geological: Soils

There are basically two extremes of soils, that are on opposite ends of the spectrum with a range of soils between them, and they are sand on the one end, and clay on the other. There can be gravel, of different types, mixed into the soil.

Clay will clump and sand will flow, and not naturally clump. Illustrating the varieties basically comes down to how much clumping, the size of the clumps, the number and variety of the clumps, and the interspersing of any gravels of whatever type.

So soil can be very difficult to illustrate, as it is mostly a texture that must be created. It is worth a good deal of study and practice, to readily be able to illustrate soils. If you are confident in your ability to illustrate trees, shrubs and grasses, with all the variety of foliage, try challenging yourself by drawing soils so that they are recognizable.

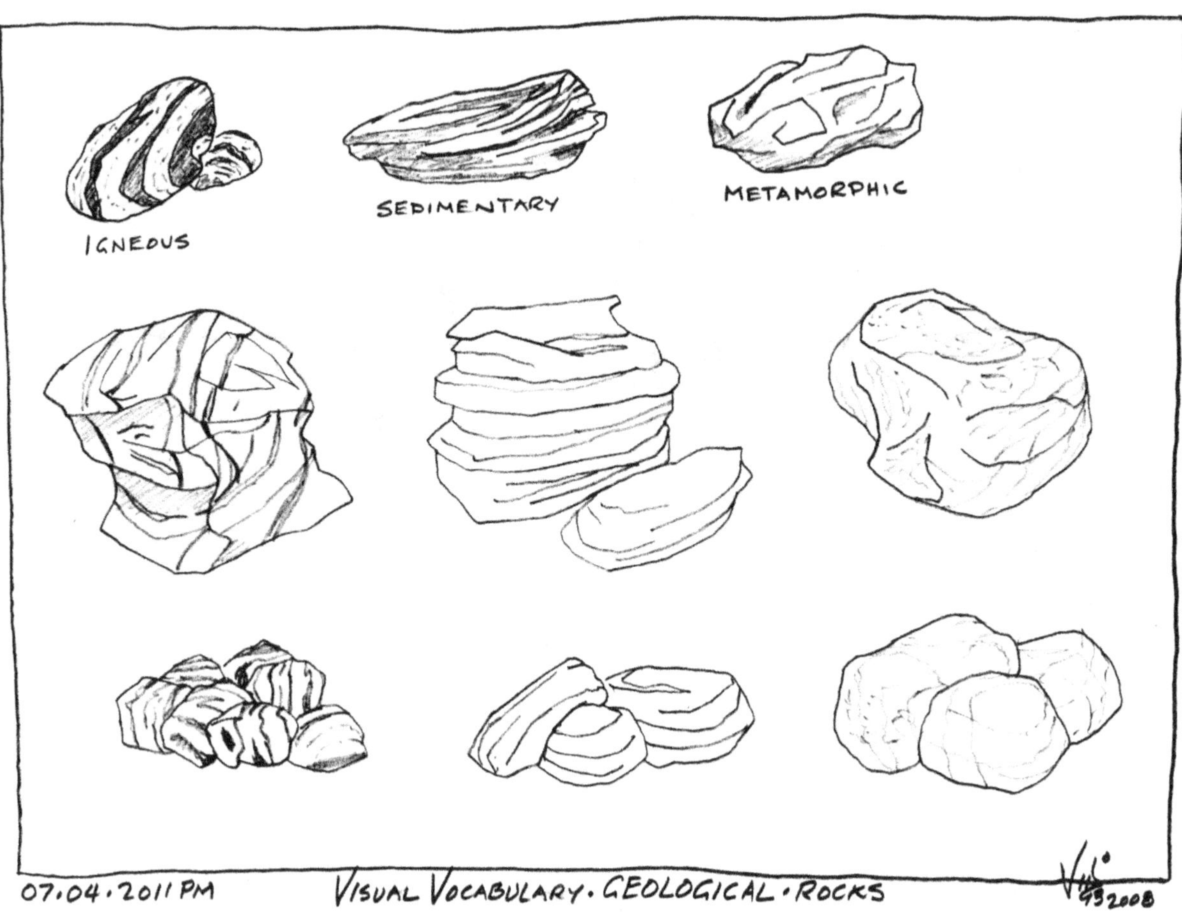

Visual Vocabulary:

Geological: Rocks

As any child can tell, as they collect them from the side of the road or at the beach, rocks are a subject that can give endless pleasure.

There are basically three types of rocks : Metamorphic, Igneous and Sedimentary. Metamorphic rocks are pressed together and made up of soils and gravels. Igneous rocks are cooled lava. Sedimentary rocks are layers of sediment from the bottom of a waterway that have been pressed together so as to have layers.

Both igneous and sedimentary rocks have striations, but sedimentary rocks usually have straight lines that form the edges of planes of sediment and circle the rock. Igneous have almost liquid looking lines that wander around forming irregular layers through the rock.

Metamorphic rocks are irregular in shape as they are usually broken off of other rocks. They can be round however, if they have been ground around such as in or under a glacier. Igneous rocks are usually round but can be broken up into irregular shapes.

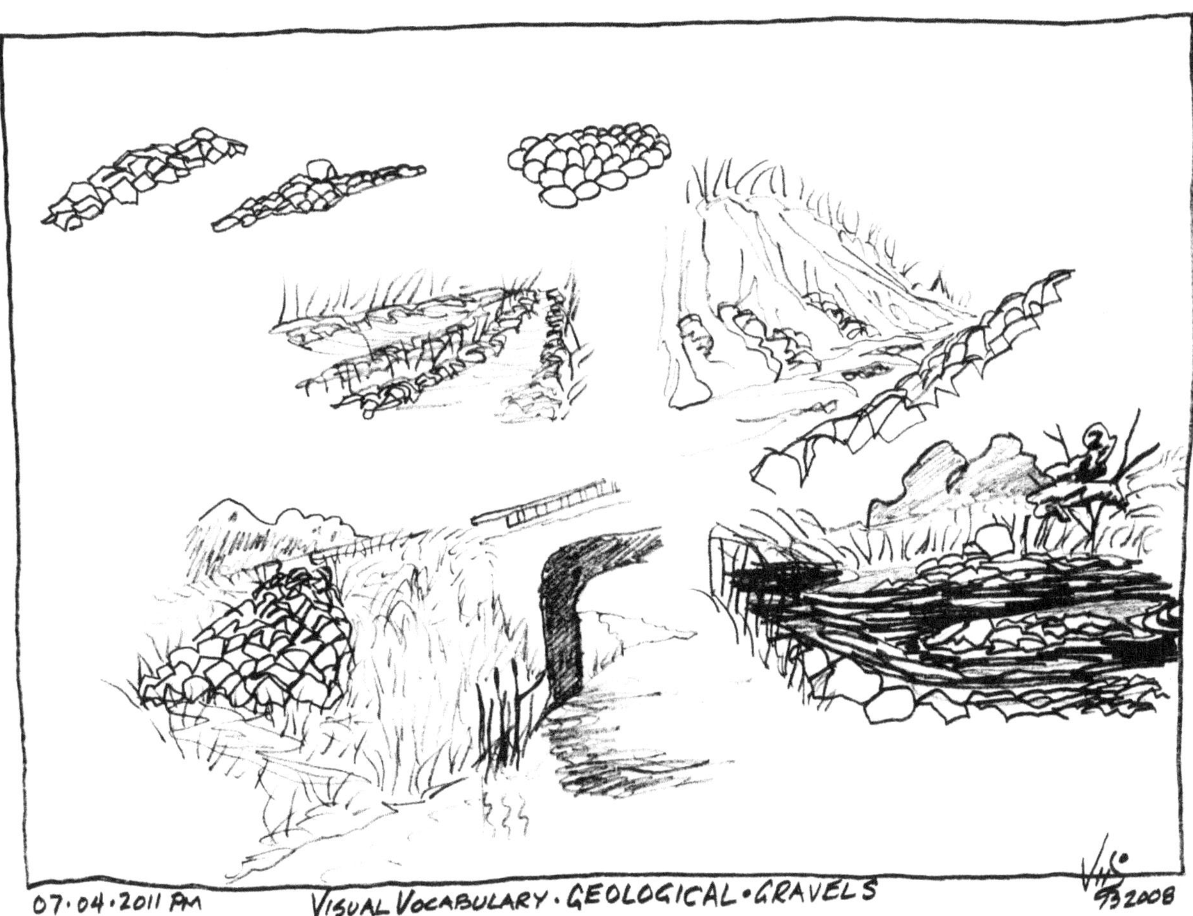

Visual Vocabulary:

Geological: Gravels

Gravels basically come down to illustrating a texture, but an understanding of different types of gravel is worth the effort of observing.

Three quarter clear crushed stone gravel is angular and rough. The gravel of a stream bed may be all rounded, or it may be large and rough. There are many types of gravels or small rock fill that are used in construction, so roadways may be a good place to start.

Even a gravel lane has a variety of textures even if it is all the same type of gravel. The travelled portion of a gravel road or lane could even be smooth, where the vehicle tires have passed over it repeatedly. The centre strip and edges are usually still loose gravel. In a gravel country road there is usually a wide centre strip that is smooth, with two loose gravel strips on either side, followed by two less smooth strips on the outside of those, and then the edge of the road is loose gravel and weeds.

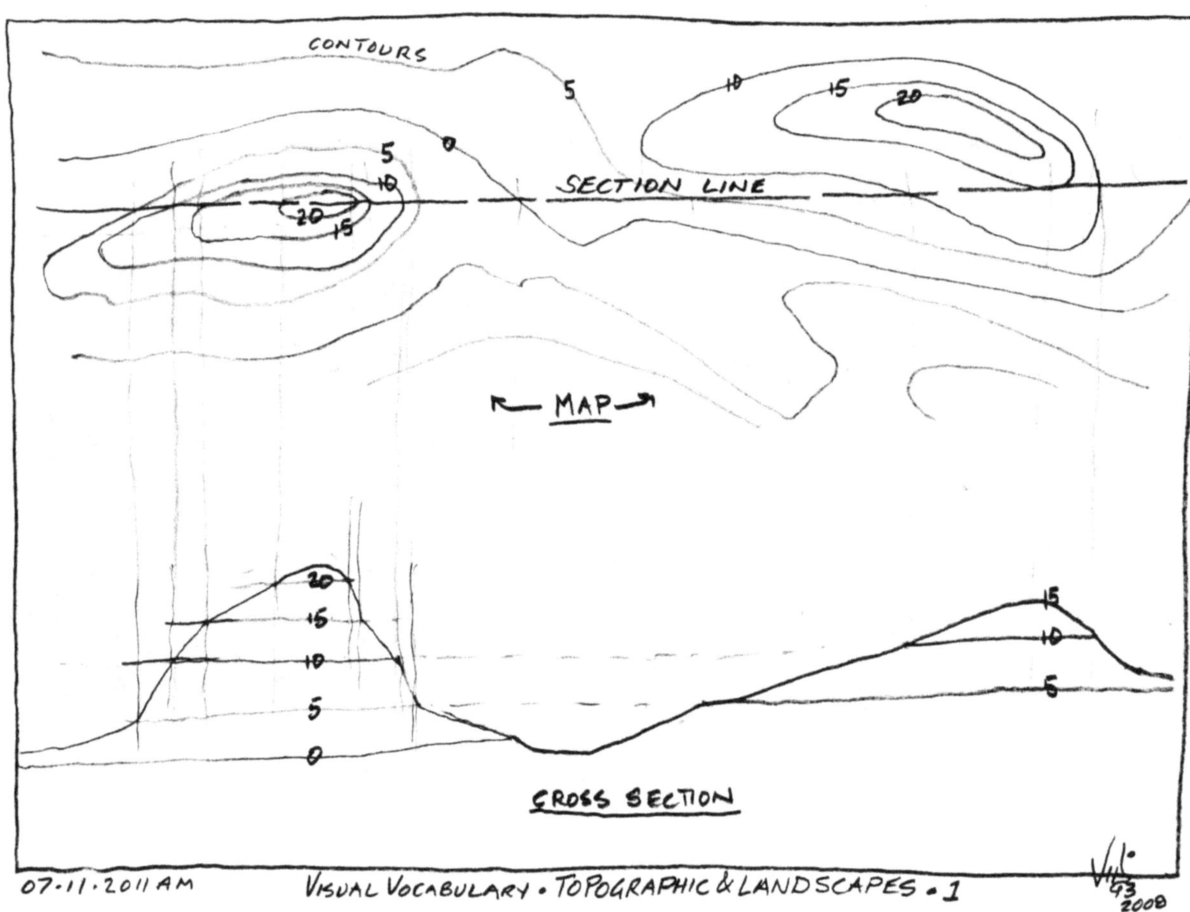

Visual Vocabulary:

Topographic and Landscapes: 1

There something to be said for being able to visualize the landscape in three dimensions, as this will allow one to keep their illustration solid .

Basically, this topographic map and elevation (cross section) are used to document the landscape drawing in the next page .

The topographic map has contour lines that give the horzontal position of places at the same elevation . If the topographic lines are close together, the area is steep . If they are far apart the area is a gradual slope .

The map is a birds eye view and the cross section is a side view .

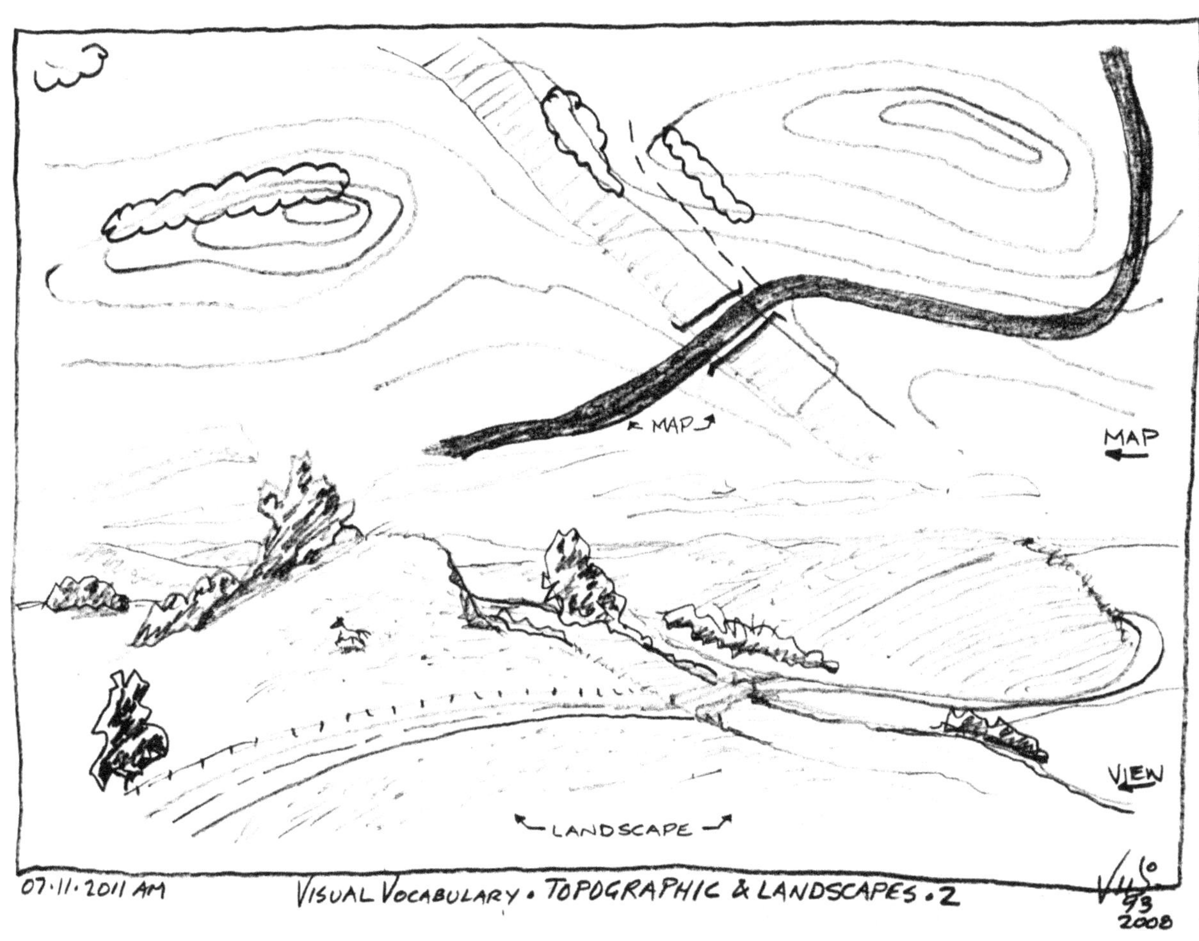

Visual Vocabulary:

Topographic and Landscapes: 2

The top illustration is a map of the topography at the top of the previous page. The illustration at the bottom is a landscape drawing of the area portrayed in the three previous illustrations on this page and the previous page.

The landscape drawing portrays the hills and valley from the top of a distant hill. The river recedes behind the hill on the left. It flows toward the right, under the bridge and in front of the hill on the right. I added a fence along the far side of the road as far as the bridge. The wooded areas are illustrated as they appear on the map. Both hills slope gradually on the visible side but drop off steeply on the far side. The horizon is reached past a jumble of random hills, and the clouds are illustrated as being swept by aerial winds that are all travelling in the same direction.

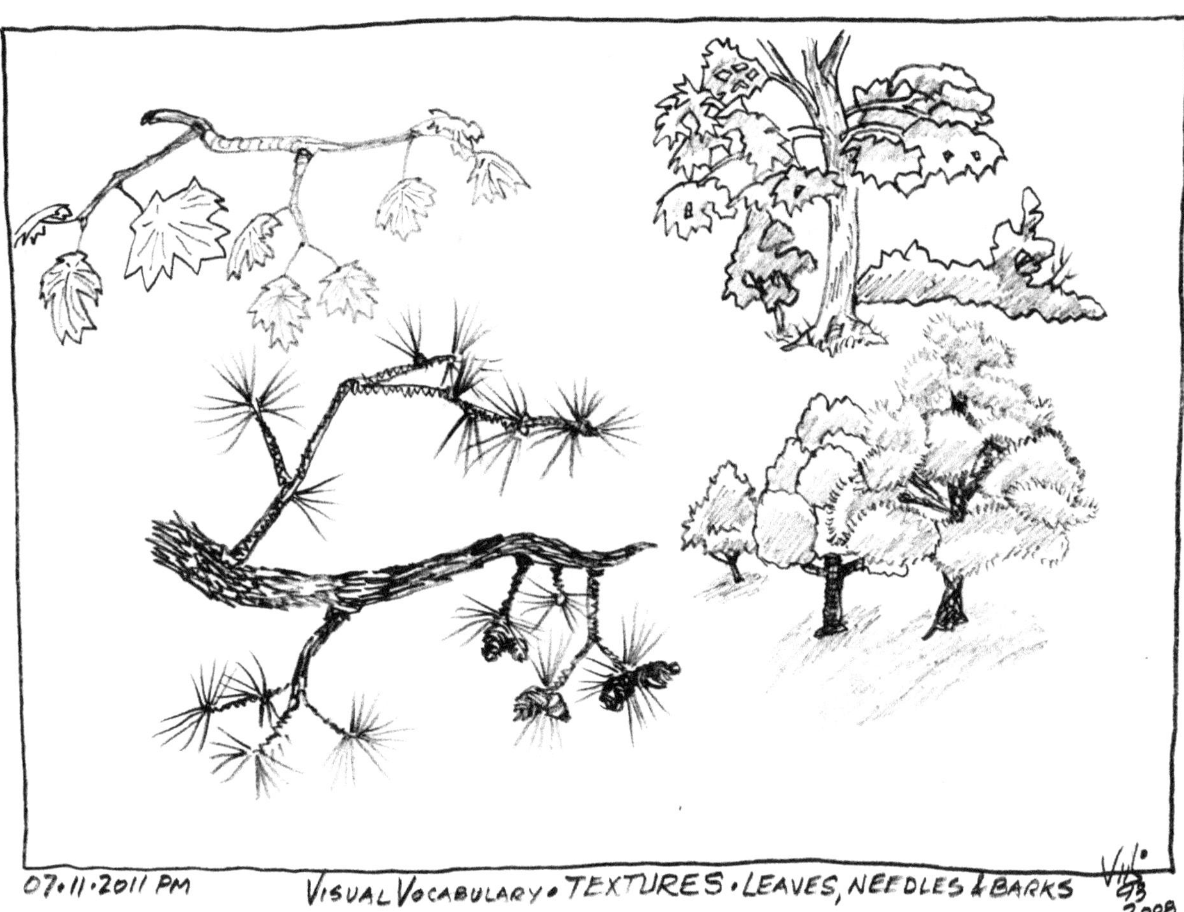

Visual Vocabulary:

Textures: Leaves, Needles & Barks

Drawing individual branches, leaves or clumps of needles is one thing, which is all right for foreground images, but as the foliage appears further away, it becomes more of a texture than a detailed drawing .

It is a good idea to develop different ways of illustrating such textures as they appear at a variety of distances .

Observation is the key to developing your own style of illustration, but at times it could be quicker to copy other illustrators' methods of illustrating foliage at various distances .

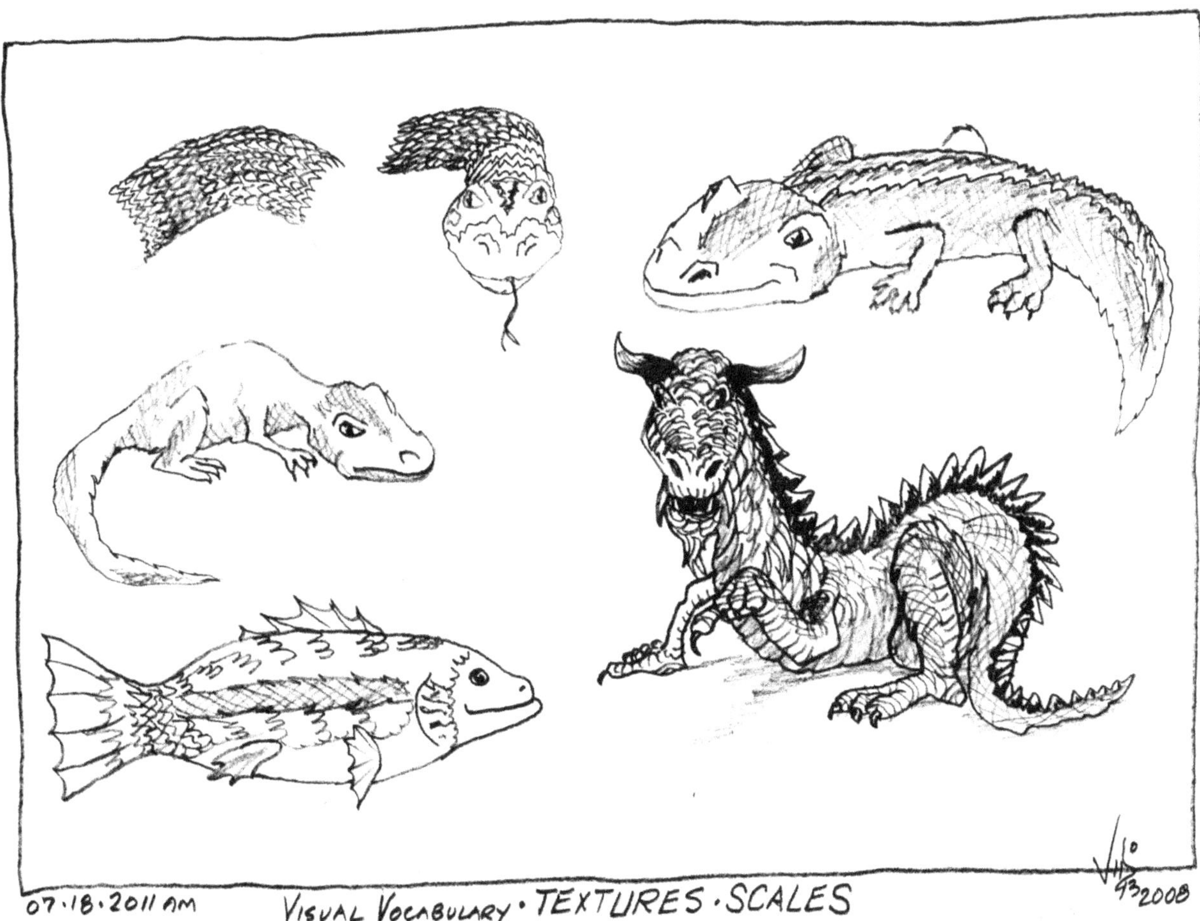

Visual Vocabulary:

Textures: Scales

Drawing individual scales, is another instance where illustrating a texture is usually more appropriate . Many styles of illustration call for a representation of scales rather than the illustration of every scale, as that would distract the from the focal point of the illustration .

The lizard and the crocodile, in this illustration, have merely representations of scales, the snake has individual scales, the dragon is a mix of individual scales and the representation of scales, as the fish is as well .

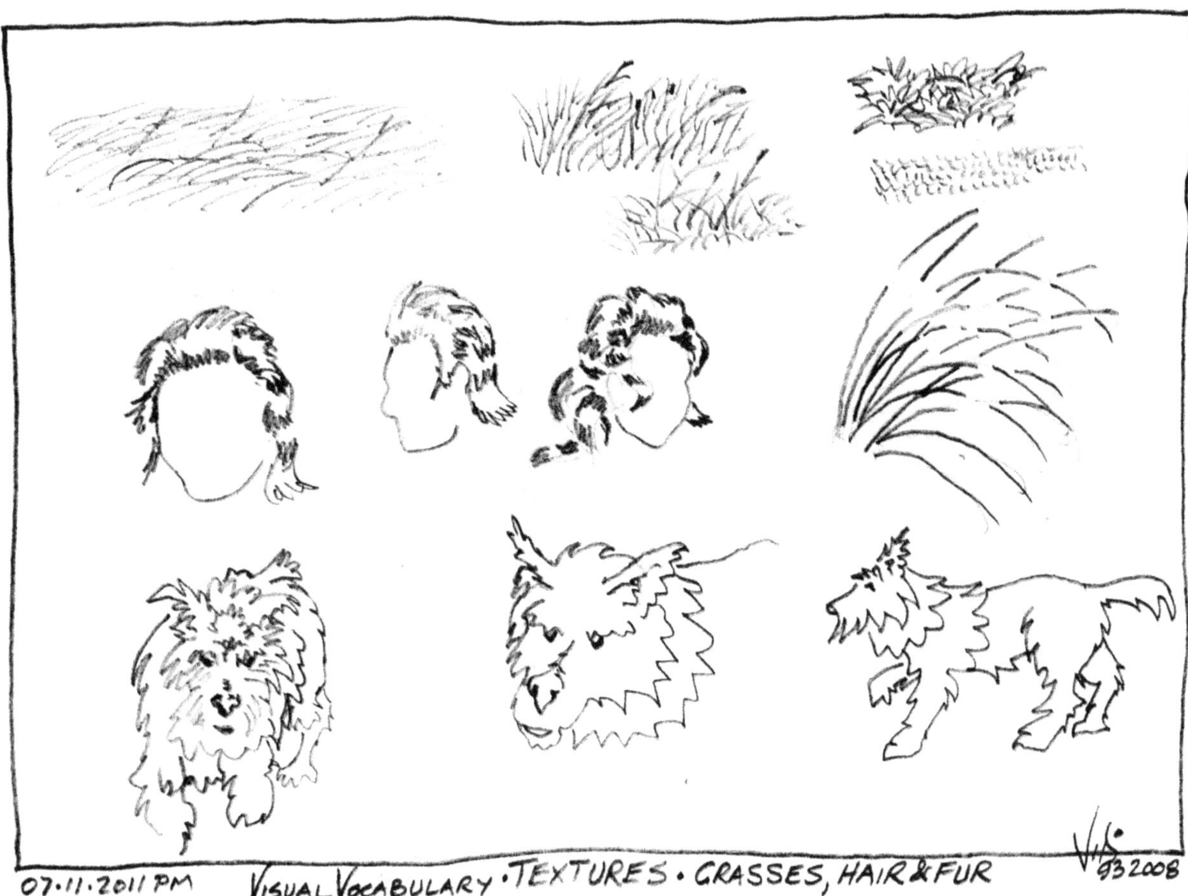

Visual Vocabulary:

Textures: Grasses, Hair & Fur

Grasses, Hair and Fur are usually linear and usually are viewed from enough of a distance to be satifactorily represented as a texture .

The outline of fur may be enough to identify it as such . Hair and grass often reflect the light and this can be used to portray the curves and flow of them .

There is a lot of flow to long hair and long grass, and this should be attended to when illustrating them . Short grass and hair may be irregular and disheveled so that the detail is useful to portray and create the effect . Remember that a suggestion may be all that is necessary .

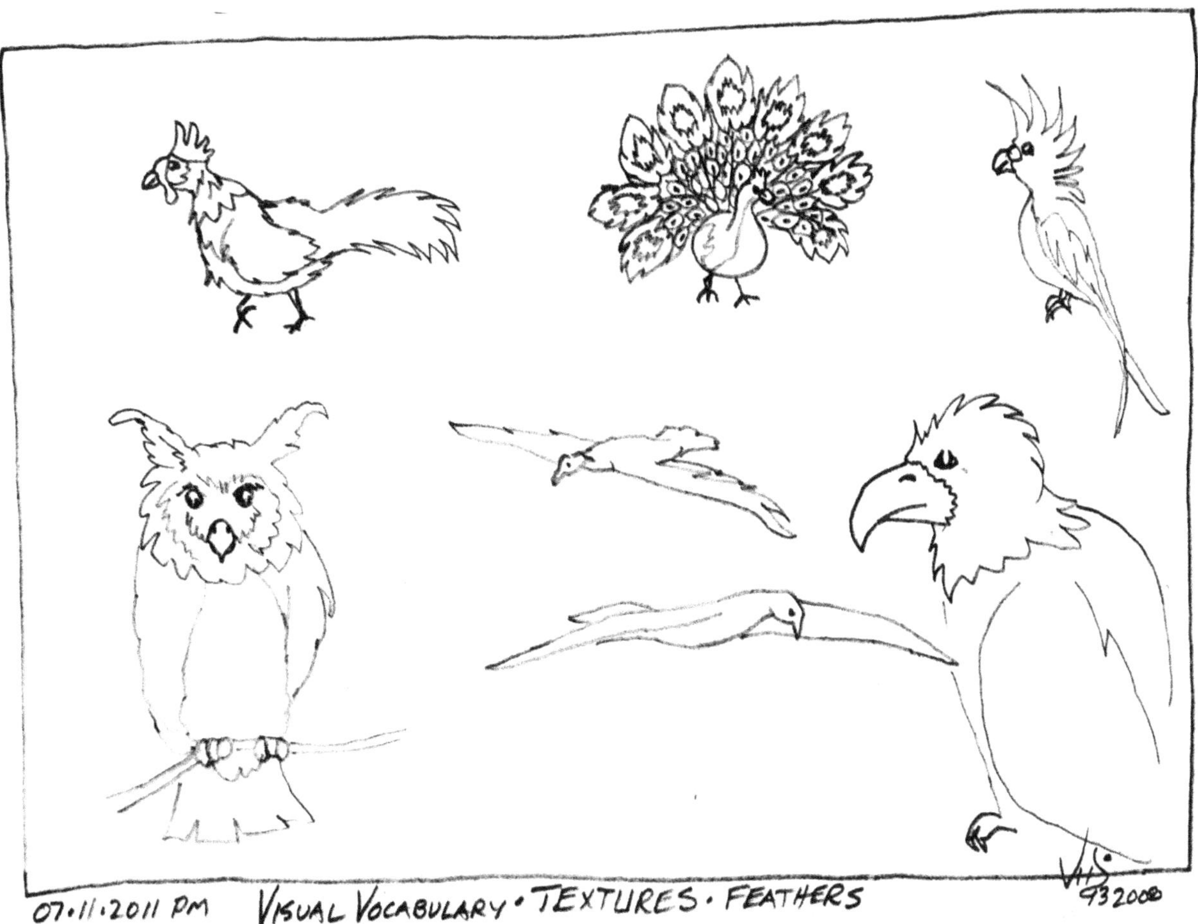

Visual Vocabulary:

Textures: Feathers

Drawing individual feathers may be worth doing as an exercise but once again the representation and outline is usually all that is needed .

A rooster or peacock tail may be disheveled, but once again, just suggesting the chaos is usually all that is needed .

In most birds, the feathers form a smooth contour outline, with regular contours where the colour changes abruptly .

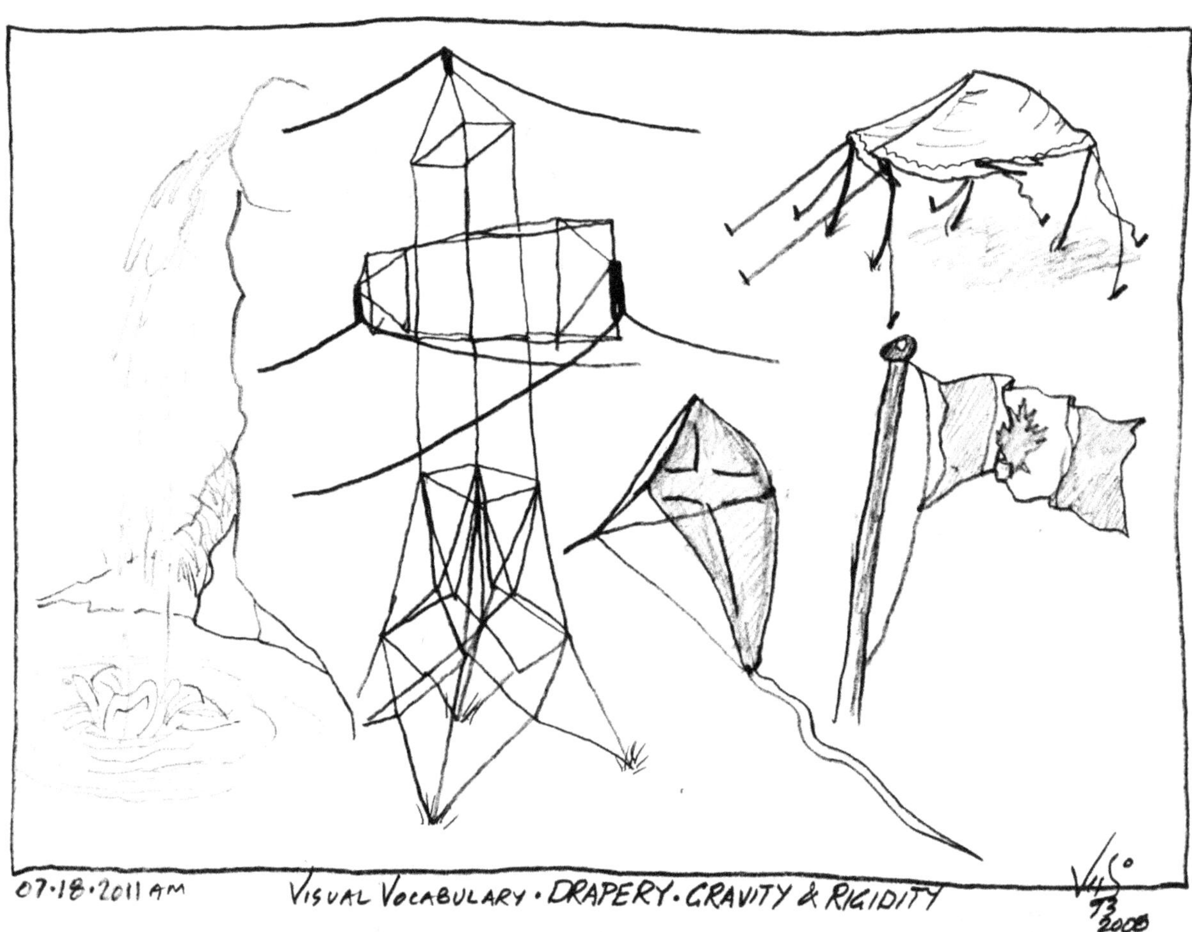

Visual Vocabulary:

Drapery: Gravity & Rigidity

Gravity pulls one way and Rigidity opposes in the opposite direction. The push and pull can be accentuated to add interesting character to one's drawing. The pull or push of the wind can be treated in the same way as gravity - a constant pull in a constant direction.

The inertia of the water as it is accellerated down from the mouth of the waterfall, is a rigidity that is pulled in the opposite direction by gravity. The hydro tower is rigid, but the hydro lines are swept down by gravity. The kite is rigid, but the wind pulls at it, again, in the opposite direction of the rigidity. The shelter and the flag are held into the pull of the wind.

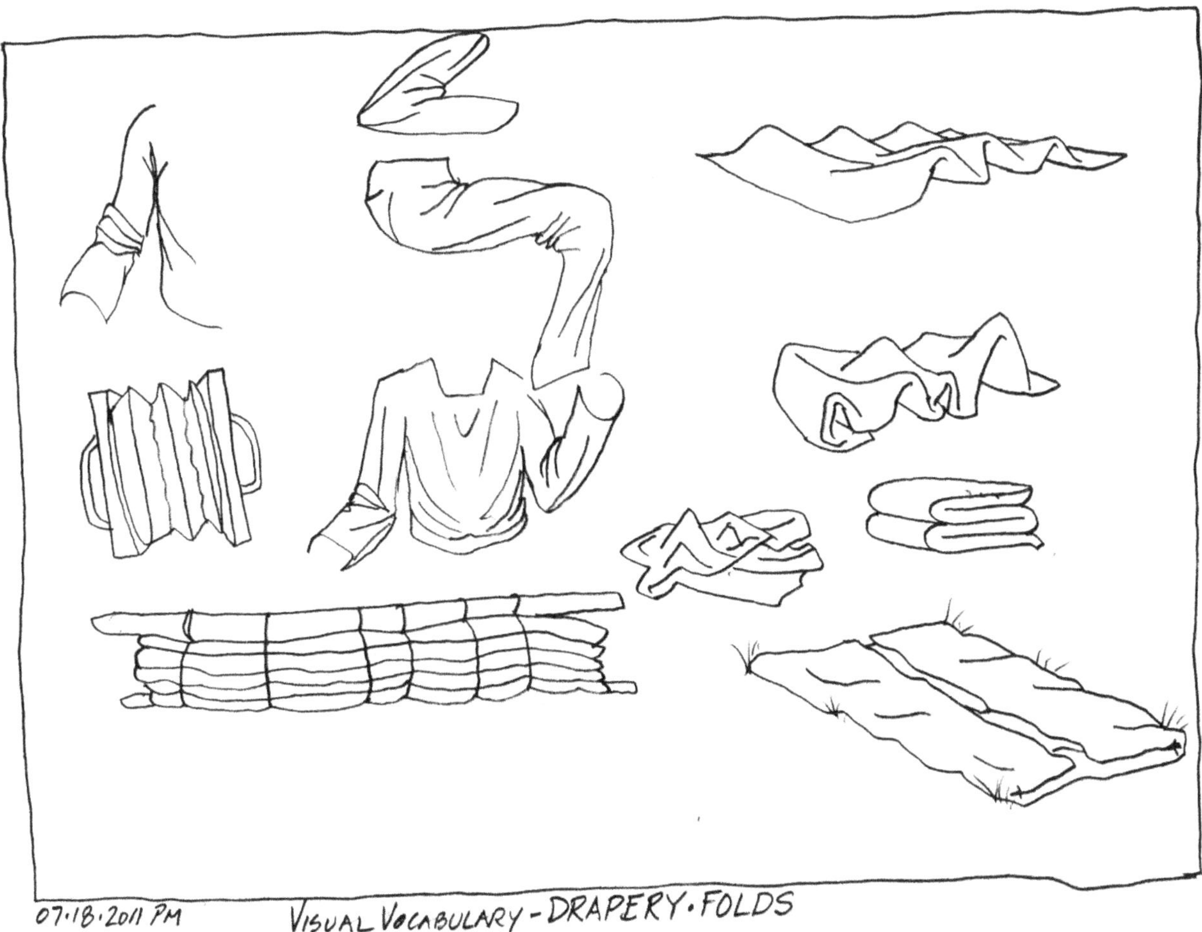

07·18·2011 PM VISUAL VOCABULARY - DRAPERY·FOLDS

Visual Vocabulary:

Drapery: Folds

Folds are almost mathematical and need to be calculated and laid out in light sketching before committing with a solid line. Careful obsevation of fabrics as one comes across them will promote a consistent method of calculating where the folds should occur, and how loose or tight they should be.

Remember that there is once again, a push and a pull to most fabrics. The pant leg when the subject is sitting on a chair, has regular areas of pull and regular areas of push, or folds.

Most fabrics fold up like an irregular accordian. There may be a wide variety of folding if there is a wide variety of fabrics.

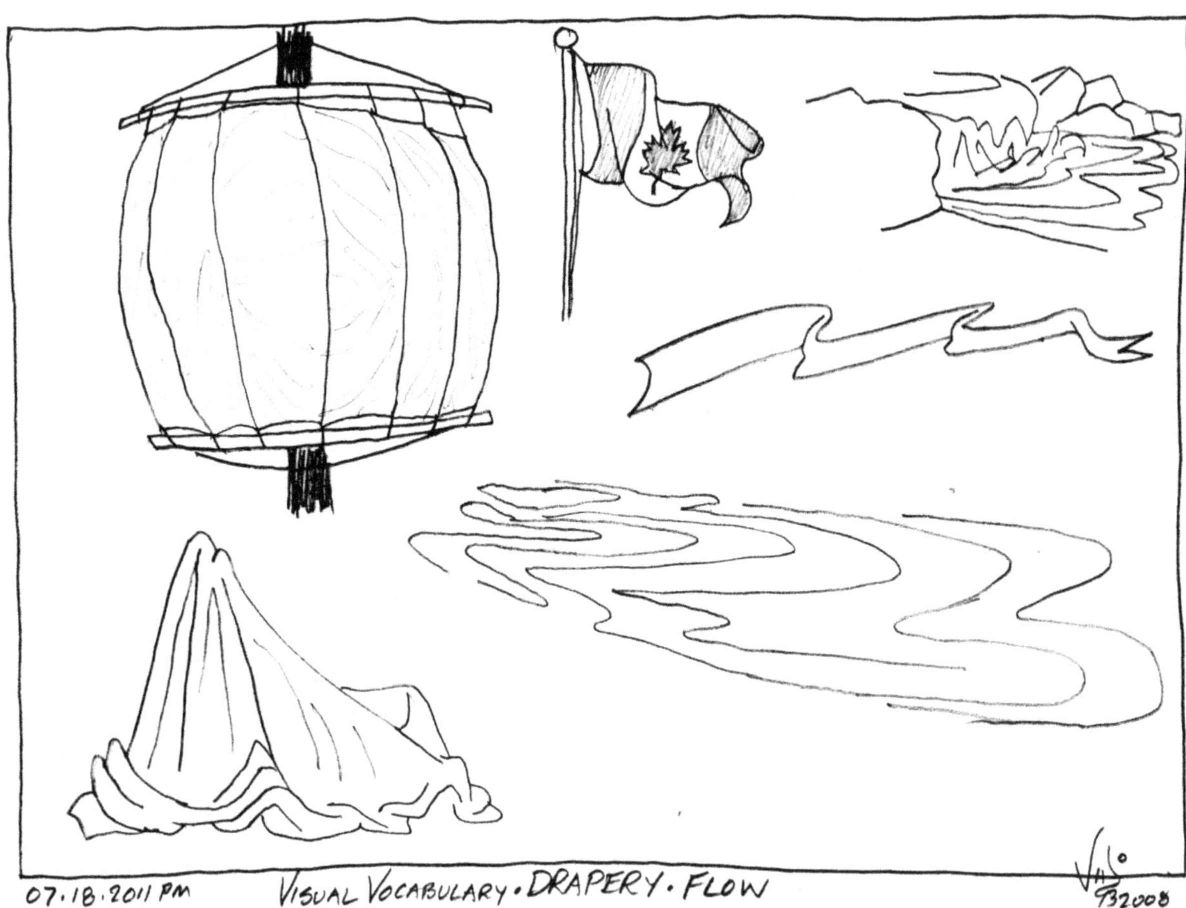

Visual Vocabulary:

Drapery: Flow

The flipside of folding is flowing. A fold is just a big crimp in a flow.

Water and flags are mostly all flow, with a smattering of folding.

Don't forget to include flow in your illustrations, and don't just show the folds.

Keep on Drawing:

This is the second of a series of pamphlets created for the Oakville OASIS Drawing Bee, and this series is intended to overcome the hurdle of beginning to draw. When one is faced with what they are going to do all day, they can flip through these pamphlets and get engrossed with the ideas of what they could be drawing.

Drawing skills are very transferable to other areas of life, but the most important transferable skills are the emotional ones of accepting one's shortcomings and carrying on to overcome them with practice and acceptance of their level of ability. No one ever got better at anything by not practicing.

As well, as the mind becomes involved in the drawing, there is a peace and almost relaxed atmosphere created, which is refreshing and beneficial to the rest of ones day.

A friend from secondary school, who went on to become an actuary, told me he thinks of me when he is bored, and wonders what I would do in such a boring situation. I was known for coming up with interesting activities, when called upon. Drawing is a great activity that anyone can do and it fills the time as well as refreshes the spirit, if one can get started and involved.

Finally, one rule I like to promote is for anyone who is critical of their drawing skill, and that is to never throw out a drawing, just hide it or put it away if one is frustrated. This is because when one completes a drawing, they are very much aware of how far the drawing came short of the image they had in their mind. But after a period of time, they forget the image they had in their head and will only see their accomplishments that they achieved in the drawing. This is encouraging and promotes further drawing.

Drawing on the Right Side of the Brain Author: ***Betty Edwards***
ISBN-13: **9780874775136** ISBN-10: **0874775132** Edition: **Revised** Binding: **Paperback**
Publisher: **Tarcher** Published: **May 1989** List Price: **$15.95**

The book cited above, is great at getting one better at drawing, but eventually, your visual vocabulary will need to be expanded, and as far as anatomy goes, I cannot recommend a better reference than the book cited below.

Atlas of Human Anatomy for the Artist Author: ***Stephen Rogers Peck***
ISBN-13: **9780195030952** ISBN-10: **0195030958** Edition: **1** Binding: **Paperback**
Publisher: **Oxford University Press** Published: **February 1982** List Price: **$19.95**

I would strongly recommend studying this book on anatomy, by memorizing the names of all the bones in the body, as well as the names of all the muscles in the body, so that you will be more fluent in the language of drawing people.

INDEX - - - - - - - - - -

TEXTBOOK --B--
Visual Vocabulary

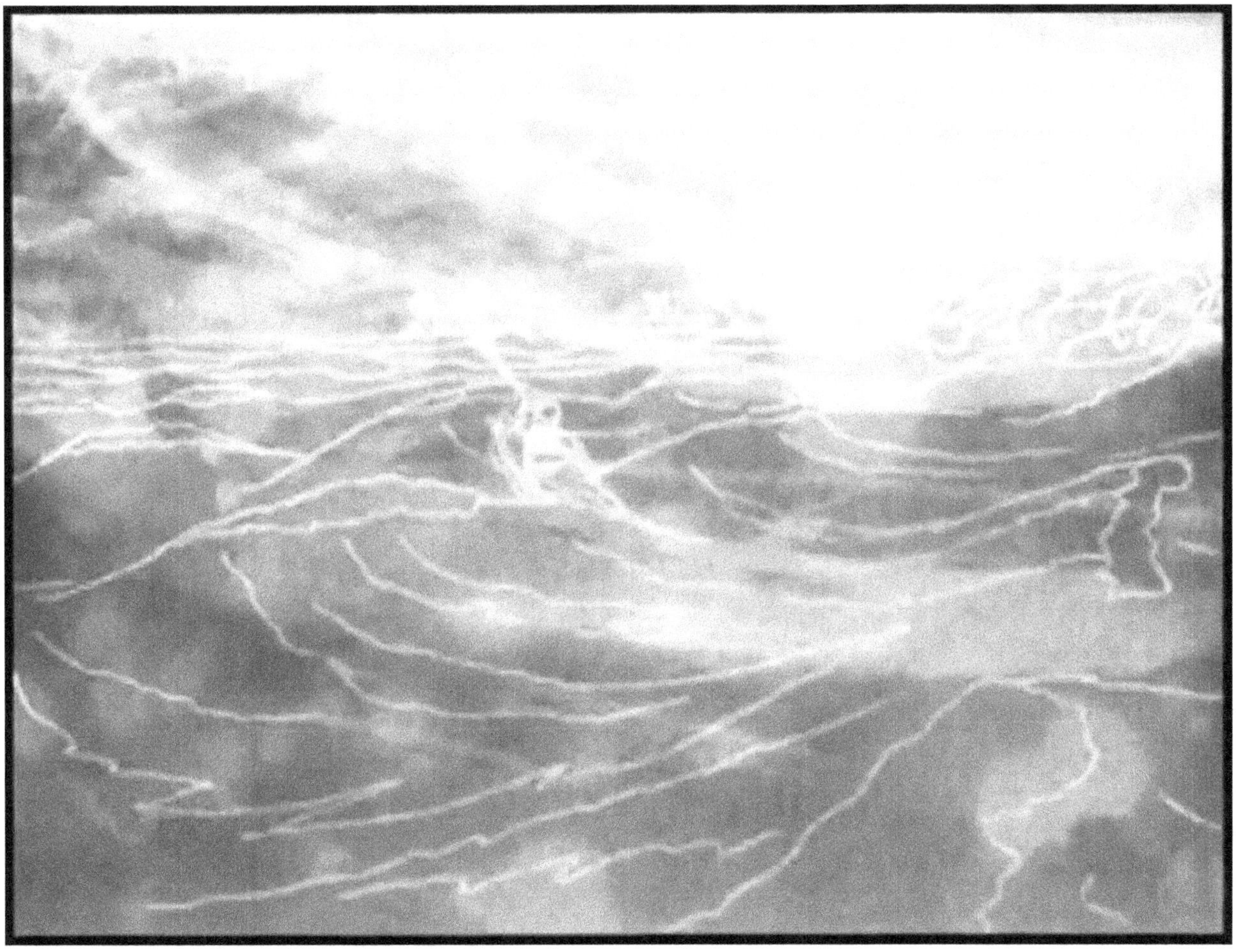

SIMPLE PERSPECTIVE
Textbook --C--

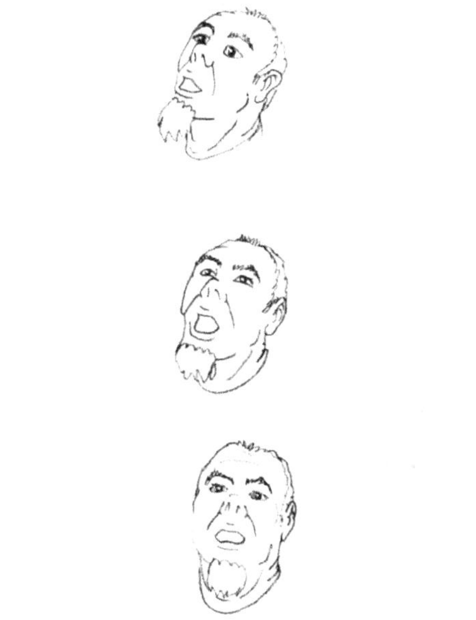

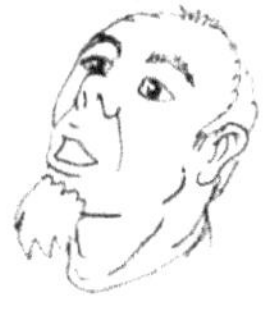

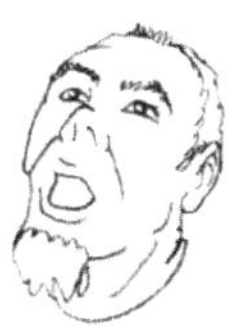

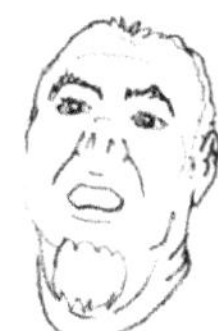

04/11/2011 PM

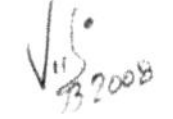

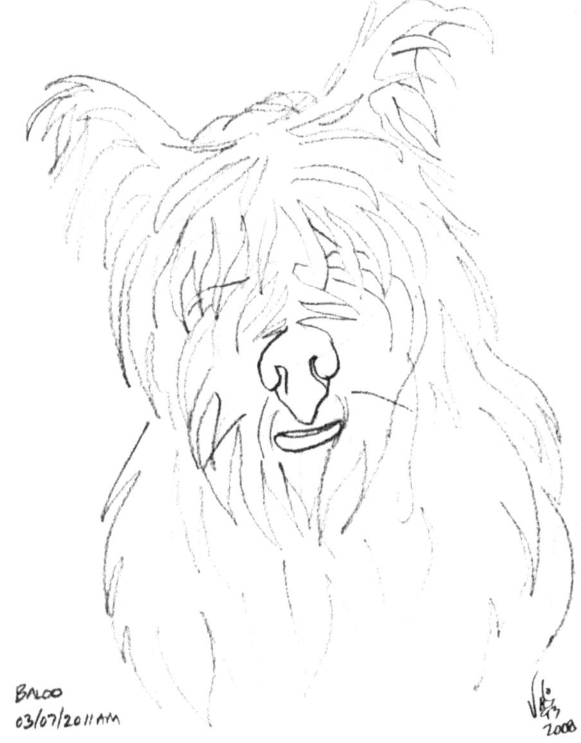

05/02/2011 AM

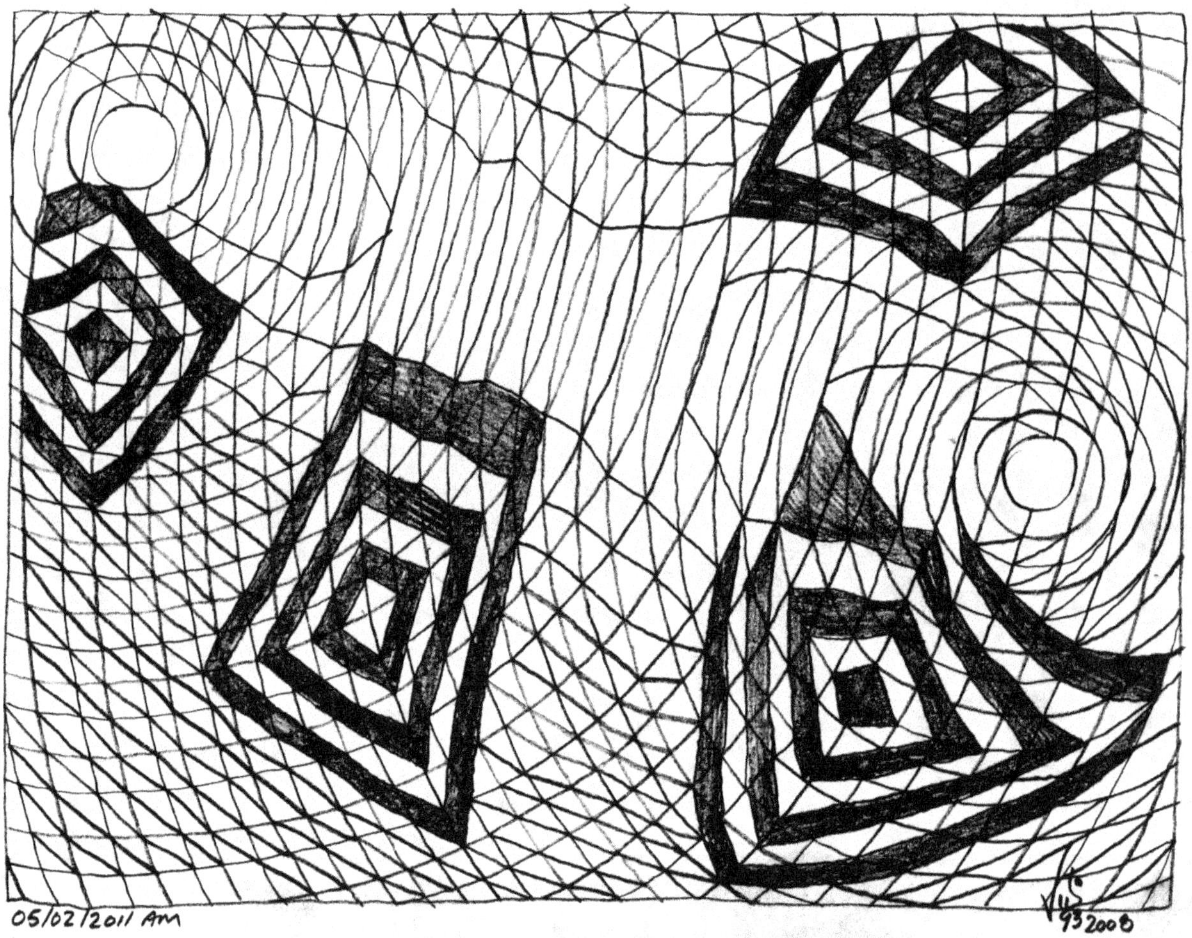

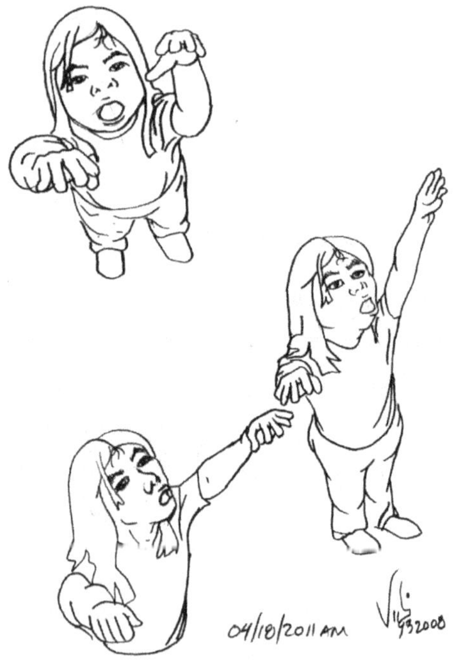
04/18/2011 AM

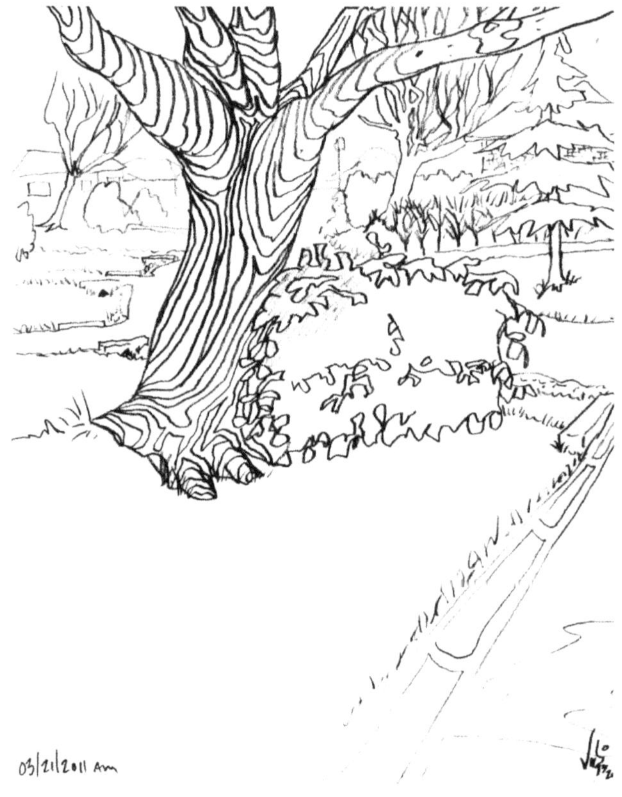
03/21/2011 Am

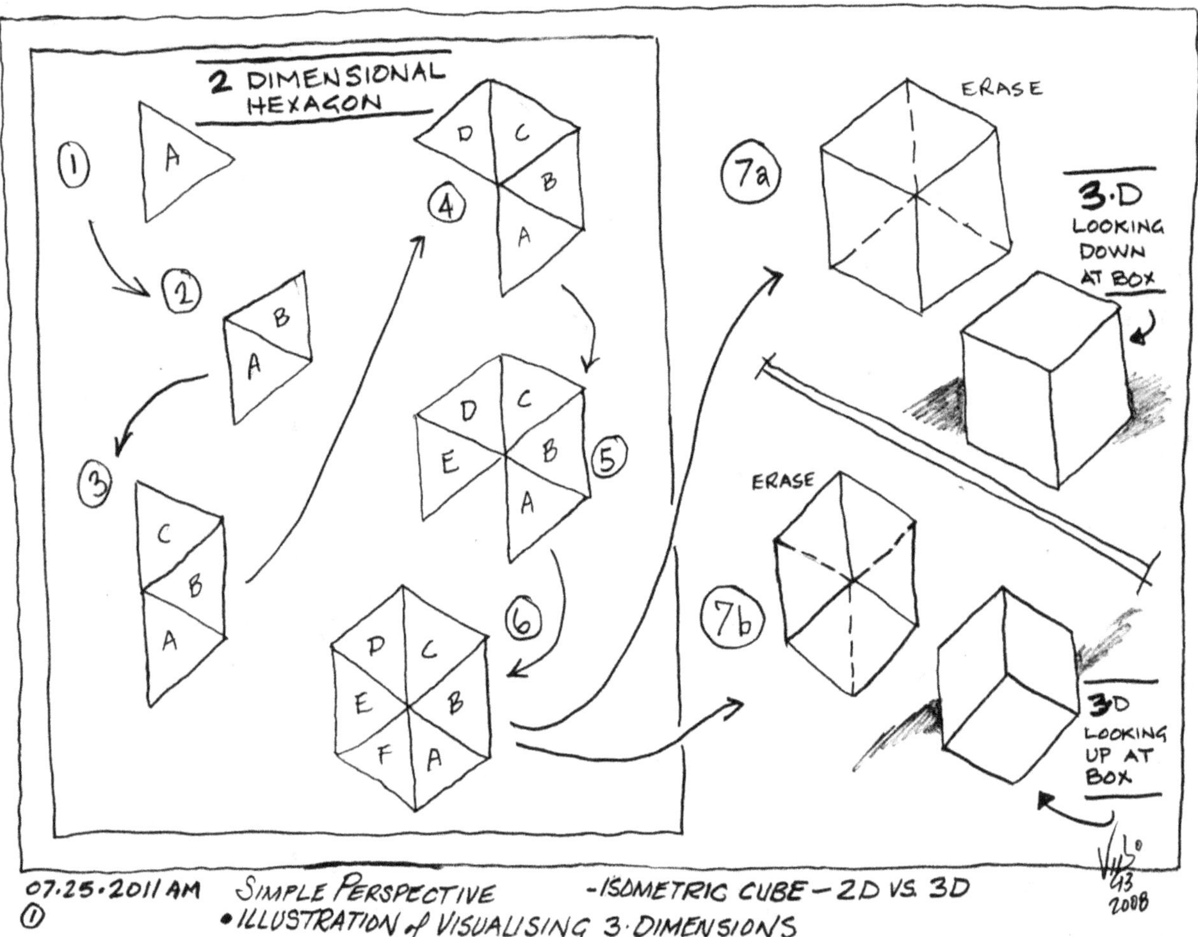

07.25.2011 AM SIMPLE PERSPECTIVE -ISOMETRIC CUBE – 2D VS. 3D
① •ILLUSTRATION of VISUALISING 3·DIMENSIONS

Illustration of Visualizing in Three Dimensions

Isometric Cube - 2D vs. 3D

One must be able to see on the page, if not imagine, the three dimensional image they are trying to create. This is different than seeing a two dimensional image on a page. The difference between the two ways of seeing a drawing must be known as the artist must be able to switch between the two ways of seeing.

This exercise starts out creating a two dimensional image and then transforms it to a three dimensional image.

Begin by drawing an equilateral triangle - a triangle with all three sides the same length; one side must be vertical. Continue by drawing adjacent triangles until one has a hexagon.

Erase three alternating lines, of which one is vertical. Do not erase two adjacent lines, and do not erase any lines on the outside edge or perimeter.

Are you now either looking up at a box or looking down at a box? This is the shift from viewing the page in two dimensions, to viewing the page as a three dimensional window. Remember how this shift feels and try to practice it often. One must be able to use both ways of viewing the image on the page. The three dimensional view is necessary for organizing the parts of the image, and the two dimensional view is good for checking the image against theory.

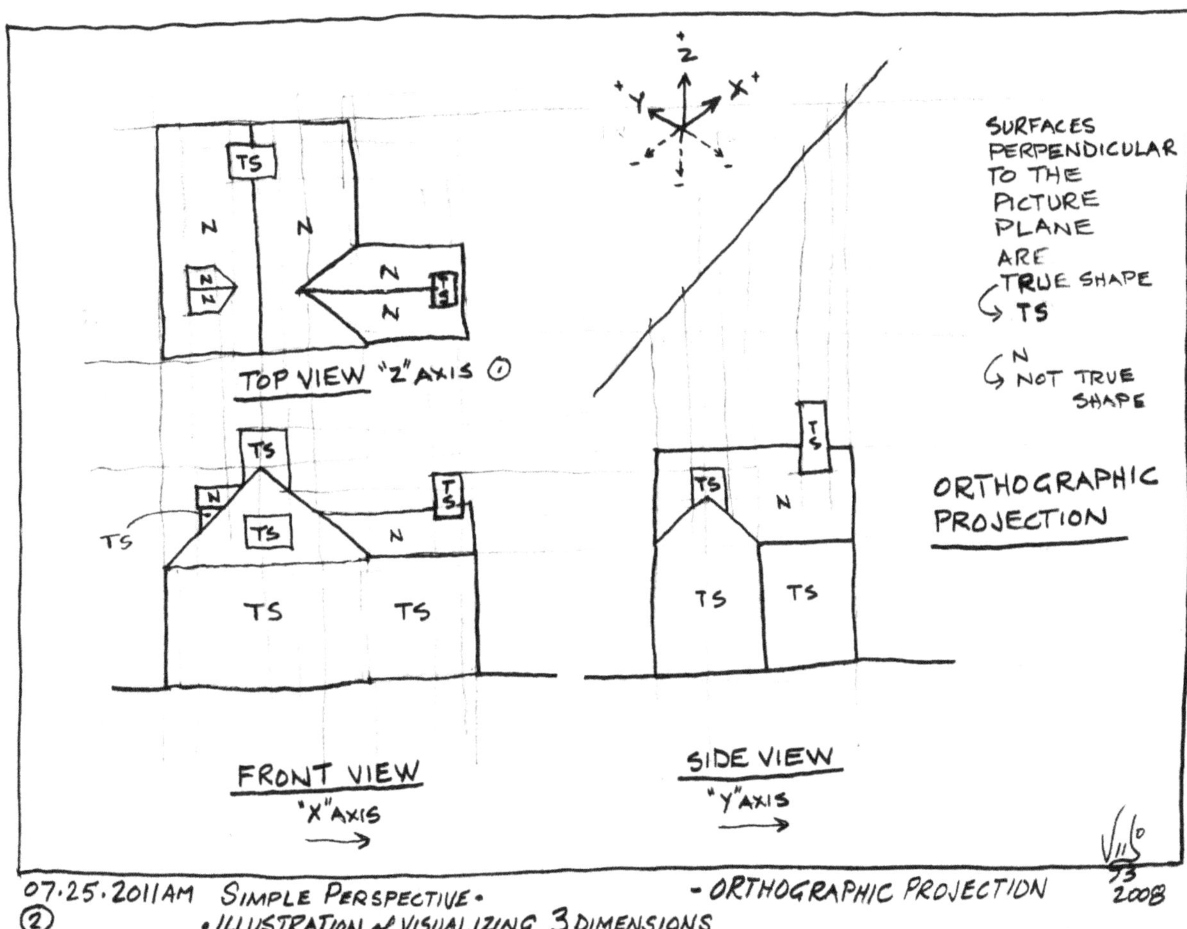

Illustration of Visualizing in Three Dimensions

Orthographic Projection

There are many ways to portray a three dimensional scene in an image. When one is drawing one must be aware of which way they are creating the image, and hopefully be trying to illustrate in Perspective. The four ways we will identify are Orthographic Projection, Isometric Projection, Oblique Projection and the purpose of this textbook - Perspective.

In a three dimensional world, three dimensions can be identified along three axes, the x, y, z axes. Orthographic Projection uses three picture planes, or images, and each of these picture planes is aligned with an axis. This means that each of the three images is situated perpendicular to the other two images, or picture planes.

Orthographic Projection shows the true shape of surfaces that are parallel to the picture plane. So if you are drawing the true shape of an image, pause and consider if it would be the true shape in the type of drawing you are creating. If not, than find your vanishing points and align the shapes accordingly.

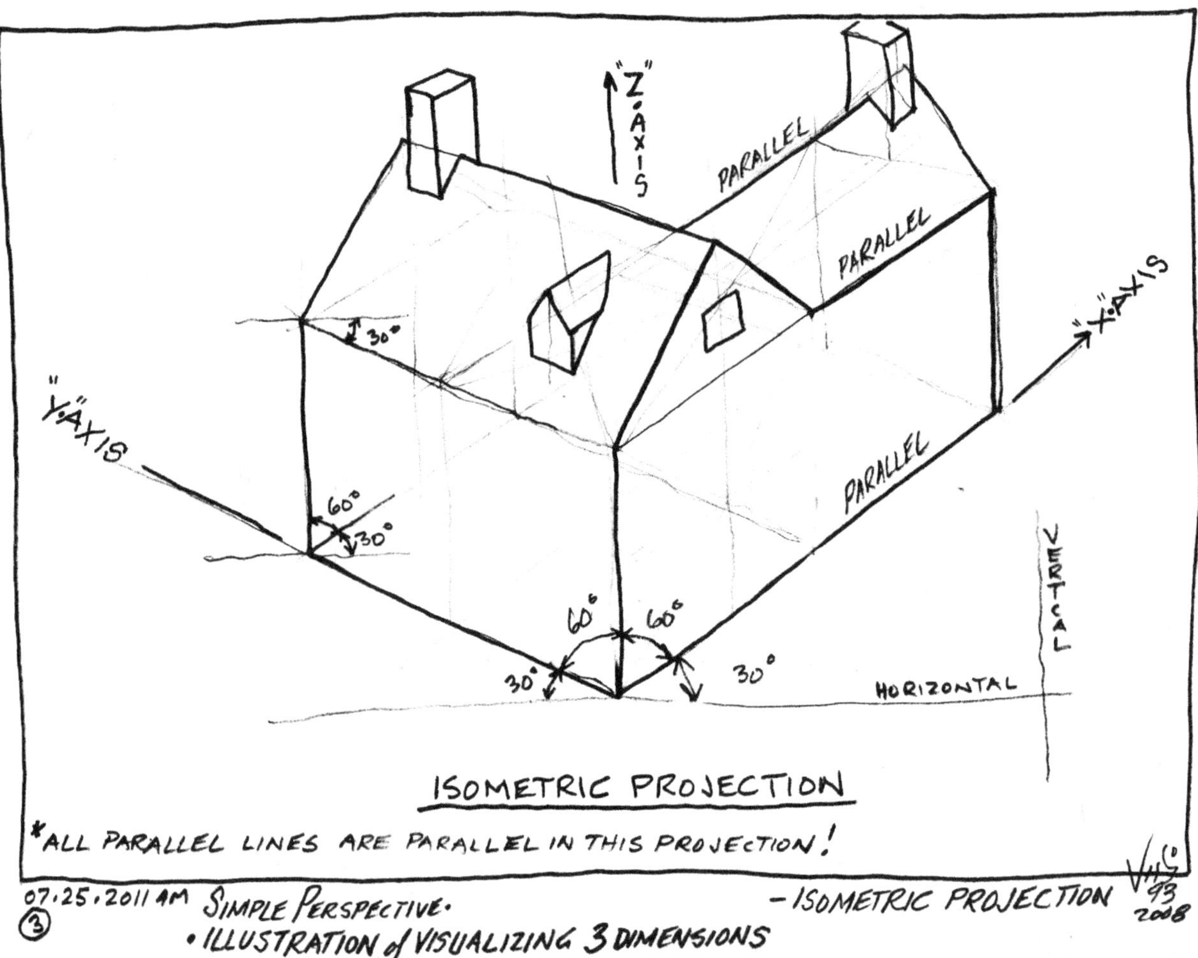

Illustration of Visualizing in Three Dimensions

Isometric Projection

A second way to portray a three dimensional scene in an image is Isometric Projection . When one is drawing one must be aware of which way they are creating the image, and hopefully be trying to illustrate in Perspective . Isometric Projection has the three axes in a set way, the left axis is at 30 degrees up from the horizontal, the right axis is at 30 degrees up from the horizontal in the other direction, and the vertical axis is vertical . The left and right axes are both at 60 degrees from the vertical and on either side .

All three axes are illustrated, and there are not any true shapes is this view . Dimensions are true along each of the three axes, but any other dimensions are distorted . So a box that is 1 unit by 2 units by 3 units, would measure one unit along one axis, two units along another axis and three units along the third axis . The diagonal dimension, not along any axis, would not be true length .

Isometric Projection is similar to Orthographic Projection in that the lengths of lines that are parallel to an axis are true length . So if you are drawing an image, pause and consider whether there would be lines that are true length in the type of drawing you are creating . If not, than find your vanishing points and measure the lengths accordingly .

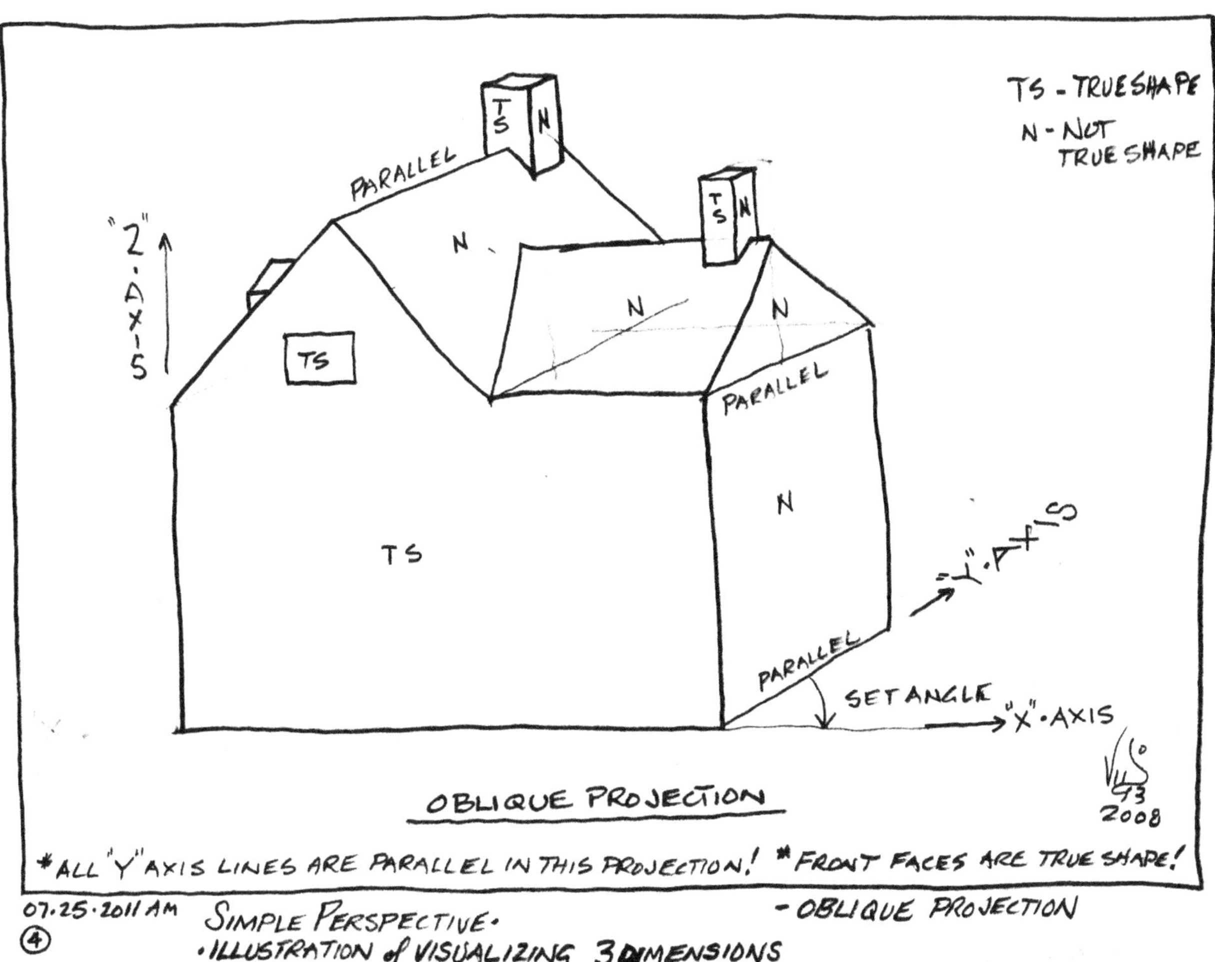

Illustration of Visualizing in Three Dimensions

Oblique Projection

Oblique Projection is a third way to portray a three dimensional scene in an image . When one is drawing one must be aware of which way they are creating the image, and hopefully be trying to illustrate in Perspective . Oblique Projection has the true shape of the front faces, those parallel to the plane formed by the horizontal and vertical axes . The depth axis is portrayed at a set angle to the horizontal axis .

The depth dimension or axis, can be at any suitable angle, about 30 degrees above the horizontal, and the depth dimensions are true length . Any other dimension that does not run along an axis, will not be true length . All depth dimensions that are parallel to the depth axis, are true length .

Oblique Projection shows the true shape of surfaces that are parallel to the picture plane . So if you are drawing the true shape of an image, pause and consider if it would be the true shape in the type of drawing you are creating . If not, than find your vanishing points and align the shapes accordingly .

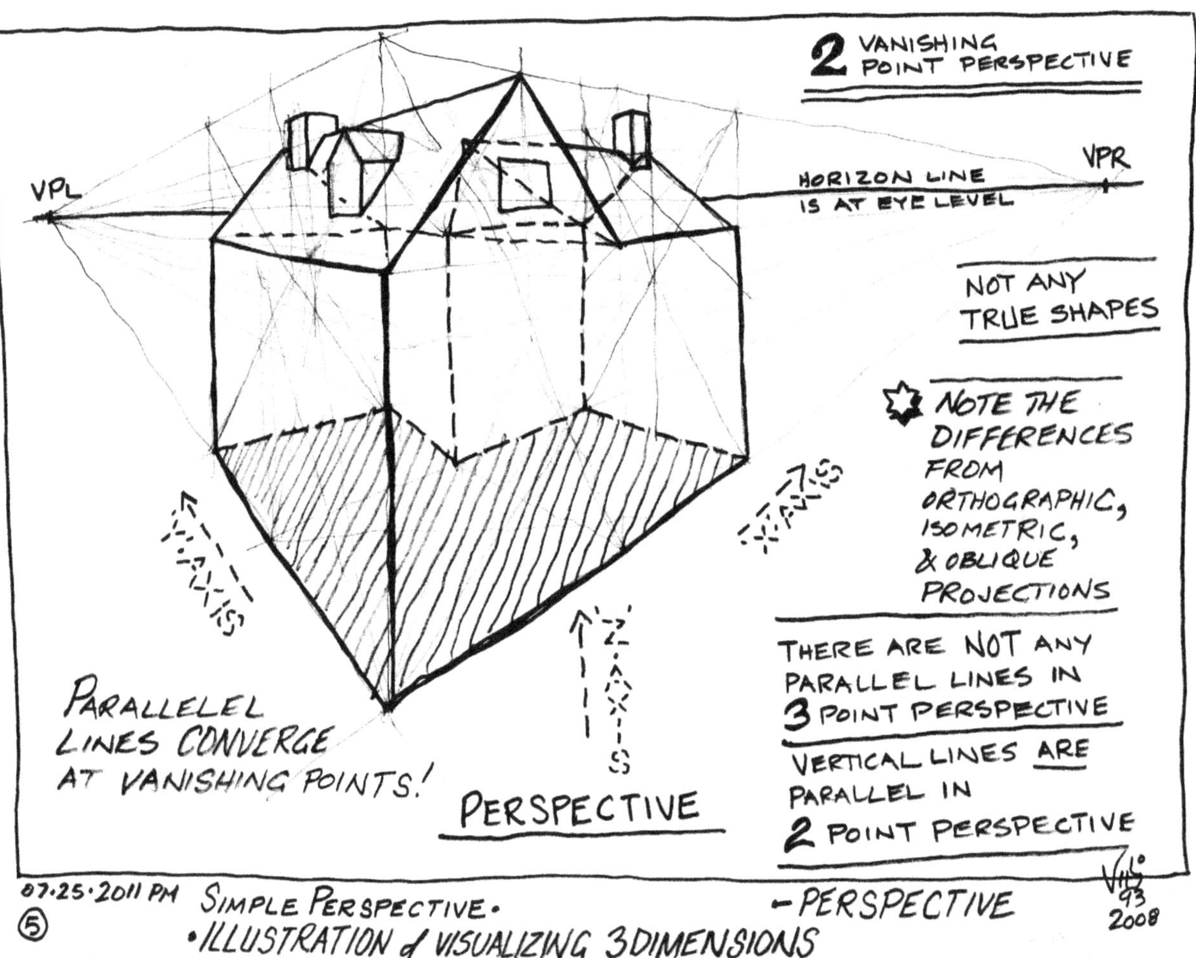
2 VANISHING POINT PERSPECTIVE
VPL
VPR
HORIZON LINE IS AT EYE LEVEL
NOT ANY TRUE SHAPES
NOTE THE DIFFERENCES FROM ORTHOGRAPHIC, ISOMETRIC, & OBLIQUE PROJECTIONS
THERE ARE NOT ANY PARALLEL LINES IN 3 POINT PERSPECTIVE
VERTICAL LINES ARE PARALLEL IN 2 POINT PERSPECTIVE
PARALLELEL LINES CONVERGE AT VANISHING POINTS!
PERSPECTIVE
07.25.2011 PM
5
SIMPLE PERSPECTIVE•
-PERSPECTIVE
•ILLUSTRATION of VISUALIZING 3DIMENSIONS
2008

Illustration of Visualizing in Three Dimensions

Perspective Projection

There are many ways to portray a three dimensional scene in an image. When one is drawing one must be aware of which way they are creating the image, and hopefully be trying to illustrate in Perspective. Perspective, although it looks very real, is only another type of projection, as once the eye moves, the vanishing points move, and this is readily apparent in 3 dimensional computer graphics, such as found in computer games. This textbook is focused on Perspective Projection.

In a three dimensional world, three dimensions can be identified along three axes, the x, y, z axes. Perspective Projection uses anywhere from one to three or more vanishing points. Usually the x and y axis are set up to converge at the left and right vanishing points, on the horizon. If the image requires a vertical vanishing point this can be added. The picture plane becomes drawing paper, and the line of sight is very close to perpendicular to the picture plane or drawing paper.

The only true shapes in Perspective Projection are those shapes in a plane that is parallel to the picture plane, so that one is looking directly at the surface of the shape. So if you are drawing the true shape of an image, pause and consider if it would be the true shape in the type of drawing you are creating. If not, than find your vanishing points and align the shapes accordingly.

Note the differences between the four types of projection and be careful not to slip into Orthographic with it's true shapes, Isometric with its true lengths, and Oblique with its true lengths and true shapes, when you are trying to create a Perspective drawing.

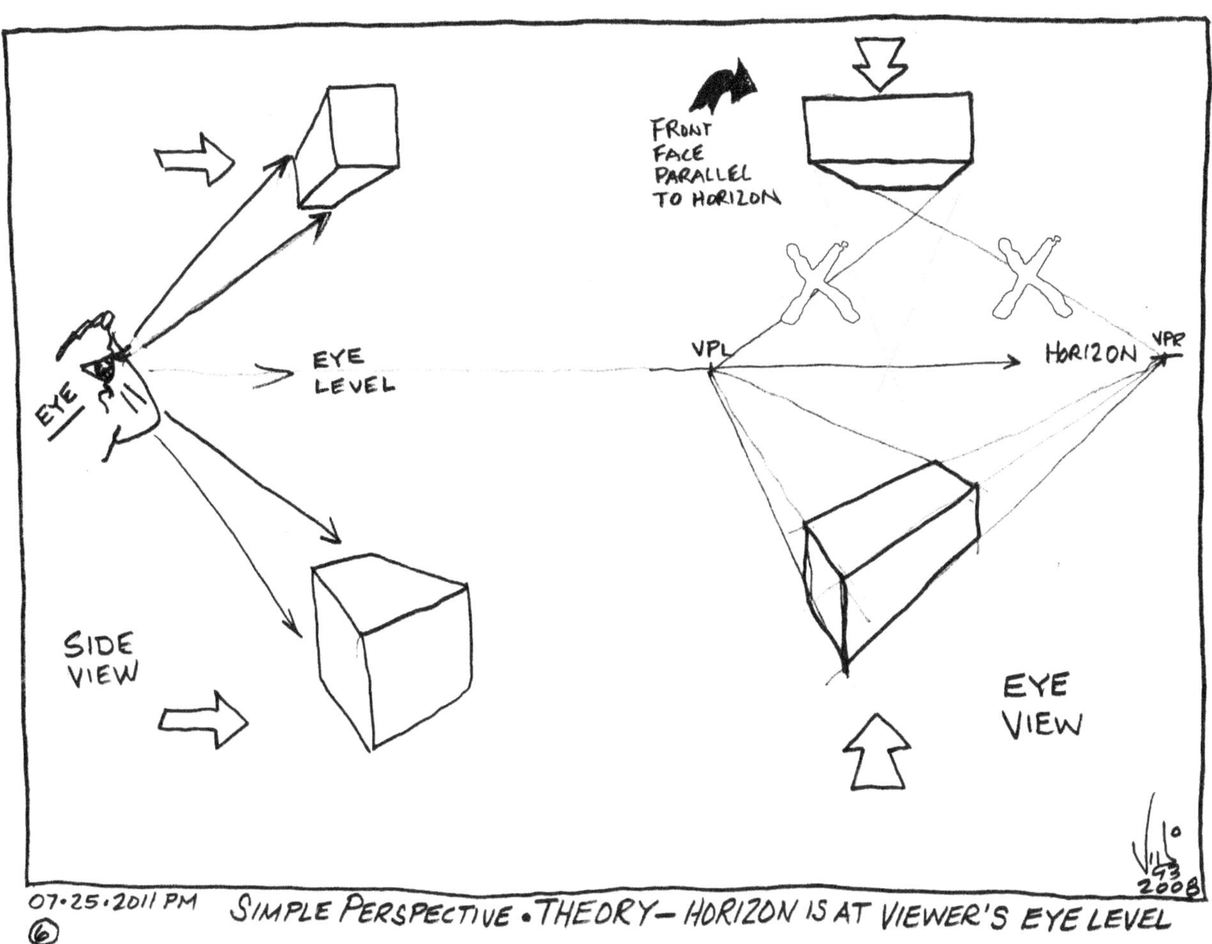

SIMPLE PERSPECTIVE • THEORY— HORIZON IS AT VIEWER'S EYE LEVEL

Theory

Horizon is at Viewer's Eye Level

Unless one is viewing the scene from an angle, such as from the viewpoint of a pilot in a plane that is not level, the horizon line will always be level, and it will always be at the eye level of the viewer. This means that any image that appears below the horizon line, the viewer will be looking down at, and any image or part of an image that appears above the horizon line, the viewer is looking up at. This is true no matter what elevation the viewer may be at. If a mountain top appears below the horizon line then the viewer is at an elevation above the mountain top.

The illustration above, shows a side view on the left, and the view from the eye on the right.

So as you begin a perspective drawing, consider whether the view will be looking up, or looking down, if not looking straight out level. If the view is looking down, then most of the image will be below the horizon line, so one would want to put the horizon line near the top of the drawing paper. If looking up, put the horizon line near the bottom of the paper.

Since most objects are in a plane that is parallel to the ground, most horizontal parallel lines will converge at a single point somewhere on the horizon.

I have no idea what I was thinking when I drew parallel lines crossing to opposite vanishing points! This is why I marked those incorrect lines with an "X" in this edition, and marked to where the correct parallel lines should recede.

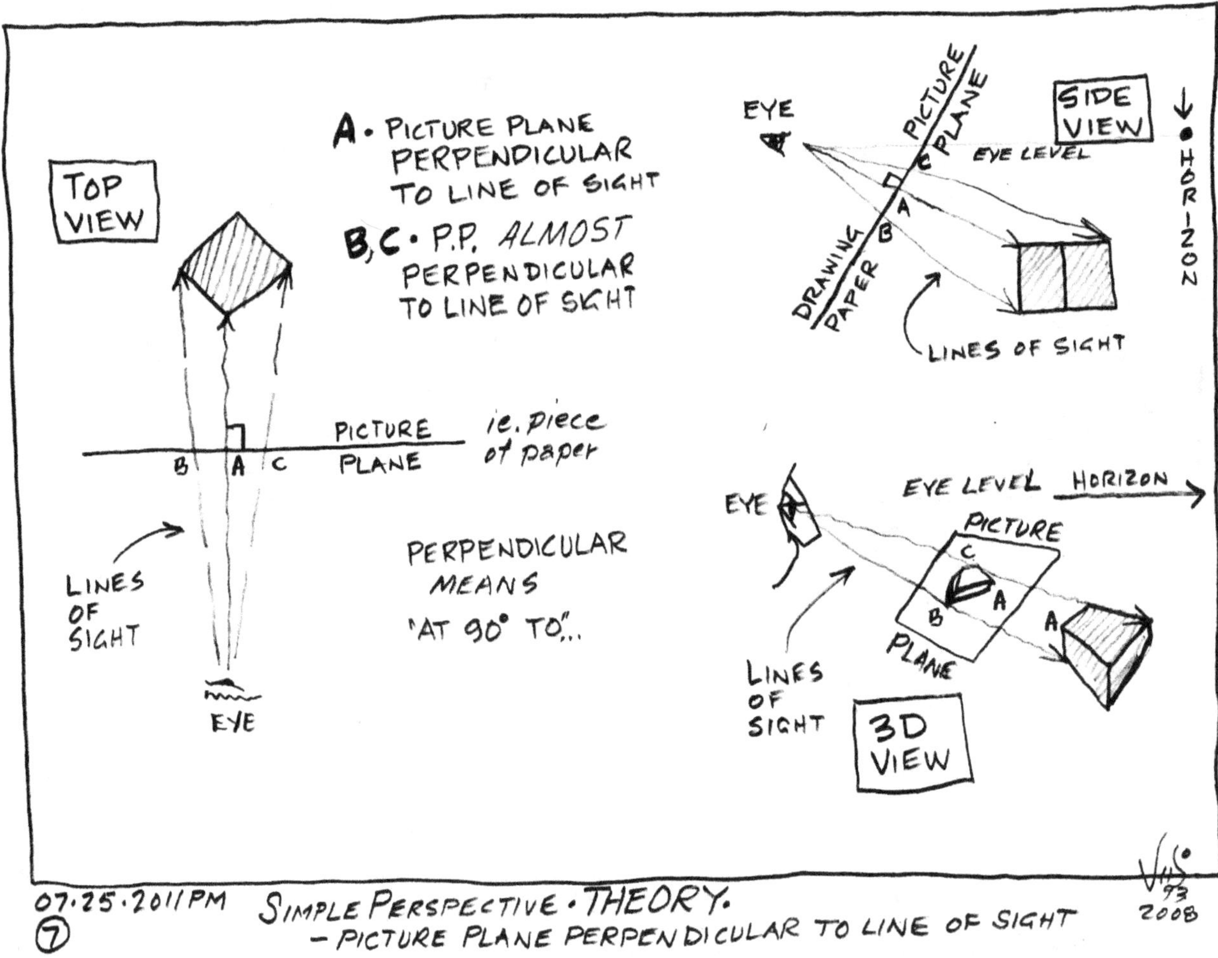

Theory

Picture Plane is Perpendicular to the Line of Sight

One need not be intimidated by this textbook, as there are many humbling errors that stand uncorrected ! The line of sight that is perpendicular to the picture plane in the top view on the left side of the image above, passed through point B on the picture plane, rather than point A, but this has been corrected in this edition .

The Picture Plane is essentially the drawing paper one is using . The Picture Plane is located between the image and the viewer . The Picture Plane is duplicated on the plane of the drawing paper .

As a matter of fact, it is possible to calculate graphically, all the heights and positions of lines in a perspective drawing, from detail orthographic top and side views, but this requires a large drawing area, and for that reason it is usually not practical . Computers are capable of this, but it depends on the software and the image processing whether it is practical even on computer . The best practice is if it looks wrong, fix it !

As one can see in the image above, not all lines of sight will be actually perpendicular to the picture plane . This means one must set up their drawing in a way that allows the majority of the lines of sight to be as close to perpenidicular to the picture plane as possible .

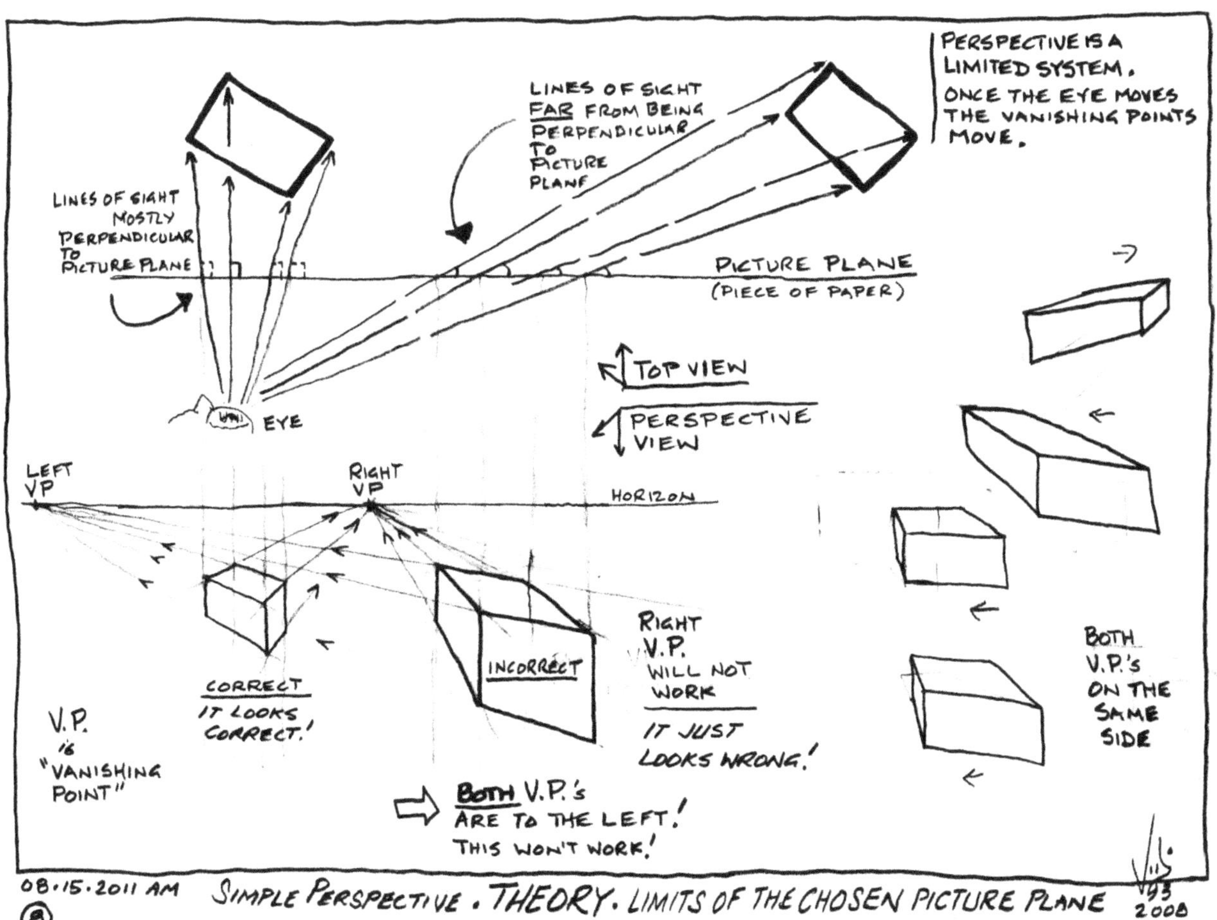
PERSPECTIVE IS A LIMITED SYSTEM. ONCE THE EYE MOVES THE VANISHING POINTS MOVE.
LINES OF SIGHT FAR FROM BEING PERPENDICULAR TO PICTURE PLANE
LINES OF SIGHT MOSTLY PERPENDICULAR TO PICTURE PLANE
PICTURE PLANE (PIECE OF PAPER)
EYE
TOP VIEW
PERSPECTIVE VIEW
LEFT VP
RIGHT VP
HORIZON
CORRECT
IT LOOKS CORRECT!
INCORRECT
RIGHT V.P. WILL NOT WORK
IT JUST LOOKS WRONG!
BOTH V.P.'s ON THE SAME SIDE
V.P. is "VANISHING POINT"
BOTH V.P.'s ARE TO THE LEFT! THIS WON'T WORK!
08.15.2011 AM
SIMPLE PERSPECTIVE . THEORY . LIMITS OF THE CHOSEN PICTURE PLANE
2008

Theory

Limits of the Chosen Picture Plane

As implied on the last page, there is a limit to how much can be included in an image. The limit arises where the line of sight becomes to far from being perpendicular to the picture plane.

A general rule, is that one may not draw to the right of the right vanishing point, nor to the left of the left vanishing point. That said, the image will even be distorted as one begins to draw in the area above or below a vanishing point. Once again, the best practice is if it looks wrong, fix it!

As one can see in the image above, when the lines of sight no longer are perpendicular to the picture plane, the image will actually begin to look wrong. This means one must set up their drawing in a way that allows the majority of the lines of sight to be as close to perpenidicular to the picture plane as possible.

Another general rule is if you cannot see something in your view without moving your eye, then do not include it in your image or drawing.

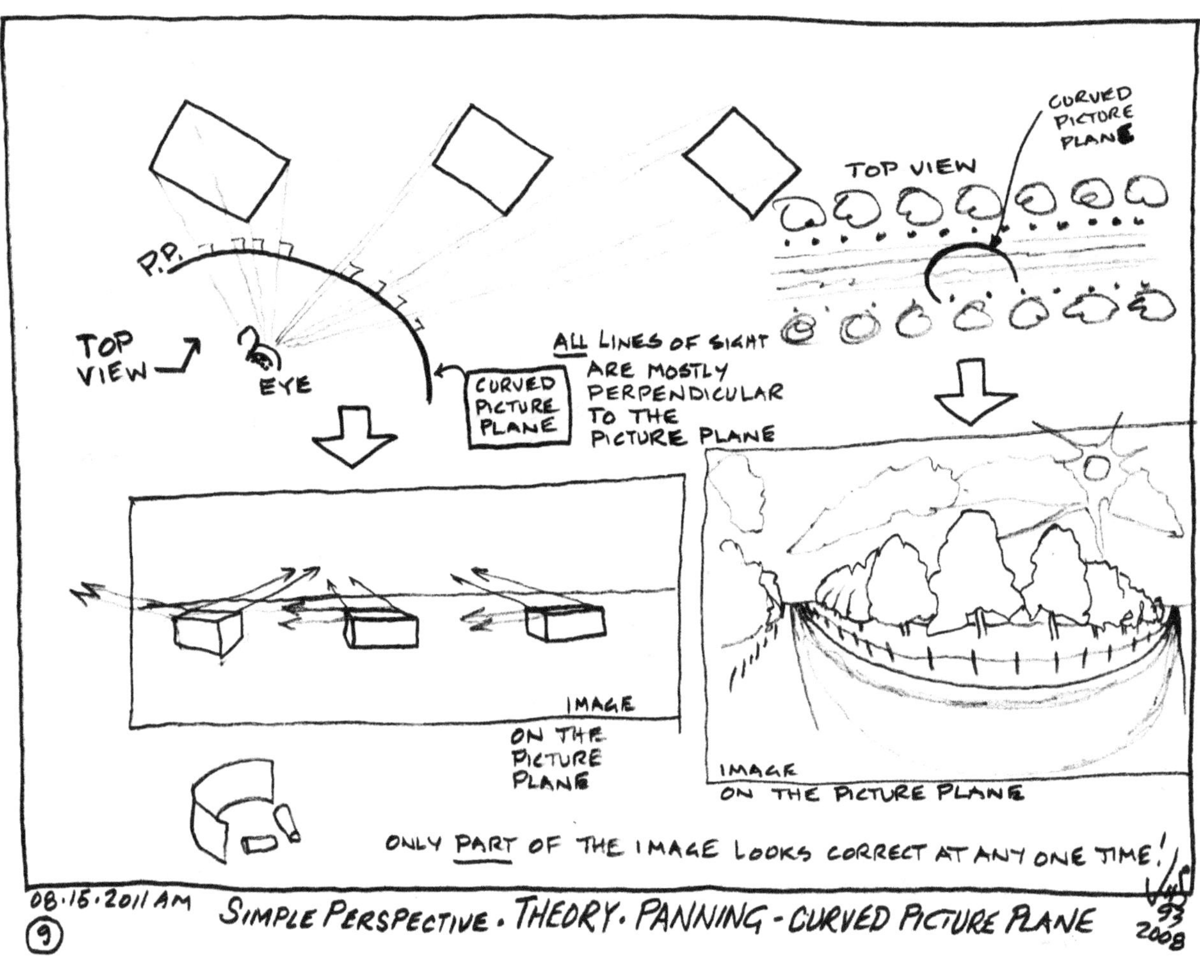

Theory

Panning - Curved Picture Plane

As stated on the last page, there is a limit to how much can be included in an image. The limit arises where the line of sight becomes too far from being perpendicular to the picture plane. But if only one part of the image is to be viewed at one time, a curved picture plane may be of use.

There are not any simple rules about vanishing points that can be stated here, when using a curved picture plane. It can be said though, that a smooth transition througout the drawing, where parallel lines, although curved, converge at infinity, and converge on the horizon, as applicable, will keep the drawing looking solid.

A good way to check it is to make an artificial frame that only allows a portion of the drawing to be viewed at a time, and using the limited view, check the drawing for abrupt changes in perspective.

A curved picture plane, in theory, keeps all lines of sight perpendicular to the picture plane. A curved picture plane, in reality, allows for the eye to move to view a larger area.

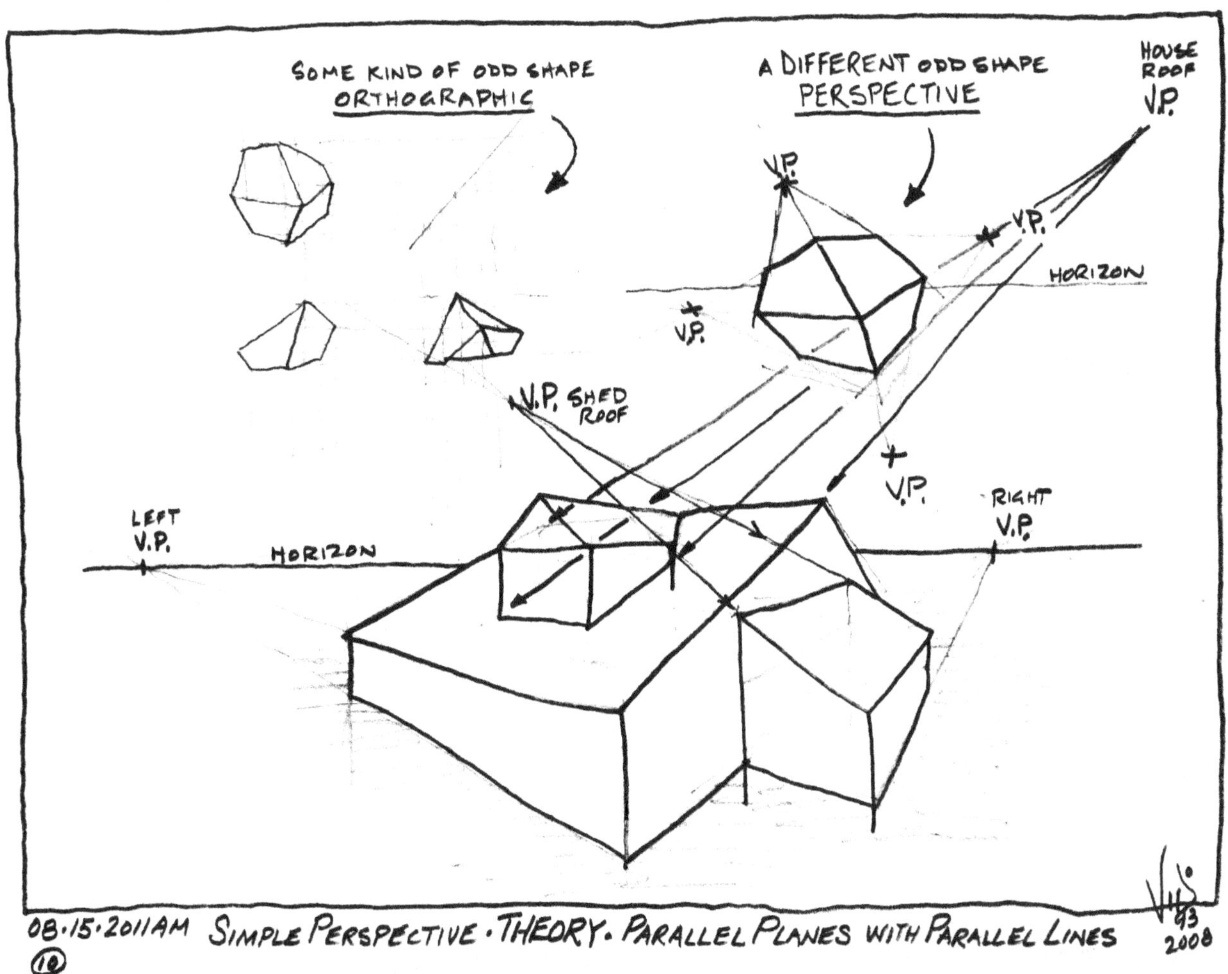

08·15·2011AM SIMPLE PERSPECTIVE · THEORY · PARALLEL PLANES WITH PARALLEL LINES
(10)

Theory

Parallel Planes with Parallel Lines

Just because a plane is not parallel to the ground plane, does not mean that receding parallel lines in that plane do not converge at a vanishing point, but rather they converge at a vanishing point that is not on the horizon .

An example of this is the lines in a sloped roof . Parallel lines in a sloped roof, such as the parallel edges of the roof, can be located by using the vanishing points on the horizon, and the vertical lines of two point perspective, but then they should converge, even if off the page, at one single point . This should be checked when drawing - do the parallel edges of the sloped roof appear to converge ?

This sort of goes back to the two Split the Angle exercises in the Warm Up section of Textbook A . As well, looking at your drawing as a two dimensional puzzle allows one to check technical things such as whether two lines appear to converge . This is most important when there are other features on the roof other than the two parallel edges that converge .

Dormers located in the roof have parallel edges in the plane of the sloped roof that are parallel to the sloped edges of the roof . An easy way to draw them is to find the point of convergance, or vanishing point of the roof edges and draw the edges of the dormer so that if extended, they would pass through the same vanishing point as the sloped edges of the roof .

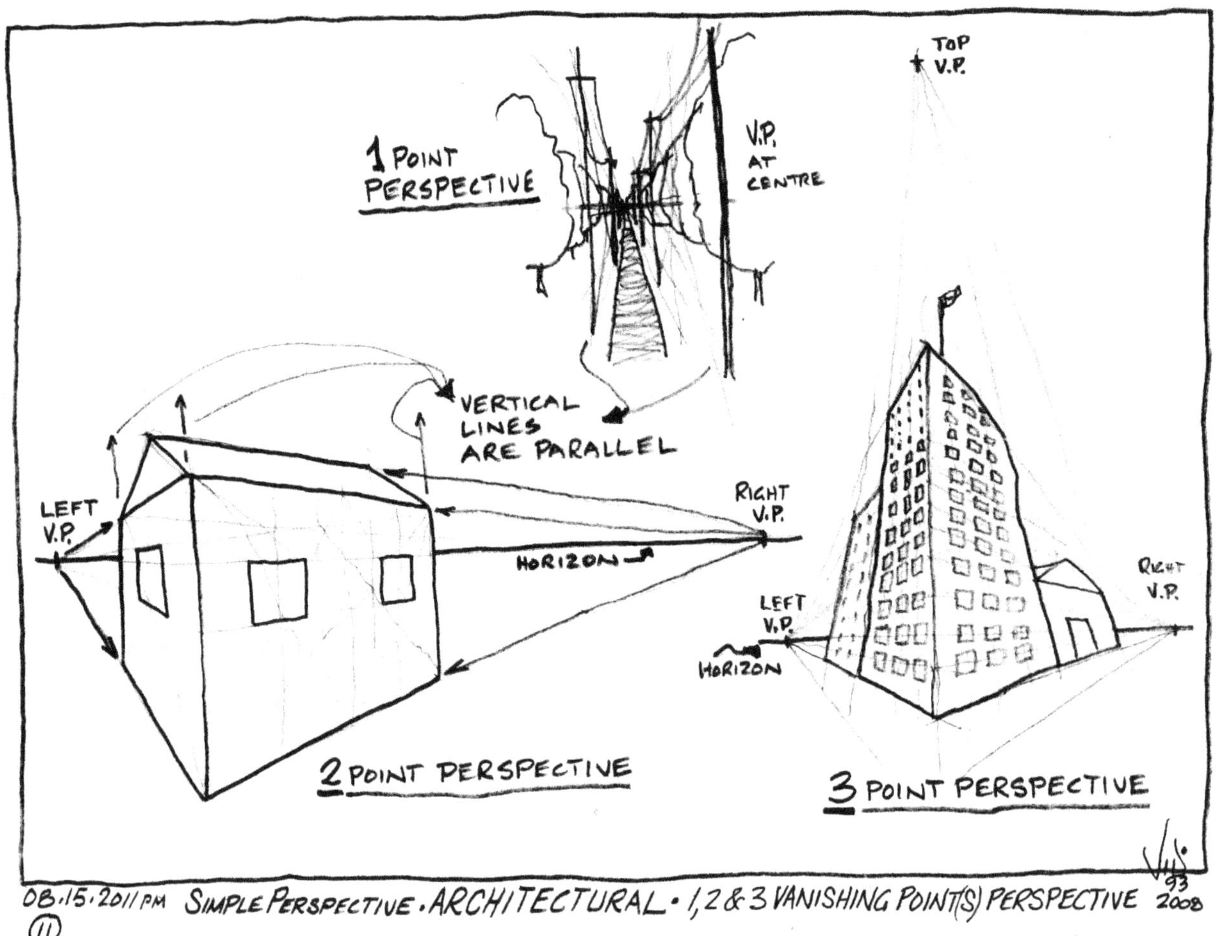

08.15.2011 PM SIMPLE PERSPECTIVE • ARCHITECTURAL • 1, 2 & 3 VANISHING POINT(S) PERSPECTIVE 2008
(11)

Architectural

1, 2 and 3 Vanishing Point Perspective

Now that it has been shown that there can be any number of vanishing points in Perspective Projection, limited only to the number a planes with parallel lines, one can understand when one should choose to use 1, 2 or 3 vanishing points.

The top centre illustration of the image above, is a 1 vanishing point perspective drawing. The vertical lines are vertical, the horizontal lines, passing across the page, are horizontal, and the receding lines, disappearing into the page, converge at the single vanishing point.

The illustration on the lower left of the image above, is a 2 vanishing point perspective drawing. Lines in the planes parallel to the ground plane may recede to either of two vanishing points, and again, the sloped edges of the roof will recede to a vanishing point that is not on the horizon. Vertical lines are vertical in this drawing.

The illustration on the lower right of the image above, is a 3 vanishing point perspective drawing. Parallel lines in parallel planes may converge at any of the three vanishing points, and if not parallel to any of the three axes, more vanishing points may be found.

The choice of how many vanishing points to use is dictated by whether the points of convergence are within the reasonable limits of the picture plane or drawing. The reason the vertical lines in the 2 point perspective drawing are drawn parallel and vertical is because the vanishing point is infinitely far away from the edges of the drawing. In the 3 point perspective, the vertical lines converge at a point that is withing the reasonable limits of the drawing or picture plane.

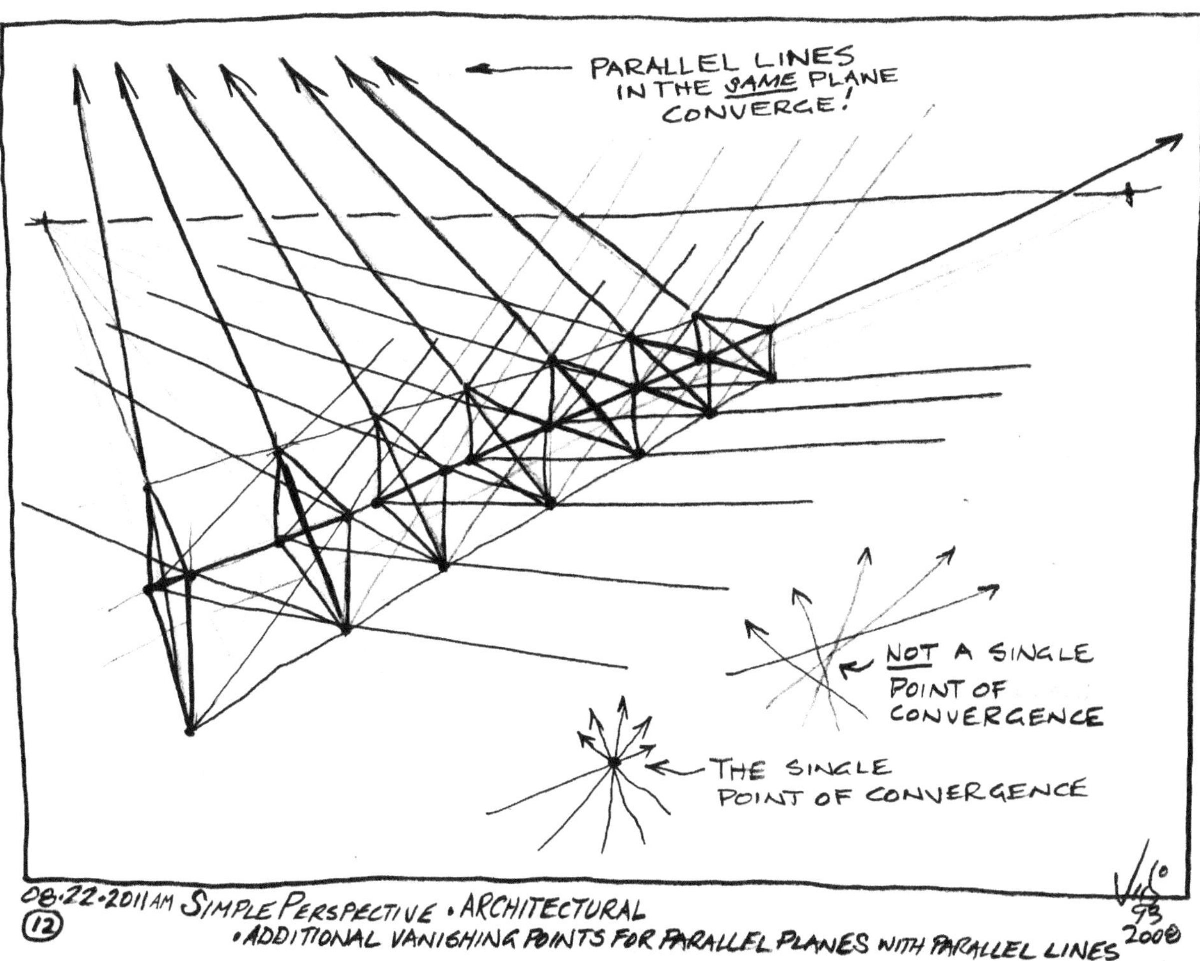

08·22·2011AM SIMPLE PERSPECTIVE • ARCHITECTURAL
⑫ • ADDITIONAL VANISHING POINTS FOR PARALLEL PLANES WITH PARALLEL LINES

Architectural

Additional Vanishing Points for Parallel Planes with Parallel Lines - 1

To discuss the idea of a vanishing point, or point of convergance of parallel lines in parallel planes, further, the illustration above has four additional vanishing points. Can you find them ?

This is a bit of a trick question. The four additional vanishing points are not on the page or picture plane. The six boxes with seven vertical walls on the ends of the boxes, have diagonals in their walls that are parallel lines in parallel planes. The dividing walls are all parallel. The sizes of these walls are the same. The diagonals in these walls are parallel and in the same plane, and they converge above and slightly off the the left, off the page. The diagonals in the floors of the boxes converge off to the left of the page. The diagonals in the front walls of the boxes converge either off the upper left of the page, or above and slightly to the right off the page. The diagonals on the back walls converge at the same point above and slightly to the right off the page.

Even with a ruler, it is hard to graphically calculate acurately enough to have the parallel lines converge at a single point. This is a good thing though, because if one knows they should converge, one can just make them converge, whereas using a ruler commits the draftsperson to the lines they have already laid down, and makes it hard to have a clean accurate drawing with single points of convergance.

One may now further appreciate the Split the Angle - Complex exercise of the Warm Ups section of Textbook A, as a good opportunity to practice drawing lines that converge at a single point off the page.

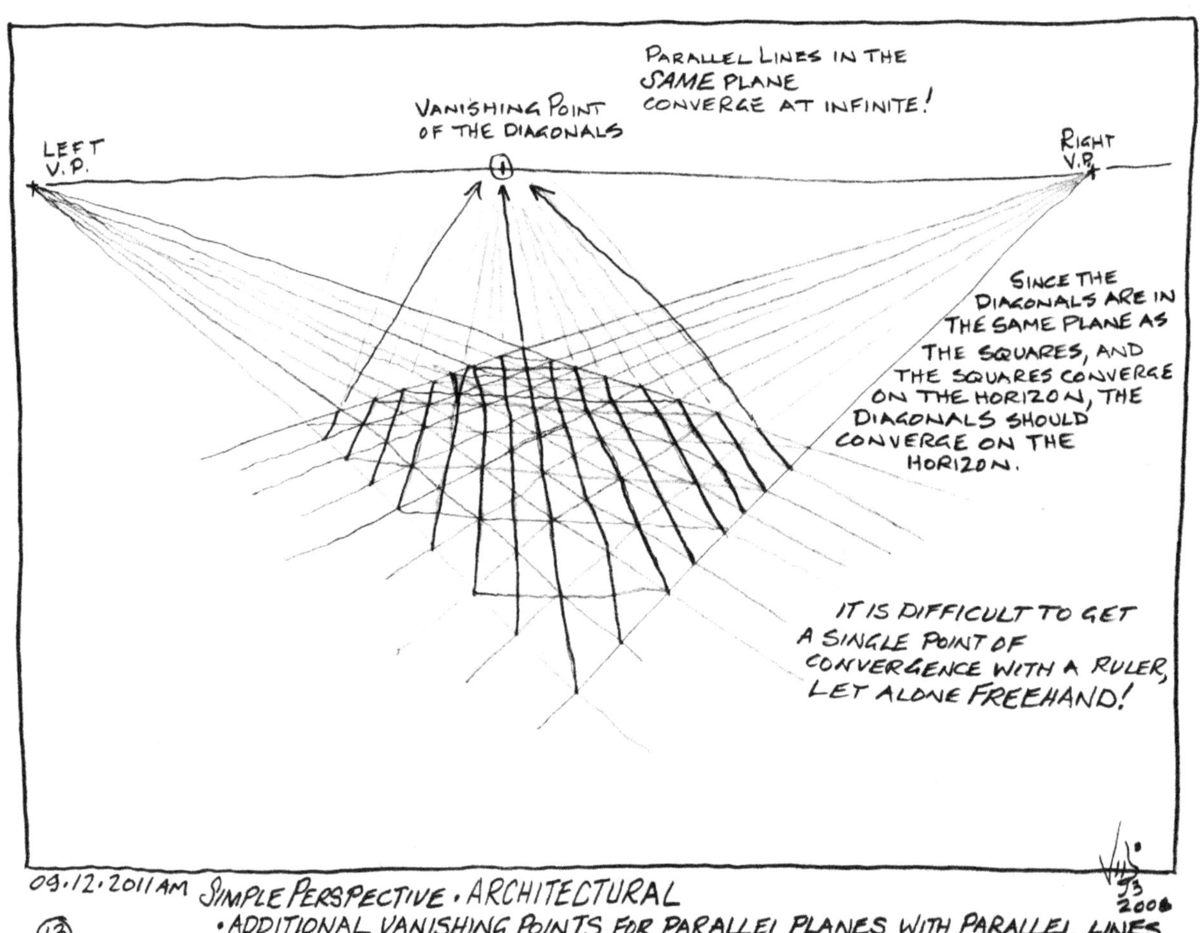

PARALLEL LINES IN THE SAME PLANE CONVERGE AT INFINITE!
VANISHING POINT OF THE DIAGONALS
LEFT V.P.
RIGHT V.P.
SINCE THE DIAGONALS ARE IN THE SAME PLANE AS THE SQUARES, AND THE SQUARES CONVERGE ON THE HORIZON, THE DIAGONALS SHOULD CONVERGE ON THE HORIZON.
IT IS DIFFICULT TO GET A SINGLE POINT OF CONVERGENCE WITH A RULER, LET ALONE FREEHAND!
09.12.2011AM SIMPLE PERSPECTIVE • ARCHITECTURAL
• ADDITIONAL VANISHING POINTS FOR PARALLEL PLANES WITH PARALLEL LINES
2006
13

Architectural

Additional Vanishing Points for Parallel Planes with Parallel Lines - 2

Another look at additional vanishing points is presented here with the diagonals of the boxes converging at a single point on the horizon, more or less . ; >

First of all, it is very difficult to graphically calculate accurately enough, the diagonals in boxes so that they converge at a single point, as obvious in the above illustration . The way to deal with this is to make the lines converge, by placing the lines as straight as possible, and as close as possible to their intersections with other lines . Do not be discouraged, as even with a ruler this is a hard thing to do, so be glad that you are not as committed as a person using a ruler, who finds themself committed to their ruled lines and unable to adjust their lines .

Even with a computer, if the lines converge far off the picture plane, the image becomes unwieldy and processing or viewing becomes very taxing . Consider yourself lucky that one may just draw it correctly in two dimensions, as they create the three dimensional image .

Parallel Planes with Parallel Lines - both the left and right vanishing points on the horizon, are for parallel lines in planes parallel to the ground plane . These points are in the ground plane . There are other vanishing points on the horizon for lines such as these diagonals . Other planes, not parallel to the ground plane, still have parallel lines converging at a single point or vanishing point .

In this discussion, remember that the left vanishing point, on the horizon, is for the set of parallel lines in the planes parallel to the ground plane, that are perpendicular to the lines in the planes parallel to the ground plane that converge at the right vanishing point, on the horizon .

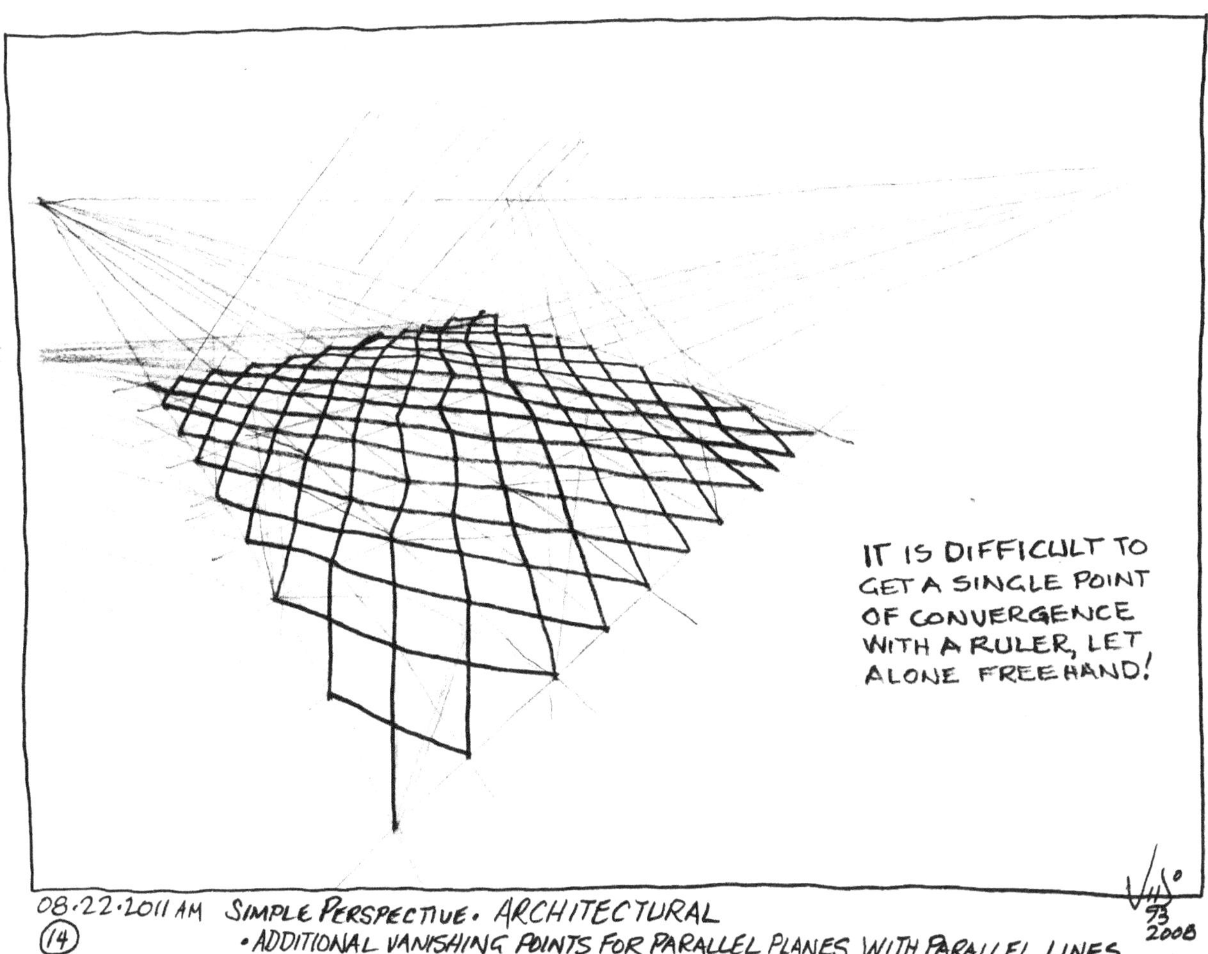
IT IS DIFFICULT TO GET A SINGLE POINT OF CONVERGENCE WITH A RULER, LET ALONE FREEHAND!

08·22·2011 AM SIMPLE PERSPECTIVE · ARCHITECTURAL
(14) · ADDITIONAL VANISHING POINTS FOR PARALLEL PLANES WITH PARALLEL LINES

Architectural

Additional Vanishing Points for Parallel Planes with Parallel Lines - 3

Another look at additional vanishing points is presented here to illustrate how important it is to judge the angle of a line as part of a two dimensional image, to verify that everything lines up, and thereby create a solid looking three dimensional image .

This is the whole idea of perspective, that overrides any technical accuracy . Everything must line up - this is the purpose of Perspective Projection . Technical accuracy is insufficient in freehand drawing as it cannot create a solid drawing . Even the use of rulers cannot create a solid drawing . And it is a mild accomplishment to achieve a computer drawing, as this is incapable of developing the skills needed to complete a painting or drawing . Industrial Light and Magic, Stephen Spielberg's special effects company that worked on the movie Jurassic Park, told prospective animators that " if you can paint on paper, we can teach you to paint on computer, but if you cannot paint on paper, a computer will not be able to help you" . The same goes for drawing - if one can draw freehand, they can keep track of all the lines in a computer drawing, otherwise they will be overwhelmed by the shear number of lines necessary in a computer drawing .

The trick is to split or divide all shapes out of an overall shape, and this is the halving of Spit the Area and Split the Angle, the exercises in the Warm Ups section of Textbook A, and the skills obtained by the accumulated practice of those exercises supplies the necessary talent when drawing Perspective Projections .

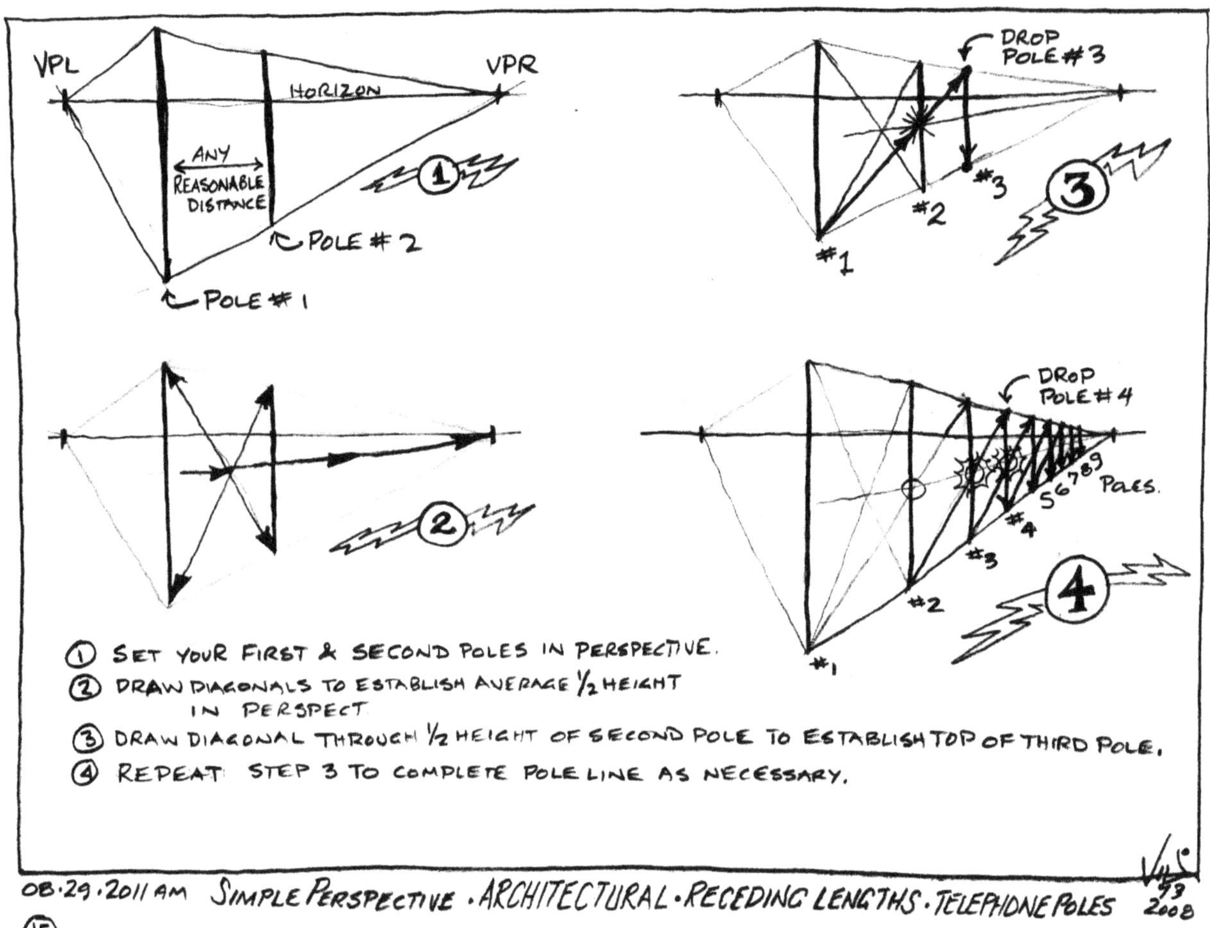

VPL
VPR
HORIZON
ANY REASONABLE DISTANCE
POLE #2
POLE #1
1
DROP POLE #3
#1
#2
#3
3
2
DROP POLE #4
#1
#2
#3
#4
5 6 7 8 9 POLES.
4
① SET YOUR FIRST & SECOND POLES IN PERSPECTIVE.
② DRAW DIAGONALS TO ESTABLISH AVERAGE ½ HEIGHT IN PERSPECT
③ DRAW DIAGONAL THROUGH ½ HEIGHT OF SECOND POLE TO ESTABLISH TOP OF THIRD POLE.
④ REPEAT STEP 3 TO COMPLETE POLE LINE AS NECESSARY.
08·29·2011 AM SIMPLE PERSPECTIVE · ARCHITECTURAL · RECEDING LENGTHS · TELEPHONE POLES
93 2008
15

Architectural

Receding Lengths - Telephone Poles

It is possible to graphically calculate the apparent length of equal length objects as they recede into the distance. Here is how to do it, by halving the given lengths.

Begin by establishing the first length, which here is a vertical telephone pole. The second length, or telephone pole must be placed within the perspective lines travelling back to a vanishing point, which in the illustration above, is the right hand vanishing point. The position of this pole is arbitrary, or just "made up" but may need to be adjusted to get the image one wants. For now just place the second telephone pole a reasonable distance from the first, with the top and bottom within the lines travelling to the right hand vanishing point.

Next, find the halfway point of the two poles by drawing diagonals from the top of the first pole to the bottom of the second pole, and from the top of the second pole to the bottom of the first pole. Then project a line back from the intersection of the two diagonals to the right hand vanishing point. You have now halved both the height of all the poles and the distance between the first and second pole.

To find the top of the third pole, draw a line from the base of the first pole, through the halfway point of the second pole, where the line passing from the intersection of the diagonals to the right hand vanishing point intersects the second pole, and continue the line you are drawing until it intersects the line from the top of the poles to the right hand vanishing point. Drop a pole, a vertical line, from this intersection to the line from the bottom of the poles that extends to the right hand vanishing point. This is your third pole.

Repeat this third step as necessary to creat the field of receding poles.

This halving by drawing diagonals has many uses. Practice this many times until you are able to understand how this halving with diagonals works.

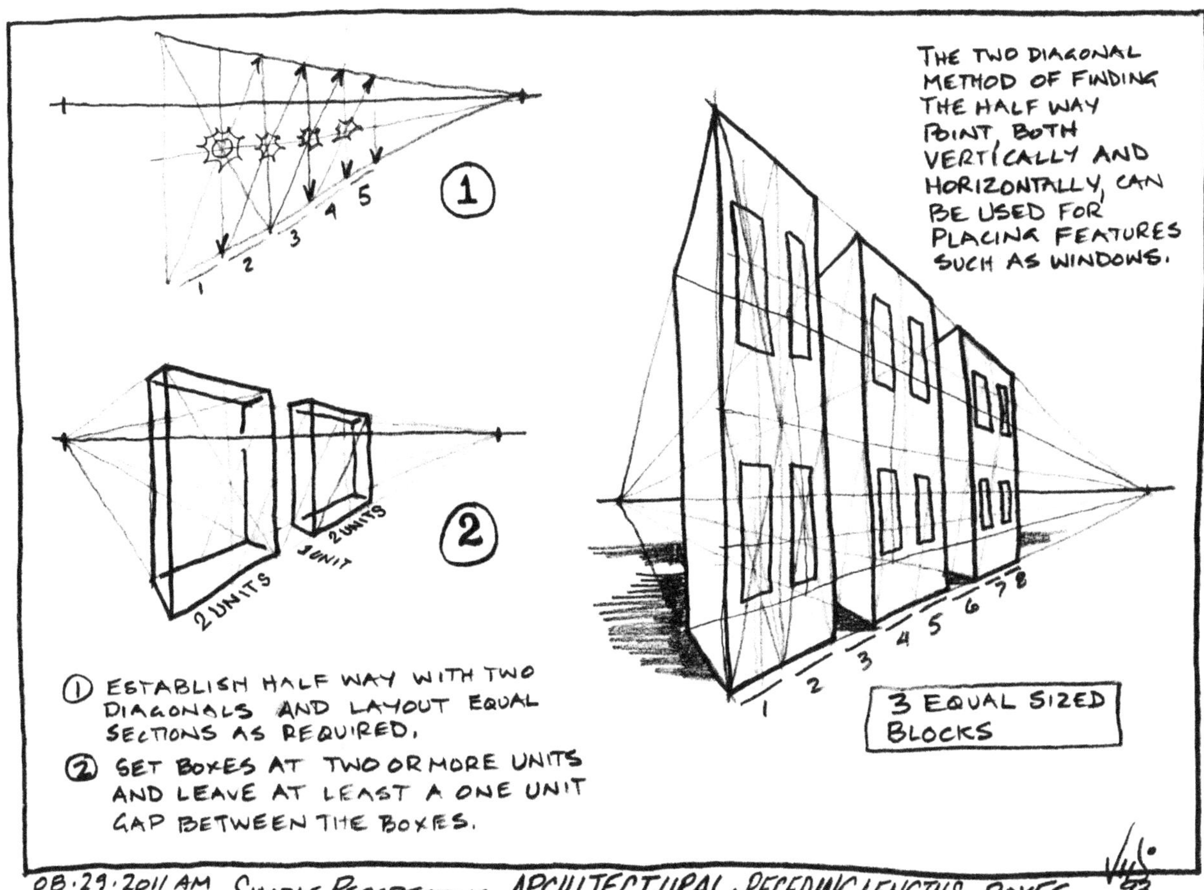

THE TWO DIAGONAL METHOD OF FINDING THE HALF WAY POINT, BOTH VERTICALLY AND HORIZONTALLY, CAN BE USED FOR PLACING FEATURES SUCH AS WINDOWS.
1
2
2 UNITS
1 UNIT
2 UNITS
3 EQUAL SIZED BLOCKS
① ESTABLISH HALF WAY WITH TWO DIAGONALS AND LAYOUT EQUAL SECTIONS AS REQUIRED.
② SET BOXES AT TWO OR MORE UNITS AND LEAVE AT LEAST A ONE UNIT GAP BETWEEN THE BOXES.
08·29·2011 AM SIMPLE PERSPECTIVE · ARCHITECTURAL · RECEDING LENGTHS · BOXES
93 2008

Architectural 16

Receding Lengths - Boxes

It is possible to graphically calculate the apparent horizontal length of equal length objects as they recede into the distance. Here is how to do it, by halving the given lengths.

Begin by establishing the first box, which here becomes an apartment block. Halve the block, with two diagonals joining the opposite corners. Draw both a vertical line through the intersection of the diagonals, and a "horizontal" line through the intersection of the diagonals that travels back to, in this case, the right hand vanishing point.

Now draw a line, from the base of the vertical line you have just dropped from the intersection of the diagonals, where it intersects the bottom of the box; through the intersection of the line from the diagonals travelling to the right hand vanishing point and the right hand side of the box; up to the line from the top of the box that travels to the right hand vanishing point. You have just located the top left corner of the next box.

What you have done is to locate the top left corner of the next box, so that the two boxes are half a box apart! Continue to build the second box by repeatedly locating the top of the next half box, using the method described above, of drawing a line from the base of the box, through the half height point on the vertical of the box, to the top point of the next half box section.

This halving by drawing diagonals has many uses. Practice this many times until you are able to understand how this halving with diagonals works.

There must be a way of transferring a length from one vanishing point line to the other vanishing point line, so as to be able to draw a cube, with all sides equal length. I have not come across, or been able to come up with, a way to do this, but I would very much like to find out how one could create a perfect cube, as this would be useful for locating spheres.

THIS HAS BEEN ACCIMPLISHED IN THE EPILOGUE BEGINNING ON PAGE 147.

Epilogue: At the end of this book, in the epilogue, there IS a solution for how to place a perfect sphere into a perspective drawing, by placing it in a perfect cube, calculated graphically.

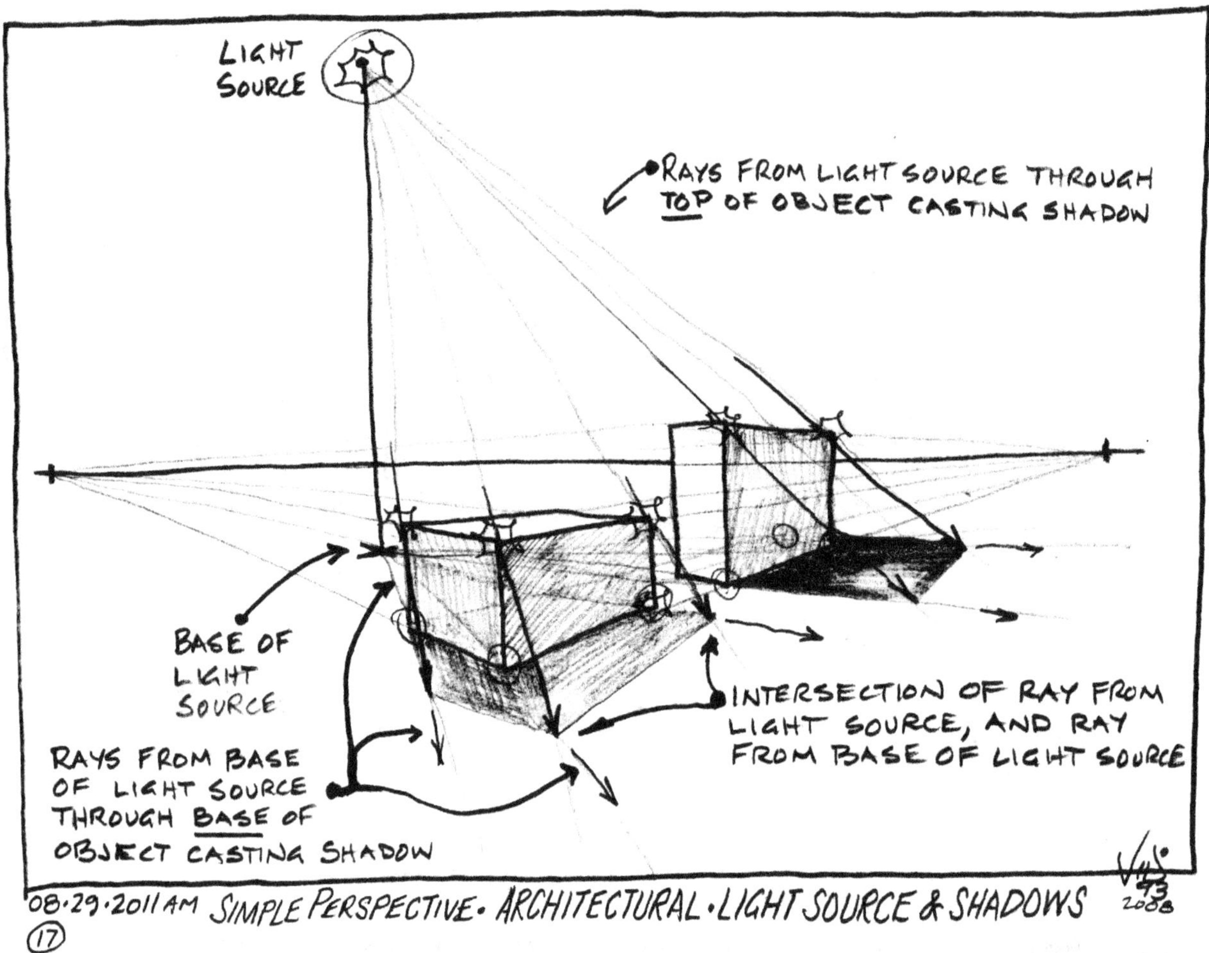

08·29·2011 AM SIMPLE PERSPECTIVE · ARCHITECTURAL · LIGHT SOURCE & SHADOWS
(17)

Architectural
Light Source and Shadows

It is possible to graphically calculate where shadows fall, and their shape, given the height of the light source and the location of the base of the light source . It should be said, that sunlight, or even daylight on a cloudy day, sends rays of light that are parallel, although shadows are indistinct on a cloudy day, with very soft edges, if at all noticable as shadows .

Begin this exercise by creating two random box shapes, similar in shape and location to the illustration above, and draw a vertical line to locate the base of the light source, and the height of the light source . Create the light source in a similar location as in the illustration above, for the ease of making this exercise work out well for you .

Now draw a line, from the base of the vertical line you have just created for the light source, through the base of each corner of the boxes that have a corresponding top corner that will cast a shadow . Next draw a ray from the light source, the top of the vertical line, through the top corner of the the base corners you have just drawn lines through in the previous step . Where these two sets of lines intersect for each corner of the boxes, are the limits of the shadows .

Since the sun is larger than the earth, all rays of light from the sun are parallel . As well, the location of the base of the sun, where it is above the ground plane, is at an infinite distance, so all rays from the location of the sun above the ground plane are from a single point on the horizon, unless the sun is shining from behind the viewer, where they will still converge at a single infinitely far away, point . So when drawing a shadow from the sun, when close to mid day, when the sun is mostly above, one could, just keep both the rays from the sun as the light source, and the rays from the location of the sun above the ground plane, parallel . If the sun is within the illustration, consider using it as a local light source .

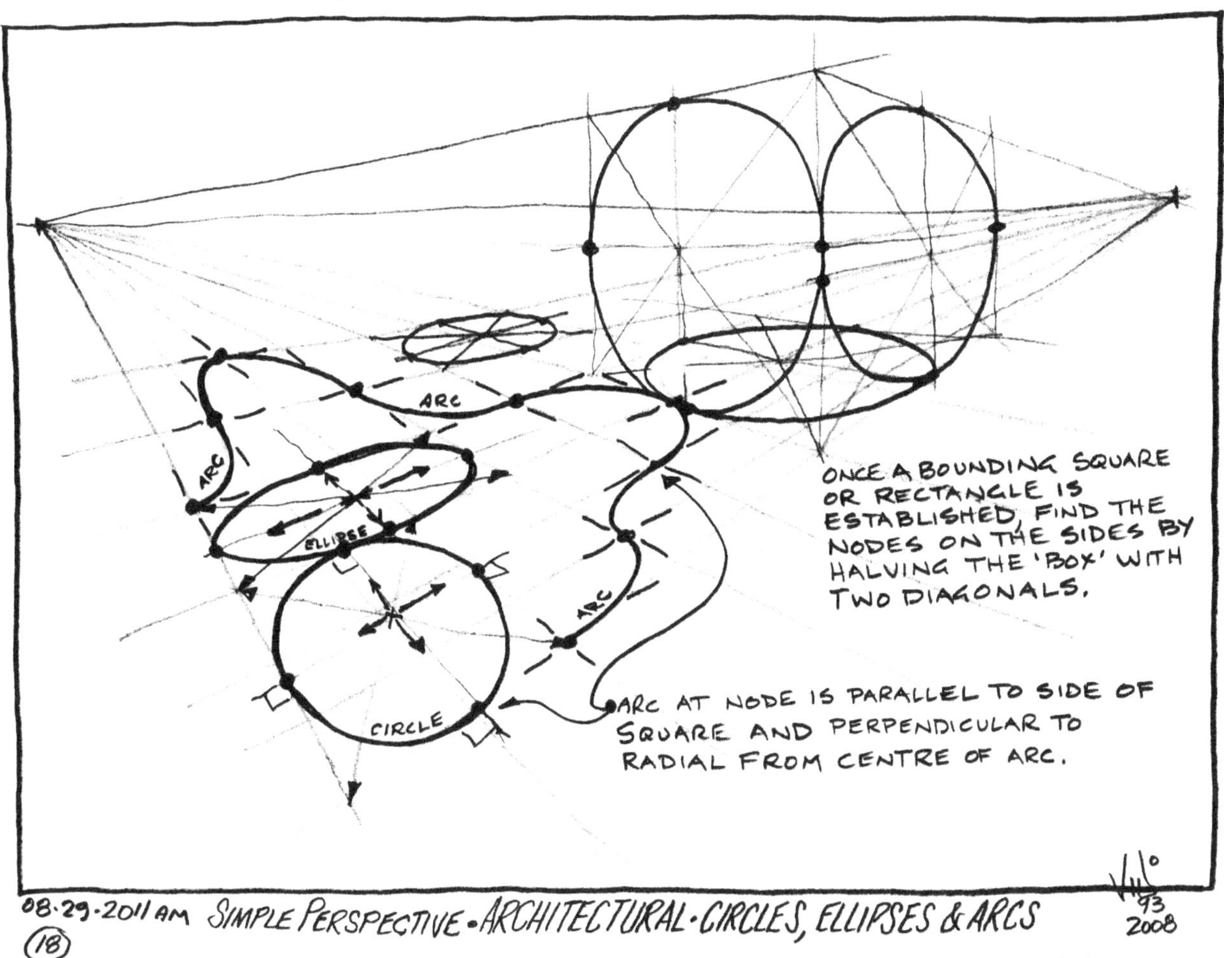

ARC
ARC
ELLIPSE
ARC
CIRCLE
ONCE A BOUNDING SQUARE OR RECTANGLE IS ESTABLISHED, FIND THE NODES ON THE SIDES BY HALVING THE 'BOX' WITH TWO DIAGONALS.
ARC AT NODE IS PARALLEL TO SIDE OF SQUARE AND PERPENDICULAR TO RADIAL FROM CENTRE OF ARC.
93
2008

08·29·2011 AM SIMPLE PERSPECTIVE • ARCHITECTURAL • CIRCLES, ELLIPSES & ARCS

(18)

Architectural
Circles, Ellipses and Arcs

Drawing circles, arcs and ellipses, as they appear in perspective, is achieved by drawing a bounding box and completing the arc within the box, after finding the nodes where the arc is tangent to the bounding box .

Landing smooth arcs where they are tangent, is the purpose of the Land the Circle exercises in the Warm Ups section of Textbook A . The practice of those exercises allows one to place a smooth curve where it needs to be located, and tangent to two or more points . The bounding box is used to locate the points where the arc, circle or ellipse needs to be tangent .

To draw a circle, begin by attempting to draw a square in perspective . Then half the square with two diagonals from corner to corner, and then draw the halfway lines from the intersection of the diagonals out to the sides of the square . Where the halfway lines intersect the four sides of the box are the locations of the nodes where the circle will be tangent - or touching the bounding box . Draw a smooth arc from node to node so that the arc is perpendicular to the halfway line and parallel to the side of the bounding box, at the node of the arc on the side of the bounding box .

This requires the ability to draw a smooth arc exactly where it is required . This is an application of the Land the Circle exercises of the Warm Ups section of Textbook A . It takes good judgement to draw a smooth arc, and there are other ways of calculating the location of the arc, such as drawing more bounding boxes within the original bounding box, but nevertheless, good judgement when placing the arc is always required .

THIS EXERCISE EMPHASIZES AND REINFORCES THE IMPORTANCE OF THE LAND THE CIRCLE EXERCISES ON PAGES 12 AND 13 OF THIS BOOK .

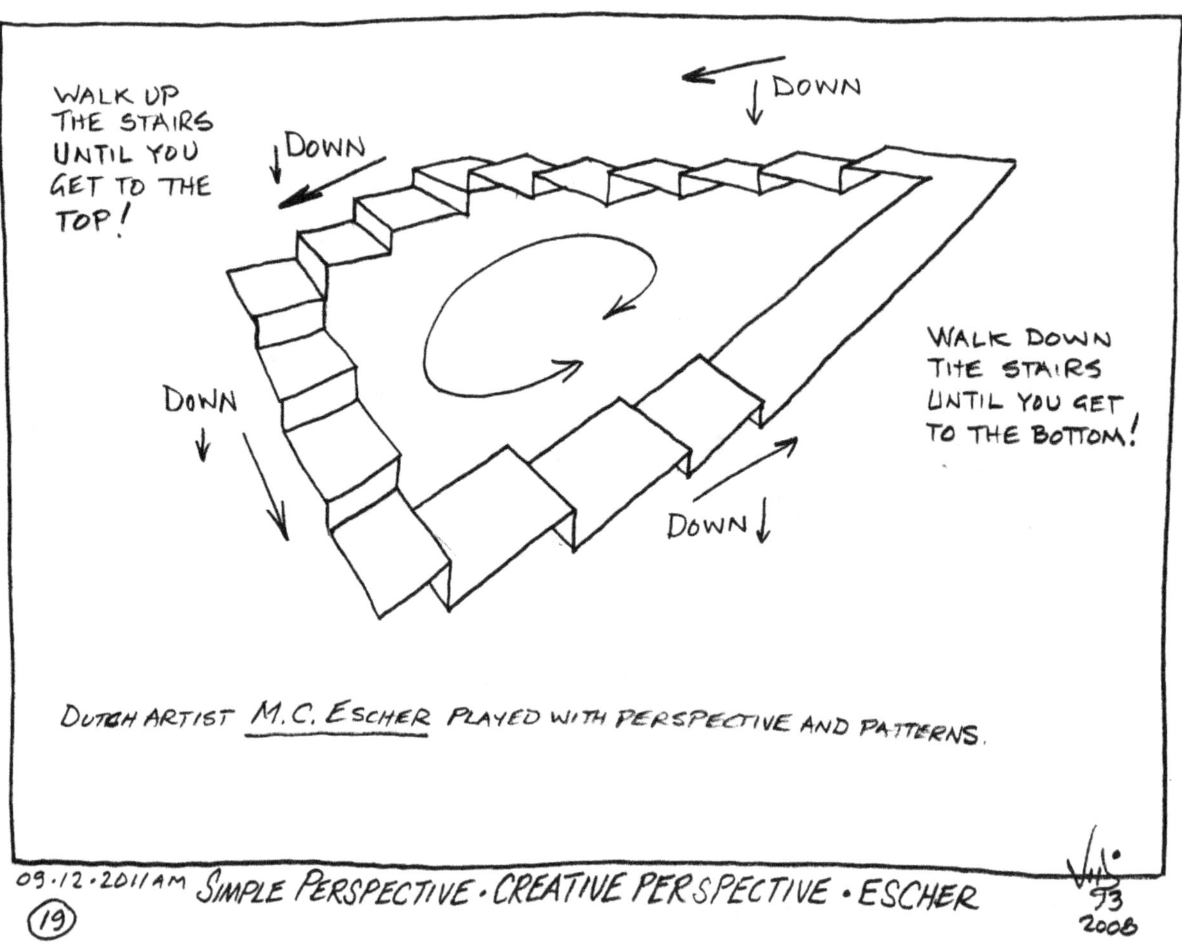
WALK UP THE STAIRS UNTIL YOU GET TO THE TOP!
DOWN
DOWN
DOWN
DOWN
WALK DOWN THE STAIRS UNTIL YOU GET TO THE BOTTOM!
DUTCH ARTIST M.C. ESCHER PLAYED WITH PERSPECTIVE AND PATTERNS.
09.12.2011AM SIMPLE PERSPECTIVE • CREATIVE PERSPECTIVE • ESCHER
19
93
2008

Creative Perspective

Escher

Dutch artist M. C. Escher played with patterns and perspective to create very interesting drawings.

Above is an example of the type of perspective drawing he would create.

This simple drawing of a set of stairs, appears to be drawn in correct perspecive, but look again. Although the perspective seems correct, the drawing is an illustration of an impossible set of stairs. One may continually walk either up or down the stairs and never reach a top or bottom.

This shows how Perspective Projection is simply a system of illustration and not a realistic portrayal of reality. When one is drawing, one must make many decisions of what to portray and what to overlook. Keeping a drawing looking solid requires that all elements of a drawing correspond to all other elements of the drawing, independently of whatever reality one may be trying to duplicate in a drawing.

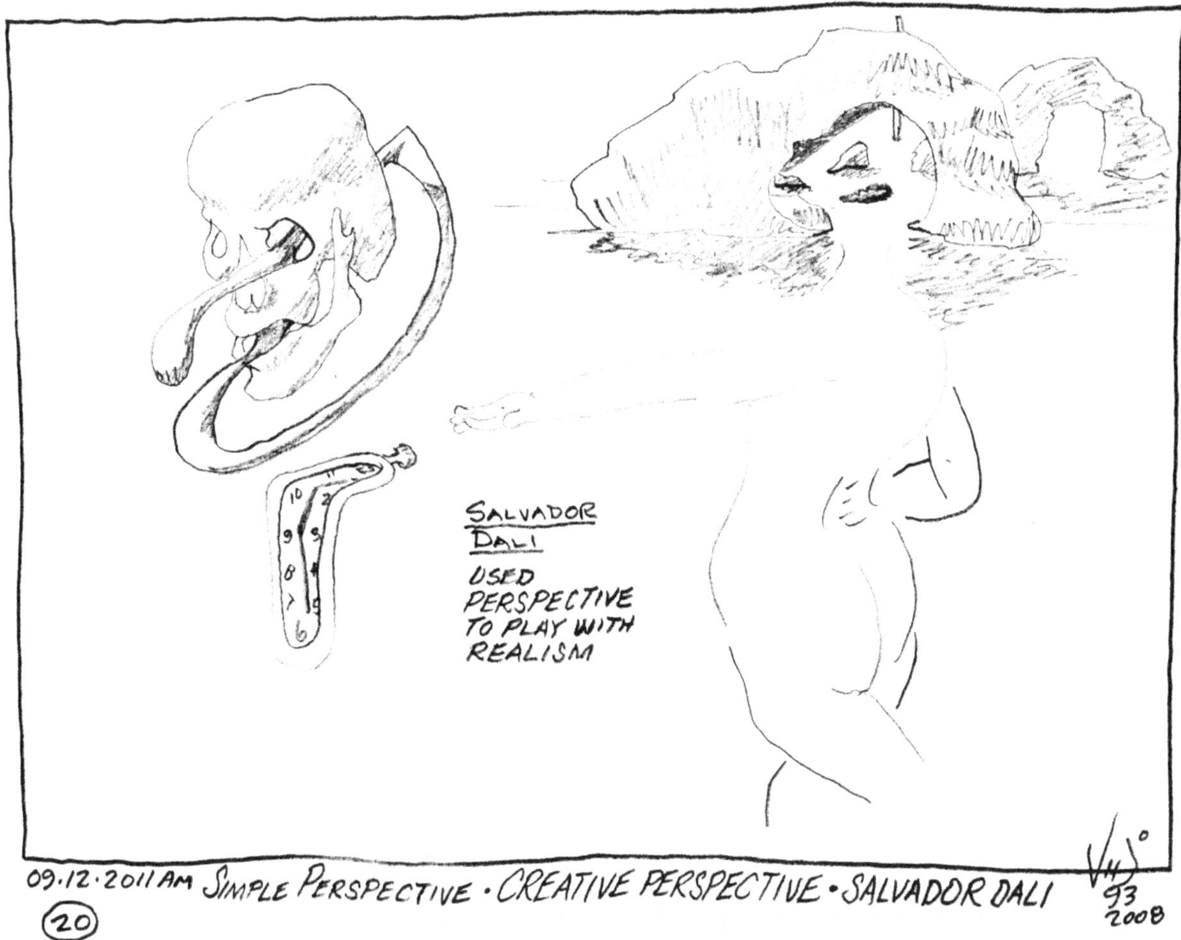
SALVADOR DALI
USED PERSPECTIVE TO PLAY WITH REALISM
09.12.2011 AM SIMPLE PERSPECTIVE • CREATIVE PERSPECTIVE • SALVADOR DALI
20
93
2008

Creative Perspective

Salvadore Dali

Spanish artist Salvador Dali used perspective to play with realism to create very interesting drawings .

Above are examples of the types of perspective drawings he would create .

The top left drawing of a skull, is a simple drawing with solid perspective, of an unnatural subject . The drawing below it, of a limp watch, also uses perspective to portray the melting watch dripping off of a surface . The drawing on the right side may flip between a drawing of the head of the figure and the cavern passing through the rock on the beach .

This shows how Perspective Projection is simply a system of illustration and not a realistic portrayal of reality . When one is drawing, one must make many decisions of what to portray and what to overlook . Keeping a drawing looking solid requires that all elements of a drawing correspond to all other elements of the drawing, independently of whatever reality one may be trying to duplicate in a drawing .

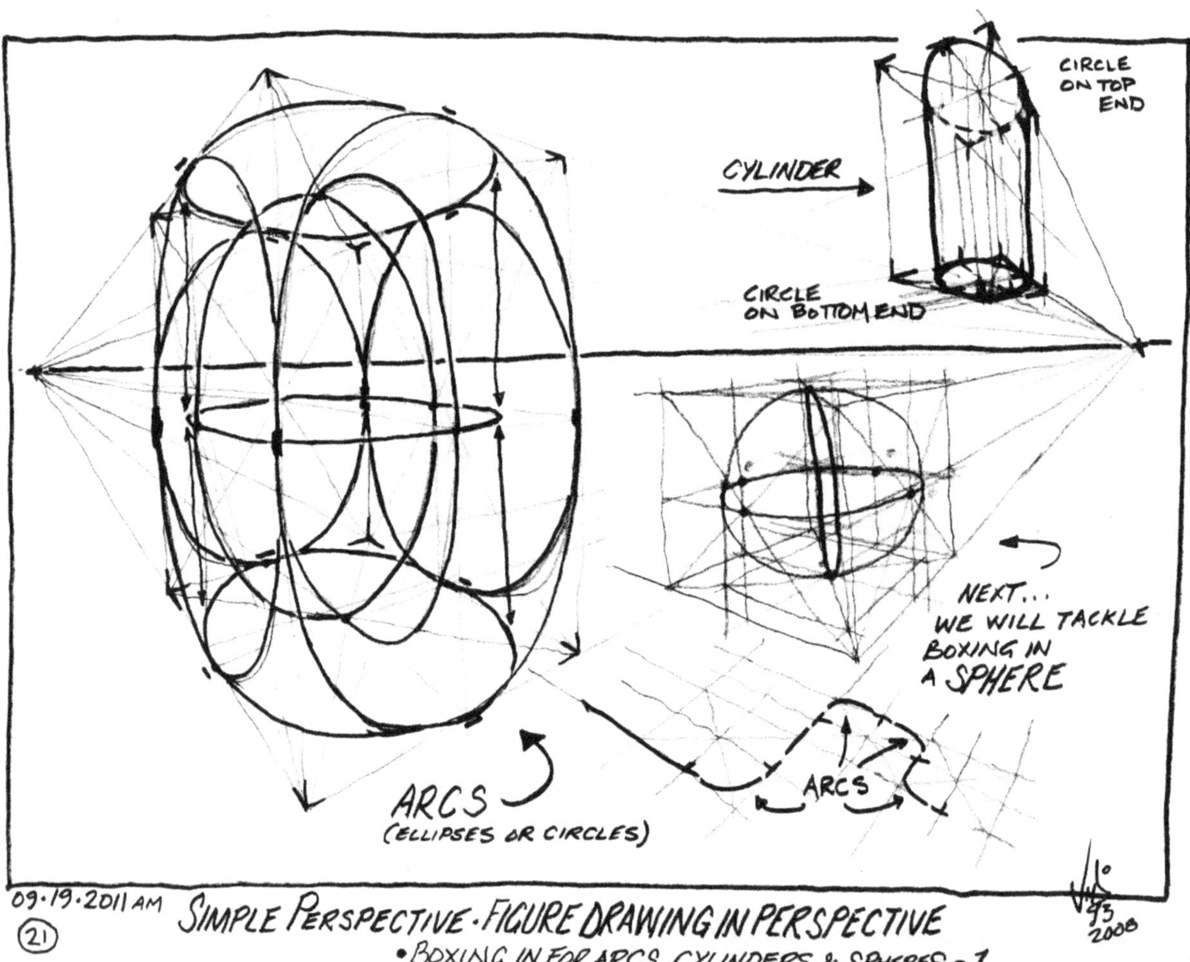

09.19.2011 AM (21) SIMPLE PERSPECTIVE · FIGURE DRAWING IN PERSPECTIVE
• BOXING IN FOR ARCS, CYLINDERS & SPHERES -1

Figure Drawing in Perspective

Boxing in for Arcs, Cylinders and Spheres - 1

As a figure can be made up of the basic shapes of cylinders and spheres, locating these shapes in perspective allows one to carve out the figure from the basic shapes by connecting them with smooth arcs.

This is a bit of a repeat of the previous exercise, but well worth touching upon again. The cylinder on the top right of the illustration is created in a box with a circle at each end. The outer limits of the cylinder are found at the extreme limits at each opposite end of the circles.

The drawing on the left side of the illustration shows all the ellipses that can be found in a bounding box. There is an ellipse on each of the top, bottom and four sides of the bounding box. Since the bounding box has been halved to find the nodes there are three more ellipses that can be drawn within the bounding box. One is vertical and recedes to the left vanishing point, another is vertical and recedes to the right vanishing point, and a third is horizontal. This makes there a total of nine circles possible within one bounding box. Be careful to choose the correct ellipse or circle when one is creating a drawing.

The shear number of possible arcs must be navigated by the artist and this is why computer illustration is not any easier than hand drawing, although more precise, because the artist must be able to find the ellipses in the maze of computer generated lines just as the artist must be able to find the ellipses in the maze of hand drawn lines.

BOXING IN A SPHERE HAS BEEN ACCIMPLISHED IN THE EPILOGUE BEGINNING ON PAGE 147.

THIS EXERCISE EMPHASIZES AND REINFORCES THE IMPORTANCE OF THE LAND THE CIRCLE EXERCISES ON PAGES 12 AND 13 OF THIS BOOK.

Epilogue: At the end of this book, in the epilogue, there IS a solution for how to place a perfect sphere into a perspective drawing, by placing it in a perfect cube, calculated graphically.

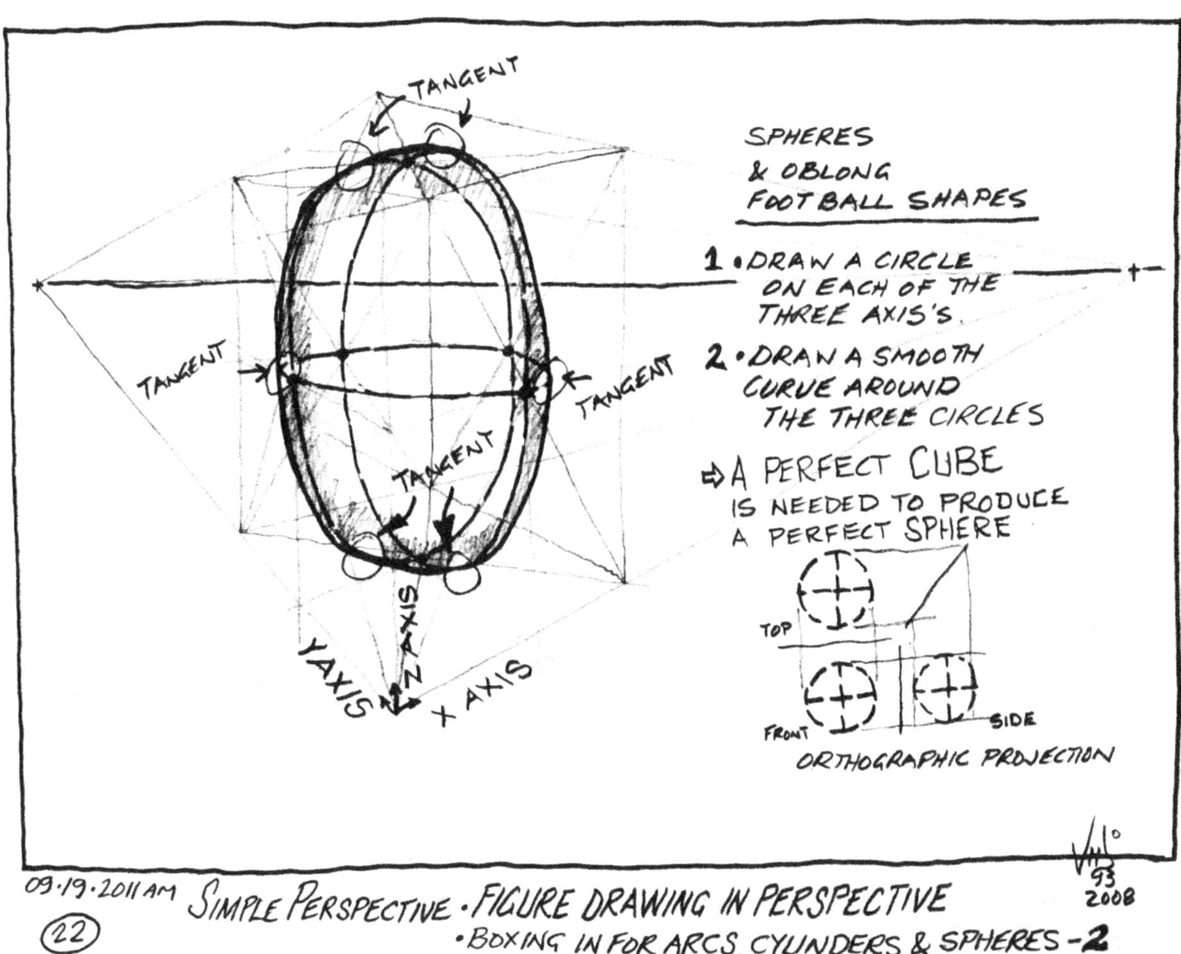

TANGENT
SPHERES
& OBLONG
FOOTBALL SHAPES
1 • DRAW A CIRCLE
ON EACH OF THE
THREE AXIS'S.
2 • DRAW A SMOOTH
CURVE AROUND
THE THREE CIRCLES
TANGENT
TANGENT
TANGENT
⇨ A PERFECT CUBE
IS NEEDED TO PRODUCE
A PERFECT SPHERE
TOP
FRONT
SIDE
ORTHOGRAPHIC PROJECTION
Y AXIS
Z AXIS
X AXIS
93
2008

09.19.2011 AM SIMPLE PERSPECTIVE • FIGURE DRAWING IN PERSPECTIVE
(22) • BOXING IN FOR ARCS, CYLINDERS & SPHERES - 2

Figure Drawing in Perspective

Boxing in for Arcs, Cylinders and Spheres - 2

As a figure can be made up of the basic shapes of cylinders, ellipses and spheres, locating these shapes in perspective allows one to carve out the figure from the basic shapes by connecting them with smooth arcs. Spheres are an important basic shape from which one can carve out a figure.

This is a bit of a repeat of the previous exercise, but well worth touching upon again. A sphere may be located within a bounding box that is a perfect cube. I wish I could come up with a way of graphically calculating a cube in perspective. Oh well . . . .

In the illustration above, the three internal ellipses have been drawn to locate the football spherical shape. There is a vertical ellipse that recedes to the left vanishing point, a vertical ellipse that recedes to the right vanishing point, and a horizontal ellipse.

To draw the outline of the football spherical shape, one must draw a smooth arc tangent to the extreme limits of the three ellipses. There are two points of tangency at the top - one for each of the vertical ellipses. There are two points of tangency in the middle - one at the left extreme of the horizontal ellipse and one at the right extreme of the horizontal ellipse. And finally, there are two points of tangency at the bottom - one for each of the vertical ellipses. Draw the outline of the spherical football shape by drawing a smooth arc tangent at these six points.

Note that the top of the shape is not the node at the top of the bounding box, because one is looking up at the top of the shape and the top node is hidden behind the shape. The same goes for the bottom node.

Epilogue: At the end of this book, in the epilogue, there IS a solution for how to place a perfect sphere into a perspective drawing, by placing it in a perfect cube, calculated graphically.

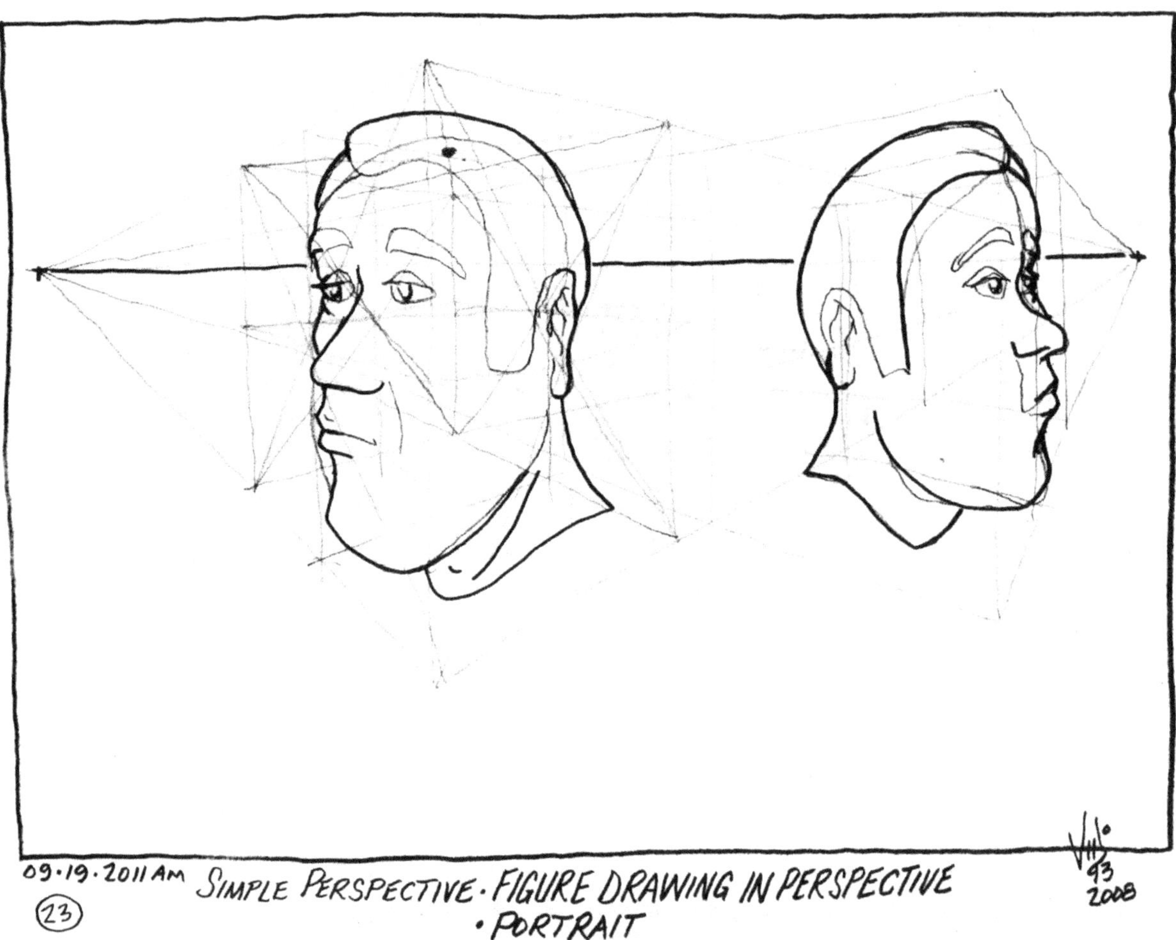

09.19.2011 AM SIMPLE PERSPECTIVE · FIGURE DRAWING IN PERSPECTIVE · PORTRAIT

(23)

Figure Drawing in Perspective

Portrait

Portraits are dealt with more thoroughly in Textbook A , but it is worth looking at portraits from the point of view of using perspective .

The idea of carving out the figure or portrait from basic shapes that are located within a bounding box is paramount for locating figures and portraits in perspective . Spheres are an important basic shape on which to build a portrait .

If one can draw a sphere in perspective, one may locate the centre line of the face, both vertically and horizontally, in perspective . Dropping the face and jaw from the basic sphere that locates the cranium, is also done in perspective by carving them out of a bounding box .

A good example is the line of the mouth . This is generally a horizontal line, that may recede to a vanishing point, so should be drawn accordingly . As well, the horizontal line locating the eyes should also recede to a vanishing point . And a line from the eyes and a line from the base of the nose, should recede to a vanishing point and help to locate the ears . This can all be done by carving out the shapes from the bounding box .

On the one hand, the reader may be disappointed by the quality of my illustrations, but on the other hand, one may take my drawings as a jumping off point and try to improve upon them, rather than be intimidated by them . Keep on drawing! !

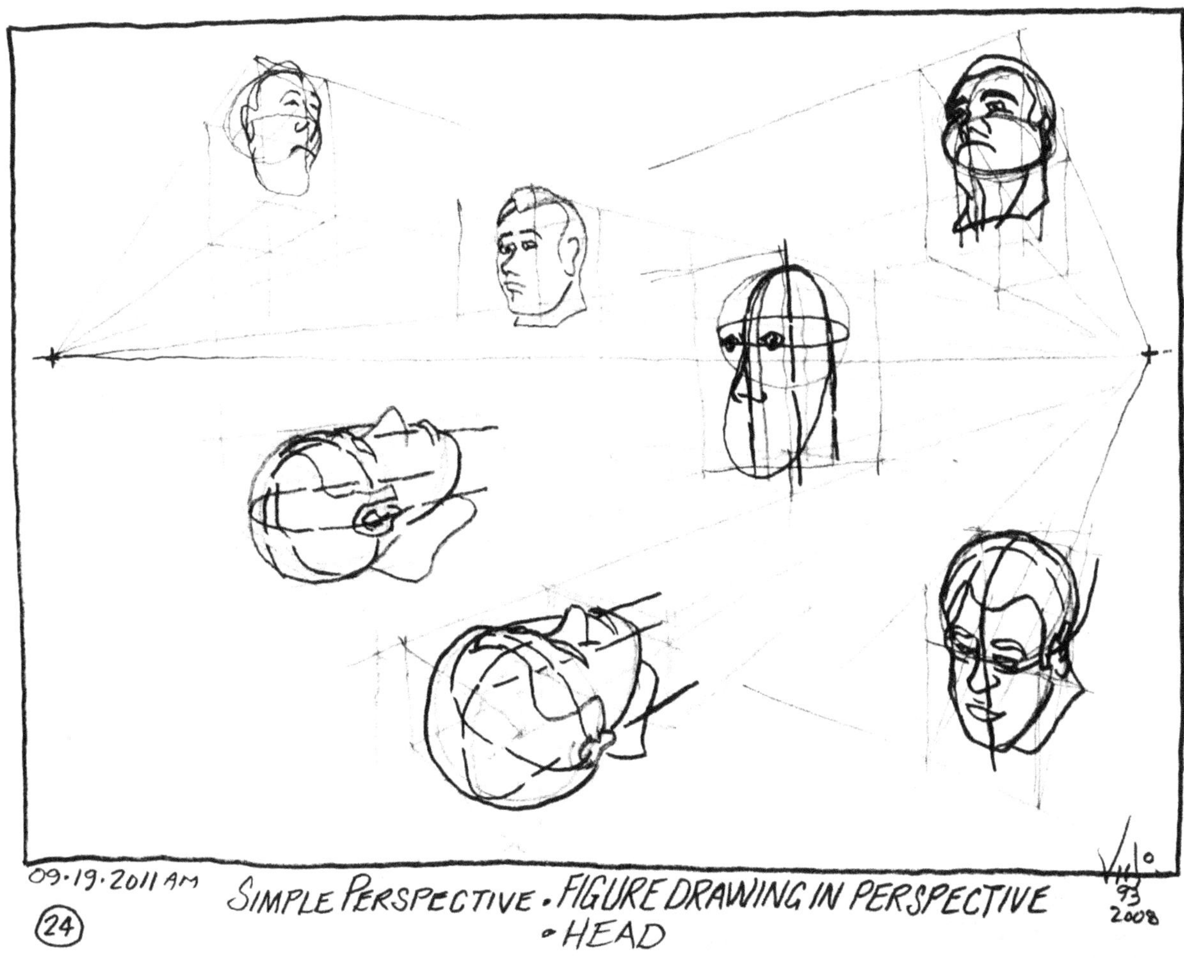

SIMPLE PERSPECTIVE • FIGURE DRAWING IN PERSPECTIVE • HEAD

Figure Drawing in Perspective

Head

Portraits are dealt with more thoroughly in Textbook A, but it is important to be able to locate the head in perspective.

The idea of carving out the figure or portrait from basic shapes that are located within a bounding box is paramount for locating figures and portraits in perspective. Spheres are an important basic shape on which to build a head.

Since it is easier to draw a box in perspective, always draw a perspective bounding box around a head, to help locate the features of the head. Keep in mind the basic ideas of perspective and do not become overburdened by graphically calculating all the details. One eye will generally be smaller and above or below the other eye, depending on the point of view. The ear is in a position perspectively relative to the eyes and nose. The mouth may be horizontal in perspective.

One need not draw an entire perspective field just to locate a head, but rather be aware of where the parallel lines in parallel planes converge, and try to keep them to a single point of convergence, usually off of the page.

On the one hand, the reader may be disappointed by the quality of my illustrations, but on the other hand, one may take my drawings as a jumping off point and try to improve upon them, rather than be intimidated by them. Keep on drawing!!

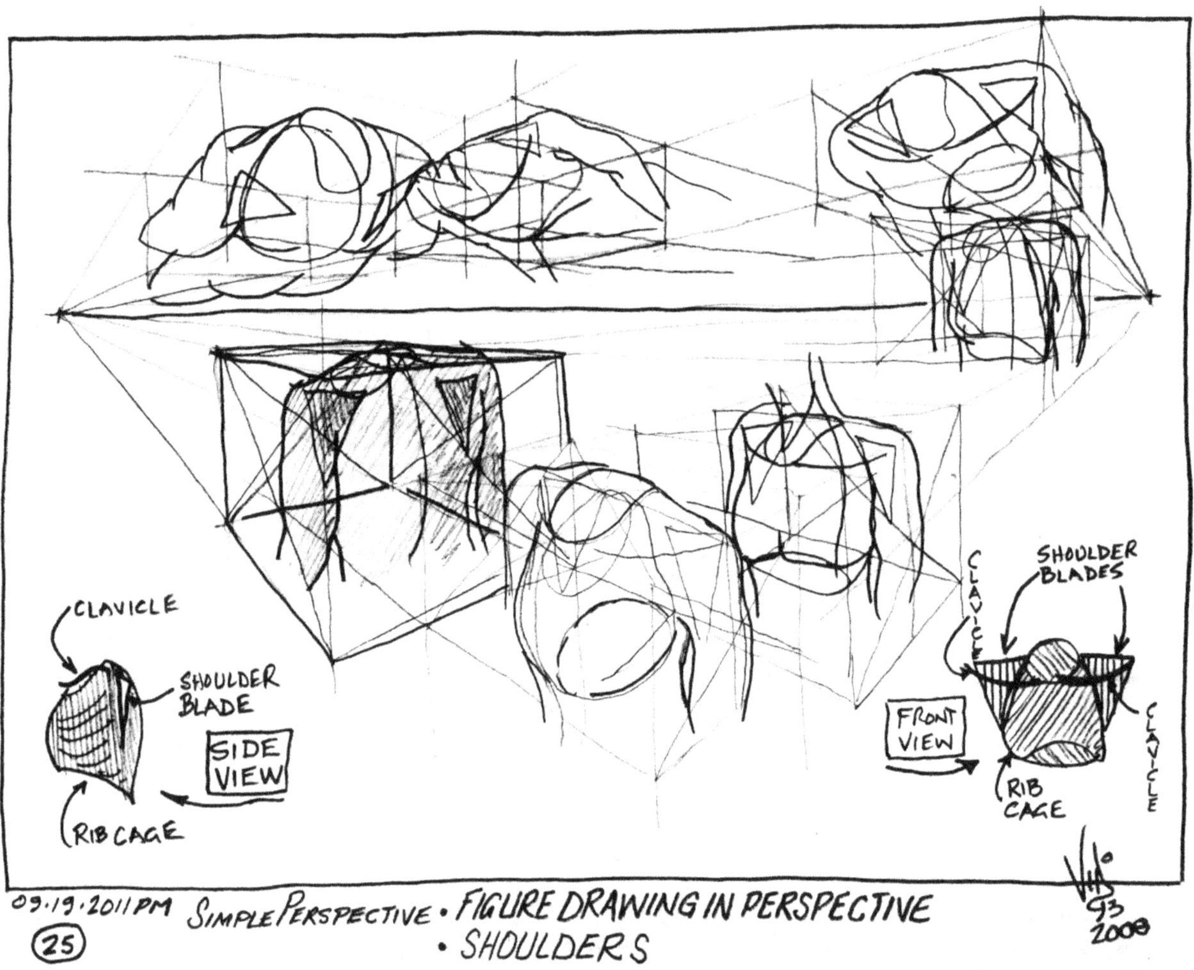

Figure Drawing in Perspective

Shoulders

Shoulders, or the shoulder carriage, can once again, be carved out of a bounding box that is drawn in perspective .

The idea of carving out the figure or portrait from basic shapes that are located within a bounding box is paramount for locating figures and portraits in perspective .

Since it is easier to draw a box in perspective, always draw a perspective bounding box around the shoulders . Keep in mind the basic ideas of perspective and do not become overburdened by graphically calculating all the details .

There are some basic shapes that make up the shoulder carriage, that is hung on the spine . The two shoulder blades can be considered as two triangles . The rib cage is somewhat egg shaped with upper and lower openings . The clavicle joins the shoulder blades to the front of the upper rib cage opening .

One need not draw an entire perspective field just to locate the shoulders, but rather be aware of where the parallel lines in parallel planes converge, and try to keep them to a single point of convergence, usually off of the page .

On the one hand, the reader may be disappointed by the quality of my illustrations, but on the other hand, one may take my drawings as a jumping off point and try to improve upon them, rather than be intimidated by them . Keep on drawing! !

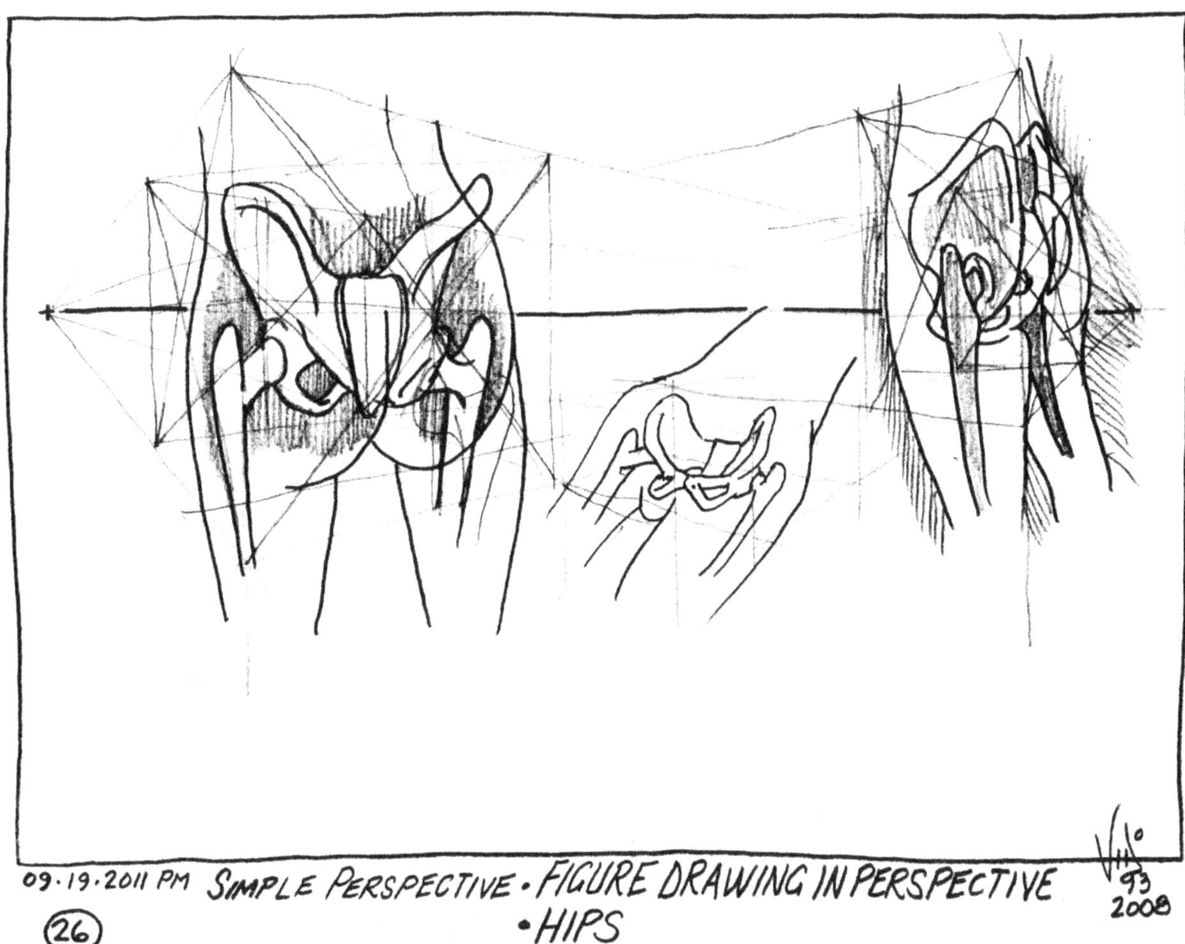

09.19.2011 PM SIMPLE PERSPECTIVE • FIGURE DRAWING IN PERSPECTIVE • HIPS

(26)

Figure Drawing in Perspective

Hips

Hips, or the hip carriage, can once again, be carved out of a bounding box that is drawn in perspective .

The idea of carving out the figure or portrait from basic shapes that are located within a bounding box is paramount for locating figures and portraits in perspective .

Since it is easier to draw a box in perspective, always draw a perspective bounding box around the hips . Keep in mind the basic ideas of perspective and do not become overburdened by graphically calculating all the details .

There are some basic shapes the make up the hip carriage, that bundles up the gut and rests on the legs . The hip carriage is like a bowl that is low on the front and high at the outer sides of the back . The spine runs down to the tailbone . The leg bones jut out and have an upper knob, before travelling down toward the ground .

One need not draw an entire perspective field just to locate the hips, but rather be aware of where the parallel lines in parallel planes converge, and try to keep them to a single point of convergence, usually off of the page .

On the one hand, the reader may be disappointed by the quality of my illustrations, but on the other hand, one may take my drawings as a jumping off point and try to improve upon them, rather than be intimidated by them . Keep on drawing!!

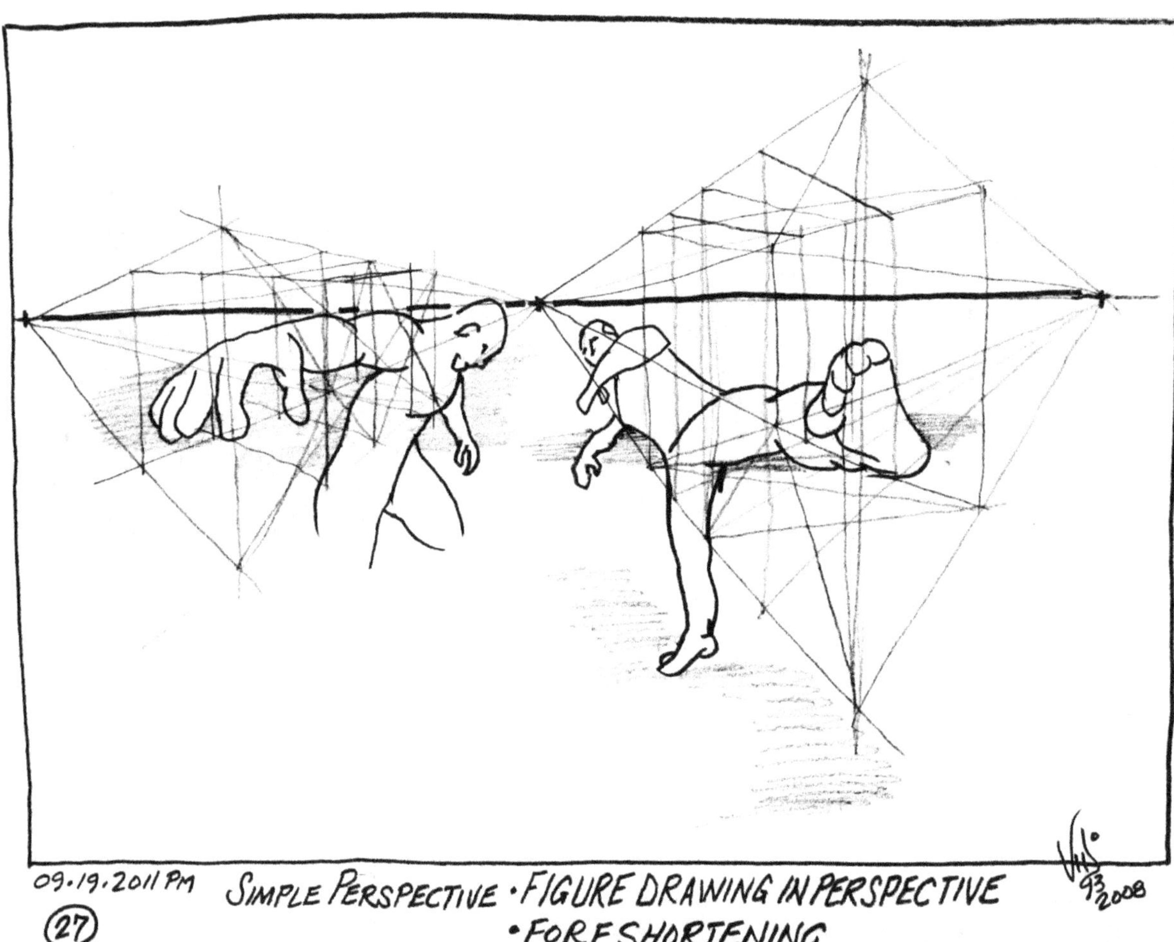

09.19.2011 PM SIMPLE PERSPECTIVE • FIGURE DRAWING IN PERSPECTIVE • FORESHORTENING

(27)

Figure Drawing in Perspective

Foreshortening

Any part of the figure, as well as the entire figure, can once again, be carved out of a bounding box that is drawn in perspective .

The idea of carving out the figure or portrait from basic shapes that are located within a bounding box is paramount for locating figures and portraits in perspective .

Since it is easier to draw a box in perspective, always draw a perspective bounding box around the figure and the various parts of the figure . Keep in mind the basic ideas of perspective and do not become overburdened by graphically calculating all the details .

There are some basic shapes the make up the figure, such as ovoids made up of ellipses, spheres made up of circles, cylinders and egg shapes, as well as bounding boxes . It is easier to locate a shape within a bounding box that is drawn in perspective, than it is to locate a shape by itself in perspective .

One need not draw an entire perspective field just to locate the figure, but rather be aware of where the parallel lines in parallel planes converge, and try to keep them to a single point of convergence, usually off of the page .

On the one hand, the reader may be disappointed by the quality of my illustrations, but on the other hand, one may take my drawings as a jumping off point and try to improve upon them, rather than be intimidated by them . Keep on drawing! !

Keep on Drawing:

This is the third of a series of pamphlets created for the Oakville OASIS Drawing Bee, and this series is intended to overcome the hurdle of beginning to draw. When one is faced with what they are going to do all day, they can flip through these pamphlets and get engrossed with the ideas of what they could be drawing.

Drawing skills are very transferable to other areas of life, but the most important transferable skills are the emotional ones of accepting one's shortcomings and carrying on to overcome them with practice and acceptance of their level of ability. No one ever got better at anything by not practicing.

As well, as the mind becomes involved in the drawing, there is a peace and almost relaxed atmosphere created, which is refreshing and beneficial to the rest of one's day.

A friend from secondary school, who went on to become an actuary, told me he thinks of me when he is bored, and wonders what I would do in such a boring situation. I was known for coming up with interesting activities, when called upon. Drawing is a great activity that anyone can do and it fills the time as well as refreshes the spirit, if one can get started and involved.

Finally, one rule I like to promote is for anyone who is critical of their drawing skill, and that is to never throw out a drawing, just hide it or put it away if one is frustrated. This is because when one completes a drawing, they are very much aware of how far the drawing came short of the image they had in their mind. But after a period of time, they forget the image they had in their head and will only see their accomplishments that they achieved in the drawing. This is encouraging and promotes further drawing.

__Drawing on the Right Side of the Brain__ Author: ***Betty Edwards***
ISBN-13: **9780874775136** ISBN-10: **0874775132** Edition: **Revised** Binding: **Paperback**
Publisher: **Tarcher** Published: **May 1989** List Price: **$15.95**

The book cited above, is great at getting one better at drawing, but eventually, your visual vocabulary will need to be expanded, and as far as anatomy goes, I cannot recommend a better reference than the book cited below.

__Atlas of Human Anatomy for the Artist__ Author: ***Stephen Rogers Peck***
ISBN-13: **9780195030952** ISBN-10: **0195030958** Edition: **1** Binding: **Paperback**
Publisher: **Oxford University Press** Published: **February 1982** List Price: **$19.95**

I would strongly recommend studying this book on anatomy, by memorizing the names of all the bones in the body, as well as the names of all the muscles in the body, so that you will be more fluent in the language of drawing people.

Other Drawings

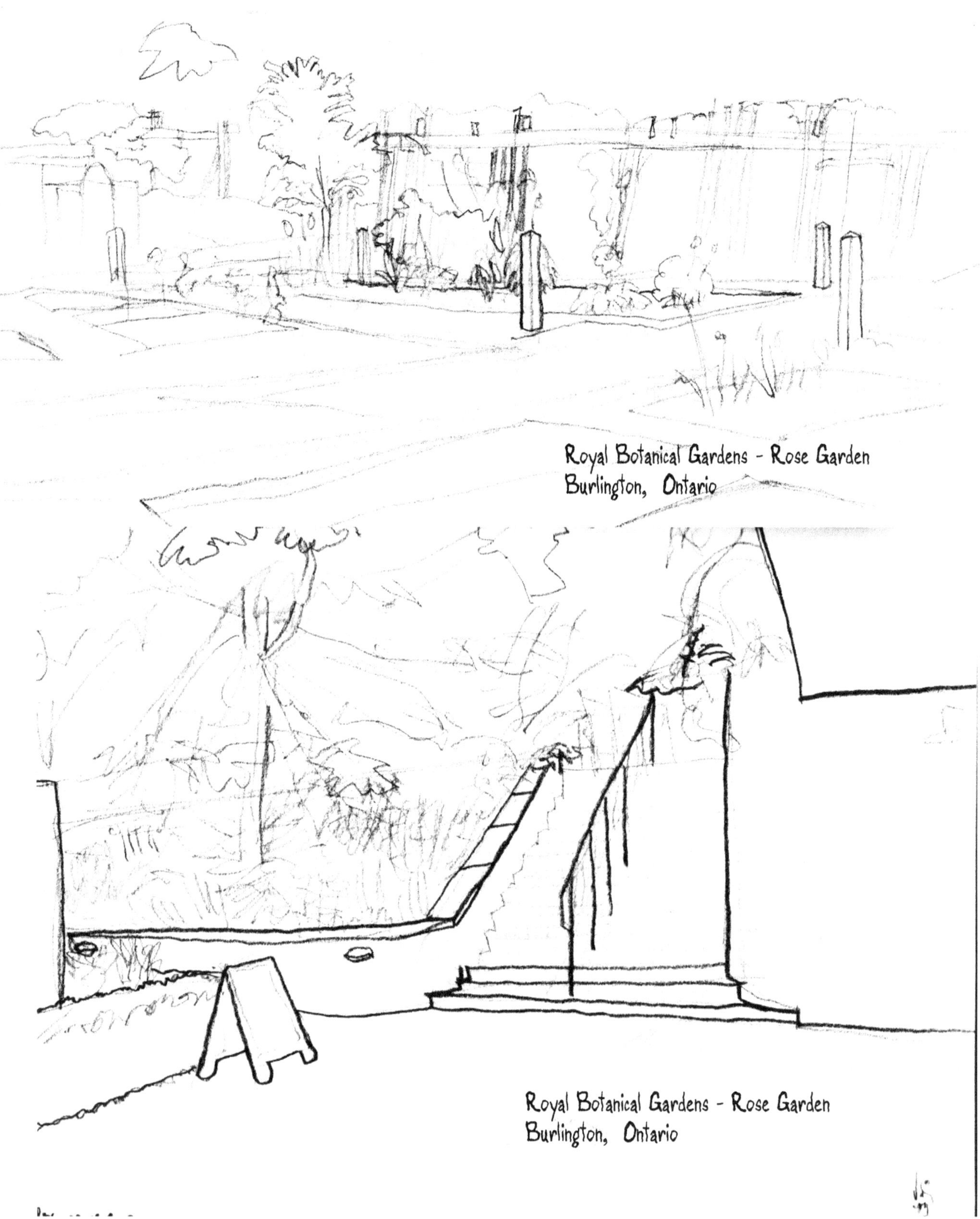

Royal Botanical Gardens - Rose Garden
Burlington, Ontario

Royal Botanical Gardens - Rose Garden
Burlington, Ontario

Other Drawings

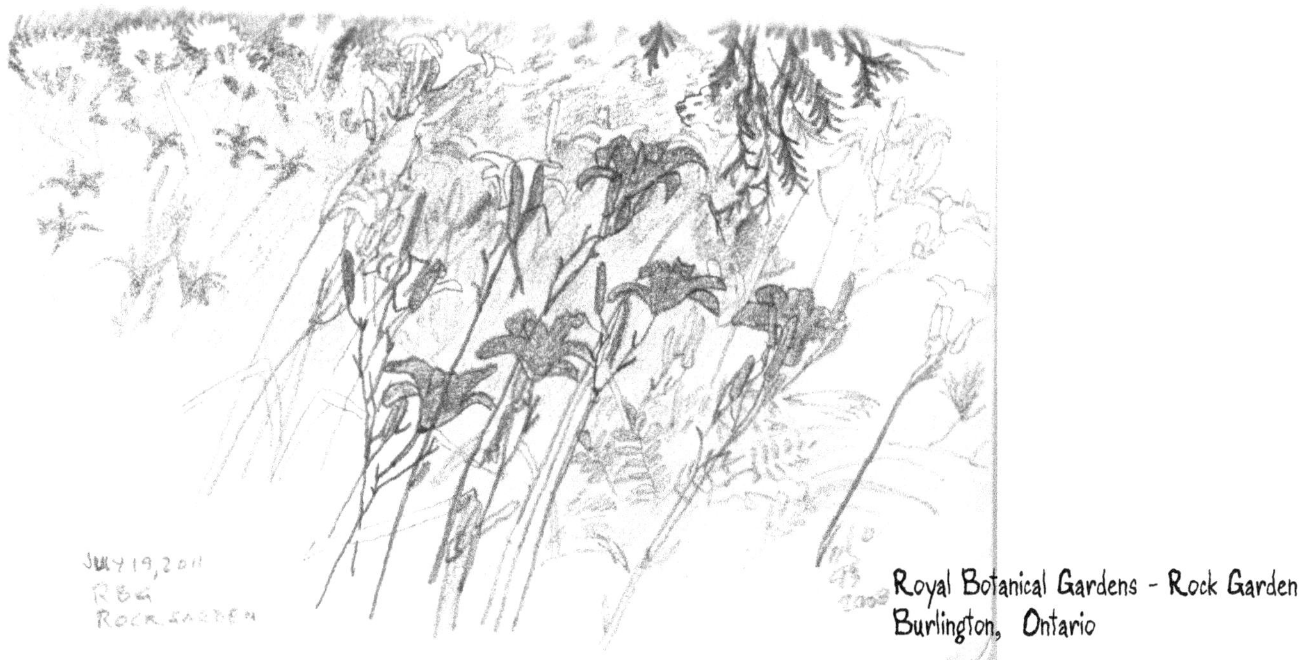

Royal Botanical Gardens - Rock Garden
Burlington, Ontario

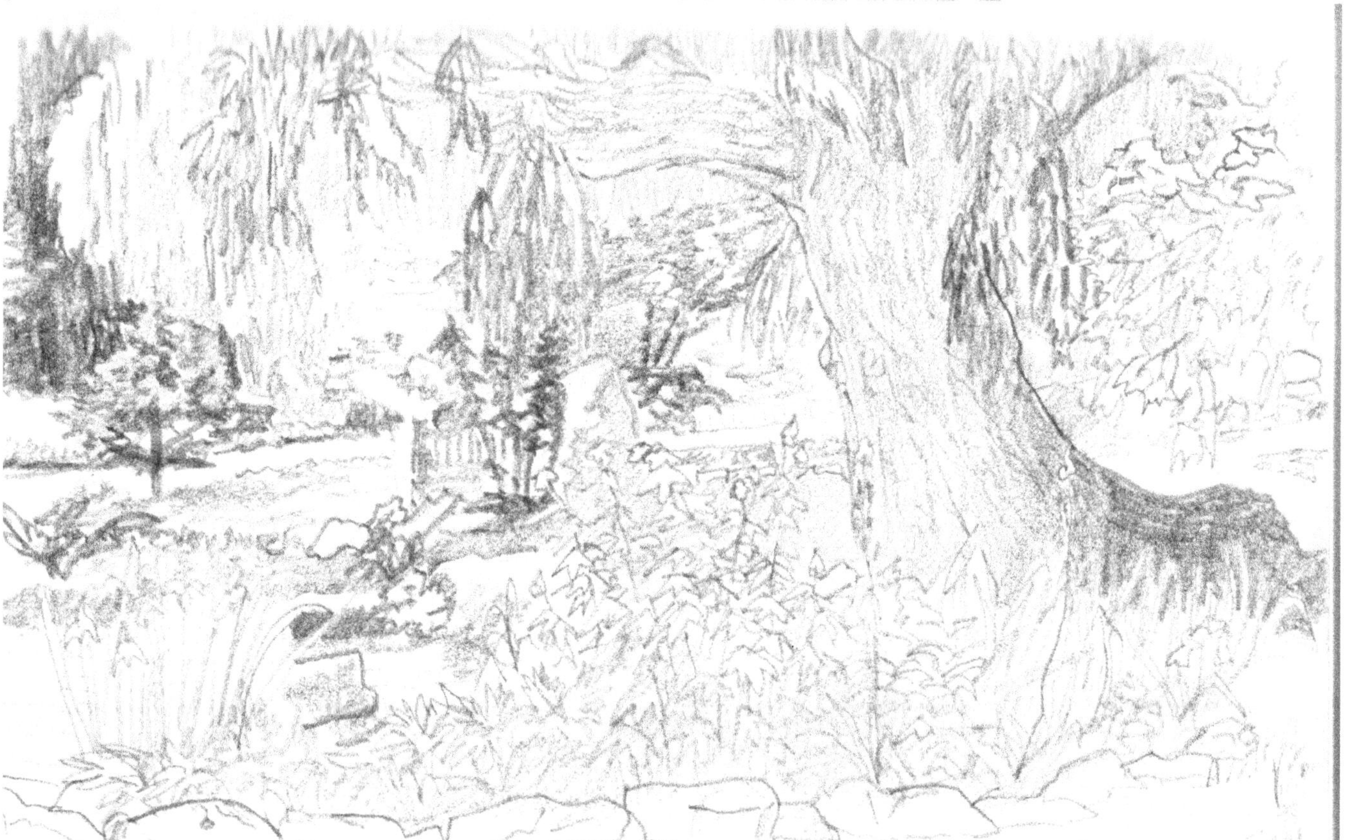

Royal Botanical Gardens - Rock Garden
Burlington, Ontario

INDEX - - - -
TEXTBOOK --C--
Simple Perspective

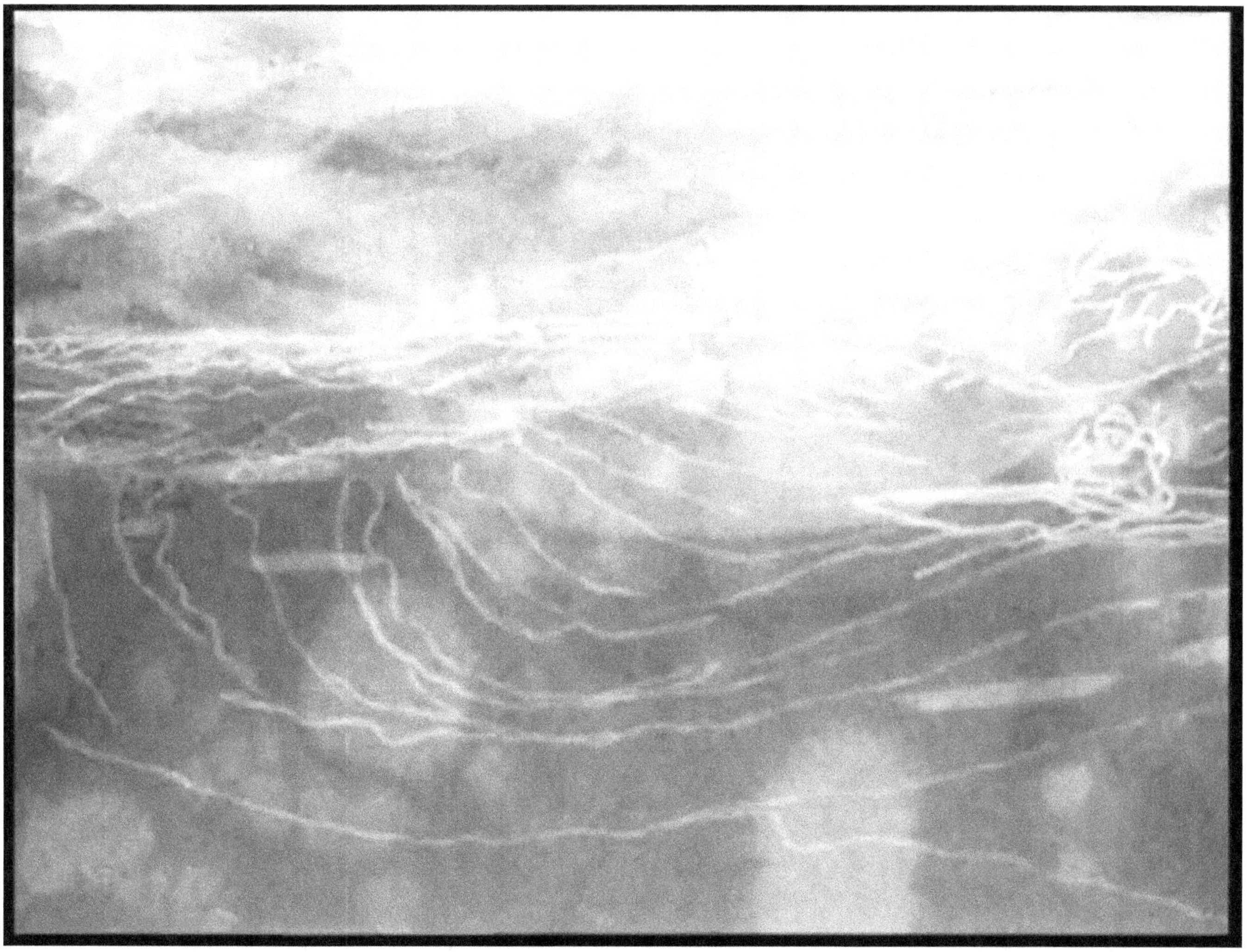

Oakville OASIS Drawing Bee

LANDSCAPES
Textbook --D--

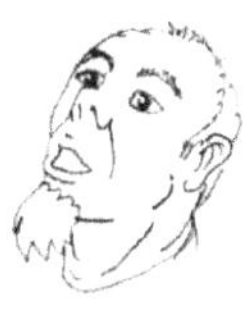

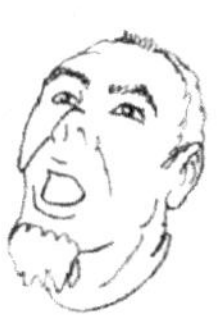

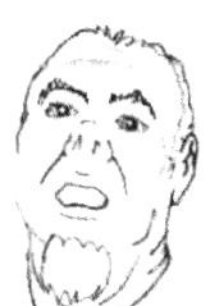

04/11/2011 PM

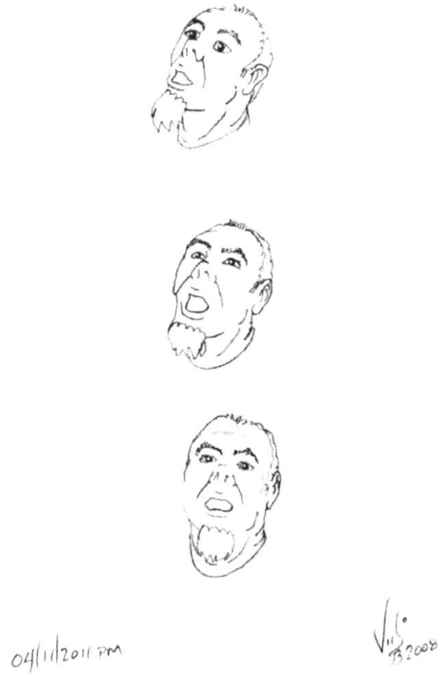

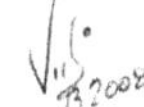

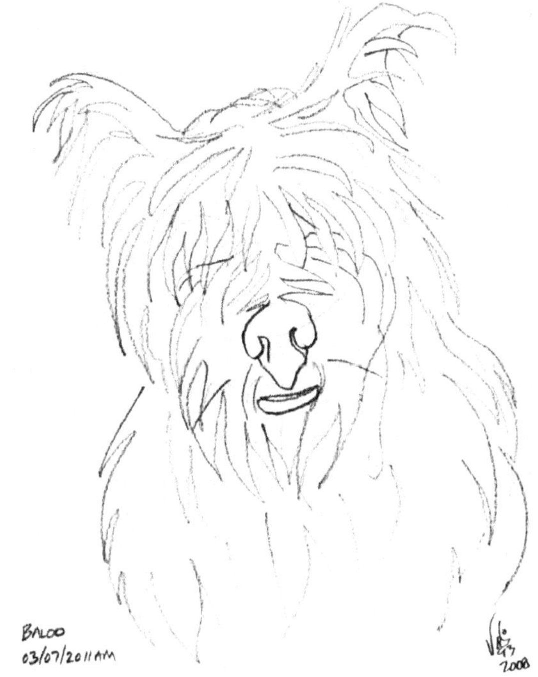

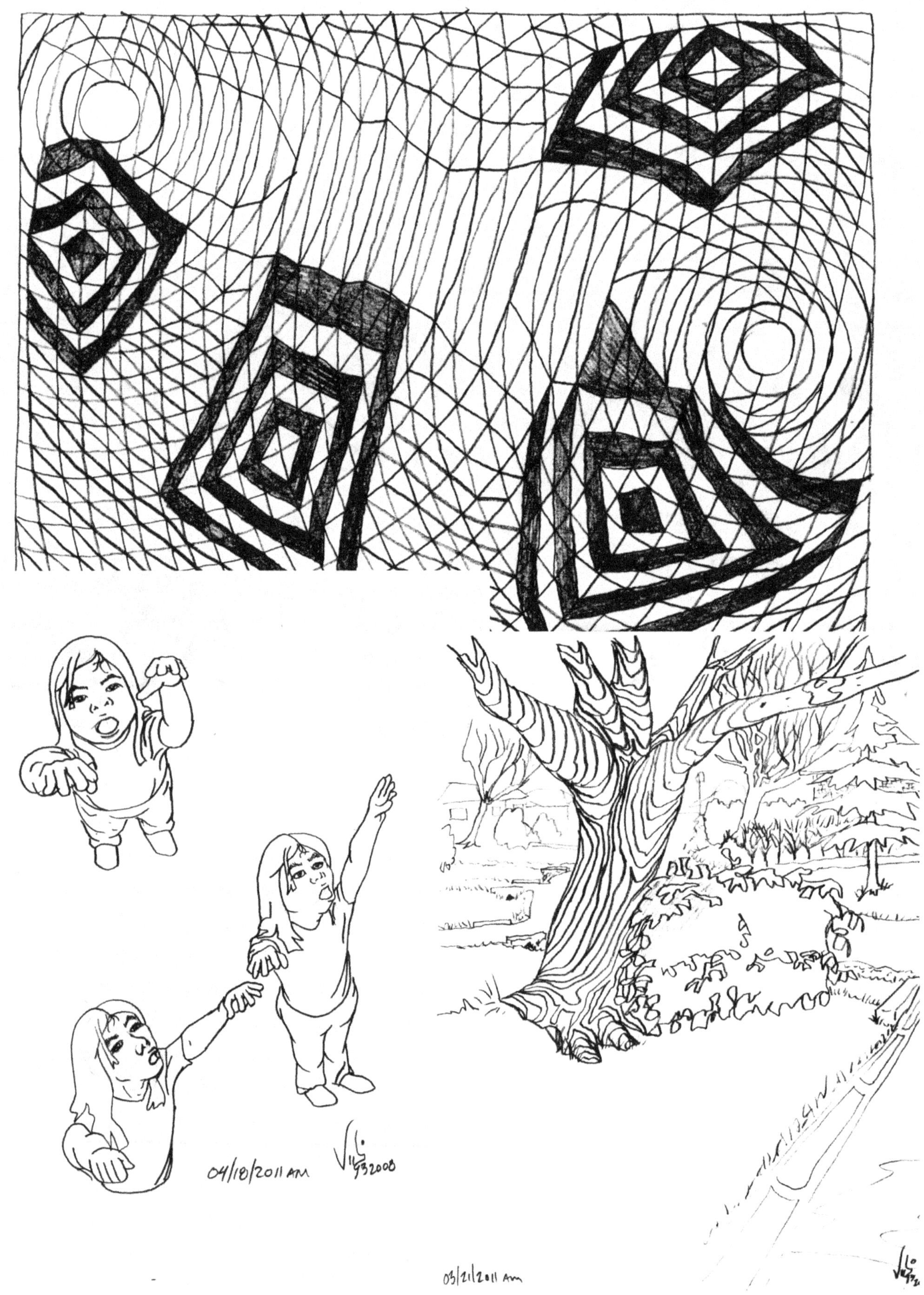

03/21/2011 Am

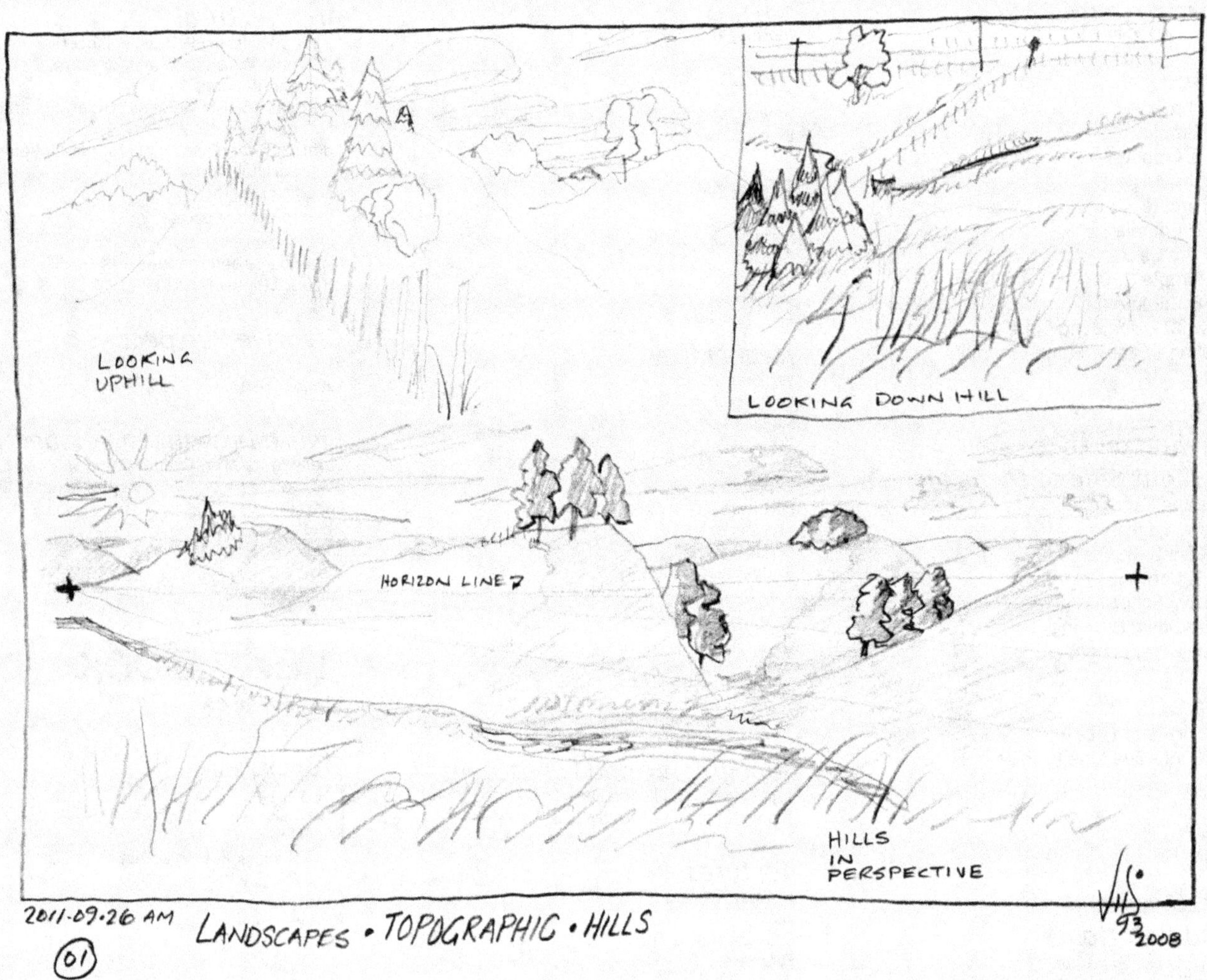

TOPOGRAPHIC
Hills

The trick to illustrating hills around one is to correctly orient the features in perspective. This means that the half sphere of a hill is oriented in perspective, with the plane on which it sits receding in one way or another according to whether one is looking up, out, or down a hill.

As well, a vertical vanishing point, for lines receding in a vertical plane, will orient the features on the hill such as trees or poles, as well as structures.

Hills themselves sit in a perspective plane, and if aligned with one another, will illustrate the perspective of that plane.

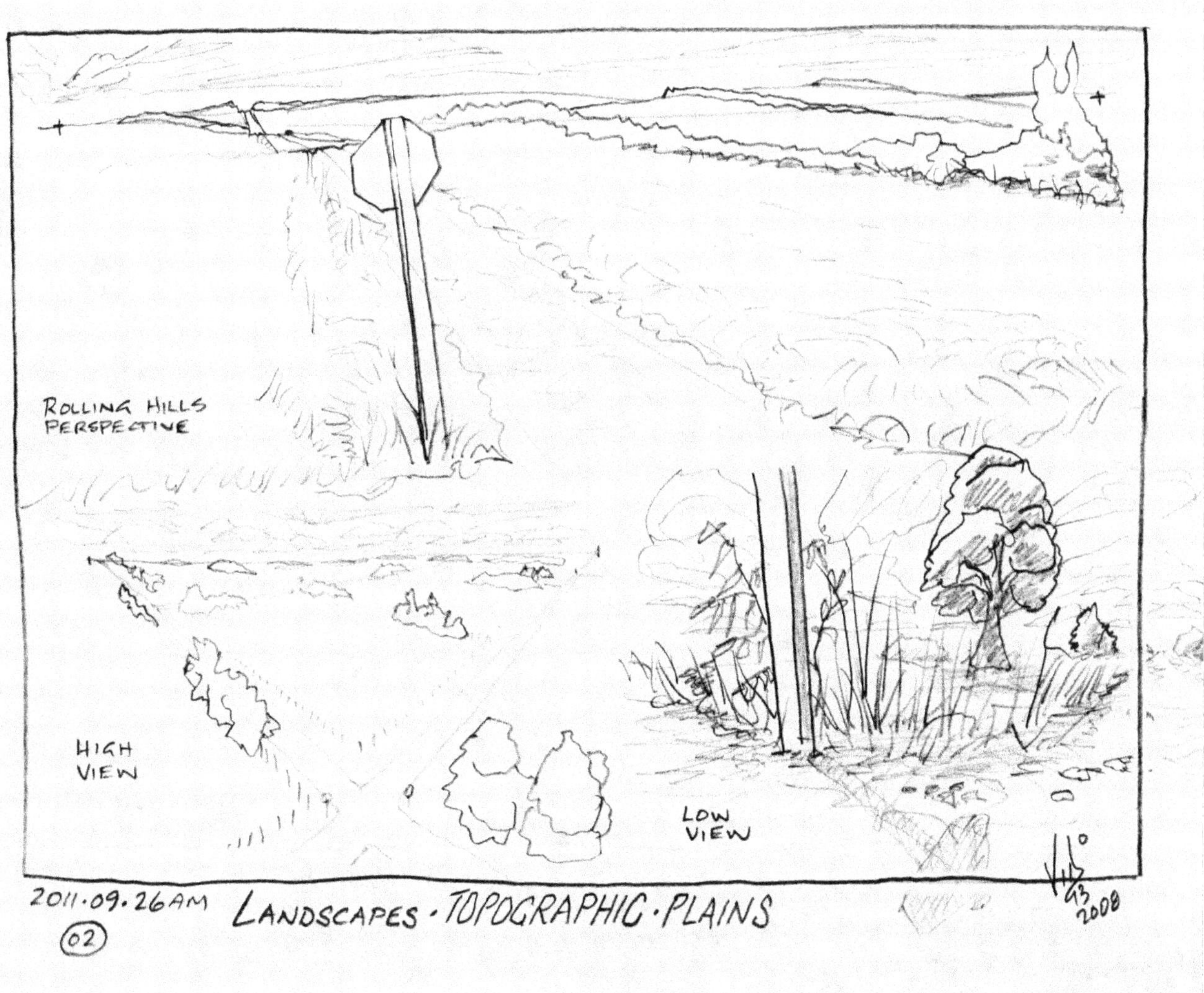

TOPOGRAPHIC

Plains

The trick to illustrating plains around one is to find something to illustrate . For what it's worth it may as well be an illustration of the ocean from the deck of a ship . This means that the view is mainly across a perspective plain . Hopefully there will be roads with hedgerows to illustrate that plane . But in Europe the roads do not follow a grid pattern so they become like random contours across the face of the plain .

Whenever I have been in the prairies, I have become very aware of the sky . This means, when illustrating a plain, pay attention to what the sky is doing, especially at dawn and dusk . Weather may be another part of one's drawing that can fill out an image .

If possible, a variety of views from various elevations can help to illustrate the plain .

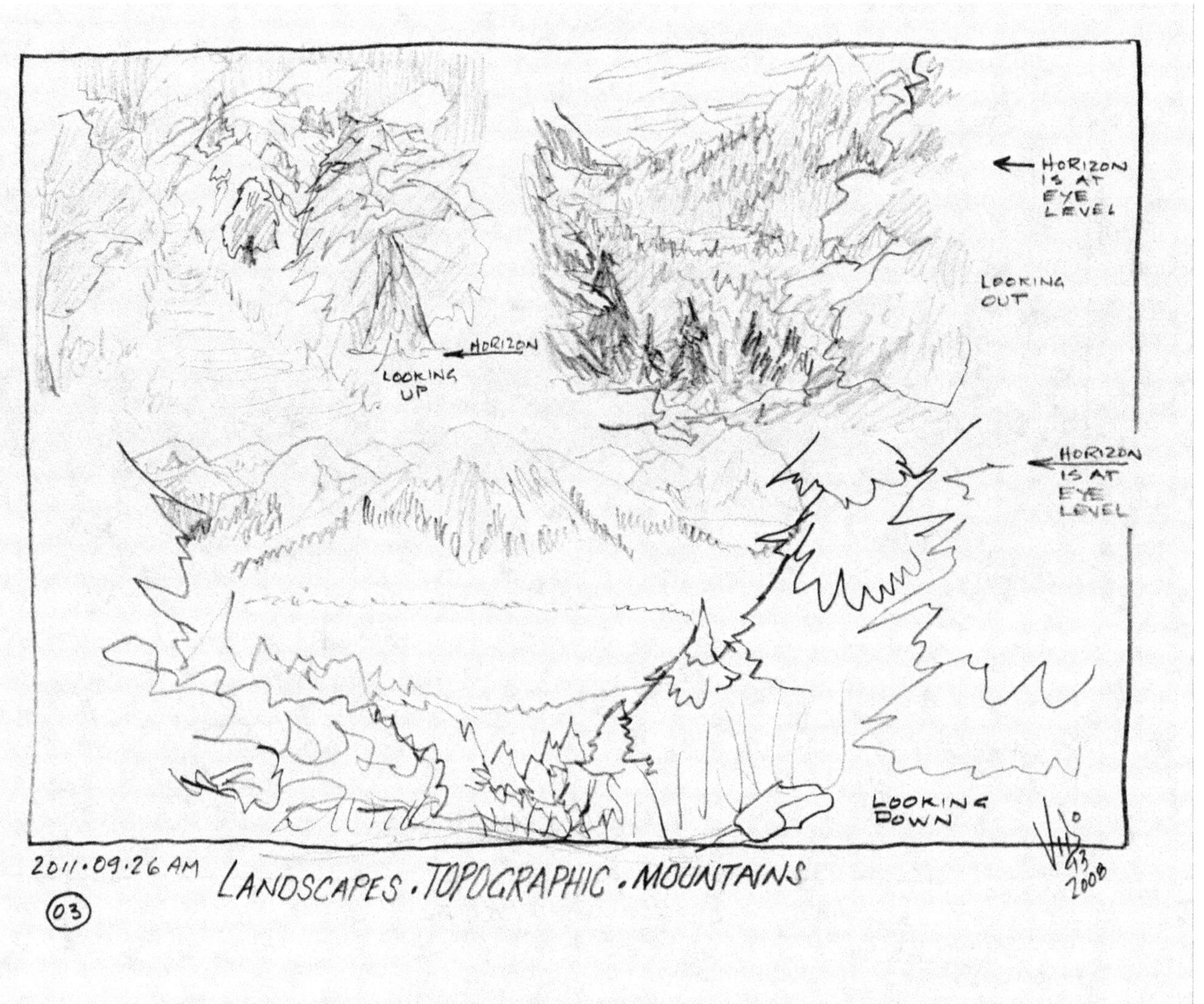

TOPOGRAPHIC

Mountains

Mountains can be so massive that it is hard to illustrate them in a regular sized drawing . One finds that if there is not an open view, the mountain becomes an incline obscurring its form . When the vantage point is on a mountain all that can be illustrated is the area below because the mountain obscures its form .

I have illustrated three views of mountains : up, out and down . This is done by positioning the horizon low, midlevel, or high in the drawing .

Because one will likely find their vantage point on some incline when approaching in amongst mountains, the view may likely be up or down, and this means one may need to make use of a vanishing point for vertical lines .

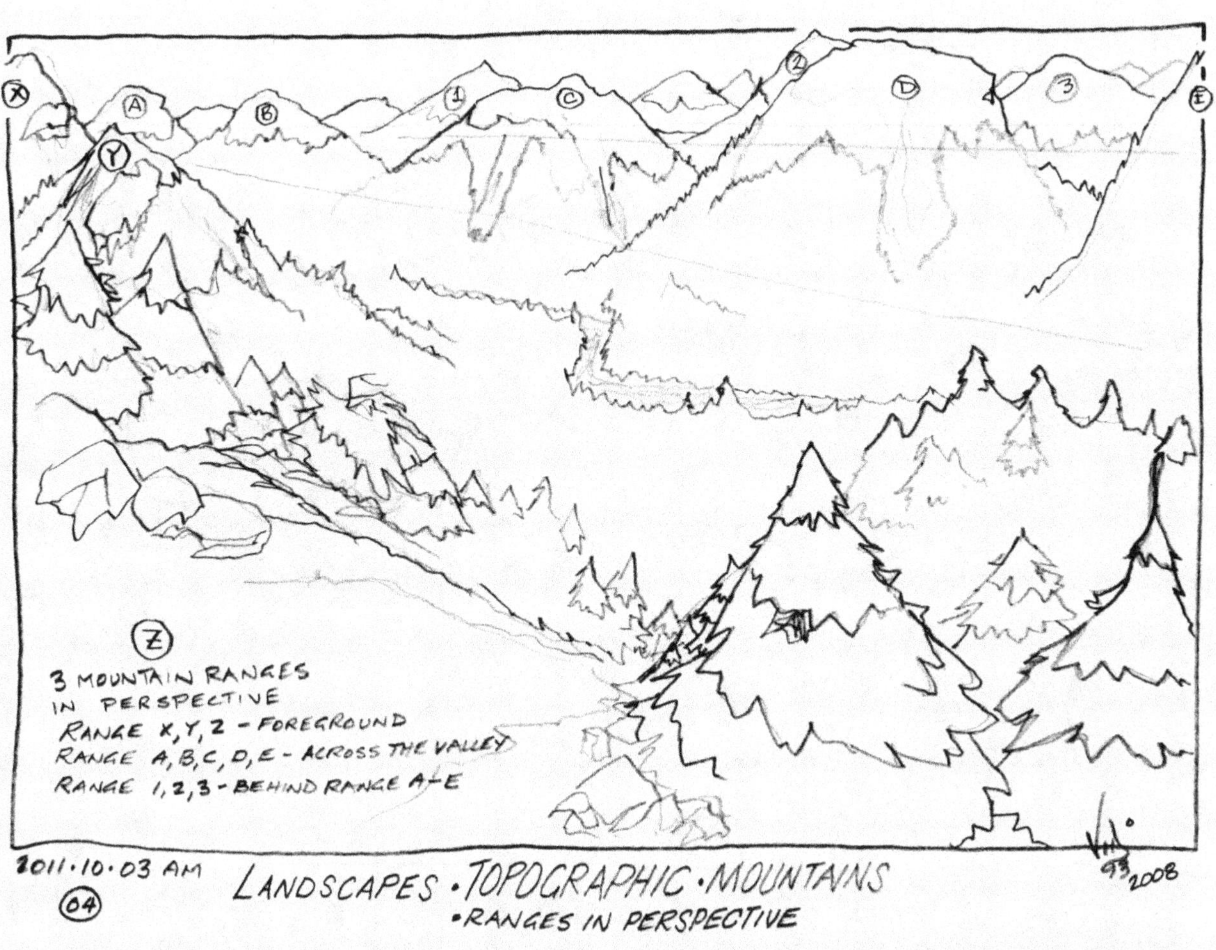

TOPOGRAPHIC

Mountains - Ranges in Perspective

Mountain ranges, although ultimately random, usually confess some sort of regular pattern that can be illustrated in perspective. Either create a pattern, if drawing from the imagination, or find a pattern in the landscape you are drawing. There may be a system of branching valleys that may even form a glacier as the snow sliding down the valleys collects into a glacier where the flow from the higher smaller valleys meets up in a lower larger valley. The pattern of the mountain ranges may be parallel lines, circular, or branching, but regardless, look for a pattern and document it in your drawing of mountain ranges.

As well, small ponds leak down the mountain in brooks that join one another in larger ponds, lakes, streams and eventually rivers. Find these small valleys near the top of the mountain and illustrate them as they grow, continuing down the mountain, joining other valleys as they descend. As well, ridges form patterns as they join up with other features whether ascending to the summit or descending to disappear in the valleys.

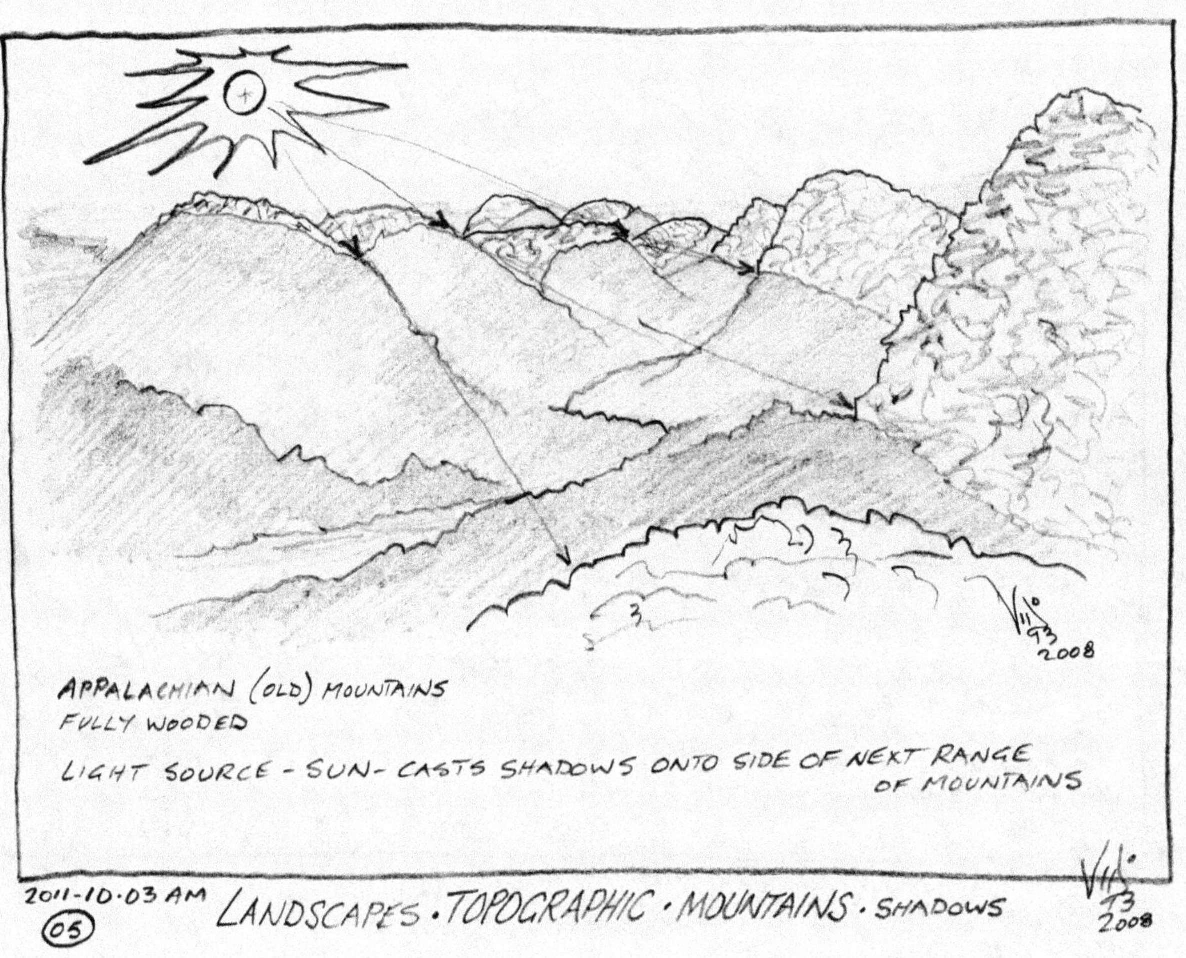

APPALACHIAN (OLD) MOUNTAINS
FULLY WOODED
LIGHT SOURCE - SUN - CASTS SHADOWS ONTO SIDE OF NEXT RANGE OF MOUNTAINS
2011-10-03 AM
05
LANDSCAPES · TOPOGRAPHIC · MOUNTAINS · SHADOWS
2008

TOPOGRAPHIC
Mountains - Shadows

Mountain ranges, unlike plains, cast massive shadows that can be used to illustrate depth in a drawing. Sort out your light source and calculate the cast shadows to illustrated them by varying the textures, contrast and details between the sunlit areas and the large shadow areas.

In the drawing on this page, at the right side, I ommited the cast shadow on the right side of the two mountains on the right ! This detracts from the illusion one should strive to create.

As well as the cast shadows on the mountainsides, other features, such as rivers, lakes, roads, rail lines and bridges will occur both within and outside of such shadows, and as they travel amongst the shadows, they can be made to further add depth to a drawing by accentuating the shadow or sunlight.

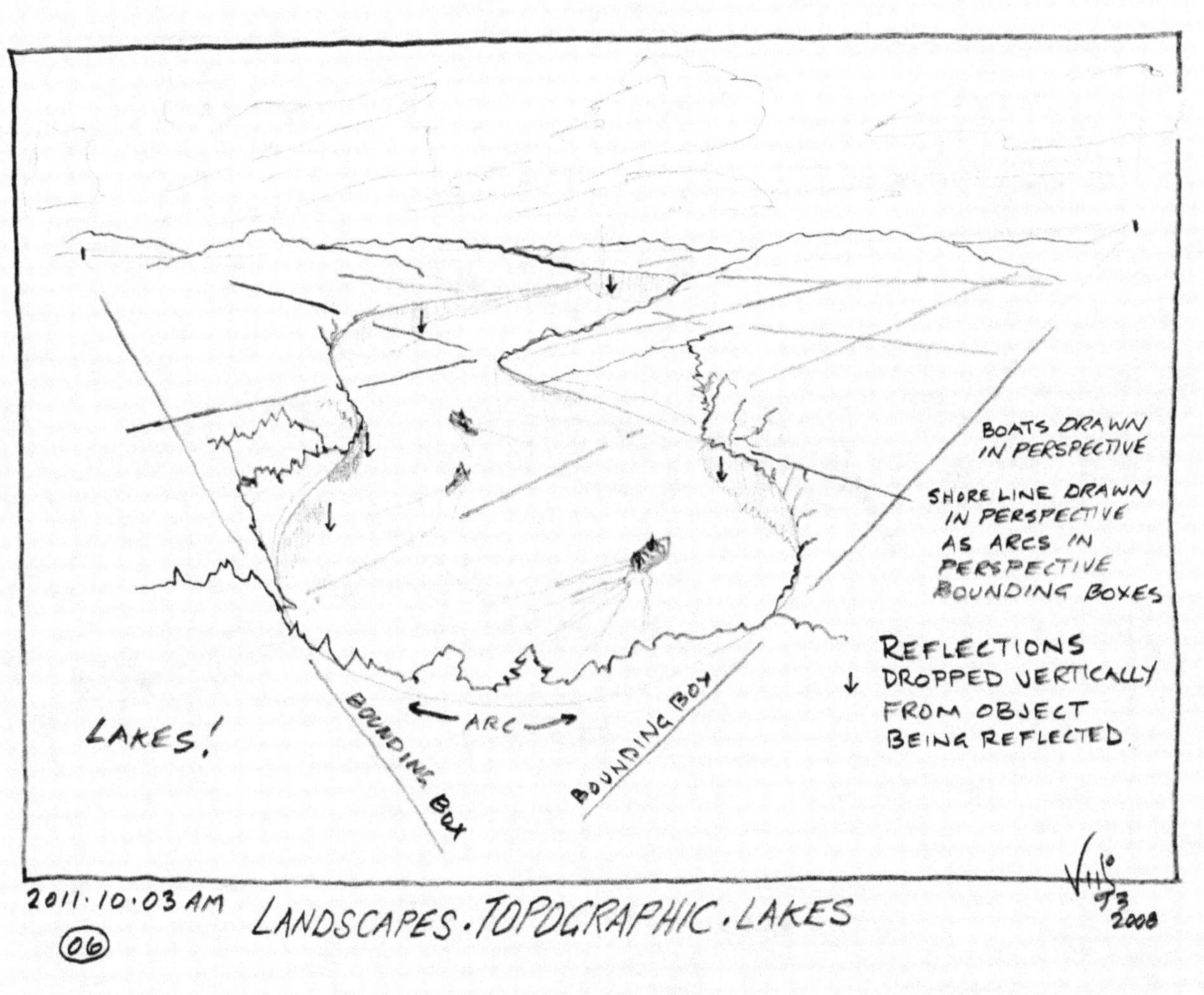
BOATS DRAWN IN PERSPECTIVE
SHORE LINE DRAWN IN PERSPECTIVE AS ARCS IN PERSPECTIVE BOUNDING BOXES
REFLECTIONS
↓ DROPPED VERTICALLY FROM OBJECT BEING REFLECTED.
LAKES!
← ARC →
BOUNDING BOX
BOUNDING BOX
2011·10·03 AM
06
LANDSCAPES·TOPOGRAPHIC·LAKES

TOPOGRAPHIC
Lakes

This is a view from a high vantage point to illustrate how a shoreline can create a perspective area that has interest. Lowering the horizon in the drawing would create a more useful view, but the idea would be the same, with penninsulas passing in front of distant shorelines creating a feeling of depth as well as making the image interesting.

The important thing that this drawing is trying to communicate is that the lake, which is basically identified by its shoreline, has a shoreline that meanders in perspective, and this illusion of perspective is what creates the illusion of a lake in one's drawing.

If one has difficulty tracing the image that should appear on the page to portray the lake in perspective, draw a perspective grid and meander the shoreline back and forth throughout that perspective grid.

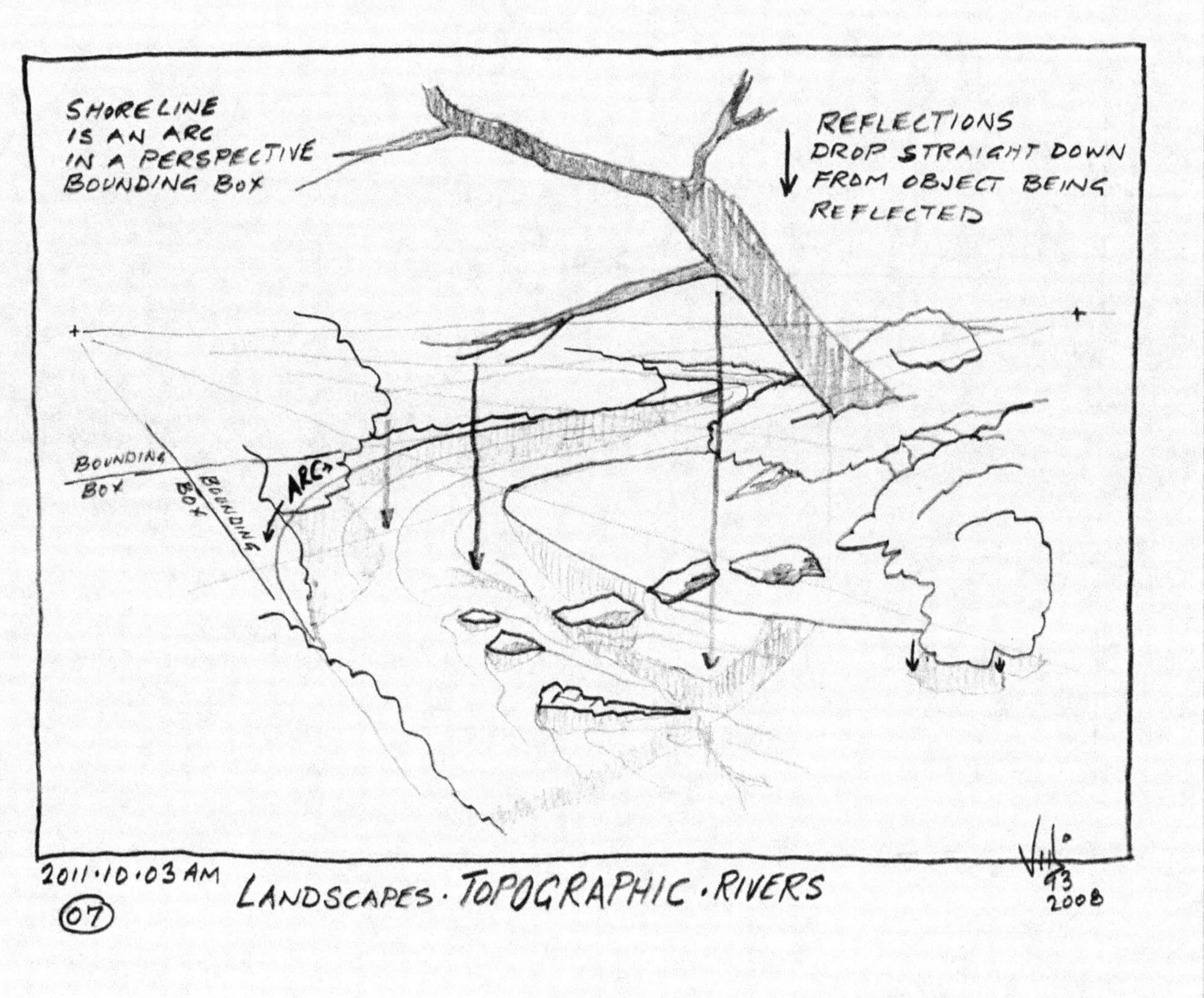
SHORELINE IS AN ARC IN A PERSPECTIVE BOUNDING BOX
REFLECTIONS DROP STRAIGHT DOWN FROM OBJECT BEING REFLECTED
BOUNDING BOX
BOUNDING BOX
ARC
2011·10·03 AM
07
LANDSCAPES · TOPOGRAPHIC · RIVERS
93
2008

TOPOGRAPHIC
Rivers

Once again, the shoreline of a river meanders through a perspective grid portraying the ground plane. Ripples, rocks and other features can be placed in the drawing by keeping them in perspective.

Reflections portray the glossy look of the water and appear directly below the object being reflected.

Keep in mind that the elevation ascends as it moves away from the water's edge and portray the features around the river at a higher elevation from the river, keeping the illusion of the perspective.

Cliffs and floodplains will alternate on the edges of the river as it will likely follow a snaking pattern between the higher sides of the river valley.

Take the opportunity to try high and low horizon lines to create more dramatic images when drawing a river.

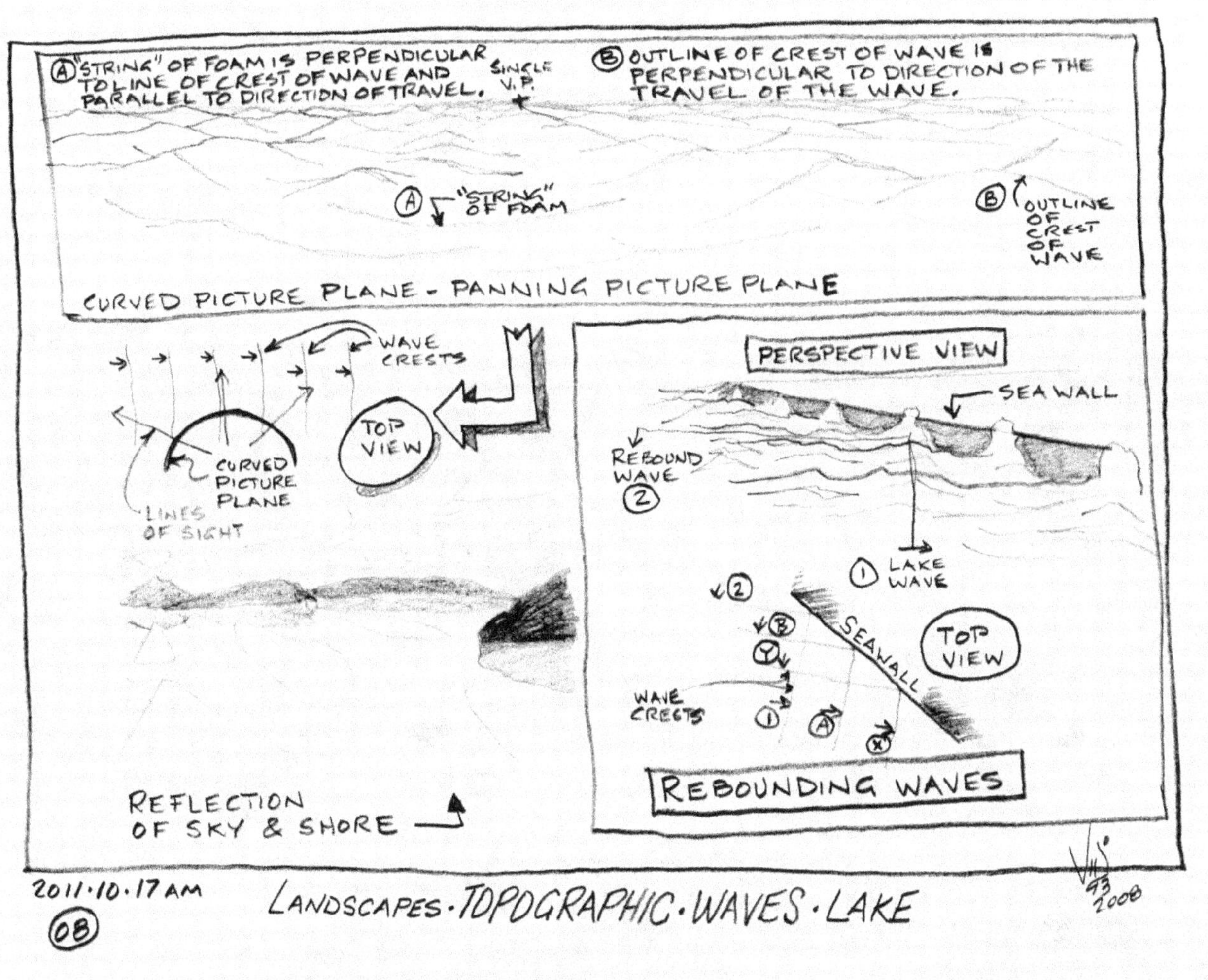

TOPOGRAPHIC

Waves - Lake

Don't confuse reflections, which are images reflected by the surface of the water, with reflecting waves, which are waves that bounce off of a severe shoreline and continue on back out onto the lake .

The illustration at the top of the drawing on this page, is a view of a lake portraying a field of waves . As the waves pass by the viewer, they must be illustrated from different angles . The waves on the left of this image are travelling toward the viewer, the waves in the middle of this image are travelling past the viewer, and the view is along the swell, and the waves on the right of the image are travelling away from the viewer .

There are only two parts of a wave that can be illustrated . The first part is the line of the crest of the wave as it appears in front of whatever is beyond . This part only appears when looking across the wave, with the wave travelling toward or away from the viewer . The second part that can be illustrated, is the string of foam left behind a breaking wave . This string runs parallel with the direction of the wave's travel, and is the only thing that can be illustrated when looking along the crest of a wave .

If waves are hitting a breakwall or seawall at a certain angle, they rebound and continue on back into the lake perpendicular, or at a 90 degree angle, to the waves approaching the seawall .

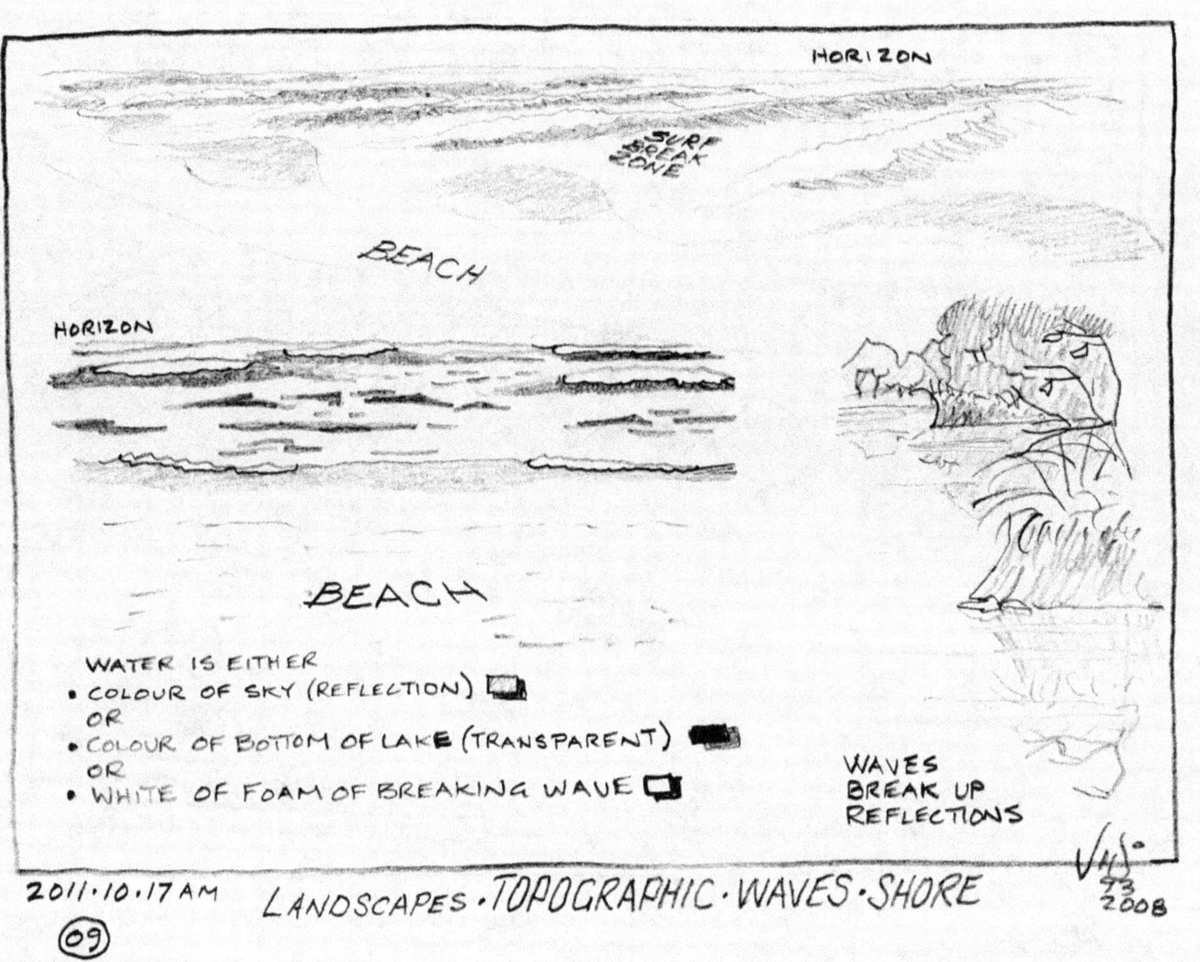

TOPOGRAPHIC

Waves - Shore

Shorelines are either rather abrupt or a beach. So the waves are either breaking onto a gradual shore, crashing onto an abrupt shore, or rebounding off of a very abrupt shore.

Crashing waves are rather easy to illustrate, although full of detail and very white.

Breaking waves, or surf, can more easily be illustrated, especially since the image is made up of only three things : foam, reflected sky or translated images of the bottom of the lake. Essentially, other than foam, the surface of the water is either directing the light from the bottom of the lake or reflecting the sky. So the if the surface is at a stong angle to the viewer it will appear dark like the bottom of the lake. Alternatively, if the surface of the water is at a low angle, it will be reflecting the distant sky, whether that sky is dark or light.

So with only these three options in one's palette, carve out your three dimensional waves, with white for the foam at the top of breaking waves, dark below the foam for the vertical surface of the wave showing the bottom of the lake, and sky tone for the areas where there is more of a calm surface of the lake. The only thing left is the little waves on the bigger swells that can be illustrated by darkening the areas where the surface of the water directs the light from below the surface.

Finally, if the surface is mostly calm, there will be detailed reflections which are broken up by small ripples.

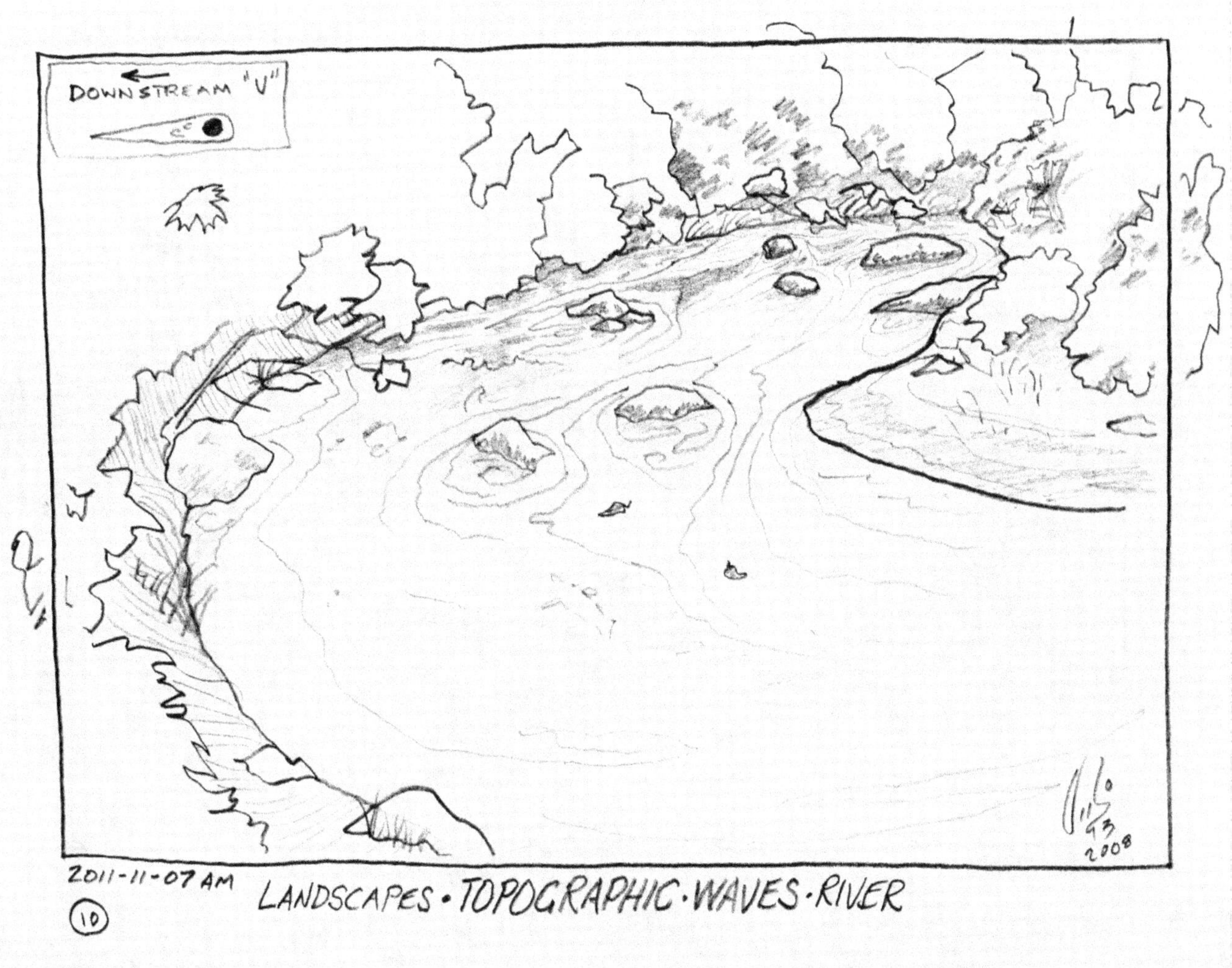

LANDSCAPES • TOPOGRAPHIC • WAVES • RIVER

TOPOGRAPHIC

Waves - River

Waves on rivers generally have very little to do with wind, and have more to do with the movement of the water beneath the surface due to the flow of the river.

Try to figure out what the ground and riverbed are doing, or becoming at the direction of the water flow, and then plan your water to flow around in response to the obstacles put up by the ground, shoreline, rocks and riverbed.

If there is a big drop off, like a weir, the water will be calm upstream as it collects behind the drop off, then flow smoothly over the drop off, to carve a deep area downstream of the drop off that is full of turbulence, before moving on down the river. Alternatively, the water may pile up behind an obstacle before moving to either side of the obstacle and subsiding as it moves down the river. This is the kind of thinking that is necessary in understanding a landscape or creating a landscape.

Another idea that can help one make sense of a river is the idea of either an upstream "V" or a downstream "V". Water bounces off the shorelines on either side and heads toward the middle of the river. This creates a "V" shape that is like an arrow pointing downstream. As well, an obstacle in a river will create an upstream "V", an "arrow" of waves that points upstream. These two "V"s, along with eddies that curl around behind obstacles, are the three main ways to illustrate the flow of a river.

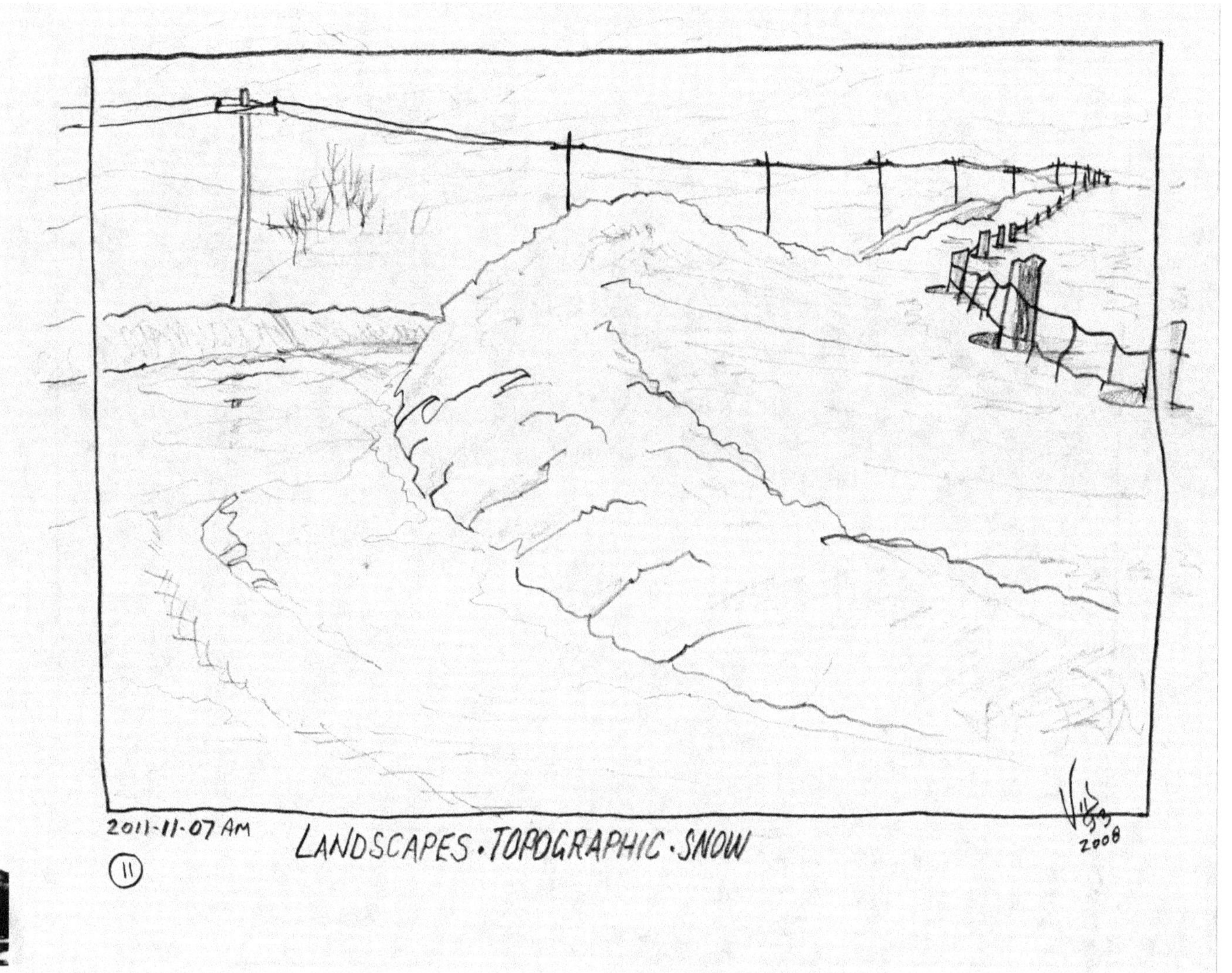

TOPOGRAPHIC
Snow

There are only three kinds of snow, once it has landed: freshly fallen, windswept and piled.

Freshly fallen snow is generally featureless, only following what lies beneath. This includes snow on steps, shrubs and branches.

Windswept snow creates drifts around obstacles, generally downwind from an obstacle, with a gap between the obstacle and the drift. As well, the wind will create waves or dunes of snow in an open area.

Piled snow is irregular, like a pile of clumps, only forming the pile as intended by the piler. This may be a plow, that creates a ridge of snow from the end of the plow. It may also be a shoveller, piling the snow in the most efficient way possible to save energy, so that the pile is only just far enough away from the cleared area so as to not fall back into the cleared area.

A landscape will likely include all three kinds of snow, interacting with each other as the layout of the landscape dictates.

Finally, don't forget tracks and reflections. Melting snow will make surfaces reflect as they become wet. Any travelled area will reveal tracks if there is a sufficient amount of snow to take an impression. This includes tire tracks as well as the footprints of animals and people.

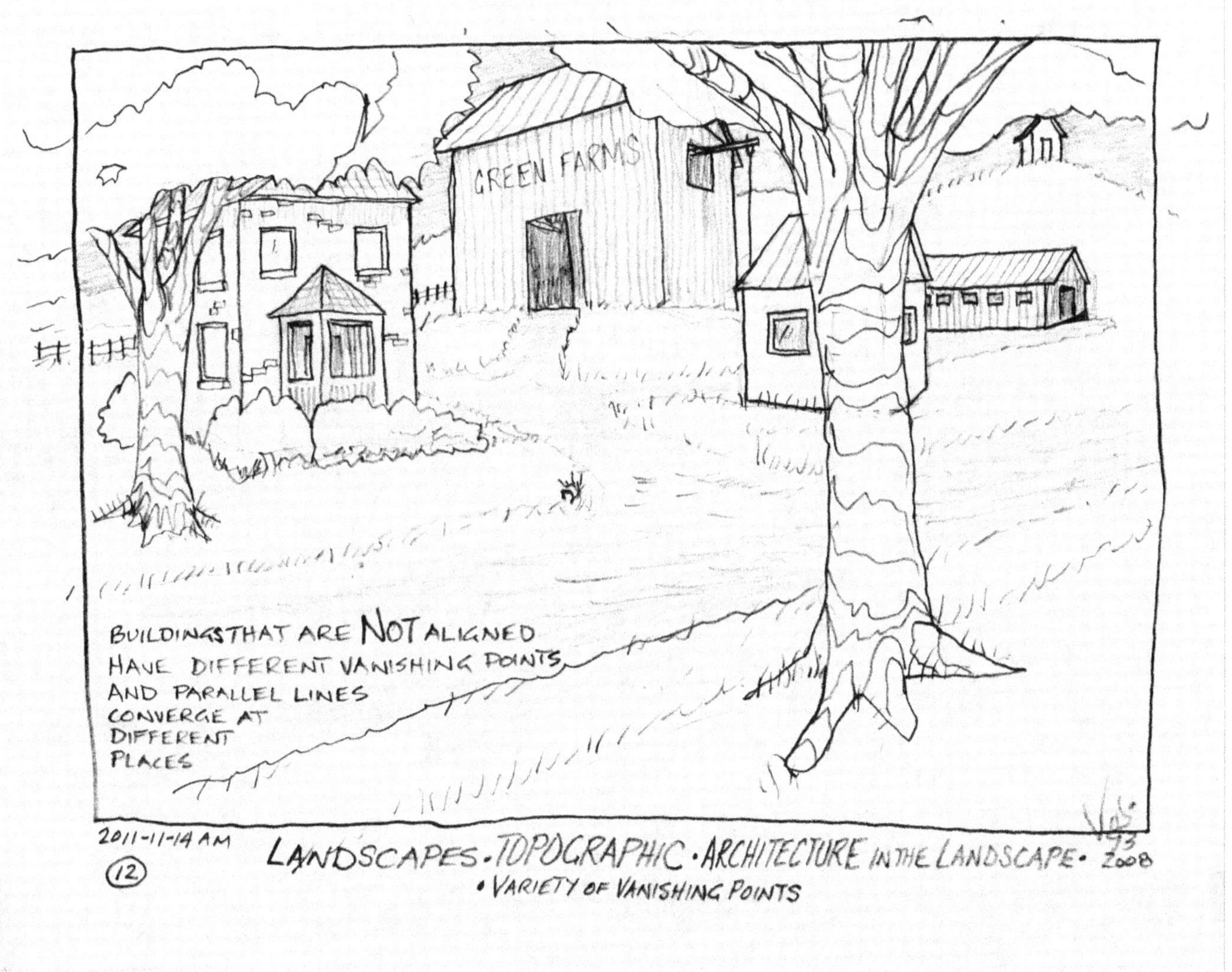

GREEN FARMS
BUILDINGS THAT ARE NOT ALIGNED
HAVE DIFFERENT VANISHING POINTS,
AND PARALLEL LINES
CONVERGE AT
DIFFERENT
PLACES
2011-11-14 AM
(12)
LANDSCAPES • TOPOGRAPHIC • ARCHITECTURE IN THE LANDSCAPE •
• VARIETY OF VANISHING POINTS
2008

TOPOGRAPHIC

Architecture in the Landscape - Variety of Vanishing Points

Not all buildings will be aligned in a grid pattern . One must establish a vanishing point where parallel lines in parallel planes converge for each orientation of any buildings . Having said this, I found it hard to vary the orientation of the buildings in this drawing .

Understanding the principles of perspective, that parallel lines in parallel planes converge at a vanishing point when they reach infinity, one can freely orient any building however randomly, and create the necessary vanishing points by merely ensuring that parallel lines have a single point of convergence .

This can be a lot of fun, once one has overcome the challenge of the fear of failure . Just remember, like a mantra, "parallel lines converge" .

When drawing a landscape with buildings, one will be surprised how quickly the scene fills up, especially when including trees and shrubs with foliage . The problem is not so much about getting the various orientations portrayed in perspective, but rather, getting everything into the picture without losing too much of one thing behind other things . This is at least what I found in doing this drawing .

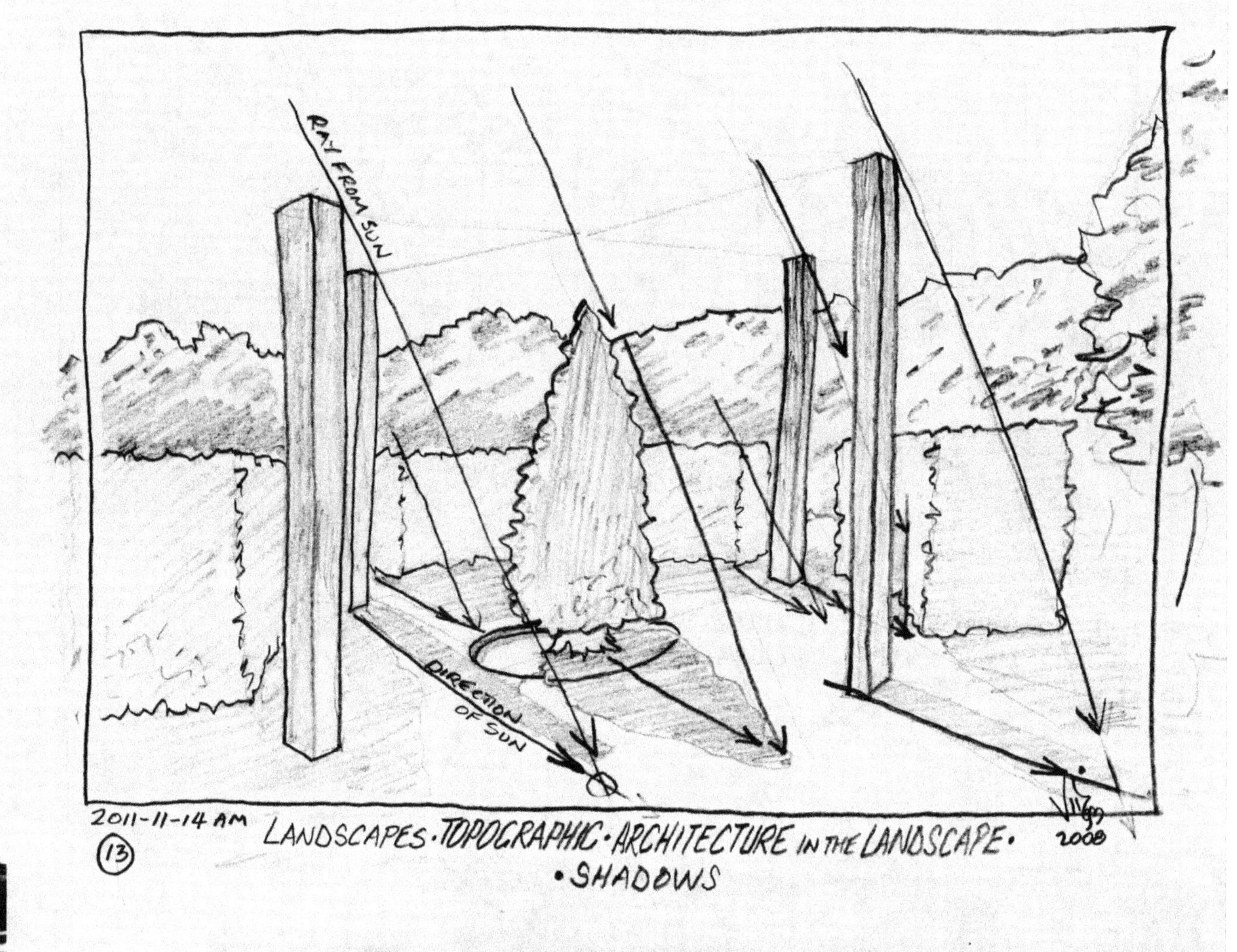

TOPOGRAPHIC

Architecture in the Landscape - Shadows

Just as discussed in Textbook -C- , on perspective, shadows fall in a line from the base of the object out in the direction of the light, away from the light source, to an extent regarding the elevation of the light source. When drawing landscapes, remember that sunlight shines in rays that are all parallel, unless the image is making use of a curved picture plane, in which case the lines of light will converge.

This rule of the direction and length of the shadow is true for trees and shrubs as well as architectural elements.

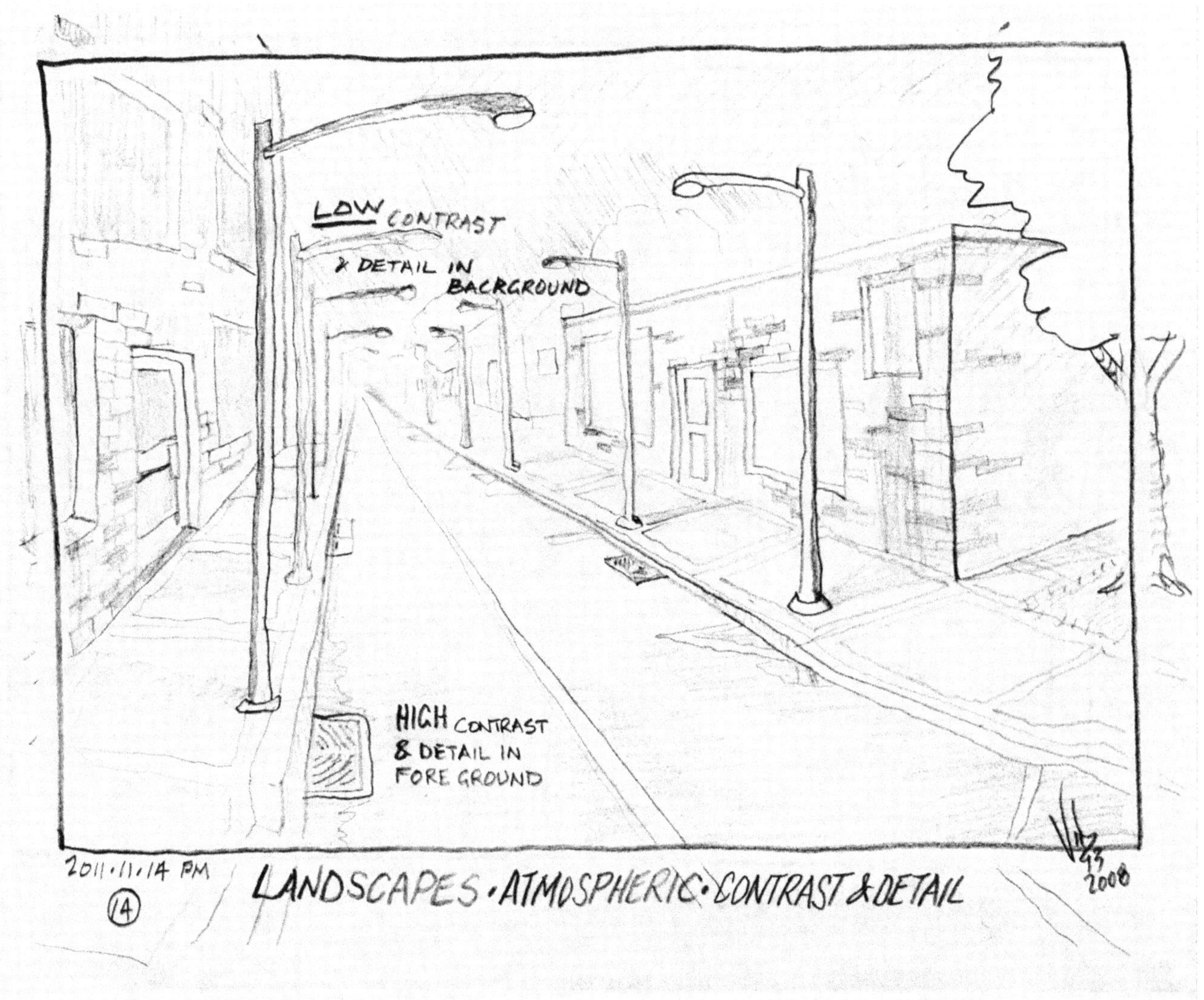

ATMOSPHERIC
Contrast & Detail

Using a street scene, where there is a lot of detail that could be drawn, I have not drawn very much detail in the distance. Individual bricks only appear in the foreground, and catchbasins are only an outline in the middle ground.

As well, the highest contrast is in the foreground, with the distant area down the road being rather muted without any black or white, only grays.

Although the illusion is that the road is just as big when it is far away, the distant road is only a very small part of the area of the drawing, so adding detail, although very tempting, is really not recommended, as it will only distract the eye.

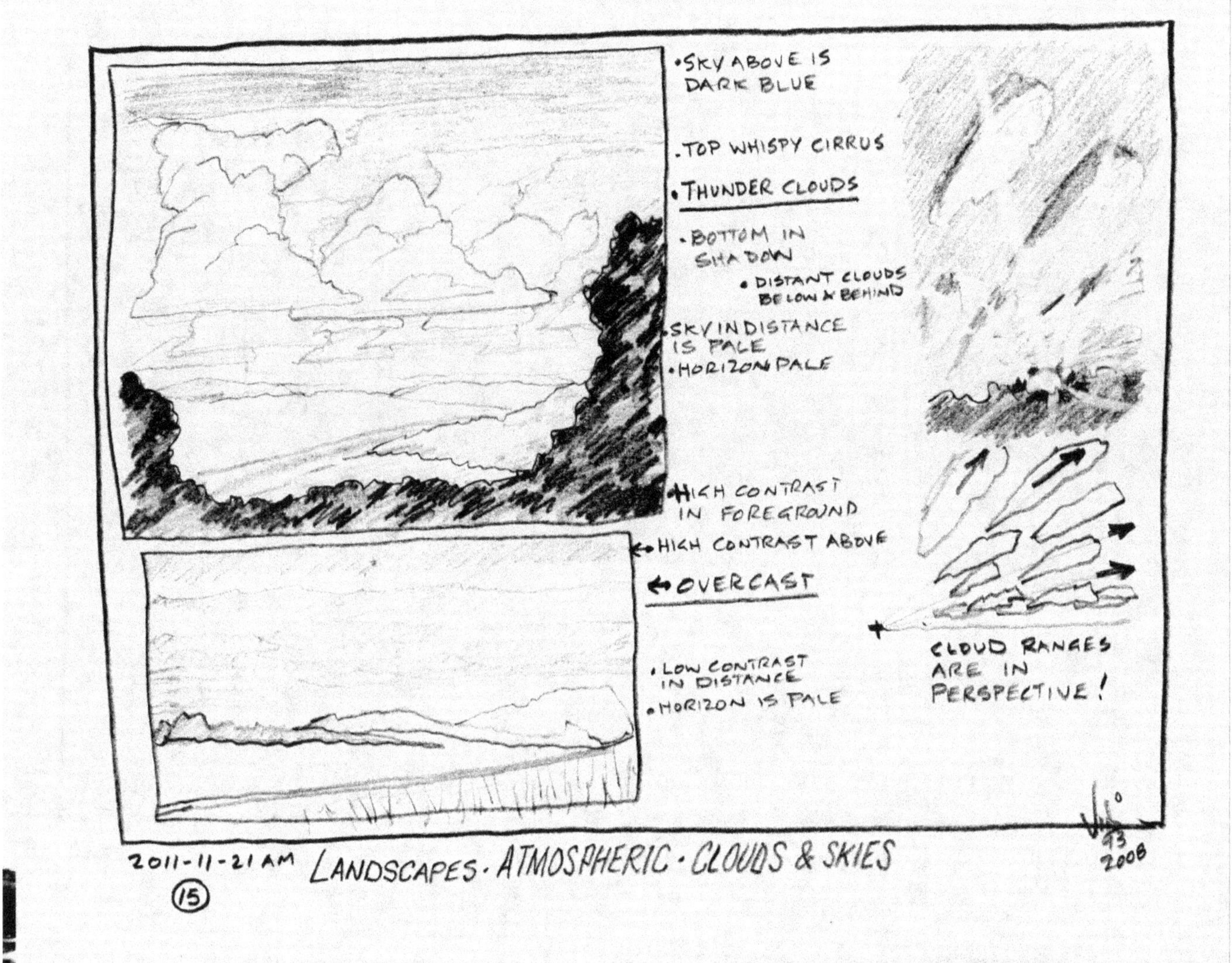

ATMOSPHERIC

Clouds & Skies

Clouds and skies are a topic that can greatly benefit from a wealth of observation, as they vary greatly, and can easily look too made up.

Try to draw the meteorlogical definitions of different cloud types to build a repertoire of clouds for your landscape drawing. These categories include cirrus, nimbus, cumulus, stratus, and combinations of the basic categories. Start with simple ones like thunderclouds with their flat bottoms and high billowing tops, or the basic overcast sky.

A clear sky is darkest above, where there is the most direct view of outer space, but still looks very blue. The distant sky is the most white, with the depth of the water vapour hazing the view to make it almost white.

Fields of clouds will be in a pattern that will appear in perspective, so be consistent with the perspective of your cloud patterns. Remember that they are above the horizon, so the bottom of the distant clouds will appear below the bottom of near clouds. Likewise, the top of near clouds will appear in front and above the top of distant clouds.

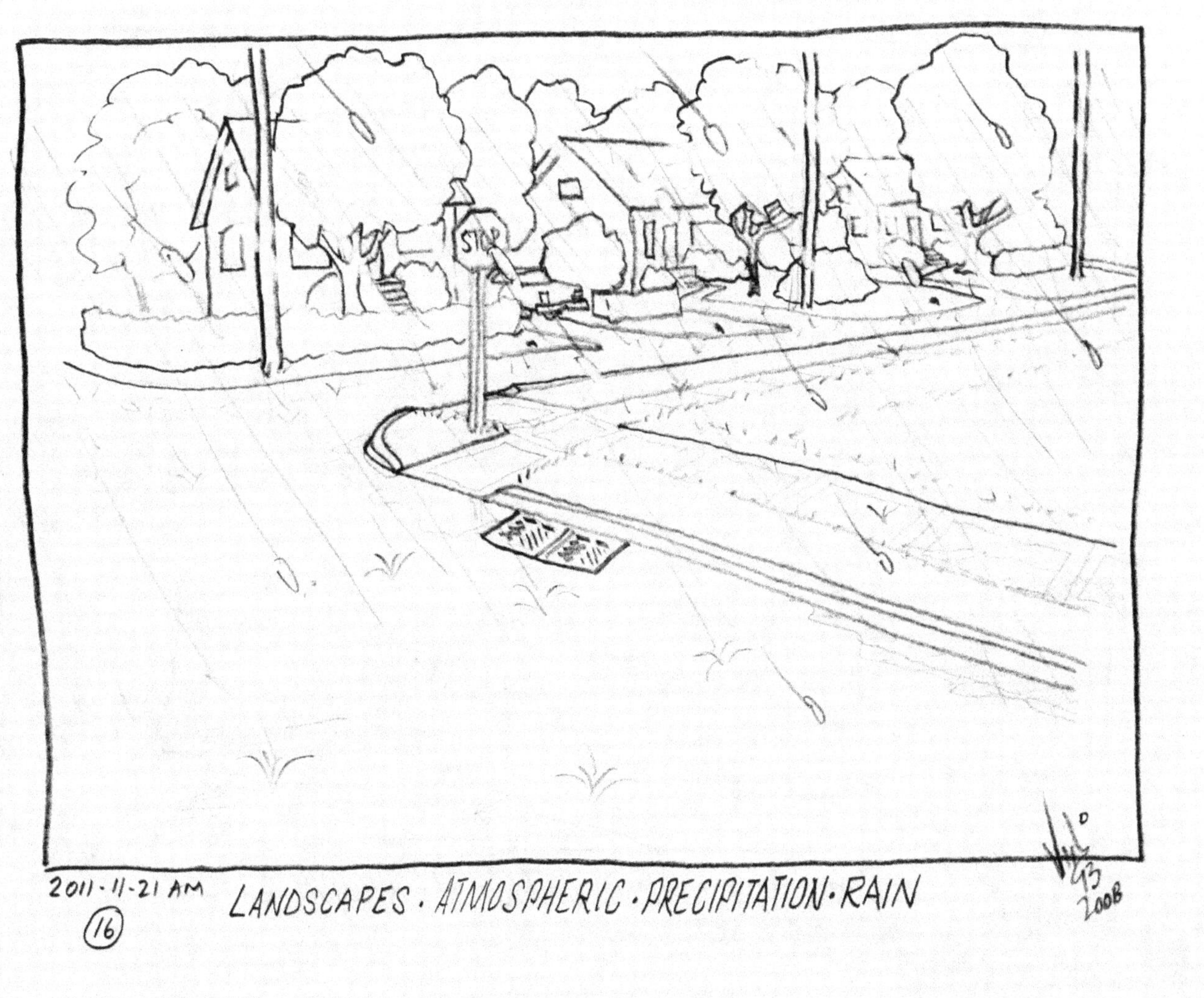

ATMOSPHERIC
Precipitation - Rain

If you are bold enough, rain can obscure a landscape, but generally it will make the distinctions between near and far landscape objects more pronounced. The details of landscape elements that are far away will be more obscured by the rain. The details of landscape elements that are closer will have less rainfall in front of them so will be more detailed.

In the foreground rain will appear as streaks across the image, and moving deeper into the depth of the drawing, the streaks will be smaller, more numerous, and obscure the landscape elements.

Rain will splash when it hits pavement or a body of water. The splashes on pavement will be less obvious in the distance. The splashes on pavement, when illustrated, will establish the perspective and contours of the pavement. Splashes in water, will obscure any potential reflection from the surface of the water, creating small ripples if close to the picture plane.

In the very near foreground, actual droplets of rain can be illustrated, along with the streak as the droplets streaks through the image. In the distance, the rain can appear cloudlike by obscuring the details, and waves of rain, illustrated by obscuring the detail of the landscape elements in the distance, can provide a dramatic effect.

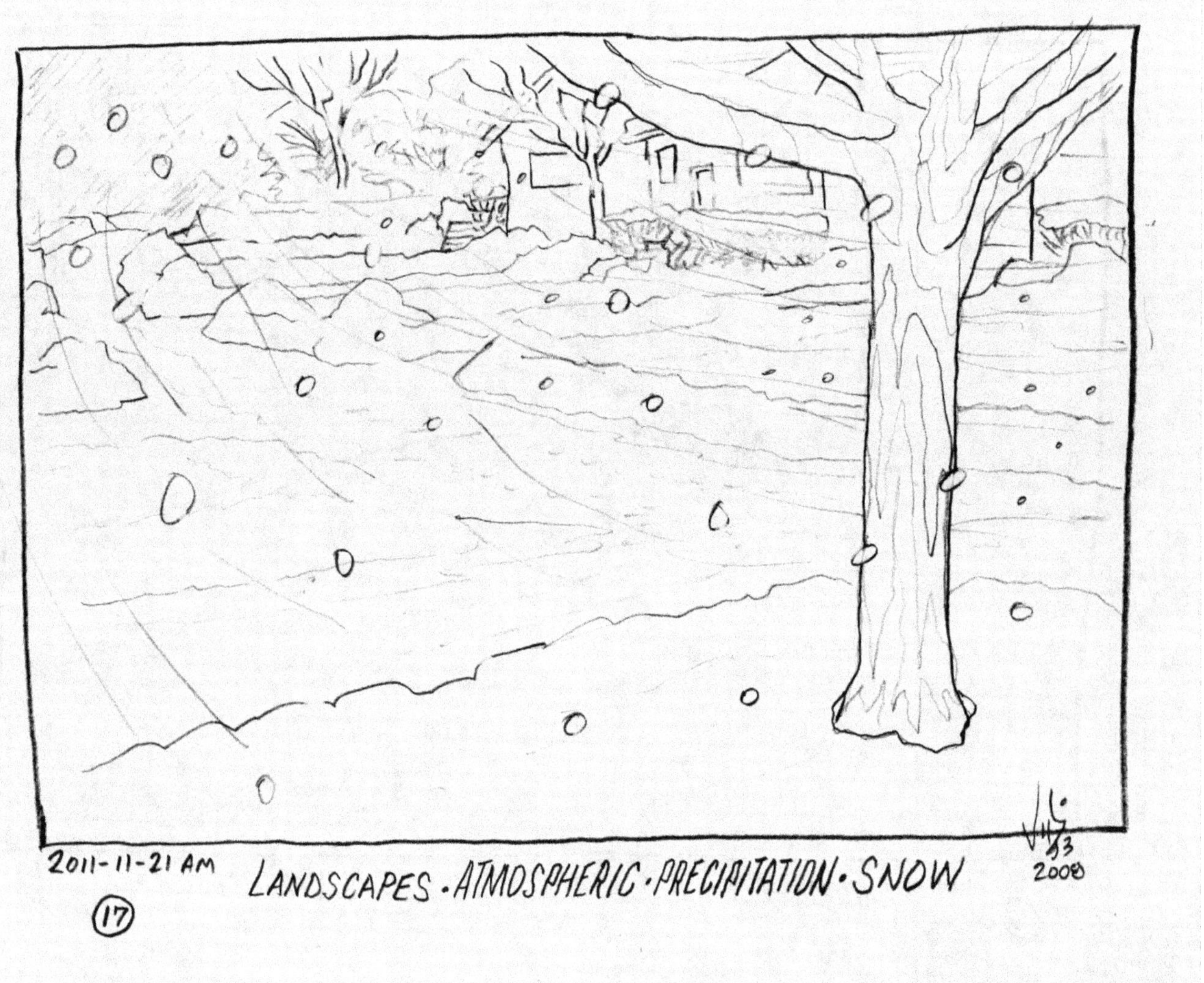

ATMOSPHERIC

Precipitation - Snow

If you are bold enough, snowfall can obscure a landscape, but generally it will make the distinctions between near and far landscape objects more pronounced. The details of landscape elements that are far away will be more obscured by the snowfall. The details of landscape elements that are closer will have less snowfall in front of them so will be more detailed.

In the foreground snowfall will appear as streaks across the image, and moving deeper into the depth of the drawing, the streaks will be smaller, more numerous, and obscure the landscape elements.

Snow will not splash when it hits pavement or a body of water. Often the wind will drift the snow across open areas, which can be illustrated by obscurring the details of the landscape elements behind the drifting snow. Snow will whisp across open areas of pavement and collect in drifts like sand dunes. Snow landing on water may obscure any potential reflection from the surface of the water.

In the very near foreground, actual snowflakes or clumps of snow can be illustrated, along with the streak as the snow streaks through the image. In the distance, the snowfall can appear cloudlike by obscuring the details, and, waves of snowfall, illustrated by obscuring the detail of the landscape elements in the distance, can provide a dramatic effect.

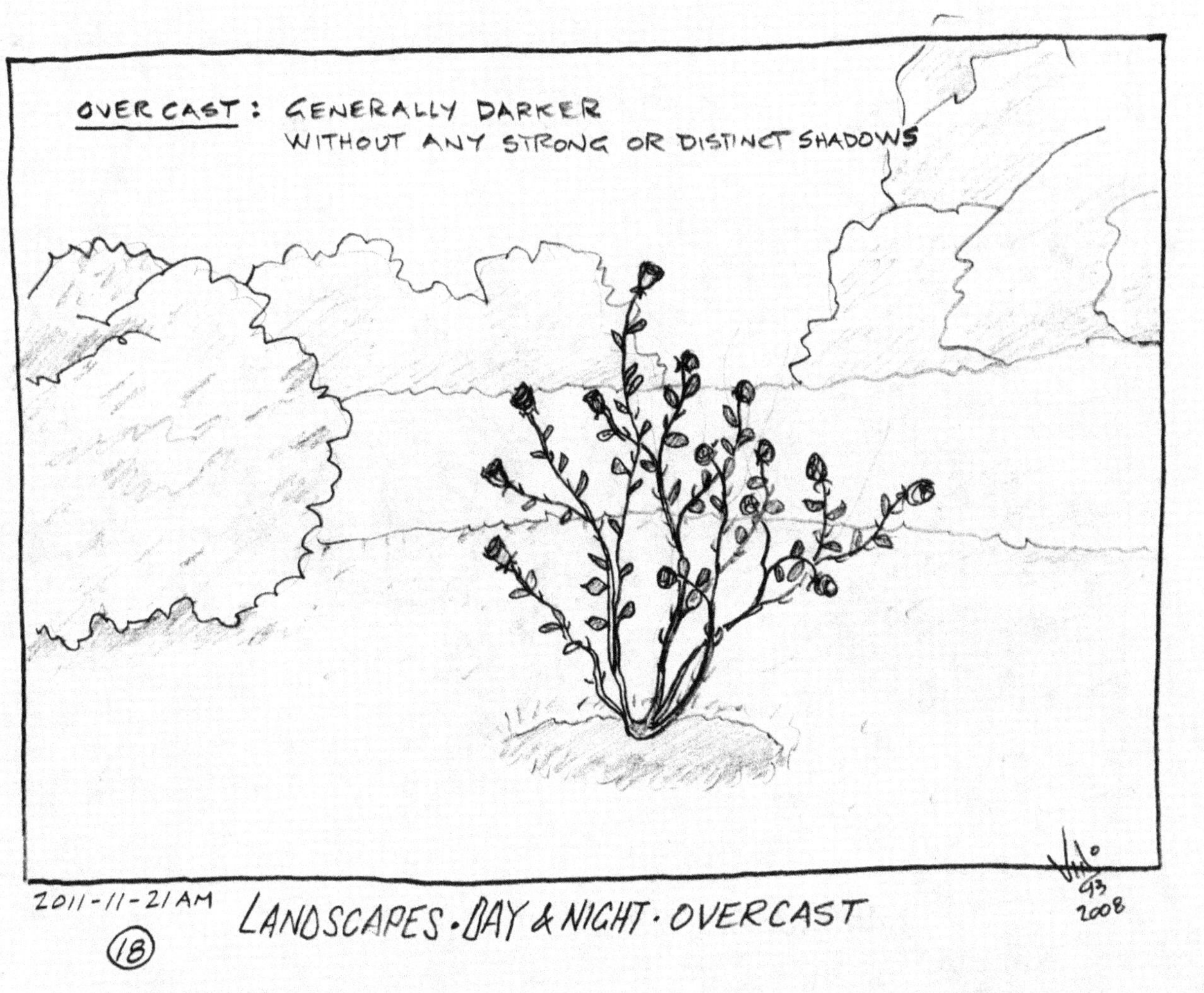
OVERCAST : GENERALLY DARKER
WITHOUT ANY STRONG OR DISTINCT SHADOWS
2011-11-21AM
18
LANDSCAPES · DAY & NIGHT · OVERCAST
93
2008

DAY and NIGHT

Overcast

The way to illustrate an overcast day, as well as showing an overcast sky, is to keep the shadows indefinite and mild, with little contrast, and avoid any strong bright areas. This muted lighting is more important than illustrating an overcast sky.

In overcast conditions, there will not be any bright white areas, and there will not be any dark black areas, as the light bounces off the sky from all angles and lightens up shadow areas. Although the image will be generally darker under overcast lighting, the shadows will be lighter, due to the light approaching from all angles as it is reflected from the overcast sky.

At night, an overcast sky will reflect the artificial light of built up areas, becoming very bright, relative to the cast shadows of the artificial light. Again, the sky will reflect light into shadow areas, lightening them up, compared to a clear night, especially with a single light source such as the moon.

So, when illustrating an overcast day, avoid pure white and pure black, and darken everything, without defining any definite shadows.

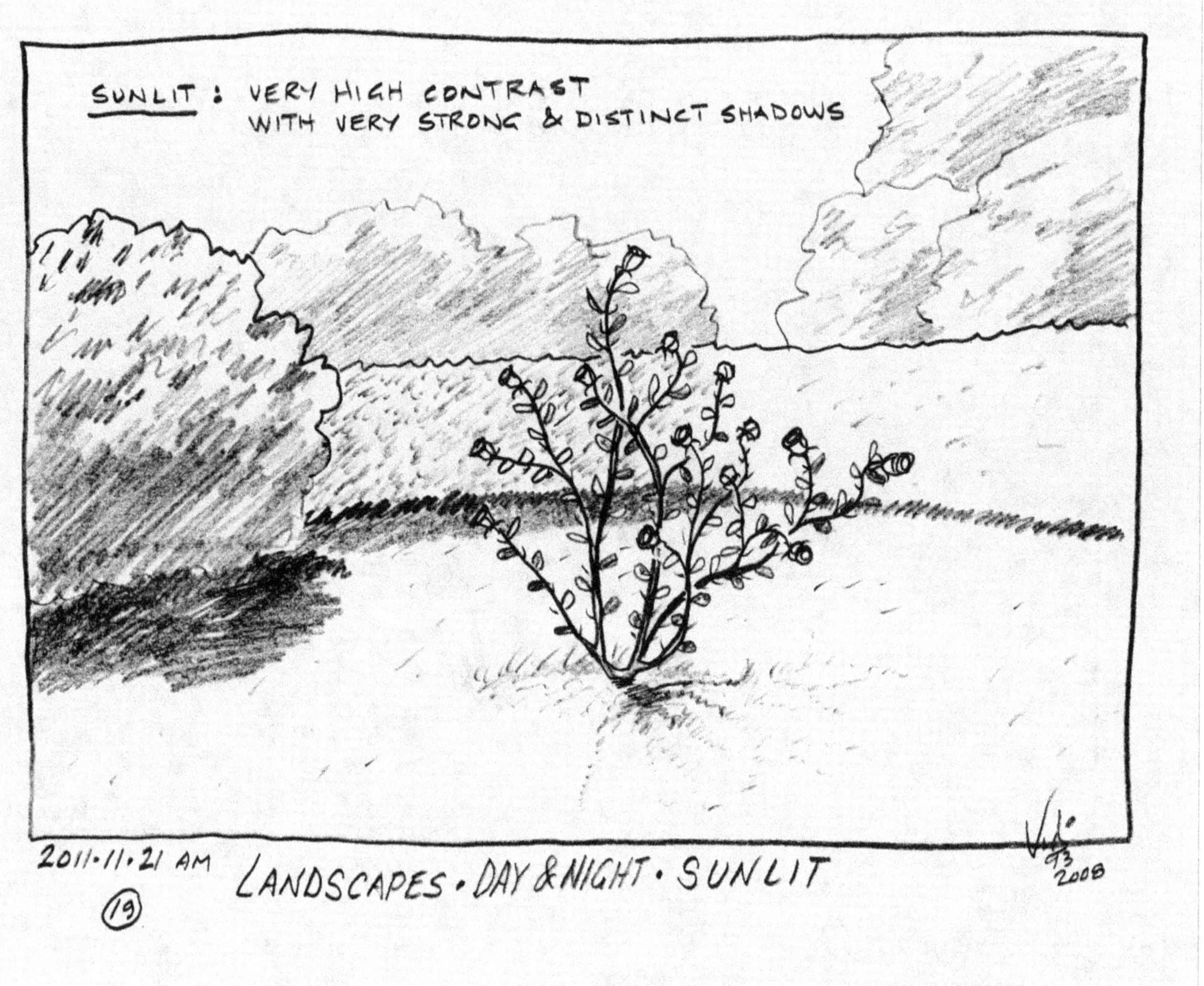
SUNLIT : VERY HIGH CONTRAST
WITH VERY STRONG & DISTINCT SHADOWS
2011·11·21 AM
19
LANDSCAPES · DAY & NIGHT · SUNLIT
2008

DAY and NIGHT

Sunlit

The way to illustrate a sunny day, as well as showing a clear sky, is to keep the shadows strong and bold, with lots of contrast between the sunlight areas and the shadow areas, and provide some pure white in the strongest lit areas. This bold lighting is more important than illustrating a clear sky or strongly shadowed clouds in the sky.

In sunlit conditions, there will be bright white areas, and there will be dark black areas, as the lighting is direct and makes strong distinctions between the lit areas and the shadow areas. Although the image will have pure white areas, those being in direct sunlight and lighter in colour to begin with, the shadows will be darker, due to the light only approaching from one angle, directly from the sun. There will be some backlight, if objects are arranged so as to reflect the bright sunlight into the shadow areas. In the drawing on this page, the light is reflecting off of the lawn and up into the shadow area of the bush on the left side. This is why the shadow area on the bush is lighter than the shadow of the bush on the ground.

At night, a clear sky will not reflect the artificial light of built up areas, so the sky will be very black. With a single light source such as the moon, the shadows will be bold and distinct.

So, when illustrating a sunlit day, have at least some pure white and pure black, and increase the contrast in everything, while defining definite shadows.

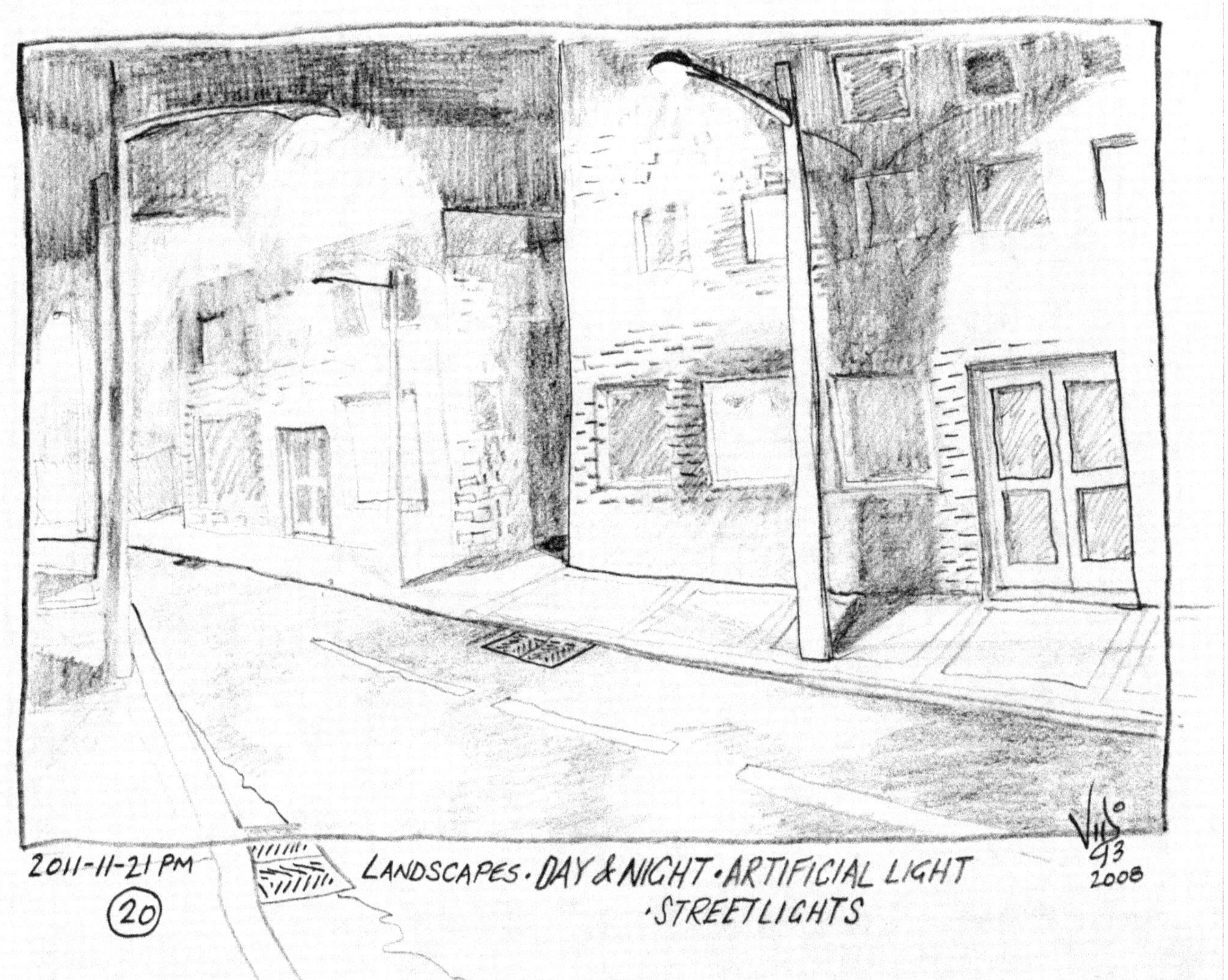

2011-11-21 PM
20
LANDSCAPES · DAY & NIGHT · ARTIFICIAL LIGHT
· STREETLIGHTS
2008

DAY and NIGHT

Artificial Light - Streetlights

Artificial light, streetlights and light coming out through windows, creates a maze of lighting and shadows, with one light source casting light into the shadows of other light sources. It can be very tricky to sort out what is darker and what is lighter. This being said, since artificial light only applys at night, any light source should be illustrated as white.

Streetlights cast shadows of their poles, as well as casting shadows of other streetlight poles. This means there will be a shadow of the pole that the streetlight is on, that runs from the sky down to the base of the pole. At some point between the streetlight and the base of the pole, the light from the next streetlight will lighten the shadow of the first streetlight. So each streetlight pole will have a darkest shadow on the top of the building that is next to it, a slightly lighter shadow where the adjacent streetlights illuminate, its own shadow running to the base of the pole, and two more pole shadows running from the base of its pole that are cast by the two adjacent streetlights.

As well, if a streetlight creates a shadow behind an obstacle such as a building or a vehicle, another streetlight will create a different shadow of the obstacle, lighting up the shadow from the first streetlight.

There are many shadows that add up or are subtracted from by the play of the light from the many streetlights, not to mention the light from windows or vehicles.

Finally, if the landscape is wet from rain, there will be at least some pure white reflections of the light sources in the wet areas.

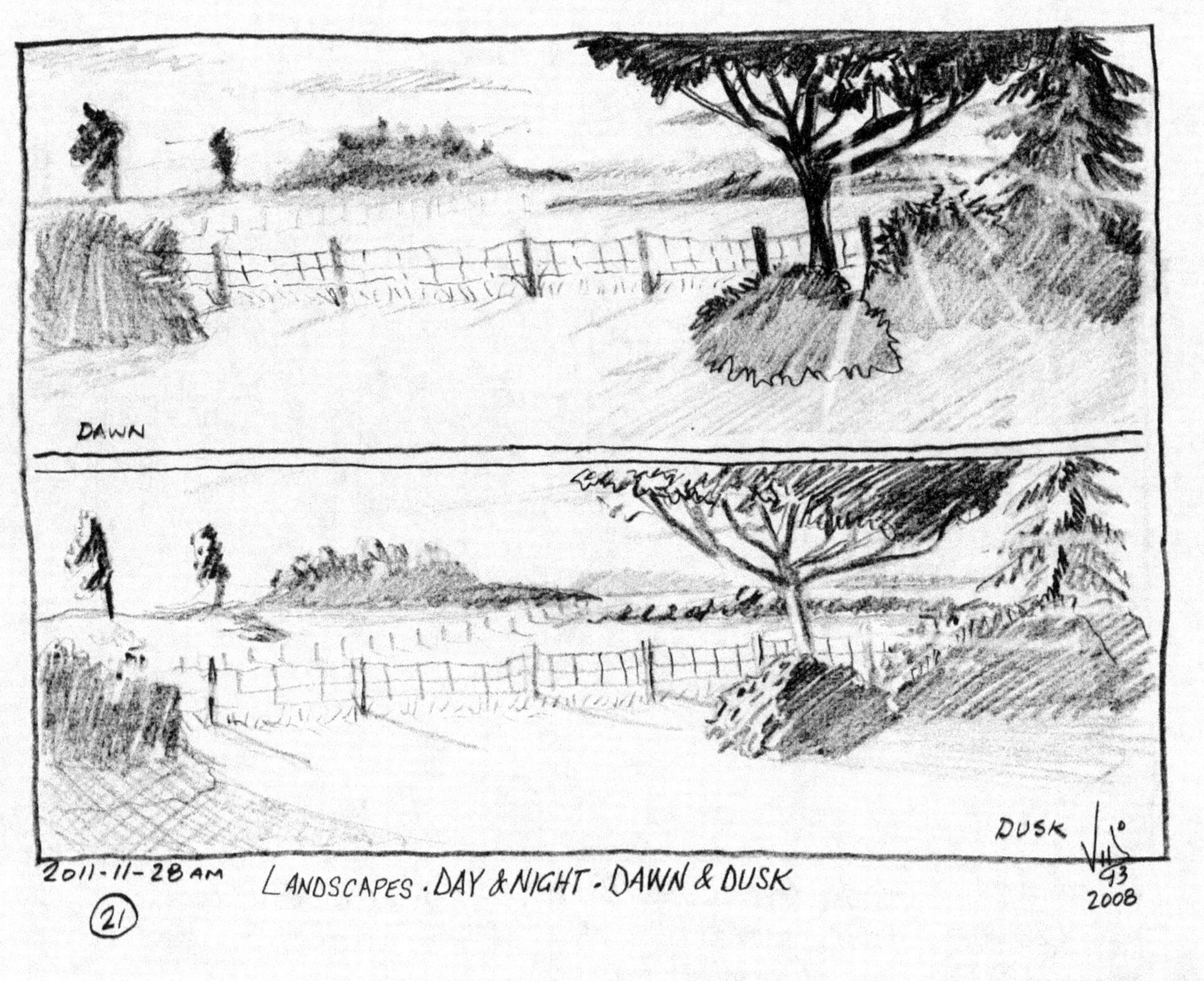

DAY and NIGHT

Dawn and Dusk

Weak sunlight at Dawn, in the summer, is usually from the East-Northeast, and sunlight at Dusk, in the evening, is usually from around the West-Northwest. In the winter, the sunrise is from the East-Southeast, and the sunset is from the West-Southwest. Dawn and Dusk both look the same, with muted light and very long, at times infinite, shadows, with only the orientation of the light and shadows revealing whether it is Dawn or Dusk.

If it is cloudy or overcast, the light just fades in or fades away, without any real shadows, or at least without any well defined strong shadows. The shadows just get more pronounced as Dawn progresses. The light just darkens, with the shadows darkening faster at first, to only be overtaken by the gathering night at Dusk.

A clear Dawn or Dusk, will have much more distinct shadows that are infinitely long at the actual sunrise or sunset, and the shadows will shorten as the sun rises, and lengthen as the sun sets. Before the sunrise, or after the sunset, there will not be any definite shadows but the glow in the sky will allow indefinite shadows in areas shaded from the sky.

Don't forget the artificial light that will come from streetlights and outdoor lights, that, if on before sunset or after sunrise, will add to the play of light at Dawn and Dusk. Many illustrations have portrayed artificial light at Dawn or Dusk.

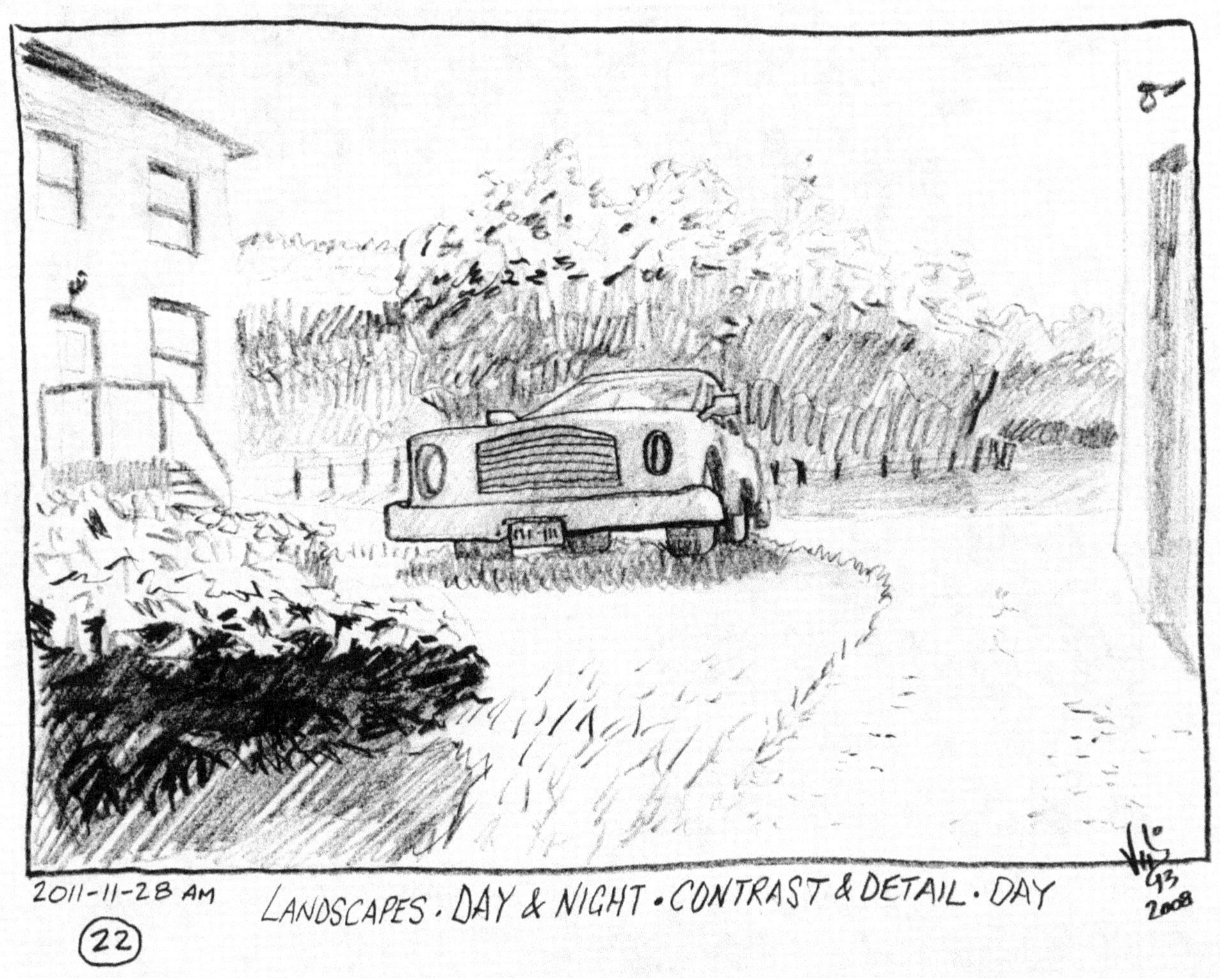

2011-11-28 AM
22
LANDSCAPES · DAY & NIGHT · CONTRAST & DETAIL · DAY

DAY and NIGHT

Contrast and Detail - Day

As well as sunlit versus overcast lighting, day and night have similar effects on contrast and detail .

In the day, sunlight is more thoroughly consistent and brighter than any light at night, but artificial light at night, although not as bright, is more controlled and direct . Sunlight will brighten backlights as it bounces off of sunlit obstacles . Sunlight makes for higher contrast between sunlit areas and shadows, and any obstacles seen against the sun will be in sharp contrast and very dark next to the bright white of sunlight .

In the drawing on this page, there is strong contrast in the top of the forest in the background . The lower area of the forest, however is backlit from the field in front of it . Even the shadow under the car is backlit from the buildings around the car . The low shrub in the front on the left side is darkest underneath, where there is little backlight, only coming from the lawn, and the shadow of the shrub on the lawn is lighter, being backlit by the building on the right .

The roof overhang on the left is very dark next to the sky, but the rest of the house is backlit from the lawn . The shadow of the building on the bay door of the building on the right is lighter because it is backlit from the lawn . The gravel drive, and the lawn between the drive and the shrub, has high contrast, especially when it is in the foreground .

The darkest darks and the brightest lights are in the foreground, as atmospheric perspective mutes the values that are farther away .

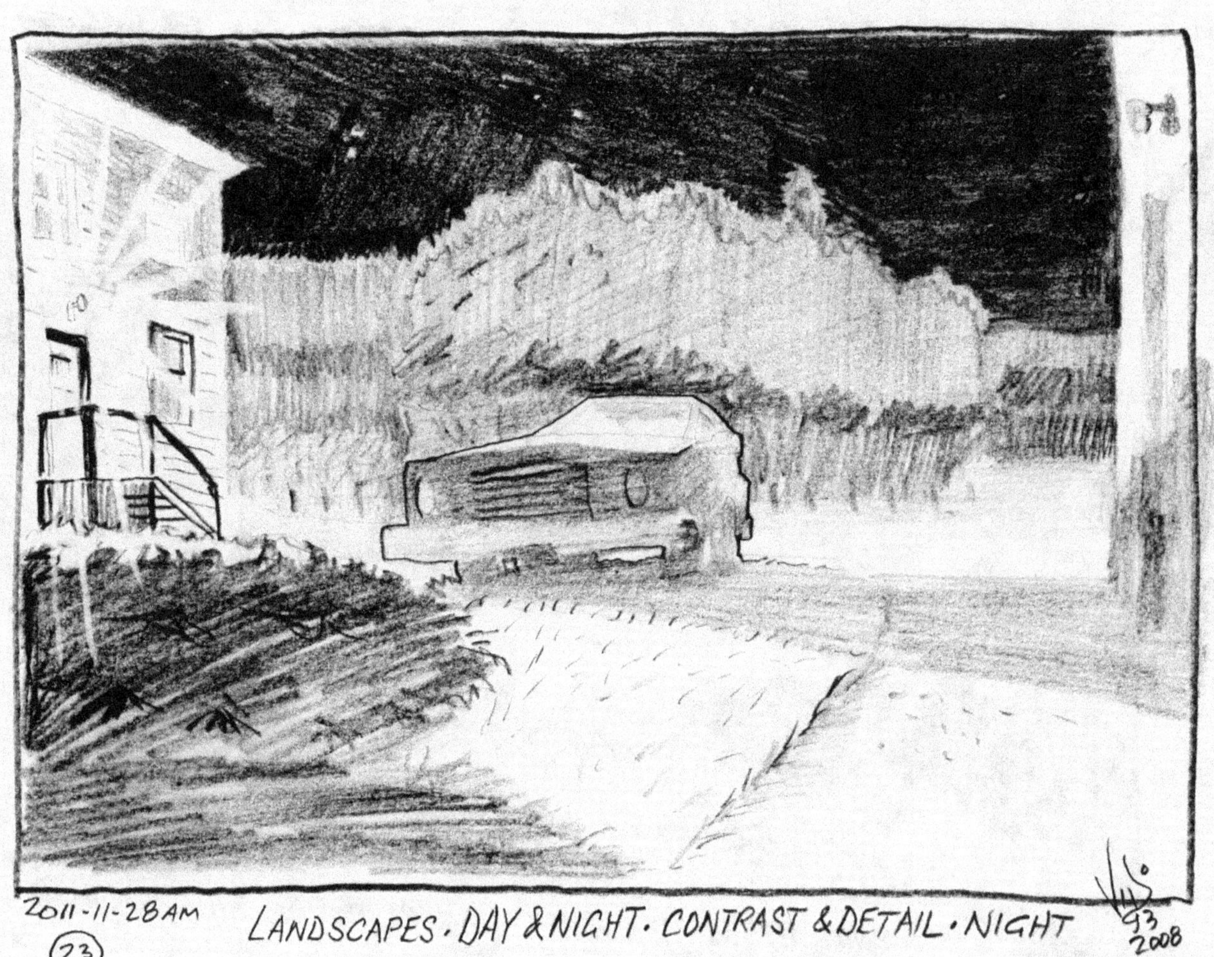

2011-11-28AM
23
LANDSCAPES · DAY & NIGHT · CONTRAST & DETAIL · NIGHT
93
2008

DAY and NIGHT
Contrast and Detail - Night

As well as sunlit versus overcast lighting, day and night have similar effects on contrast and detail .

The night, although not as bright, is usually artificially lit and artificial light is more controlled and direct . Artificial light is from a smaller closer source than the moon or the sun, so shadows are smaller and more defined since the light source is closer . There are few backlights since the light source is weaker . Nevertheless, objects seen against a lightsource will be almost black in comparison to the light source being white .

In the drawing on this page, the clear sky is pure black, with a few spots of white representing stars . The woods in the distance reflect stray light from the buildings, but even without, would be lighter than the black sky .

The shadows are longer since the light sources are lower .

The roof overhang on the left is very bright next to the black sky, being lit from the light at the door . The railings of the porch are dark since the light source is behind them . They appear very dark since they are relatively close to the light source at this distance . The shadow of the car on the bay door of the building on the right is lighter because it is backlit from the lawn . The light above the bay door on the right is not illuminated . The gravel drive, and the lawn between the drive and the shrub, has high contrast, especially when it is in the foreground .

The darkest darks and the brightest lights are in the foreground, as atmospheric perspective mutes the values that are farther away .

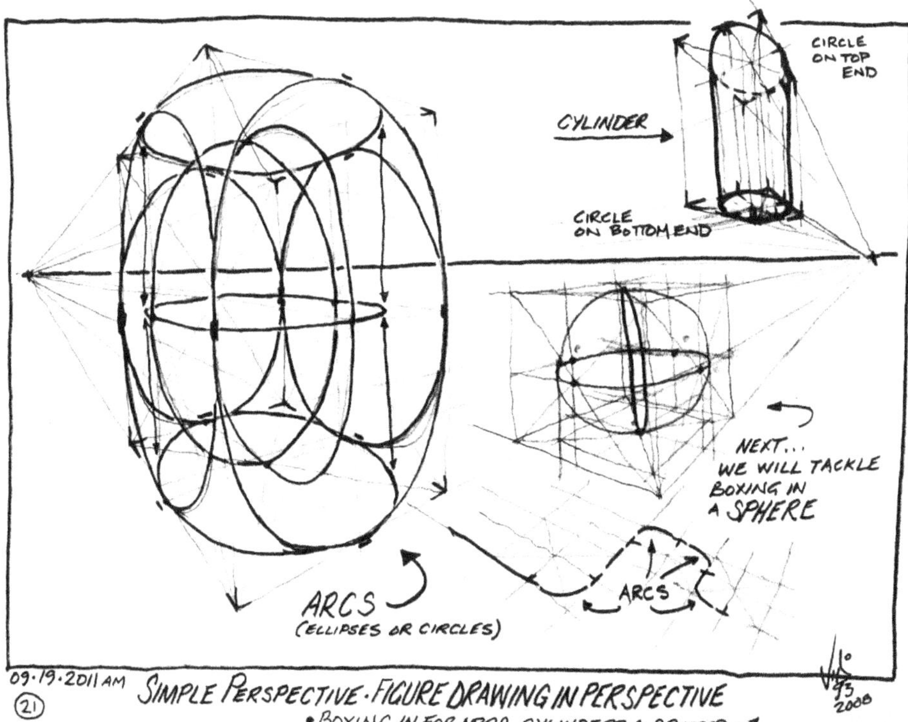

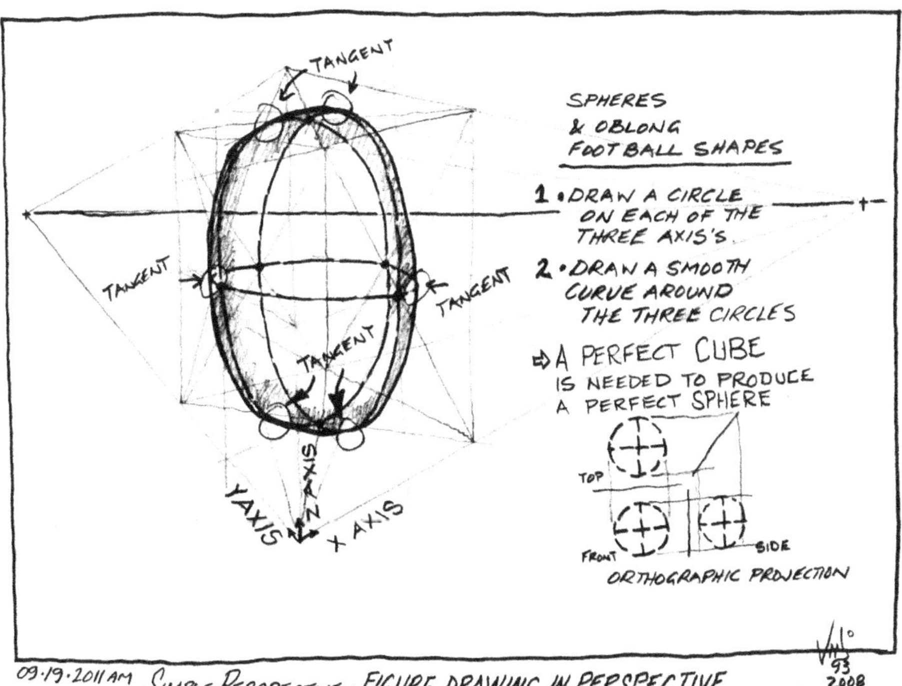

TANGENT
SPHERES & OBLONG FOOTBALL SHAPES
1 • DRAW A CIRCLE ON EACH OF THE THREE AXIS'S.
2 • DRAW A SMOOTH CURVE AROUND THE THREE CIRCLES
⇨ A PERFECT CUBE IS NEEDED TO PRODUCE A PERFECT SPHERE
TANGENT
TANGENT
TANGENT
Y AXIS
Z AXIS
X AXIS
TOP
FRONT
SIDE
ORTHOGRAPHIC PROJECTION
09·19·2011 AM SIMPLE PERSPECTIVE · FIGURE DRAWING IN PERSPECTIVE
•BOXING IN FOR ARCS, CYLINDERS & SPHERES -2
22

Here in this Epilogue, written in the fall of 2015, are ten steps to a single drawing that tackles the problem posed by these two perspective exercises from pages 110 & 111, of the Simple Perspective textbook C section of this publication.

Essentially, an eliptoid can be placed in a box. To correctly place a sphere in a box, the box must be a perfect cube, with all the edges and sides exactly the same as all the other edges and sides.

The trick is to calculate graphically, a perfect cube. This, as I have recently figured out, is accomplished by realizing that a right angle, a 90 degree angle, when split into two equal 45 degree angles, will always appear as the two halves being equal, no matter what angle such an angle is viewed at or oriented.

Having a 45 degree angle allows us to extend such a line out to the opposite corner of a face of a box so as to indicate the equal length on the opposite edge.

Just follow along and it may become clear as we go along.

Enjoy !!!

2015-09-30 A

PLACING A SPHERE IN A GRAPHICALY CALCULATED PERFECT CUBE.

2015-09-30 A 2015-10-04 B

PLACING A SPHERE IN A GRAPHICALY CALCULATED PERFECT CUBE.

Now, given three edges of three separate cubes, one vertical and two horizontal, the lines back to both vanishing points on the horizon are drawn.

Again, it is very important to practice good draftsmanship, acquired from the first four exercises of this book that train the ability to draw straight well placed lines, and the ability to split an angle with a straight line that runs through the vertex of the angle.

At this point the drawing may seem to be proficient, but as this exercise progresses, inaccuracies will compound. See if you can spot any inaccuracies or poor draftsmanship at this point in the exercise, not having compounded any errors yet.

Now here is the important part of creating a perfect cube in perspective - splitting the angle between the edge and the lines drawn from each vertex of that edge, back to the vanishing points. Since any angle, when split, will appear to have been split into two equal angles,

NO MATTER WHAT ORIENTATION THE ANGLE IS AT, OR HOW IT PRESENTS, so a right angle, a 90 degree angle, when split, will create two equal 45 degree angles, that appear equal no matter how they are viewed - they will appear equal from any viewpoint.

When these splitting lines are extended, they intersect the other edge at exactly the same distance from the other end of the given edge, as the distance the vertex of the angle split, is from the other end of the given edge. The line splitting the angle measures out the other edge of the cube!

Now, drawing the lines from the new vertices of the new cube edges, back to the vanishing points, complete the bottom squares of each of the three cubes.

Poor draftsmanship is present in this drawing - can you spot it ? But even though the draftsmanship may be poor, if it can be spotted, it can be corrected, and furthermore, a straight edge or ruler cannot correct poor draftsmanship if the draftsperson cannot see the angles and intersections correctly. Drawings like this cannot be created with a ruler, even if the drawing is very large, even 24" x 36", as the vanishing points will need to be placed at least a few feet off of such a large page, and usually beyond the edge of the desk! Even if that were possible it would be hard to maintain such points. For practical reasons it is absolutely necessary to see the perspective, keeping in mind that parallel lines in parallel planes must appear to converge at a single point.

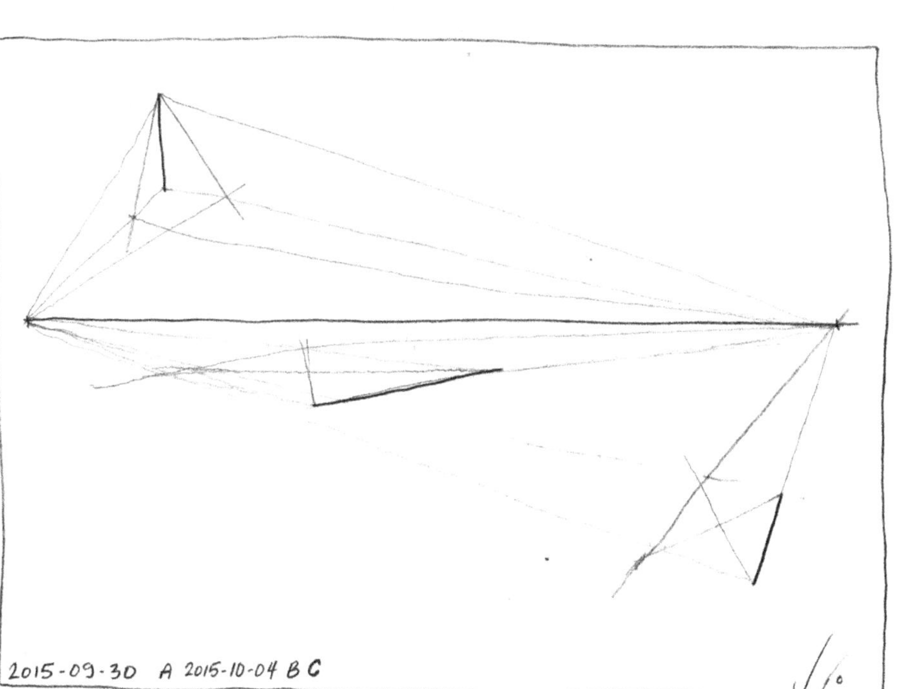

PLACING A SPHERE IN A GRAPHICALY CALCULATED PERFECT CUBE.

In this drawing we are only using two vanishing points, and vertical lines remain vertical in this drawing. So in this step vertical lines are simply extended above the four vertices of each bottom of the cubes.

Note how the top left cube has a bottom that does not look square, the same as the other two cubes. But also note that the bottom right cube bottom appears to have been corrected when the vertical at the back corner is placed and extended. Watch how this turns out.

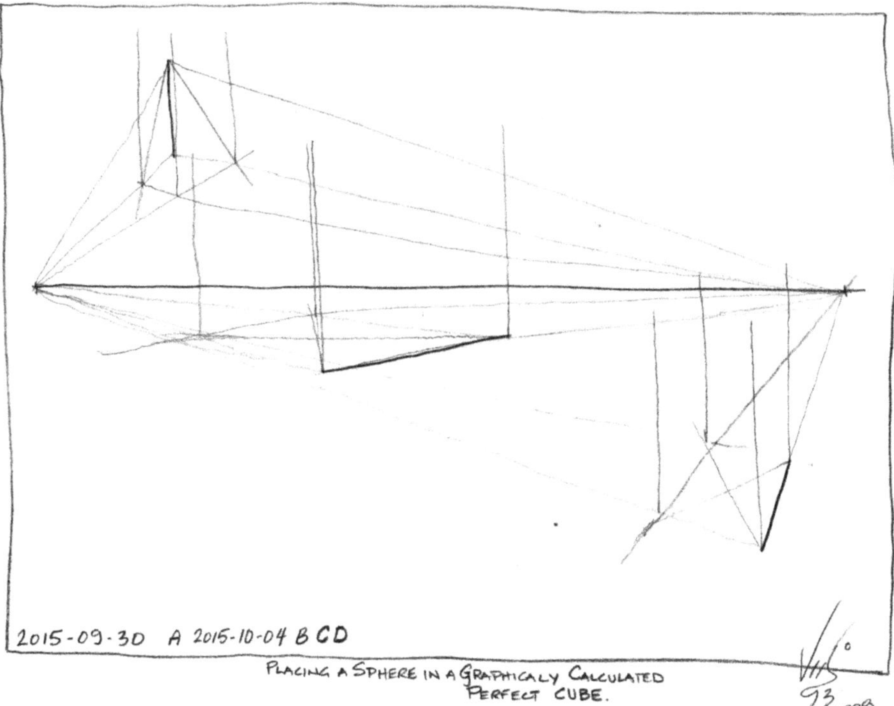

PLACING A SPHERE IN A GRAPHICALY CALCULATED PERFECT CUBE.

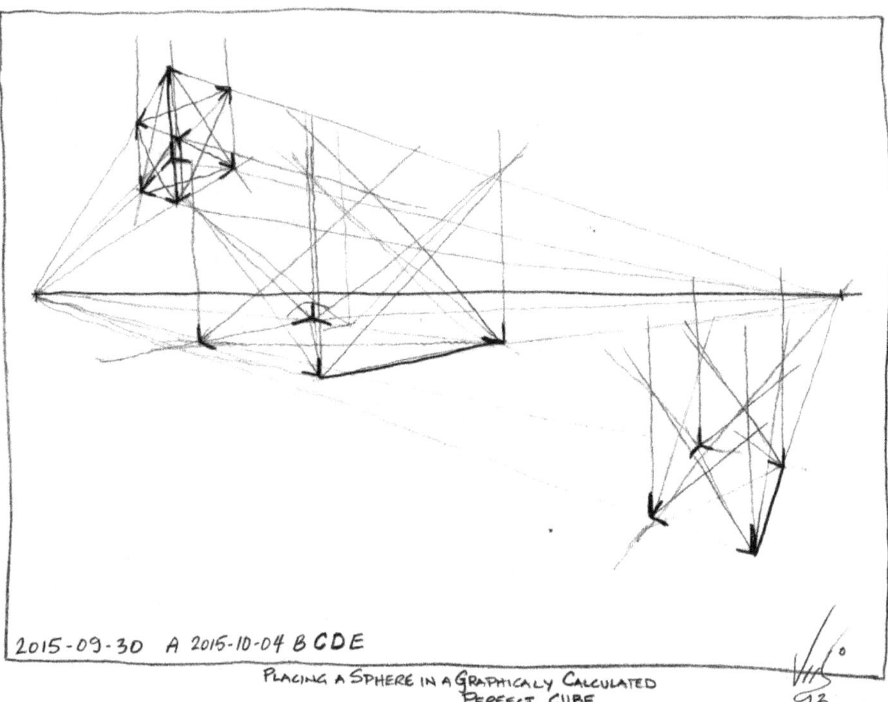

In the top left cube, the lines back to the vanishing points from the two new vertices are drawn, and a third vertice at the top back corner is created. Note that this vertice should be confirmed by three individual lines running through it - the vertical from the bottom corner and the two lines to the vanishing points from two of the new vertices. Diagonal lines connecting opposite corners of each face of the cube are drawn on this upper left cube.

The two lower cubes, in this step, again split the angles created by the verticals of the last step and the four edges of the bottoms of each cube. This locates the four top vertices of each cube on the vertical lines drawn up from each of the four vertices at the bottom of each cube.

Again, each vertice should be confirmed by three lines intersecting at each new vertice - the two angle splitting lines from the bottom vertices, and the vertical line from that vertice's bottom vertice.

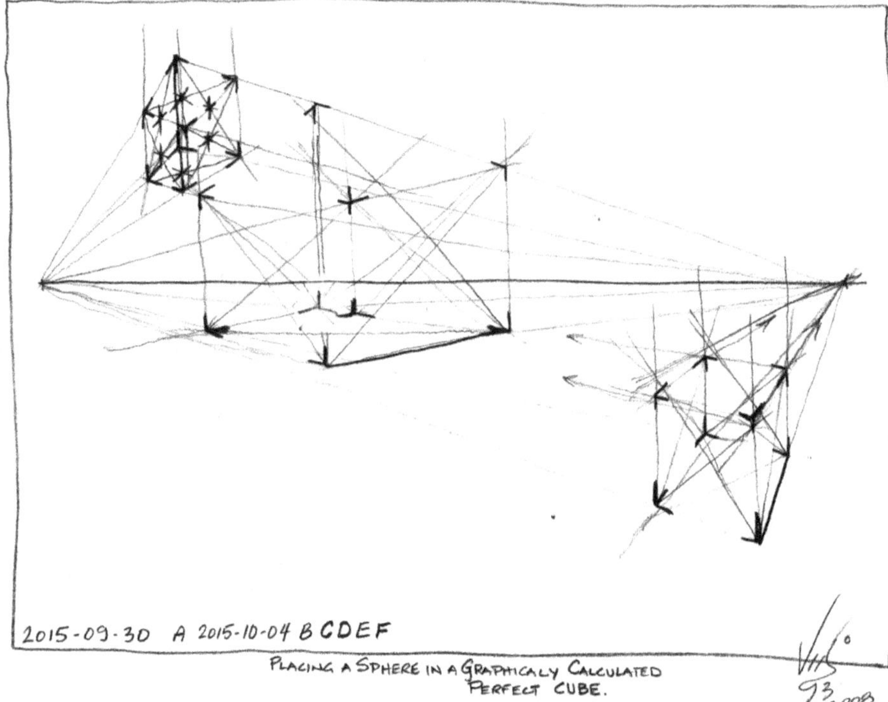

In this step, the centres of each of the six faces of the top left cube are identified. These centres will be tangent to the three circles that will set up the sphere. Is this cube looking like a perfect cube, with all sides equal?

In the middle cube, an obvious error is being corrected at the back bottom corner. Yet even with this correction, do the eight vertices portray a perfect cube?

The eight vertices of each of the two lower cubes are located in this step. Note that a few of the vertices are not consistently located by three lines, so the vertice is located where it seems that it should be located. The important thing, not only that the sphere ends up correctly located, is that it still looks round, like a sphere! A sphere from any angle appears as a circle in any two dimensional drawing.

In this step, the upper left cube now has the three sphere layout circles drawn tangent to the six faces of the cube. Does the cube look like a perfect cube, with all sides equal? Do the circles look like perfect elipses ? They should look like perfect elipses. The trick is to see the elipses as you draw them tangent to the faces of the cubes. Drawing "ordinate" lines at each centre of each face helps to make the ellipses or "circles" tangent.
The centres of each face of the two lower cubes are now located at where the diagonals from opposite corners of each face intersect.

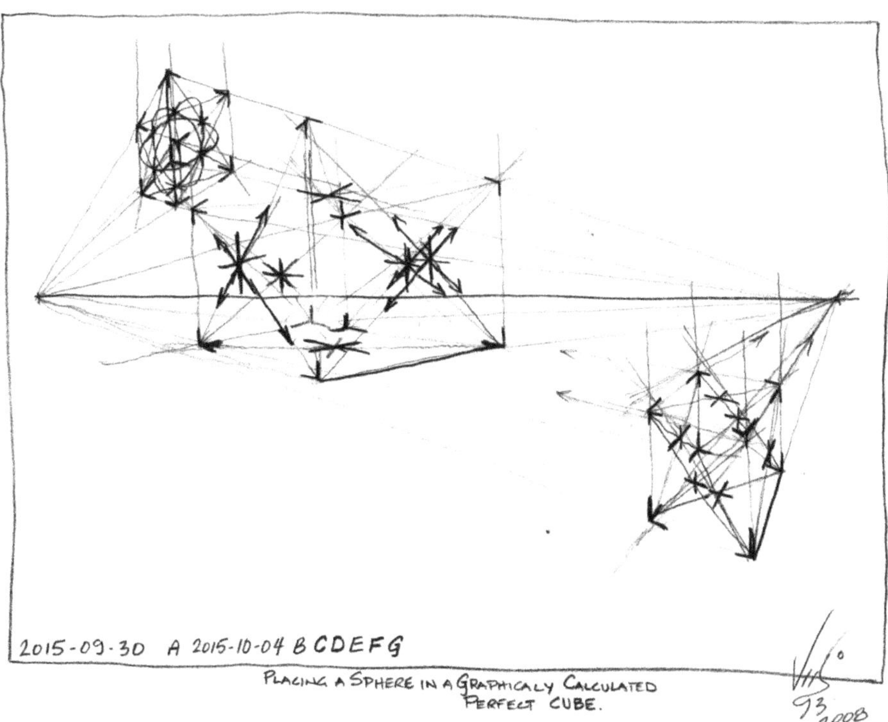

Here the upper left cube's sphere has been drawn based on the three layout circles. One must draw the sphere's perimeter tangent to the outer extremes of the three ellipses that represent the three circles placing the sphere.
Does this sphere look round, like a circle? No it does not. This is because the bounding box was not a perfect cube. Even with the layout circles being pretty good ellipses, the cube's inaccuracies produced an inaccurate sphere.
In the middle cube two layout circles have been drawn, paying attention to them being tangent to the centres of the faces, but they are not smooth ellipses. It cannot be emphasized enough how important the fifth and sixth exercises of Landing the Circle, in this book, are to the practice of drawing. What goes around comes around, and circles come around a lot, tangentially!

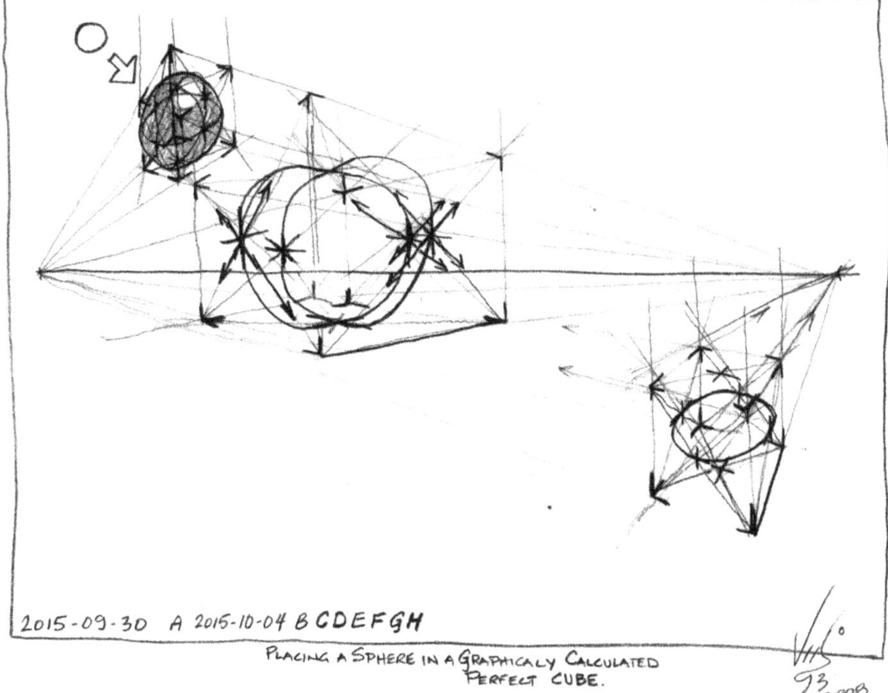

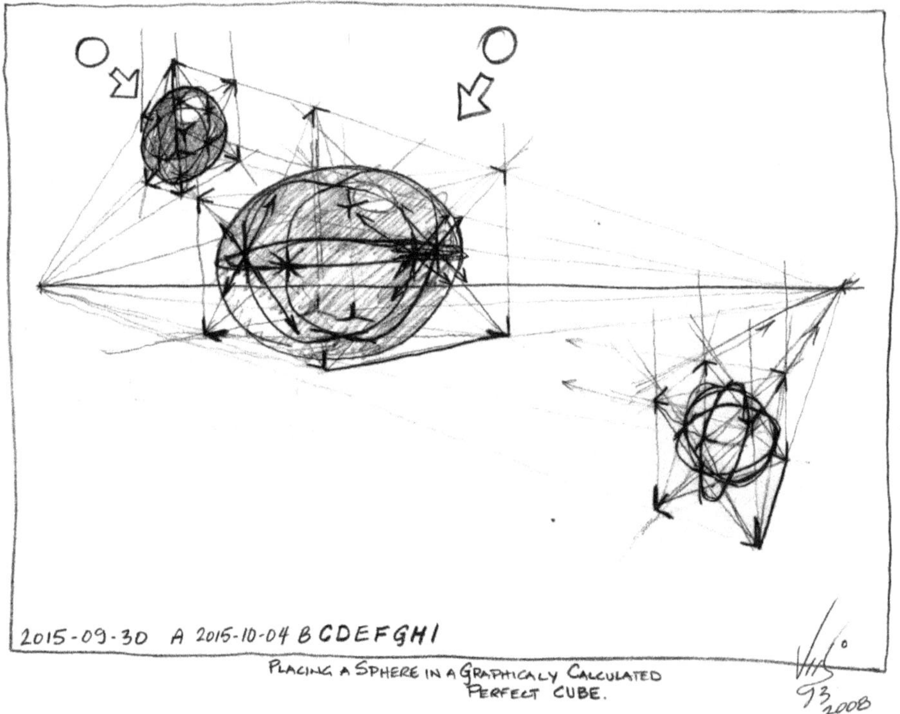

In this step the sphere of the middle cube has been drawn, but the circle of the sphere is not tangent to the extremes of the layout circles, at the bottom of the sphere. This may have been to correct ellipses that were not smooth.
Nevertheless, this sphere is not round, like a circle, because the bounding box is not a perfect cube.

The layout circles are drawn in the lower right cube. Does this cube look promising? Will the sphere be round? The ellipses look smoother than those in the other two bounding boxes.

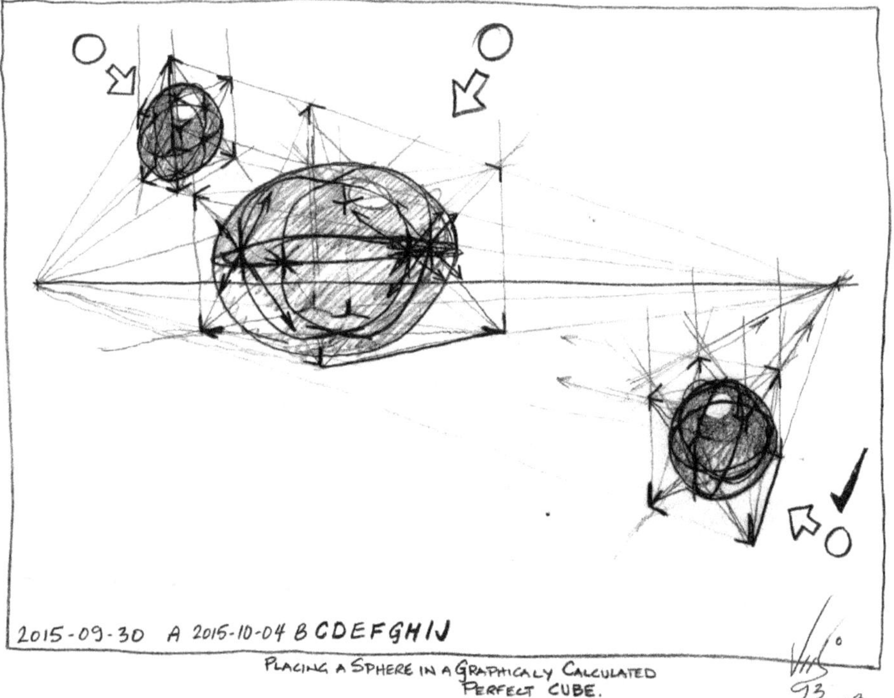

Here, at the final step, is the completed drawing.
The sphere in the lower right is complete and yes, it does look round! The circle of the sphere is tangent to the extremes of the layout ellipses or "circles".
Looking back now, one can see the errors in the layout of the cubes. With this experience, look forward when you draw, and try to see the image in the picture plane as you lay it out, to verify the accuracy of your draftsmanship.
As well, this will help you visualize a split angle, a split area, and a well placed tangent or concentric circle.

I was very pleased when I realized how to graphically calculate a perfect cube. I hope this book has been pleasing to you, and helped you find JOY, at least in drawing!

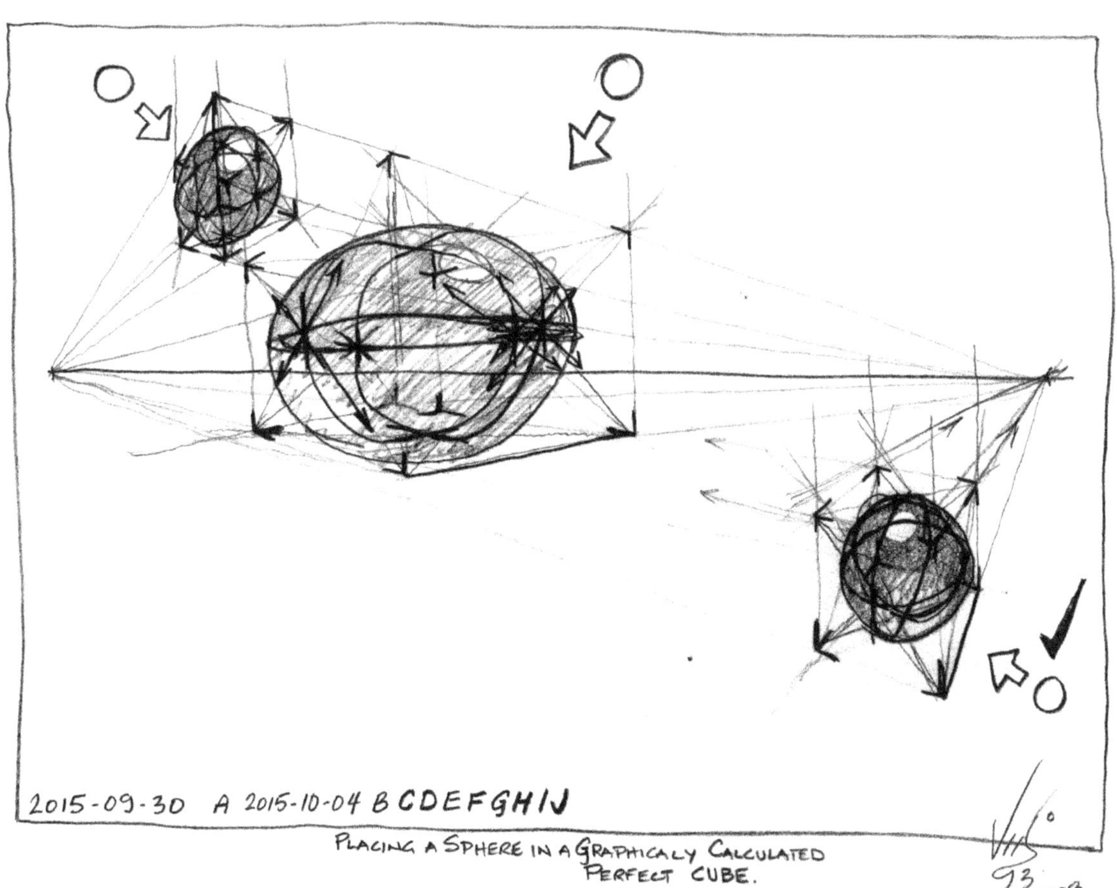

PLACING A SPHERE IN A GRAPHICALY CALCULATED PERFECT CUBE.

Sometimes it is just necessary to shut down or occupy the analytical and logical side of the brain to allow the spatial and relational side of the brain to address the task at hand.

I hope this Epilogue of placing a sphere in perspective has allowed your analysis to appreciate the relational demands of a good drawing. Analysis cannot accomplish this on its own, yet it is necessary to identify errors that creep in from, at the very least, a shaky hand.

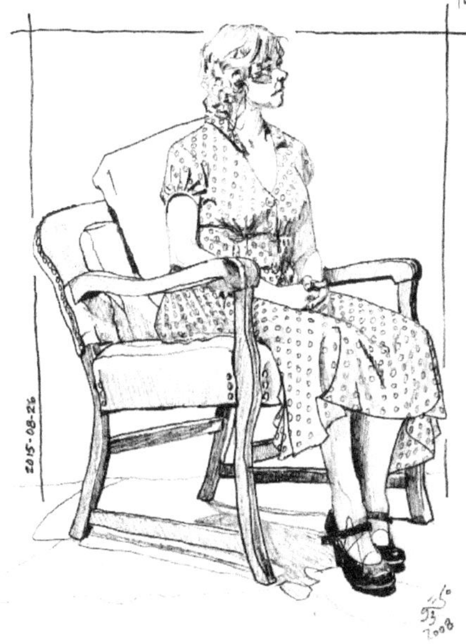

This drawing I completed from a woman posing at the Art Gallery of Burlington, has a layout error in it. I was lost in the details, so I laid out the drawing with the upper and lower extremes of the image at the top and bottom of my page. I then laid out the left and right extremes of the image at the left and right sides of my page. Then everything fit in and the drawing seemed to progress well.

Does she look like a young girl in a big chair ? This is because the proportions of the image were not the same as the proportions of the drawing page, so the drawing is wider than it should be !

Accurate analysis is necessary, in a well educated way, respectful of the relationships in which it exists. If the parts do not relate to the whole, or if the whole does not account for the parts, the effort fails, especially when drawing and courting !

TEXTBOOK --A--

Warm Ups

from

Drawing on the
Right Side of the Brain

Portraits

Still Life

Drawing on the Right Side of the Brain Author: ***Betty Edwards***
ISBN-13: **9780874775136** ISBN-10: **0874775132** Edition: **Revised** Binding: **Paperback**
Publisher: **Tarcher** Published: **May 1989** List Price: **$15.95**

TEXTBOOK --B--
Visual Vocabulary

People -

Animals -

Plants

Mechanical

Geological

Topographic and Landscapes

Textures

Drapery

TEXTBOOK --C--
Simple Perspective

Illustration of Visualizing in Three Dimensions

Theory

Architectural

Creative Perspective

Figure Drawing in Perspective

TEXTBOOK --D--

Landscapes

Topographic

Atmospheric

Day and Night

R David Foster

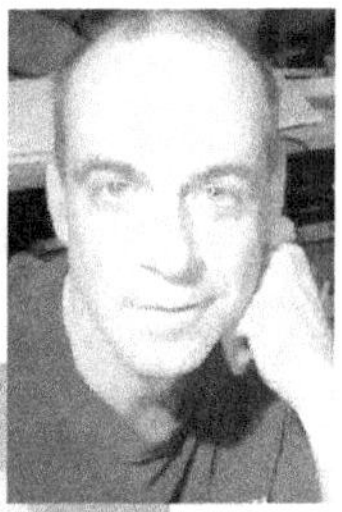

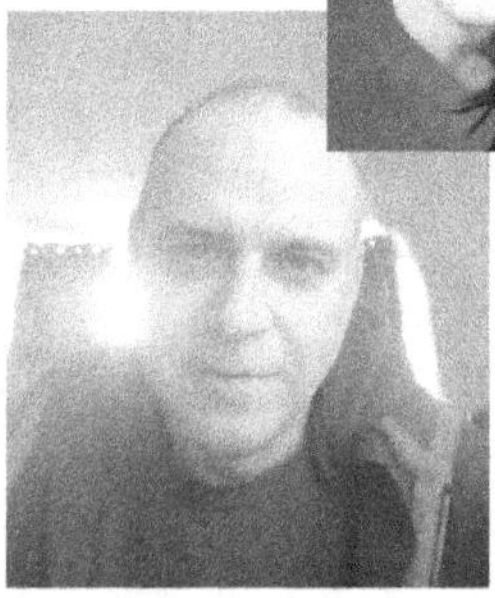

- began the Oakville OASIS Drawing Bee in March 2010, with funding from the Canadian Mental Health Association (CMHA), Halton Region Branch, and it continues today with Paul Tomas leading it. Before that, around 2005, David ran a workshop in drawing and watercolour painting, again under CMHA at the request of Clarisse Berardicurti. His other accomplishments are a 35mm animated film entitled **HYPOTHERMIA /** ***My Kayak Prayer,*** completed in 2008, that was supported by the Liaison of Independent Film of Toronto and the Ontario Arts Council. He is now devoting the largest portion of his available time to his animated series HESUS JOY CHRIST, of which there are 5 episodes completed. He regularly updates his blog entitled . . . . . .

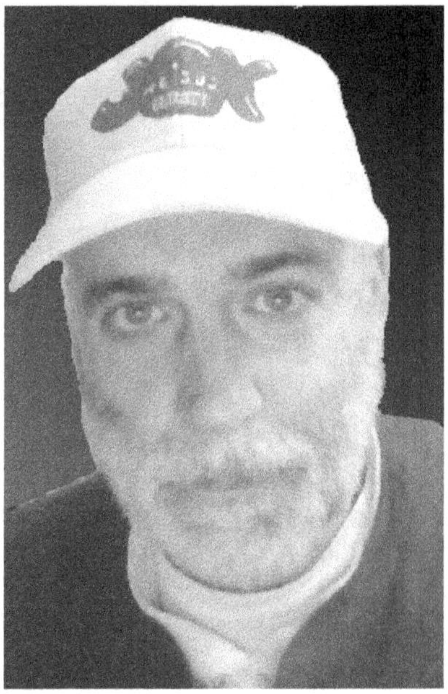

Vid'93 Bein' To Wordie . . . . at ***www.vid93.blogspot.com*** .

David is currently a member of the Oakville Arts Council, and the Art Gallery of Burlington (AGB) - Burlington Fine Arts Association. He attends the Wednesday Sketch Group, at the AGB when he is available and inspired and appreciates the opportunity to practice life drawing, portrait drawing, and still life drawing, from life.

David has always drawn, with the exception being when he was in high school, when he only practiced technical drawing or drafting. So his self taught experience far exceeds his formal artistic education, giving due credit to his father's generous exposure and encouragment towards art, and the benefits of the exercises provided by the book ***Drawing on the Right Side of the Brain***, by Betty Edwards. David achieved honours in the Art Fundamentals Intensive program at Sheridan College in Oakville, Ontario, before being accepted into the Classical Animation Program in 1993, only to fail out by the end of first year. The Art Fundamentals instructors did not want him to waste his talent in Animation, but he had a love for the potential of the medium of Animation, which exceeded the discouragement of the animation instruction.

Search **"vid932008"** *on* **www.google.ca** *for a website with all of it !*

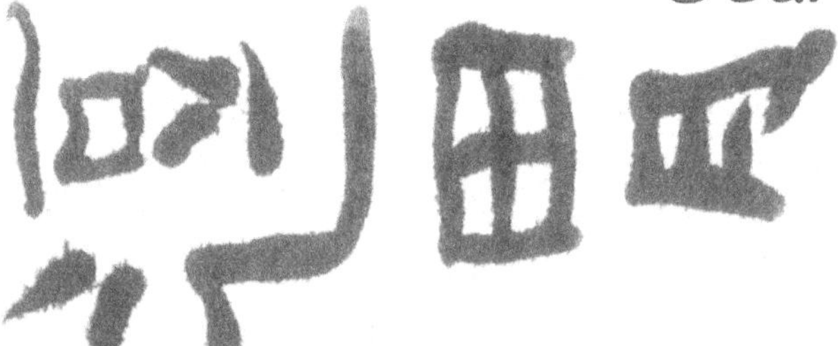

vid932008@gmail.com

www.vid93.blogspot.com

http://sites.google.com/site/vid932008/

www.ingramcontent.com/pod-product-compliance
Lightning Source LLC
Chambersburg PA
CBHW080915170526
45158CB00008B/2116
9780991785223